TEACHINGS OF PRESIDENTS OF THE CHURCH
BRIGHAM YOUNG

Published by
The Church of Jesus Christ of Latter-day Saints
Salt Lake City, Utah

Contents

Title	Page

Introduction

The prophet Brigham Young taught the restored gospel of Jesus Christ in a basic, practical way that gave inspiration and hope to the Saints struggling to build a home in the wilderness. Though more than a century has now passed, his words are still fresh and appropriate for us today as we continue the work of building the kingdom of God.

President Young declared that as members of The Church of Jesus Christ of Latter-day Saints we possess the "doctrine of life and salvation for all the honest-in-heart" (*DBY*, 7).* He promised that those who receive the gospel in their hearts will have awakened "within them a desire to know and understand the things of God more than they ever did before in their lives" and will begin to "inquire, read and search and when they go to their Father in the name of Jesus he will not leave them without a witness" (*DBY*, 450).

This book reflects the desire of the First Presidency and the Quorum of the Twelve Apostles to deepen the doctrinal understanding of Church members and to awaken within them a greater desire to know the things of God. It will inspire and motivate individuals, priesthood quorums, and Relief Society classes to inquire, read, search, and then go to their Father in Heaven for a witness of the truth of these teachings.

Each chapter contains two sections—"Teachings of Brigham Young" and "Suggestions for Study." The first section consists of extracts from Brigham Young's sermons to the early Saints. Each statement has been referenced, and the original spelling and punctuation have been preserved; however, the sources cited will not be readily available to most members. These original sources are not necessary to have in order to effectively study or teach from this book. Members need not purchase additional references and commentaries to study or teach these chapters. The text provided in this book, accompanied by the scriptures, is sufficient for instruction. Members should prayerfully read and study President Young's teachings in order to gain new insights into gospel principles and discover how those

---

*For an explanation of the abbreviations used in this book to show the sources from which President Young's statements have been taken, see "Works Cited and Abbreviations Used" on page 360.

principles apply to their everyday lives. By faithfully and prayerfully studying these selections, Latter-day Saints will have a greater understanding of gospel principles and will more fully appreciate the profound and inspired teachings of this great prophet.

The second section of each chapter offers a series of questions that will encourage thoughtful contemplation, personal application, and discussion of President Young's teachings. Members should refer to and carefully reread his words on the principle being discussed. Deep and prayerful study of these teachings will inspire members to greater personal commitment and will help them resolve to follow the teachings of the Savior, Jesus Christ.

If individuals and families prayerfully follow the principles in this book, they will be blessed and inspired to greater dedication and spirituality, as were the early Saints who heard these words directly from the lips of the "Lion of the Lord" (*HC,* 7:434)—the prophet, seer, and revelator, President Brigham Young.

Instructions to Teachers

Teaching these lessons will require careful advance reading, study, and prayerful preparation. Become very familiar with the teachings and plan various ways to present and teach these principles in the class setting. Lessons should help class members see how gospel principles apply to daily living. Encourage discussions about how these principles can influence our feelings about our Father in Heaven, Jesus Christ, ourselves, our families, and our neighbors. Invite participants to live according to the principles being taught.

Involve as many people as possible during the instruction period by inviting them to read aloud, answer questions, or share experiences. You can make special assignments when preparing lessons, being sensitive to the readiness of class members to participate. Carefully avoid controversy. Rely upon the scriptures for support and understanding. Humbly seek the Lord's Spirit, and the brothers and sisters you teach will be blessed. As the Lord has promised, "Wherefore, he that preacheth and he that receiveth, understand one another, and both are edified and rejoice together" (D&C 50:22).

Historical Summary

1801, June 1:	Born in Whitingham, Windham County, Vermont.
1815–21:	Mother dies; Brigham begins to earn his own way in life, eventually becoming a carpenter (14; numbers in parentheses show his age).
1824:	Marries Miriam Angeline Works (23).
1832:	Baptized into the Church and ordained an elder. Wife dies (31).
1834:	Marries Mary Ann Angell. Acts as captain in march of Zion's Camp (33).
1835, February 14:	Ordained as one of the original members of the Quorum of the Twelve (34).
1839–41:	Serves a mission to Great Britain (38–40).
1844–47:	Joseph Smith is martyred. Brigham Young leads the Church as President of the Quorum of the Twelve (43–46).
1847:	Receives section 136 of the Doctrine and Covenants. Sees Joseph Smith in vision and is given valuable instruction. Leads the exodus from Winter Quarters to the Salt Lake Valley and returns to Winter Quarters (45–46).
1847, December 27:	Sustained as President of the Church at Kanesville (Council Bluffs), Iowa (46).
1851:	Becomes governor of the Territory of Utah (49).
1853, April 6:	Lays the cornerstone for Salt Lake Temple (52).
1857–58:	Utah War. Released as governor after eight-year term (56–57).
1867:	The Tabernacle is completed. Reorganizes the Relief Society (66).
1869:	The railroad comes to Utah. The Young Women's Mutual Improvement Association is organized (68).
1875:	The Young Men's Mutual Improvement Association is organized (74).
1877, April 6:	Dedicates the St. George Temple. Gives new emphasis to the proper organization of the priesthood (75).
1877, August 29:	Dies in Salt Lake City, Utah (76).

President Young about 1847–50. "I wanted to thunder, and roar out the gospel to the nations. It burned in my bones like fire pent up. . . . Nothing would satisfy me but to cry abroad in the world what the Lord is doing in the latter days" (*DNW,* 24 Aug. 1854, 1).

The Ministry of Brigham Young

Brigham Young was the second President of The Church of Jesus Christ of Latter-day Saints, the colonizer and builder of a great commonwealth of Latter-day Saints in the American West, and a devoted husband and father. He was a faithful disciple and Apostle of the Lord Jesus Christ. "Jesus is our captain and leader," he testified (DNW, 24 May 1871, 5). "My faith is placed upon the Lord Jesus Christ, and my knowledge I have received from him," he affirmed (DNW, 21 Nov. 1855, 2). His life was centered in building up and sustaining the kingdom of the Lord Jesus Christ on the earth.

Experiences from the Life of Brigham Young

Learning through hard work.

Brigham Young was born in Vermont in 1801, the ninth of 11 children of John and Abigail Howe Young. He grew to manhood on the heavily wooded lands of central New York state, where his family's home and the surrounding land became his classroom (see *DNW,* 22 Apr. 1857, 4). His parents were poor, he later said. "We never had the opportunity of letters [formal education] in our youth, but we had the privilege of picking up brush, chopping down trees, rolling logs, and working amongst the roots, and of getting our shins, feet and toes bruised" (*DNW,* 12 Aug. 1857, 4). Young Brigham worked hard to help clear the land, farm it, and help with household chores. He never forgot his father's strict moral training or how his mother "taught her children all the time to honour the name of the Father and the Son, and to reverence the [Bible]; she said, Read it, observe its precepts, and apply them to your lives as far as you can; do everything that is good; do nothing that is evil; and if you see any persons in distress, administer to their wants" (*MSS,* 1853, 55). Brigham's mother died when he was 14 years old.

By age 16 Brigham had become an apprentice carpenter, joiner, painter, and glazier. He took pride in his craft and said he considered "honest, reliable work, such as would endure, for those who employed me" to be "a part of my religion" (Brigham Young to George Hickox, 19 Feb. 1876, BYP).

At age 23 he married Miriam Angeline Works. Two daughters were born to the young couple. Brigham supported his family by making and repairing chairs, tables, and cupboards and installing windows, doors, stairways, and fireplace mantels. On his father's farm in Mendon, New York, he constructed a home and woodworking shop next to a small stream, using a waterwheel to power his mill machinery.

When Miriam contracted tuberculosis, Brigham assumed much of the burden of her work in addition to his own. As she became progressively more bedridden, he regularly prepared breakfast for the family, dressed his daughters, cleaned up the house, and "carried his wife to the rocking chair by the fireplace and left her there until he could return in the evening," when he cooked supper, got his family into bed, and finished the household chores (*LSBY,* 5). His experiences in his youth and early marriage in caring for children and managing a home taught him much about family cooperation and housekeeping. Years later he counseled the Saints on these subjects and teasingly boasted that he could beat "most of the women in [the] community at housekeeping" (*DNW,* 12 Aug. 1857, 4).

Gaining a witness of the Spirit.

Brigham and Miriam joined the Methodist Church the year they were married, but Brigham continued to wrestle with religious questions. He sought a church organized according to the pattern Jesus had established, after the pattern of the New Testament with a "system of ordinances" (*DNW,* 19 July 1866, 3) and all the gifts of the gospel. Because of the missionary efforts of Joseph Smith's brother Samuel, Brigham Young's family obtained two copies of the Book of Mormon in April 1830, just one month after the book was published. Some of Brigham's brothers and sisters read it and declared its truth, but Brigham himself did not immediately accept it (see LL, 33). "'Hold on,' says I. . . . 'Wait a little while; what is the doctrine of the book, and of the revelations the Lord has given? Let me apply my heart to them.' . . . I examined the matter studiously, for two years, before I made up my mind to receive that book. I knew it was true, as well as I knew that I could see with my eyes, or feel by the touch of my fingers, or be sensible of the demonstration of any sense. Had not this been the case, I never would have embraced it to this day" (*MSS,* 15:45).

Brigham Young had to know for himself. He later taught the Saints that God did not intend them "to be led entirely by another person, suspending their own understanding, and pinning their faith upon another's sleeve" (*DNW,* 24 Aug. 1854, 1). "It is my duty to know the mind of the Lord concerning myself," he told them (*DNW,* 22 Sept. 1875, 4). "It is your privilege and duty to live so that you know when the word of the Lord is spoken to you and when the mind of the Lord is revealed to you" (*DNW,* 22 Sept. 1875, 4).

Missionaries from a branch of the Church in Columbia, Pennsylvania, passed through Mendon in 1831, preaching that the heavens had been opened and that the gospel and the holy priesthood were restored through Joseph Smith. After Brigham and other family members and friends visited the Columbia Branch, he believed he had found the religion he had long sought, but he struggled to decide if he could actually sacrifice everything for it. Then, as one of the missionaries bore testimony, "the Holy Ghost proceeding from that individual illuminate[d] my understanding, and light, glory, and immortality [were] before me," he remembered. He said that he was encircled and filled by them, and he knew for himself that the testimony of the man was true (*DNW,* 9 Feb. 1854, 4). On 15 April 1832, a cold and snowy day, Brigham Young was baptized in his own millstream, confirmed, and ordained an elder (see *DNW,* 2 Apr. 1862, 1). "According to the words of the Savior, I felt a humble, child-like spirit, witnessing unto me that my sins were forgiven," he recalled (*MHBY-1,* 3). Miriam entered the waters of baptism about three weeks afterward (*MHBY-1,* 3). All of Brigham Young's immediate family members were baptized, and they remained faithful Latter-day Saints.

In the late summer of 1832, after returning from missionary travels in the nearby countryside, Brigham nursed Miriam through the final weeks of her consumptive illness. She died in September 1832.

Sacrificing to build and defend the kingdom of God.

Brigham Young turned his full attention and energy to the Church. Anxious to meet the Prophet Joseph Smith, he left immediately for Kirtland, Ohio, with his brother Joseph and close friend Heber C. Kimball. They found Joseph Smith chopping wood with his brothers. Brigham's "joy was full at the privilege of shaking the hand of the Prophet of God" and receiving "the sure testimony, by the Spirit of prophecy, that he was all that any man could believe him to be, as a true Prophet" (*MHBY-1,* 4). This marked the beginning of one of Brigham Young's most important relationships. When he returned to New York, he gave away many of his possessions and reduced his business in order to dedicate more of his time to the Church. Assured that Vilate Kimball, Heber's wife, would care for his daughters, he served a series of missions. He held meetings and baptized in the countryside surrounding Mendon. He also traveled into upper New York and Ontario, Canada, to preach the gospel and bear witness that Joseph Smith was a prophet of God.

Desiring to obey the Prophet's counsel to gather with the Saints, in September 1833 Brigham Young moved his family from Mendon to Kirtland. There, Brigham "had the privilege of listening to the teachings of the Prophet and enjoying the society of the Saints, working hard at [his] former trade" (*MHBY-1*, 7). He helped construct homes, the Kirtland Temple, and several public buildings.

On 18 February 1834 he married Mary Ann Angell; over the next 10 years, six children were born into their family. Mary Ann, Brigham recorded, "labored faithfully for the interest of my family and the kingdom" (*MHBY-1*, 8).

During his years in Kirtland (1833–38), Brigham learned that building the kingdom of God requires obedience and sacrifice. In the spring of 1834, he volunteered to march with Zion's Camp, a group of 205 men recruited by Joseph Smith to take aid and provisions to the Saints who had been forced from their homes in Jackson County, Missouri. "We performed a journey of two thousand miles on foot," Brigham recalled (*DNW,* 8 Oct. 1856, 2). He remembered that because of the extreme hardships and sickness "we had grumblers in that camp." The men needed to be tutored in patience and cooperation and so, said Brigham, "Joseph [Smith] led, counseled and guided the company," particularly the men who had "uneasy, unruly and discontented spirits" (*DNW,* 3 Dec. 1862, 1). The difficult journey strengthened Brigham's loyalty to Joseph Smith and provided priceless schooling in obedience to God and His prophet (see *DNW,* 3 Aug. 1854, 2).

Nine veterans of Zion's Camp, including Brigham Young, were selected to be members of the first Quorum of the Twelve Apostles at a special conference on 14 February 1835 (see D&C 18:26–32). Brigham Young was ordained by the laying on of hands and blessed "that he may go forth and gather the elect, preparatory to the great day of the coming of the Lord." He and other members of the quorum, "called to preach the Gospel of the Son of God to the nations of the earth" (*HC,* 2:196), left in May 1835 for a four-month mission to the eastern states. He returned to the eastern states as a missionary during the summers of 1836 and 1837.

Elder Young supervised the painting and finishing of the Kirtland Temple. He was present when the Prophet Joseph introduced preliminary ordinances there, and he attended the March 1836 dedication services with hundreds of Saints who had made great sacrifices to build the first temple in this dispensation (see *MHBY-1,* 12; *HC,* 2:428).

Before Elder Young could fully savor the unity developed by such experiences, several dissenters became so vocal in their opposition to the Prophet that they tried to wrest from him the leadership of the Church. In January 1838 Elder Young confronted these apostates in the Kirtland

Temple: "I rose up, and in a plain and forcible manner told them that Joseph was a Prophet, and I knew it, and that they might rail and slander him as much as they pleased, they could not destroy the appointment of the Prophet of God, they could only destroy their own authority, cut the thread that bound them to the Prophet and to God and sink themselves to hell" (*MHBY-1*, 16).

Shouldering responsibility.

Brigham Young remembered waiting with Joseph Smith "scores and scores of nights ready to receive the mob who sought [the Prophet's] life" (*DNSW*, 15 May 1877, 1). He was so uncompromising in his support of the Prophet that the apostates, he recounted, "threatened to destroy me" (*MHBY-1*, 23–24). He fled Kirtland and went to western Missouri, joining Joseph Smith and other Church leaders whose lives had been threatened. But as large numbers of Latter-day Saints continued to migrate into western Missouri, other settlers there became alarmed, fearful of political and economic domination by the Saints. Tensions erupted in the summer and fall of 1838 and culminated when the governor ordered the state militia to exterminate the Latter-day Saints or drive them from the state. The imprisonment of Joseph Smith and other key leaders and the apostasy or death of several members of the Quorum of the Twelve thrust new responsibilities on Brigham Young, now President of the Quorum. He and Apostle Heber C. Kimball were the only members of the Church's presiding quorums available to guide and assist the Saints in their difficult winter exodus from Missouri. Under their direction, the Saints covenanted to help the poor, to bring every Latter-day Saint out of the state, and to prepare to gather once again.

The exiled Saints built a new city in Commerce, Illinois, which they later named Nauvoo. President Young stayed there only a few months, however, because the Prophet Joseph received a revelation calling the Quorum of the Twelve to serve missions in England. In the fall of 1839, President Young left Illinois determined to assume the new responsibility despite the ill health he and his family were suffering. He later recalled that he could not walk very far without help and that his sister Fanny begged him not to go. He responded: "'Sister Fanny, I never felt better in my life.' She was a very eccentric woman and, looking at me, with tears in her eyes, she said 'you lie.' I said nothing, but I was determined to go to England or to die trying. My firm resolve was that I would do what I was required to do in the Gospel of life and salvation, or I would die trying to do it" (*DNSW*, 2 Aug. 1870, 1).

Eight members of the Quorum of the Twelve served missions in the British Isles during 1840 and 1841, and Brigham Young, as Quorum

President, directed their labors. During that momentous year the Twelve achieved remarkable success. As President Young prepared to leave Liverpool in April 1841, he reflected with gratitude on God's "dealings with me and my brethren of the Twelve during the past year of my life. . . . It truly seemed a miracle to look upon the contrast between our landing and departing from Liverpool. We landed in the spring of 1840, as strangers in a strange land and penniless, but through the mercy of God we have gained many friends, established Churches in almost every noted town and city in the kingdom of Great Britain, baptized between seven and eight thousand, printed 5,000 Books of Mormon, 3,000 Hymn Books, 2,500 volumes of the *Millennial Star,* and 50,000 tracts, and emigrated to Zion 1,000 souls, . . . and have left sown in the hearts of many thousands the seeds of eternal truth, which will bring forth fruit to the honor and glory of God, and yet we have lacked nothing to eat, drink or wear: in all these things I acknowledge the hand of God" (*MHBY-1,* 96–97).

By wholeheartedly shouldering new responsibilities, President Young and his fellow Apostles had enlarged not only their personal capacities but the capacity of the quorum to work unitedly and effectively for the Church. Joseph Smith trusted their "united wisdom" and announced in Nauvoo in August 1841 "that the time had come when the Twelve should be called upon to stand in their place next to the First Presidency" (*HC,* 4:403). The Twelve were given greater responsibilities, including preaching the gospel, settling immigrants, purchasing land, and building the Nauvoo Temple.

Before the temple was completed, Joseph Smith privately introduced President Young and other members of the Twelve to temple ordinances, including baptism for the dead, the temple endowment, and family sealings, anticipating that the Twelve would teach these ordinances to the members of the Church. The Prophet met with the Twelve in the spring of 1844 to confer on them all of the keys and authority necessary to carry forward the work of the kingdom. "I roll the burthen [burden] and responsibility of leading this Church off from my shoulders on to yours," the Prophet proclaimed. "Now, round up your shoulders and stand under it like men; for the Lord is going to let me rest a while" (undated Certificate of the Twelve, BYP).

Within three months the Prophet Joseph Smith was dead. While President Young was serving a summer mission in the Boston area, he learned that Joseph and Hyrum Smith had been murdered by a mob at Carthage, Illinois. Upon hearing the news, he asked himself "whether Joseph had taken the keys of the kingdom with him from the earth," but he immediately felt assured that the keys of the kingdom rested with the Twelve (*MHBY-1,* 171). Returning at once to Nauvoo, he found that Joseph's First Counselor, Sidney Rigdon, had offered to take over leadership of the Church, and a general assembly of Saints had already been called to sustain a new leader. President Young spoke to the gathering of Saints with forceful plainness:

"For the first time in my life, for the first time in your lives, for the first time in the kingdom of God in the 19th century, without a Prophet at our head, do I step forth to act in my calling in connection with the Quorum of the Twelve, as Apostles of Jesus Christ unto this generation—Apostles whom God has called by revelation through the Prophet Joseph, who are ordained and anointed to bear off the keys of the kingdom of God in all the world.

" . . . Now, if you want Sidney Rigdon or William Law to lead you, or anybody else, you are welcome to them; but I tell you, in the name of the Lord that no man can put another between the Twelve and the Prophet Joseph. Why? Because Joseph was their file leader, and he has committed into their hands the keys of the kingdom in this last dispensation, for all the world" (*HC,* 7:232, 235).

Many witnesses noted that President Young looked and sounded like the Prophet Joseph as he spoke, a powerful manifestation of divine approval. The nearly 5,000 Saints assembled sustained the Twelve as the governing quorum of the Church. Three days following the meeting in which President Young had told the Saints he "wanted the privilege to weep and mourn for thirty days at least" (*HC,* 7:232), he quietly expressed his grief: "It has been a time of mourning [since] the day that Joseph and Hyrum were brought in from Carthage to [Nauvoo]. It was judged by many both in and out of the church that there was more than five barrels of tears shed. I cannot bear to think anything about it" (*MHBY-1,* 177).

During nearly a decade of service as an Apostle of Jesus Christ, Brigham Young had been learning the ways of the Lord. His willingness to work hard, obey, sacrifice, and accept responsibility and his capacity for receiving and acting on the promptings of the Spirit prepared him to preside over the Latter-day Saints, first as President of the Quorum of the Twelve and after December 1847 as President of the Church. Under his extraordinary leadership, which spanned some 33 years, he taught the Saints how to build Zion in the American West and in their own hearts, families, and wards. "Brother Joseph, the Prophet, has laid the foundation for a great work, and we will build upon it," he promised the Saints in August 1844. "We can build a kingdom such as there never was in the world" (*HC,* 7:234). His unwavering faith in God; his dedication, experience, and sense of humor; his love for gospel doctrine and ordinances; and his understanding of priesthood order and Church organization enabled him to move the Saints toward oneness of heart and mind.

An artist's depiction of the Saints crossing the frozen Mississippi River during the exodus from Nauvoo, Illinois, in February 1846.

Gathering the Saints to build the kingdom of God.

President Brigham Young led the exodus of the Latter-day Saints from Nauvoo to the Salt Lake Valley in the Rocky Mountains. This permitted the Saints to gather in a way that had not been possible in Ohio, Missouri, or Illinois. When President Young looked out at the valley of the Great Salt Lake on 24 July 1847, he was certain he had found the refuge that Joseph Smith had foreseen for the Saints in the West and that he himself had seen in vision as being the right place. "The spirit of light rested upon me and hovered over the valley, and I felt that there the Saints would find protection and safety," Brigham wrote (*MHBY-2,* 564). Here the Saints could find the time and space needed to establish themselves as a people apart from the world.

The gathering in the West, which began with the arrival of President Young and the pioneer company in July 1847, continued for decades. Eighty thousand Saints made the difficult journey westward before 1869 when the railroad made travel easier. Even after that, Saints continued to leave their homes and often their families to gather to Zion. Their geographical move symbolized a spiritual move away from the world. President Young declared that God had called Saints "together from the uttermost parts of the earth . . . to become of one heart and of one mind in all our operations and endeavors to establish Christ's spiritual and temporal kingdom upon earth, to prepare for the coming of the Son of Man in power and great glory" (*DNSW,* 21 Jan. 1868, 2). He expected and required a great deal of his people in building Zion temporally and spiritually. They not only journeyed to the tops of the mountains but also gave of their means to help other Saints follow them in gathering.

Under President Young's direction, Saints left the Salt Lake Valley to colonize approximately 400 settlements in the American West. They worked to raise their own food, make their own clothing, and establish local industries so they could become economically self-sufficient. They learned to depend on the Lord and one another.

Not all of the economic enterprises that President Young directed the Saints to undertake were successful. Economic success, however, was not his primary concern. Ultimately he was less concerned with raising crops and money than he was with helping his people to become a holy nation. He knew from experience that they would grow from working hard and accepting responsibility. "This is a good place to make Saints," he told a congregation of members in Salt Lake City in 1856 (*DNW,* 10 Sept. 1856, 5).

For several years, Brigham Young served the area named Deseret (later to become the state of Utah) as territorial governor and superintendent of Indian affairs. In time he was replaced by federal appointees. He spent years trying to resolve conflicts between the Latter-day Saints and the United States government over the Saints' desire for political independence. He endured criticism and ridicule from ministers, journalists, reformers, and politicians who attacked him and his people for their religious beliefs and their social, economic, and political practices. But such challenges did not alter his clear understanding of the need to "make Saints" and thereby build Zion. President Young declared: "I have looked upon the community of the Latter-day Saints in vision, and beheld them organized as one great family of heaven; each person performing his several duties in his line of industry, working for the good of the whole more than for individual aggrandizement; and in this I have beheld the most beautiful order that the mind of man can contemplate, and the grandest results for the upbuilding of the kingdom of God and the spread of righteousness upon the earth" (*DNSW,* 21 Jan. 1868, 2).

Building Zion through priesthood ordinances and organization.

President Young recognized that Zion could not be built through hard work alone. Zion must be directed through the priesthood, which he knew to be the "Government of the Son of God" (*DNW,* 10 Aug. 1864, 2). He knew that the Saints could "become of one heart and of one mind in all . . . operations and endeavors" (*DNSW,* 21 Jan. 1868, 2), only according to a "pure and holy form of government" (*DNSW,* 8 Nov. 1870, 3). He taught that Church members could be sanctified only by participating in priesthood ordinances; thus, priesthood ordinances and organization were central to his teachings and leadership.

From 1844 to 1846, President Young and the Twelve made completion of the Nauvoo Temple an urgent priority. Endowments and sealings were performed there even before construction ended. "Such has been the anxiety manifested by the Saints to receive the ordinances, and such the anxiety on our part to administer to them; that I have given myself up entirely to the work of the Lord in the Temple night and day, not taking more than four hours sleep, upon an average, per day, and going home but once a week," President Young recorded in his diary (*MHBY-2,* 10). Between 10 December 1845 and 7 February 1846, approximately 5,615 Saints received the ordinance of the endowment and numerous families were sealed. Just over a year later, three days after arriving in the Salt Lake Valley, President Young designated the lot where the Salt Lake Temple would be built. It was to be at the center of the city and at the center of Saints' lives. The great temple, which took 40 years to build, was not completed until after President Young had died, but he designated other sacred places where temple endowments and sealings could be performed for the living while waiting for the temple to be finished. At the dedication of the lower stories of the St. George Temple on 1 January 1877, a few months before his death, President Young spoke energetically about resuming ordinance work for the dead: "When I think upon this subject, I want the tongues of seven thunders to wake up the people. Can the fathers be saved without us? No. Can we be saved without them? No" (*MS,* 39:119).

Temple ordinances were critical to binding together generations and to passing sacred truths from one generation to another. Latter-day Saints born or converted in the last half of the nineteenth century would not experience the persecutions in Missouri or personally remember the Prophet Joseph Smith. With the passage of time, fewer of them would be involved in pioneering and colonizing experiences, but they too would need to learn sacred truths about building Zion. President Young encouraged efforts to teach the gospel to the youth of the Church and worked to refine Church organization, expressing a desire to "rear up a generation of men and women who shall love and maintain truth and righteousness in the earth" (*MFP,* 2:288). Ward Sunday Schools for children, first established in 1849, began working unitedly under a central board in 1867. At President Young's request, and beginning with his own daughters, associations were organized in 1869 to strengthen young women in their gospel understanding and commitment to provident living. In 1875, similar associations were formed to teach young men and give them leadership experience.

Recognizing that Zion cannot be built without the sisters, President Young reestablished the Relief Society in 1867 as it had been organized in Nauvoo by the Prophet Joseph Smith. The women assisted bishops in providing relief to the poor and afflicted, encouraged families to make at home whatever they needed, taught one another the gospel, and supervised the teaching of younger women and children.

During the last year of his life, President Young put the priesthood quorums in order. He divided and reorganized stakes, increasing the number of stakes from eight to eighteen. He directed the organization of elders quorums and instructed the elders in their temporal and spiritual responsibilities. He emphasized the ward as the primary local unit of Church activity and expanded the role of the bishop as head of the ward. Members of the Quorum of the Twelve who had been presiding over local units were released from those positions so they could carry out their callings as special witnesses of Jesus Christ to the nations. By the time of his death on 29 August 1877, the Church was organized as most Saints recognize it today.

President Young's commitment to building Zion through colonization, economic enterprise, sacred temple ordinances, and priesthood organization is woven through the fabric of his sermons. No one sermon could capture the comprehensiveness of his vision. "I have only touched a little of the great Gospel Sermon," he declared at the end of one discourse (*MSS,* 15:49). The fulness of the gospel, he believed, could only be taught little by little, line upon line. "The gospel of the Son of God," he said, " . . . is from eternity to eternity. When the vision of the mind is opened, you can see a great portion of it, but you see it comparatively as a speaker sees the faces of a congregation. To look at, and talk to each individual separately, and thinking to become fully acquainted with them, only to spend five minutes with each would consume too much time, it could not easily be done. So it is with the visions of eternity; we can see and understand, but it is difficult to tell" (*DNW,* 26 Oct. 1854, 2). Through his teaching and his leadership, President Brigham Young always tried to help the Saints both see and understand the eternal truths of the gospel.

Brigham Young's life was centered in teaching the gospel and building up and sustaining the kingdom of God. "The Kingdom of heaven is first and foremost with us," he told the Saints (*DNW,* 27 July 1864, 2).

Perhaps the leadership given by President Young has been best described by the Apostles who were serving at the time of his death: "During the thirty three years that he has presided over the Church, since the martyrdom of the Prophet Joseph, his knees have never trembled, his hands have never shook; he never faltered or quailed. However threatening the surroundings or prospects may have been, he has never been dismayed; but at those times he has exhibited such serene confidence and faith, and uttered such words of encouragement, as to comfort and sustain all the people, and to call forth their love and admiration. The Lord, however, not only blessed him with valor, but He endowed him with great wisdom. His counsels, when obeyed, have been attended with salvation, and as an organizer and administrator he has no superior. . . .

"His labors the Lord has crowned with most remarkable success, his words he has honored and fulfilled, and those who have obeyed his counsel he has blessed and upheld. The time will yet come when his presidency over the Church of Jesus Christ of Latter-day Saints will be pointed to as an epoch of wonderful events" (*MFP,* 2:298).

Suggestions for Study

- How did Brigham Young come to know the Church was true?
- How did Brigham Young's willingness to be obedient and make sacrifices help him build and defend the kingdom of God?
- What can members of the Church today learn from Brigham Young's constant support of the Prophet Joseph Smith?

- What were some of the events in Brigham Young's life that prepared him to preside over the Church? How is the Lord preparing each of us to serve in the kingdom of God?

- What did President Young say was the express purpose for the gathering of the Saints? In what ways did President Young build up the kingdom of God?

- What did Brigham Young say is the "Government of the Son of God"? How did President Young magnify his priesthood?

- What is required to "rear up a generation of men and women who shall love and maintain truth and righteousness in the earth"? What did Brigham Young do to accomplish this? Why is this so important today?

- How did President Young help the Saints to see and understand the eternal truths of the gospel? Why do you feel it will be beneficial to study and ponder the teachings of Brigham Young over the next two years?

The Salt Lake Temple in the 1880s. The Saints felt a great
desire to build a temple to their God.

The Gospel Defined

The world knows President Brigham Young as a great colonizer who directed the transformation of a desert wilderness into a beautiful habitation. More important, he was a profound teacher of the restored gospel of Jesus Christ who inspired the early Saints to live the well-defined doctrine of a religion that assures everyone an opportunity to return to the presence of God.

Teachings of Brigham Young

The gospel of Jesus Christ encompasses a system of laws and ordinances that leads to salvation.

Our religion is nothing more nor less than the true order of heaven—the system of laws by which the gods and the angels are governed. Are they governed by law? Certainly. There is no being in all the eternities but what is governed by law (*DBY,* 1).

The Gospel of the Son of God that has been revealed is a plan or system of laws and ordinances, by strict obedience to which the people who inhabit this earth are assured that they may return again into the presence of the Father and the Son. The laws of the Gospel are neither more nor less than a few of the principles of eternity revealed to the people, by which they can return to heaven from whence they came (*DBY,* 1).

When we talk of the celestial law which is revealed from heaven, that is, the Priesthood, we are talking about the principle of salvation, a perfect system of government, of laws and ordinances, by which we can be prepared to pass from one gate to another, and from one sentinel to another, until we go into the presence of our Father and God (*DBY,* 130).

We may receive the truth, and know, through every portion of the soul, that the Gospel is the power of God unto salvation; that it is the way to life eternal (*DBY,* 90).

Our religion, in common with everything of which God is the Author, is a system of law and order. He has instituted laws and ordinances for the government and benefit of the children of men, to see if they would obey them and prove themselves worthy of eternal life by the law of the celestial worlds (*DBY,* 1).

The Lord has not established laws by which I am compelled to have my shoes made in a certain style. He has never given a law to determine whether I shall have a square-toed boot or a peaked-toe boot; whether I shall have a coat with the waist just under my arms, and the skirts down to my heels; or whether I shall have a coat like the one I have on. Intelligence, to a certain extent, was bestowed both upon Saint and sinner, to use independently, aside from whether they have the law of the Priesthood or not, whether they have ever heard of it or not (*DBY,* 63).

You know that it is one peculiarity of our faith and religion never to ask the Lord to do a thing without being willing to help him all that we are able; and then the Lord will do the rest. I shall not ask the Lord to do what I am not willing to do (*DBY,* 43).

The gospel of Jesus Christ embraces all truth.

All truth is for the salvation of the children of men—for the benefit and learning—for their furtherance in the principles of divine knowledge; and divine knowledge is any matter of fact—truth; and all truth pertains to divinity (*DBY,* 11).

Be willing to receive the truth, let it come from whom it may; no difference, not a particle. Just as soon receive the Gospel from Joseph Smith as from Peter, who lived in the days of Jesus. Receive it from one man as soon as another. If God has called an individual and sent him to preach the Gospel that is enough for me to know; it is no matter who it is, all I want is to know the truth (*DBY,* 11).

"Mormonism," so-called, embraces every principle pertaining to life and salvation, for time and eternity. No matter who has it. If the infidel has got truth it belongs to "Mormonism." The truth and sound doctrine possessed by the sectarian world, and they have a great deal, all belong to this Church. As for their morality, many of them are, morally, just as good as we are. All that is good, lovely, and praiseworthy belongs to this Church and Kingdom. "Mormonism" includes all truth. There is no truth but what belongs to the Gospel. It is life, eternal life; it is bliss; it is the fulness of all things in the gods and in the eternities of the gods (*DBY,* 3).

In a word, if "Mormonism" is not my life, I do not know that I have any. I do not understand anything else, for it embraces everything that comes within the range of the understanding of man. If it does not circumscribe every thing that is in heaven and on earth, it is not what it purports to be (*DBY,* 2).

I want to say to my friends that we believe in all good. If you can find a truth in heaven, earth or hell, it belongs to our doctrine. We believe it; it is ours; we claim it (*DBY,* 2).

16

[The gospel] embraces all morality, all virtue, all light, all intelligence, all greatness, and all goodness. It introduces a system of laws and ordinances (*DBY,* 3).

Such a plan incorporates every system of true doctrine on the earth, whether it be ecclesiastical, moral, philosophical, or civil; it incorporates all good laws that have been made from the days of Adam until now; it swallows up the laws of nations, for it exceeds them all in knowledge and purity, it circumscribes the doctrines of the day, and takes from the right and the left, and brings all truth together in one system, and leaves the chaff to be scattered hither and thither (*DBY,* 3–4).

It is our duty and calling, as ministers of the same salvation and Gospel, to gather every item of truth and reject every error. Whether a truth be found with professed infidels, or with the Universalists, or the Church of Rome, or the Methodists, the Church of England, the Presbyterians, the Baptists, the Quakers, the Shakers, or any other of the various and numerous different sects and parties, all of whom have more or less truth, it is the business of the Elders of this Church (Jesus, their Elder Brother, being at their head) to gather up all the truths in the world pertaining to life and salvation, to the Gospel we preach, . . . to the sciences, and to philosophy, wherever it may be found in every nation, kindred, tongue, and people and bring it to Zion (*DBY,* 248).

All knowledge and wisdom and every good that the heart of man can desire is within the circuit and circle of the faith we have embraced (*DBY,* 446).

It embraces every fact there is in the heavens and in the heaven of heavens—every fact there is upon the surface of the earth, in the bowels of the earth, and in the starry heavens; in fine, it embraces all truth there is in all the eternities of the Gods (*DBY,* 448).

Our religion measures, weighs, and circumscribes all the wisdom in the world—all that God has ever revealed to man. God has revealed all the truth that is now in the possession of the world, whether it be scientific or religious. The whole world are under obligation to him for what they know and enjoy; they are indebted to him for it all, and I acknowledge him in all things (*DBY,* 2).

It comprehends all true science known by man, angels, and the gods. There is one true system and science of life; all else tends to death. That system emanates from the Fountain of life (*DBY,* 2).

Truth will abide when error passes away. Life will remain when they who have rejected the words of eternal life are swallowed up in death. I like the truth because it is true, because it is lovely and delightful, because it is so glorious in its nature, and so worthy the admiration, faith and consideration of all intelligent beings in heaven or on the earth (*DBY,* 9).

17

I delight in this, because truth is calculated to sustain itself; it is based upon eternal facts and will endure, while all else will, sooner or later, perish (*DBY*, 11).

Every individual that lives according to the laws that the Lord has given to his people, and has received the blessings that he has in store for the faithful, should be able to know the things of God from the things which are not of God, the light from the darkness, that which comes from heaven and that which comes from somewhere else. This is the satisfaction and the consolation that the Latter-day Saints enjoy by living their religion; this is the knowledge which every one who thus lives possesses (*DBY*, 35).

How easy it is to live by the truth. Did you ever think of it, my friends? Did you ever think of it, my brethren and sisters? In every circumstance of life, no matter whether among the humble or lofty, truth is always the surest guide and the easiest to square our lives by (*DBY*, 11).

Our religion is simply the truth. It is all said in this one expression—it embraces all truth, wherever found, in all the works of God and man that are visible or invisible to mortal eye (*DBY*, 2).

Through the power of the priesthood, the gospel is the means of salvation for all of God's children.

The Gospel which we preach is the Gospel of life and salvation. The Church which we represent is the Church and Kingdom of God, and possesses the only faith by which the children of men can be brought back into the presence of our Father and God. The Lord has set his hands to restore all things as in the beginning, and by the administration of his holy Priesthood, save all who can be saved, cleanse from the world the consequences of the Fall and give it to the hands of his Saints (*DBY*, 4).

The Priesthood . . . is a perfect order and system of government, and this alone can deliver the human family from all the evils which now afflict its members, and insure them happiness and felicity hereafter (*DBY*, 130).

The Gospel and the Priesthood are the means he employs to save and exalt his obedient children to the possession with him of the same glory and power to be crowned with crowns of glory, immortality and eternal lives (*DBY*, 5).

All the acts we perform should be governed by the guidance of the Priesthood (*DBY*, 133).

There is no ordinance that God has delivered by his own voice, through his Son Jesus Christ, or by the mouths of any of his Prophets, Apostles or Evangelists, that is useless. Every ordinance, every commandment and requirement is necessary for the salvation of the human family (*DBY*, 152).

With regard to the ordinances of God, we may remark that we yield obedience to them because he requires it; and every iota of his requirements has a rational philosophy with it. . . . That philosophy reaches to all eternity, and is the philosophy that the Latter-day Saints believe in. Every particle of truth that every person has received is a gift of God. We receive these truths, and go on from glory to glory, from eternal lives to eternal lives, gaining a knowledge of all things, and becoming Gods, even Sons of God (*DBY,* 152).

The Gospel of Jesus Christ is the opening avenue—the open gate in the road or way from earth to heaven, through which direct revelation comes to the children of men in their various capacities, according to their callings and standing in the society in which they live. The Gospel of salvation is a portion of the law that pertains to the kingdom where God resides; and the ordinances pertaining to the holy Priesthood are the means by which the children of men find access to the way of life, wherein they can extend their travels until they return to the presence of their Father and God (*DBY,* 6).

The laws and ordinances which the Lord has revealed in these latter days, are calculated to save all the sons and daughters of Adam and Eve (*DBY,* 1).

We declare it to all the inhabitants of the earth from the valleys in the tops of these mountains that we are the Church of Jesus Christ of Latter-day Saints . . . and we have the doctrine of life and salvation for all the honest-in-heart in all the world (*DBY,* 7).

Suggestions for Study

The gospel of Jesus Christ encompasses a system of laws and ordinances that leads to salvation.

- According to President Young, the gospel of Jesus Christ is the "power of God unto salvation." How does his statement compare with the Savior's definition of the gospel in 3 Nephi 27:13–14?

- What is the role of the gospel of Jesus Christ in bringing to pass the immortality and eternal life of man? (See also Moses 1:39; Abraham 3:25.) Why do we need a system of laws and ordinances to return to God's presence? In what way are God's laws and ordinances of "benefit [to the] children of men"? (See also 2 Nephi 2:13, 16.)

- President Young taught that God is "governed by law." How can knowing that God is governed by law help us? (See also D&C 82:10.)

- President Young described the gospel as an orderly system. In what matters does God expect us to use our own sound judgment? (See also D&C 58:26–29.)

The gospel of Jesus Christ embraces all truth.

- President Young challenged Latter-day Saints to be seekers of truth. Why do we need to understand that the gospel of Jesus Christ embraces all truth? Why should we accept truth from wherever it might be found? What can we learn from President Young's statement that "all truth pertains to divinity"?

- What do President Young's statements teach about accepting and loving people of other faiths?

- How can we distinguish between truth and error? (See also 1 Corinthians 2:11, 14; Moroni 7:12–17.) Why is the ability to "gather every item of truth and reject every error" so important in the latter days?

- How does knowing gospel truths affect how we live our lives? Why is truth always "the surest guide and the easiest to square our lives by"? How are our lives affected when we live by lies and deception? (See also D&C 88:86.)

Through the power of the priesthood, the gospel is the means of salvation for all of God's children.

- What is the relationship between the priesthood and the gospel of Jesus Christ? Why are priesthood ordinances essential in the gospel plan?

- What is the role of local priesthood quorums, groups, and committees in being ministers of the gospel? What is the place of the Relief Society in teaching truth and building faith in the gospel of Jesus Christ? What experiences have you had with someone providing Christlike service? How have such experiences influenced you?

- President Young taught that the gospel is "the open gate in the road or way from earth to heaven." What responsibility is placed on those who have accepted the restored gospel to spread their witness of its laws, ordinances, and truth? (See also Matthew 28:19–20; Proverbs 22:6.)

Living the Gospel

As a great colonizer, civic and Church leader, and provider for his family, President Brigham Young exemplified the living, practical gospel. He emphasized in his teachings and in his life that the gospel of Jesus Christ is the way to salvation for mankind and also "is a matter-of-fact religion, and taketh hold of the every-day duties and realities of this life" (DBY, 12).

Teachings of Brigham Young

Our personal growth in the gospel comes little by little and line upon line as we live the principles we learn.

W e . . . take all the laws, rules, ordinances and regulations contained in the Scriptures and practice them as far as possible, and then keep learning and improving until we can live by every word that proceeds out of the mouth of God (*DBY,* 3).

We have the Gospel of life and salvation, to make bad men good and good men better (*DBY,* 6).

In conversation not long since with a visitor who was returning to the Eastern States, said he, "You, as a people consider that you are perfect?" "Oh no;" said I, "not by any means. . . . The doctrine that we have embraced is perfect; but when we come to the people, we have just as many imperfections as you can ask for. We are not perfect; but the Gospel that we preach is calculated to perfect the people so that they can obtain a glorious resurrection and enter into the presence of the Father and the Son" (*DBY,* 7).

The people [cannot receive the laws] in their perfect fulness; but they can receive a little here and a little there, a little today and a little tomorrow, a little more next week, and a little more in advance of that next year, if they make a wise improvement upon every little they receive; if they do not, they are left in the shade, and the light which the Lord reveals will appear darkness to them, and the kingdom of heaven will travel on and leave them groping. Hence, if we wish to act upon the fulness of the knowledge that the Lord designs to reveal, little by little, to the inhabitants of the earth, we must improve upon every little as it is revealed (*DBY*, 4).

I . . . feel to urge upon the Latter-day Saints the necessity of a close application of the principles of the Gospel in our lives, conduct and words and all that we do; and it requires the whole man, the whole life to be devoted to improvement in order to come to knowledge of the truth as it is in Jesus Christ. Herein is the fulness of perfection. It was couched in the character of our Savior; although but a scanty portion of it was made manifest to the people, in consequence of their not being able to receive it. All they were prepared to receive he gave them. All we are prepared to receive the Lord gives us; all that the nations of the earth are prepared to receive he imparts unto them (*DBY*, 11–12).

It is written of the Savior in the Bible that he descended below all things that he might ascend above all. Is it not so with every man? Certainly it is. It is fit, then, that we should descend below all things and come up gradually, and learn a little now and again, receive "line upon line, precept upon precept, here a little and there a little" [see Isaiah 28:9–10; D&C 98:12] (*DBY*, 60) until we can reach into eternity and embrace a fulness of his glory, excellency and power (*DBY*, 3).

The spiritual and temporal aspects of the gospel are one.

With God, and also with those who understand the principles of life and salvation, the Priesthood, the oracles of truth and the gifts and callings of God to the children of men, there is no difference in spiritual and temporal labors—all are one. If I am in the line of my duty, I am doing the will of God, whether I am preaching; praying, laboring with my hands for an honorable support; whether I am in the field, mechanic's shop, or following mercantile business, or wherever duty calls, I am serving God as much in one place as another; and so it is with all, each in his place, turn and time (*DBY*, 8).

In the mind of God there is no such a thing as dividing spiritual from temporal, or temporal from spiritual; for they are one in the Lord [see D&C 29:34–35] (*DBY*, 13).

Anything that pertains to the building up of the Lord's kingdom on earth, whether it be in preaching the Gospel or building temples to his name, we have been taught to consider a spiritual work, though it evidently requires the strength of the natural body to perform it (*DBY*, 13).

We cannot even enter the temple when it is built, and perform those ordinances which lead to spiritual blessings, without performing a temporal labor. Temporal ordinances must be performed to secure the spiritual blessings the Great Supreme has in store for his faithful children. Every act is first a temporal act. The Apostle says, faith comes by hearing [see Romans 10:17]. What should be heard to produce faith? The preaching of the Word. For that we must have a preacher; and he is not an invisible spirit, but a temporal, ordinary man like ourselves, and subject to the same regulations and rules of life. To preach the Gospel is a temporal labor, and to believe on the Lord Jesus Christ is the result of a temporal labor. To be baptized is a temporal labor, both to the person administered to and the administrator. I am a living witness to the truth of this statement, for I have made my feet sore many a time, and tired myself out traveling and preaching, that by hearing the Gospel the people might have faith. The blessings we so earnestly desire will come to us by performing the manual labor required, and thus preparing all things necessary to receive the invisible blessings Jehovah has for his children (*DBY,* 13–14).

The gospel is a guide for daily life—a practical religion.

The religion of Jesus Christ is a matter-of-fact religion, and taketh hold of the every-day duties and realities of this life (*DBY,* 12).

The principles of eternity and eternal exaltation are of no use to us, unless they are brought down to our capacities so that we practice them in our lives (*DBY,* 14).

I reduce the Gospel to the present time, circumstances and condition of the people (*DBY,* 8).

That system that brings present security and peace is the best to live by, and the best to die by; it is the best for doing business; it is the best for making farms, for building cities and temples, and that system is the law of God. But it requires strict obedience. The rule of right, and the line which God has drawn for the people to walk by insures peace, comfort, and happiness now and eternal glory and exaltation; but nothing short of strict obedience to God's law will do this (*DBY,* 8).

At times when I think of addressing you, it occurs to me that strict sermonizing upon topics pertaining to the distant future, or reviewing the history of the past, will doubtless please and highly interest a portion of my hearers; but my judgment and the spirit of intelligence that is in me teach that, by taking such a course, the people could not be instructed pertaining to their every-day duties. For this reason, I do not feel impressed to instruct you on duties to be performed a hundred years hence, but rather to give those instructions pertaining to the present, to our daily walk and conversation, that we may know how to benefit ourselves under the passing time, and present privileges, and be able to lay a foundation for future happiness (*DBY,* 12).

My mission to the people is to teach them with regard to their every-day lives. I presume there are many here who have heard me say, years and years ago, that I cared very little about what will take place after the Millennium. Elders may preach long discourses concerning what took place in the days of Adam, what occurred before the creation, and what will take place thousands of years from now, talking of things which have occurred or that will occur yet, of which they are ignorant, feeding the people on wind; but that is not my method of teaching. My desire is to teach the people what they should do now, and let the Millennium take care of itself. To teach them to serve God and to build up his Kingdom is my mission. I have taught faith, repentance, baptism for the remission of sins, and the laying on of hands for the reception of the Holy Ghost. We are to be taught with regard to our every-day life in a temporal point of view (*DBY,* 8–9).

We do not allow ourselves to go into a field to plough without taking our religion with us; we do not go into an office, behind the counter to deal out goods, into a counting house with the books, or anywhere to attend to or transact any business without taking our religion with us. If we are railroading or on a pleasure trip our God and our religion must be with us (*DBY,* 8).

We want the Saints to increase in goodness, until our mechanics, for instance, are so honest and reliable that this Railroad Company will say, "Give us a 'Mormon' Elder for an engineer, then none need have the least fear to ride, for if he knows there is danger he will take every measure necessary to preserve the lives of those entrusted to his care." I want to see our Elders so full of integrity that they will be preferred by this Company for their engine builders, watchmen, engineers, clerks, and business managers. If we live our religion and are worthy the name of Latter-day Saints, we are just the men that all such business can be entrusted to with perfect safety; if it can not it will prove that we do not live our religion (*DBY,* 232–33).

Our religion incorporates every act and word of man. No man should go to merchandising unless he does it in God; no man should go to farming or any other business unless he does it in the Lord. No man of council should sit to judge the people but what should judge in the Lord, that he may righteously and impartially discern between right and wrong, truth and error, light and darkness, justice and injustice (*DBY,* 9).

On reading carefully the Old and New Testaments we can discover that the majority of the revelations given to mankind anciently were in regard to their daily duties; we follow in the same path. The revelations contained in the Bible and the Book of Mormon are examples to us, and the book of Doctrine and Covenants contains direct revelation to this Church; they are a guide to us, and we do not wish to do them away; we do not want them to become obsolete and to set them aside. We wish to continue in the revelations of the Lord Jesus Christ day by day, and to have his Spirit with us continually. If we can do this, we shall no more walk in darkness but we shall walk in the light of life (*DBY,* 12).

If we wish to enjoy the Spirit of Zion, we must live for it. Our religion is not merely theory; it is a practical religion, to bring present enjoyment to every heart (*DBY,* 12).

The work of building up Zion is in every sense a practical work; it is not a mere theory. A theoretical religion amounts to very little real good or advantage to any person. To possess an inheritance in Zion or in Jerusalem only in theory—only in imagination—would be the same as having no inheritance at all. It is necessary to get a deed of it, to make an inheritance practical, substantial and profitable. Then let us not rest contented with a mere theoretical religion, but let it be practical, self-purifying and self-sustaining, keeping the love of God within us, walking by every precept, by every law, and by every word that is given to lead us (*DBY,* 12).

And if I today attend to what devolves upon me to do, and then do that which presents itself tomorrow, and so on, when eternity comes I will be prepared to enter on the things of eternity. But I would not be prepared for that sphere of action, unless I could manage the things that are now within my reach. You must all learn to do this (*DBY,* 11).

The very object of our existence here is to handle the temporal elements of this world and subdue the earth, multiplying those organisms of plants and animals God has designed shall dwell upon it (*DBY,* 15).

Life is for us, and it is for us to receive it today, and not wait for the Millennium. Let us take a course to be saved today, and, when evening comes, review the acts of the day, repent of our sins, if we have any to repent of, and say our prayers; then we can lie down and sleep in peace until the morning, arise with gratitude to God, commence the labors of another day, and strive to live the whole day to God and nobody else (*DBY,* 16).

The responsibility to take care of ourselves and our families is an important practical application of the gospel.

I have tried continually to get this people to pursue a course that will make them self-sustaining, taking care of their poor, the lame, the halt and the blind, lifting the ignorant from where they have no opportunity of observing the ways of the world, and of understanding the common knowledge possessed among the children of men, bringing them together from the four quarters of the world, and making of them an intelligent, thrifty and self-sustaining people (*DBY,* 16).

My warfare is, and has been for years, to get the people to understand that if they do not take care of themselves they will not be taken care of; that if we do not lay the foundation to feed and clothe and shelter ourselves we shall perish with hunger and with cold; we might also suffer in the summer season from the direct rays of the sun upon our naked and unprotected bodies (*DBY,* 16–17).

Who are deserving of praise? The persons who take care of themselves or the ones who always trust in the great mercies of the Lord to take care of them? It is just as consistent to expect that the Lord will supply us with fruit when we do not plant the trees; or that when we do not plow and sow and are saved the labor of harvesting, we should cry to the Lord to save us from want, as to ask him to save us from the consequences of our own folly, disobedience and waste (*DBY,* 293).

Instead of searching after what the Lord is going to do for us, let us inquire what we can do for ourselves (*DBY,* 293).

While we have a rich soil in this valley, and seed to put in the ground, we need not ask God to feed us, nor follow us round with a loaf of bread begging of us to eat it. He will not do it, neither would I, were I the Lord. We can feed ourselves here; and if we are ever placed in circumstances where we cannot, it will then be time enough for the Lord to work a miracle to sustain us (*DBY,* 294).

If you cannot provide for your natural lives, how can you expect to have wisdom to obtain eternal lives? God has given you your existence—your body and spirit, and has blest you with ability, and thereby laid the foundation of all knowledge, wisdom, and understanding, and all glory and eternal lives. If you have not attained ability to provide for your natural wants, and for a wife and a few children, what have you to do with heavenly things? (*DBY,* 13).

Look to yourselves in your capacity as Relief Societies in this city and throughout the mountains. Look at your condition. Consider it for yourselves, and decide whether you will go to and learn the influence which you possess, and then wield that influence for doing good and to relieve the poor among the people (*DNW,* 17 Aug. 1869, 3).

Suggestions for Study

Our personal growth in the gospel comes little by little and line upon line as we live the principles we learn.

- Why does the Lord teach us gospel truths "a little today and a little tomorrow"? (See also Isaiah 28:9–10; 2 Nephi 28:30; D&C 98:12.) What must we do to receive a greater portion of gospel truths? (See also Alma

12:9–11.) What might happen if we are given more truth than we are prepared to receive?

- Why is living a principle of the gospel sometimes essential to learning that principle? (See also John 7:17; D&C 93:28.)
- How do we limit what God can teach us?

The spiritual and temporal aspects of the gospel are one.

- President Young said there is "no such a thing as dividing spiritual from temporal." How should an understanding of that statement affect our approach to our daily tasks?

The gospel is a guide for daily life—a practical religion.

- President Young taught the Saints to apply the principles of the gospel in a practical way in their daily lives. How should the gospel influence our decisions about our family, occupation, and other responsibilities?
- What do you think President Young meant when he said that we should not go "anywhere to attend to or transact any business without taking our religion with us"? How can we take our religion with us everywhere we go and still be sensitive to the beliefs of others? How can we rely more on the Spirit to help us take our religion with us wherever we are?
- In addition to missionary work and Church service, what is our responsibility in the community?

The responsibility to take care of ourselves and our families is an important practical application of the gospel.

- What did President Young teach about our responsibility to take care of ourselves? How can we become self-reliant in spiritual, educational, physical, emotional, and economic ways? How can we help others do so?
- Why is self-reliance an important part of the gospel?
- President Young spoke of the virtue and necessity of providing for ourselves. What blessings come into our lives as we do this? Under what circumstances does President Young say the Lord will "work a miracle to sustain us"?

An artist's perception of Joseph Smith's First Vision. President Young said that Joseph Smith "took heaven, . . . and brought it down to earth" by revealing the true nature of the Godhead (*DBY,* 458).

CHAPTER 4

Knowing and Honoring
the Godhead

God the Father, His Son Jesus Christ, and the Holy Ghost constitute the Godhead. President Brigham Young taught the Latter-day Saints to worship God the Father and address prayers to Him in the name of Jesus Christ. He taught further that God the Father was once a man on another planet who "passed the ordeals we are now passing through; he has received an experience, has suffered and enjoyed, and knows all that we know regarding the toils, sufferings, life and death of this mortality" (DBY, 22).

Teachings of Brigham Young

God the Father designed and governs countless worlds, created mankind, and is a personage who can be known and worshiped.

We believe in one God, one Mediator and one Holy Ghost [see Articles of Faith 1:1]. We cannot believe for a moment that God is destitute of body, parts, passions, or attributes. Attributes can be made manifest only through an organized personage. All attributes are couched in and are the results of organized existence (*DBY,* 23).

Some would have us believe that God is present everywhere. It is not so. He is no more every where present in person than the Father and Son are one in person (*DBY,* 23–24).

God is considered to be everywhere present at the same moment; and the Psalmist says, "Whither shall I flee from thy presence?" [Psalm 139:7]. He is present with all his creations through his influence, through his government, spirit and power, but he himself is a personage of tabernacle, and we are made after his likeness (*DBY,* 24).

Some believe or conceive the idea that to know God would lessen him in our estimation; but I can say that for me to understand any principle or being, on earth or in heaven, it does not lessen its true value to me, but on the contrary, it increases it; and the more I can know of God, the dearer and more precious he is to me, and the more exalted are my feelings towards him (*DBY,* 18).

29

Let every person be the friend of God [see James 2:23] (*DBY,* 18).

The great architect, manager and superintendent, controller and dictator [absolute ruler] who guides this work is out of sight to our natural eyes. He lives on another world; he is in another state of existence; he has passed the ordeals we are now passing through; he has received an experience, has suffered and enjoyed, and knows all that we know regarding the toils, sufferings, life and death of this mortality, for he has passed through the whole of it, and has received his crown and exaltation and holds the keys and the power of this Kingdom; he sways his scepter, and does his will among the children of men, among Saints and among sinners, and brings forth results to suit his purpose among kingdoms and nations and empires, that all may redound to his glory and to the perfection of his work (*DBY,* 22).

He presides over the worlds on worlds that illuminate this little planet, and millions on millions of worlds that we cannot see; and yet he looks upon the minutest object of his creations; not one of these creatures escapes his notice; and there is not one of them but his wisdom and power has produced (*DBY,* 20).

Our Father in Heaven begat all the spirits that ever were, or ever will be, upon this earth [see Hebrews 12:9]; and they were born spirits in the eternal world. Then the Lord by his power and wisdom organized the mortal tabernacle of man. We were made first spiritual, and afterwards temporal (*DBY,* 24).

It is written that God knows all things and has all power [see 1 Nephi 9:6] (*DBY,* 20).

He is the Supreme Controller of the universe. At his rebuke the sea is dried up, and the rivers become a wilderness. He measures the waters in the hollow of his hand, and meteth out heaven with a span, and comprehendeth the dust of the earth in a measure, and weigheth the mountains in scales, and the hills in a balance; the nations to him are as a drop in a bucket, and he taketh up the isles as a very little thing; the hairs of our heads are numbered by him, and not a sparrow falleth to the ground without our Father; and he knoweth every thought and intent of the hearts of all living, for he is everywhere present by the power of his Spirit—his minister, the Holy Ghost. He is the Father of all, is above all, through all, and in you all [see Ephesians 4:6]; he knoweth all things pertaining to this earth, and he knows all things pertaining to millions of earths like this (*DBY,* 19).

He has given form, motion and life to this material world; has made the great and small lights that bespangle the firmament above; has allotted to them their times and their seasons, and has marked out their spheres. He has caused the air and the waters to teem with life, and covered the hills and plains with creeping things, and has made man to be a ruler over his creations (*DBY,* 18).

God is the source, the fountain of all intelligence, no matter who possesses it, whether man upon the earth, the spirits in the spirit-world, the angels that dwell in the eternities of the Gods, or the most inferior intelligence among the devils in hell. All have derived what intelligence, light, power, and existence they have from God—from the same source from which we have received ours. Every good and perfect gift cometh from God [see James 1:17]. Every discovery in science and art, that is really true and useful to mankind has been given by direct revelation from God, though but few acknowledge it. It has been given with a view to prepare the way for the ultimate triumph of truth, and the redemption of the earth from the power of sin and Satan (*DBY,* 18).

Many have tried to penetrate to the First Cause of all things; but it would be as easy for an ant to number the grains of sand on the earth. It is not for man, with his limited intelligence, to grasp eternity in his comprehension. . . . It would be as easy for a gnat to trace the history of man back to his origin as for man to fathom the First Cause of all things, lift the veil of eternity, and reveal the mysteries that have been sought after by philosophers from the beginning. What then, should be the calling and duty of the children of men? Instead of inquiring after the origin of Gods—instead of trying to explore the depths of eternities that have been, that are, and that will be, instead of endeavoring to discover the boundaries of boundless space, let them seek to know the object of their present existence, and how to apply, in the most profitable manner for their mutual good and salvation, the intelligence they possess. Let them seek to know and thoroughly understand things within their reach, and to make themselves well acquainted with the object of their being here, by diligently seeking unto a super-power for information and by the careful study of the best books (*DBY,* 25).

Jesus Christ, the Only Begotten Son of the Father in the flesh, atoned for the sins of all who repent.

The Latter-day Saints believe in Jesus Christ, the only begotten Son of the Father [in the flesh], who came in the meridian of time, performed his work, suffered the penalty and paid the debt of man's original sin by offering up himself, was resurrected from the dead, and ascended to his Father; and as Jesus descended below all things, so he will ascend above all things. We believe that Jesus Christ will come again, as it is written of him: "And while they looked steadfastly toward heaven as he went up, behold two men stood by them in white apparel; which also said, Ye men of Galilee, why stand ye gazing up into heaven? this same Jesus which is taken from

31

you into heaven, shall so come in like manner as ye have seen him go into heaven [Acts 1:10–11]" (*DBY,* 26).

Our faith is concentrated in the Son of God, and through him in the Father (*DBY,* 26).

The Latter-day Saints and every other person who is entitled to salvation, and all except those who have sinned against the Holy Ghost, may know that Jesus is the Christ in the same way that Peter knew it [see Matthew 16:13–19]. Miracles do not give this knowledge to mankind, though they may serve as collateral evidence to strengthen the believer. The miracles of Jesus were known to the Jews, yet they suffered him to be put to death as a deceiver of mankind and one possessed of a devil (*DBY,* 28).

Jesus undertook to establish the Kingdom of God upon the earth. He introduced the laws and ordinances of the Kingdom (*DBY,* 29).

He did nothing of himself. He wrought miracles and performed a good work on the earth; but of himself he did nothing. He said, "As I have seen my Father do, so do I" [see John 5:19]. "I came not to do my will, but the will of him that sent me" [see John 5:30]. We must come to the conclusion that the Son of God did not suggest, dictate, act, or produce any manifestation of his power, of his glory, or of his errand upon the earth, only as it came from the mind and will of his Father (*DBY,* 26).

"I and my Father are one," [John 10:30] says Jesus; what, one body? No. . . . They are no more one person than I and one of my sons are one person. If my son receives my teaching, will walk in the path I mark out for him to walk in, if his faith is the same as mine, his purpose is the same, and he does the work of his father as Jesus did the work of his Father, then is my son one with me in the scriptural sense (*DBY,* 28).

The Lord has revealed to us a plan by which we may be saved both here and hereafter. God has done everything we could ask, and more than we could ask. The errand of Jesus to earth was to bring his brethren and sisters back into the presence of the Father; he has done his part of the work, and it remains for us to do ours. There is not one thing that the Lord could do for the salvation of the human family that he has neglected to do; and it remains for the children of men to receive the truth or reject it; all that can be accomplished for their salvation, independent of them, has been accomplished in and by the Savior. . . . He is now King of kings and Lord of lords, and the time will come when every knee will bow and every tongue confess [see Mosiah 27:31], to the glory of God the Father, that Jesus is the Christ [see Philippians 2:10–11]. That very character that was looked upon, not as the Savior, but as an outcast, who was crucified between two thieves and treated with scorn and derision, will be greeted by all men as the only Being through whom they can obtain salvation (*DBY,* 27).

The Holy Ghost is a personage of spirit who bears witness to truth.

The Holy Ghost, we believe, is one of the characters that form . . . the Godhead. Not one person in three, nor three persons in one; but the Father, Son, and Holy Ghost are one in essence, as the hearts of three men who are united in all things. He is one of the three characters we believe in, whose office it is to administer to those of the human family who love the truth. I have stated that they are one, as the hearts of three men might be one. Lest you should mistake me, I will say that I do not wish you to understand that the Holy Ghost is a personage having a tabernacle, like the Father and the Son; but he is God's messenger that diffuses his influence through all the works of the Almighty (*DBY,* 30).

The Holy Ghost is [the Father and the Son's] minister to bring truths to our remembrance, to reveal new truths to us, and teach, guide, and direct the course of every mind, until we become perfected and prepared to go home, where we can see and converse with our Father in Heaven (*DBY,* 26).

I have proven to my satisfaction, according to the best knowledge I can gather, that man can be deceived by the sight of the natural eye, he can be deceived by the hearing of the ear, and by the touch of the hand; that he can be deceived in all of what is called the natural senses. But there is one thing in which he cannot be deceived. What is that? It is the operations of the Holy Ghost, the Spirit and power of God upon the creature. It teaches him of heavenly things; it directs him in the way of life; it affords him the key by which he can test the devices of man, and which recommends the things of God. Not only the Saints who are present, and who gathered to Zion, but those of every nation, continent, or island who live the religion taught by our Savior and his Apostles, and also by Joseph Smith; they also bear the same testimony, their eyes have been quickened by the Spirit of God, and they see alike, their hearts have been quickened, and they feel and understand alike, and there are no disputations among them with regard to the doctrines of the Savior (*DBY,* 31).

Without the power of the Holy Ghost a person is liable to go to the right or the left from the straight path of duty; they are liable to do things they are sorry for; they are liable to make mistakes; and when they try to do their best, behold they do that which they dislike (*DBY,* 31).

I want to see men and women breathe the Holy Ghost in every breath of their lives, living constantly in the light of God's countenance (*DBY,* 31).

Suggestions for Study

God the Father designed and governs countless worlds, created mankind, and is a personage who can be known and worshiped.

- What did President Young teach about the importance of knowing God the Father? (See also John 17:3.) How does knowing someone affect our relationship with that person? What things have helped you come to know God the Father?

- How can God's influence be "considered to be everywhere present at the same moment"? What are some examples of Heavenly Father's concern for even the "minutest object of his creations"?

- The doctrine that God was once a man and has progressed to become a God is unique to this Church. How do you feel, knowing that God, through His own experience, "knows all that we know regarding the toils [and] sufferings" of mortality?

- President Young taught that all good and true discoveries in science and art have "been given by direct revelation from God." How have inspired advances in these areas helped to move God's work forward?

- What does President Young say is the "calling and duty of the children of men"? How can we better understand things within our reach and be acquainted with our purpose on earth? Where should we seek for such understanding?

Jesus Christ, the Only Begotten Son of the Father in the flesh, atoned for the sins of all who repent.

- What did President Young teach about Jesus Christ and His mission on earth?

- The first principle of the gospel is faith in the Lord Jesus Christ. In what ways does having faith in the Son of God change our lives? (See also Jacob 4:10–11 and Moroni 7:41–42.)

- President Young taught that every Latter-day Saint may know that Jesus is the Christ in the same way that the Apostle Peter knew (see also Matthew 16:13–19). How may someone come to know that Jesus is the Christ? Why do miracles by themselves not provide enough knowledge for a person to know that Jesus is the Christ? Why is this knowledge so important to our salvation?

- Whose errand did Jesus perform when He ministered to the inhabitants of the earth? What can we learn from Jesus' example and apply to our lives? How can we learn and accept our own errands from the Lord?

- President Young reminded us that one day "every knee will bow and every tongue confess" that Jesus is the Christ (Mosiah 27:31; see also Philippians 2:9–11). Living as a true disciple of Jesus Christ is more difficult than merely saying that Jesus is the Christ. What can give you the strength to live the gospel as a dedicated disciple?

The Holy Ghost is a personage of spirit who bears witness to truth.

- What is the mission of the Holy Ghost? How does He work in the lives of God's children?
- How is the personage of the Holy Ghost different from that of God the Father and His Son Jesus Christ? (See also D&C 130:22.) In what way are the three members of the Godhead "one"?
- How is the Holy Ghost the minister for the Father and the Son?
- What experiences have you had that testify to you of the Holy Ghost's ability to teach and guide you?

President Brigham Young taught that "all who attain to any glory whatever, in any kingdom, will do so because Jesus has purchased it by his atonement" (*DBY,* 30).

Accepting the Atonement of Jesus Christ

Regarding the Atonement, President Brigham Young wrote the following to one of his sons: "To obtain the full benefit of that infinite atonement made by our Lord and Savior is within our reach—is ours—fully and completely, but only so, on condition of our faithfulness in observing our covenants and obligations to keep the divine commandments given to us" (LBY, 259). President Young taught that all hopes for salvation are founded on the Atonement of the Savior, Jesus Christ.

Teachings of Brigham Young

Jesus Christ offered mankind an infinite atonement.

The Latter-day Saints are believers in the atonement of the Savior, and I would like to have the Elders of Israel understand as far as they can all the points of doctrine in regard to the redemption of the human family, that they may know how to talk about and explain them (*DNSW,* 18 Aug. 1874, 2).

Jesus came to establish his spiritual kingdom, or to introduce a code of morals that would exalt the spirits of the people to godliness and to God, that they might thereby secure to themselves a glorious resurrection and a title to reign on the earth when the kingdoms of this world should become the kingdoms of our God and his Christ. He also came to introduce himself as the Savior of the world, to shed his blood upon the altar of atonement, and open up the way of life to all believers (*DNW,* 13 Aug. 1862, 1).

Joseph [Smith] told us that Jesus was the Christ—the Mediator between God and man—and the Savior of the world. He told us that there was no other name in the heavens nor under the heavens, neither could there be, by which mankind could be saved in the presence of the Father, but by and through the name and ministry of Jesus Christ, and the atonement he made on Mount Calvary. Joseph also told us that the Savior requires strict obedience to all the commandments, ordinances and laws pertaining to his kingdom, and that if we would do this we should be made partakers of all the blessings promised in his Gospel (*DNW,* 22 Oct. 1862, 1).

The moment the atonement of the Savior is done away, that moment, at one sweep, the hopes of salvation entertained by the Christian world are destroyed, the foundation of their faith is taken away, and there is nothing left for them to stand upon. When it is gone all the revelations God ever gave to the Jewish nation, to the Gentiles, and to us are rendered valueless, and all hope is taken from us at one sweep (*DBY,* 27).

Through the gift of the Atonement, which only Christ could give, God's children may inherit a kingdom of glory.

The Latter-day Saints believe in the Gospel of the Son of God, simply because it is true. They believe in baptism for the remission of sins, personal and by proxy; they believe that Jesus is the Savior of the world; they believe that all who attain to any glory whatever, in any kingdom, will do so because Jesus has purchased it by his atonement (*DBY,* 30).

Jesus was appointed, from the beginning, to die for our redemption, and he suffered an excruciating death on the cross (*DBY,* 27).

I can say to you in regard to Jesus and the atonement (it is so written, and I firmly believe it), that Christ has died for all. He has paid the full debt, whether you receive the gift or not. But if we continue to sin, to lie, steal, bear false witness, we must repent of and forsake that sin to have the full efficacy of the blood of Christ. Without this it will be of no effect; repentance must come, in order that the atonement may prove a benefit to us. Let all who are doing wrong cease doing wrong; live no longer in transgression, no matter of what kind; but live every day of your lives according to the revelations given, and so that your examples may be worthy of imitation. Let us remember that we never get beyond the purview of our religion—never, never! (*DBY,* 156–57).

Jesus will bring forth, by his own redemption, every son and daughter of Adam, except the sons of perdition, who will be cast into hell. . . . It is true that every person who does not sin away the day of grace, and become an angel to the Devil, will be brought forth to inherit a kingdom of glory (*DBY,* 382).

Jesus is the first begotten from the dead, as you will understand. Neither Enoch, Elijah, Moses, nor any other man that ever lived on earth, no matter how strictly he lived, ever obtained a resurrection until after Jesus Christ's body was called from the tomb by the angel. He was the first begotten from the dead. He is the Master of the resurrection—the first flesh that lived here after receiving the glory of the resurrection (*DBY,* 374).

This was no miracle to him. He had the issues of life and death in his power; he had power to lay down his life and power to take it up again. This is what he says, and we must believe this if we believe the history of the Savior and the sayings of the Apostles recorded in the New Testament. Jesus had this power in and of himself; the Father bequeathed it to him; it was his legacy, and he had the power to lay down his life and take it again (*DBY*, 340–41).

Christ's Atonement makes forgiveness possible to those who have faith, repent, and obey God.

Darkness and sin were permitted to come on this earth. Man partook of the forbidden fruit in accordance with a plan devised from eternity, that mankind might be brought in contact with the principles and powers of darkness, that they might know the bitter and the sweet, the good and the evil, and be able to discern between light and darkness, to enable them to receive light continually (*DBY*, 61).

This Gospel will save the whole human family; the blood of Jesus will atone for our sins, if we accept the terms he has laid down; but we must accept those terms or else it will avail nothing in our behalf (*DBY*, 7–8).

To be Saints indeed requires every wrong influence that is within them, as individuals, to be subdued, until every evil desire is eradicated, and every feeling of their hearts is brought into subjection to the will of Christ (*DBY*, 91).

It requires all the atonement of Christ, the mercy of the Father, the pity of angels and the grace of the Lord Jesus Christ to be with us always, and then to do the very best we possibly can, to get rid of this sin within us, so that we may escape from this world into the celestial kingdom (*DBY*, 60).

Suggestions for Study

Jesus Christ offered mankind an infinite atonement.

- Why did Jesus come to earth and establish His "spiritual kingdom"? For what other reasons did He come to earth? How did Jesus "open up the way of life to all believers"? How can we teach our families so as to "exalt [their] spirits . . . to godliness and to God"?

- How can we be "saved in the presence of the Father" and "be made partakers of all the blessings promised in his Gospel"?

- According to President Young, what would happen to the Christian world if the Atonement of Jesus Christ were done away with? (See also 2 Nephi 9:6–9.)

- Review the following scriptures to learn about other aspects of the Atonement: Mosiah 13:28, 32–35; Alma 7:11–12; 34:9–12; Moroni 8:8–12; D&C 88:6.

Through the gift of the Atonement, which only Christ could give, God's children may inherit a kingdom of glory.

- Jesus was appointed in the premortal existence "to die for our redemption." He redeems us from physical and spiritual separation from God. This is called the Atonement. President Young stated that Christ's Atonement "has paid the full debt, whether you receive the gift or not." (See also Helaman 14:15–18.) How do we receive the full benefit from the Atonement?
- President Young taught that all who attain to any glory in any kingdom will do so because Jesus purchased it by His Atonement. How did He pay for Adam's debt? How did He pay for our debt? (See also 2 Nephi 2:8–10.)
- How was Jesus able to be the "Master of the resurrection"?

Christ's Atonement makes forgiveness possible to those who have faith, repent, and obey God.

- Why were "darkness and sin permitted to come on this earth"? What are the consequences of the fall of Adam? (See also 2 Nephi 2:22–25.)
- The Atonement provides redemption from our sins on terms "laid down" by our Redeemer. What are those terms? (See also 2 Nephi 2:26; D&C 18:44.)
- What divine help can we draw on in order to "escape from this world into the celestial kingdom"? What is required of us?

The Communication between God and Man

President Brigham Young taught that our "first and foremost duty [is] to seek the Lord until we open the path of communication from God to our own soul." Shortly after the Prophet Joseph Smith's death, Brigham Young told of a dream in which Joseph visited and instructed him: "Joseph stepped toward us, and looking very earnestly, yet pleasantly, said: 'Tell the people to be humble and faithful, and be sure to keep the spirit of the Lord and it will lead them right. Be careful and not turn away the small still voice; it will teach them what to do and where to go; it will yield the fruits of the Kingdom. . . . Tell the brethren that if they will follow the spirit of the Lord, they will go right'" (JH). All God's children have the privilege of being enlightened by the Spirit of Christ and receiving personal revelation through the Holy Ghost as they earnestly seek the Lord.

Teachings of Brigham Young

The Spirit of Christ is given to all God's children to enlighten them and help them know good from evil.

The Spirit of the Lord enlightens every man that comes into the world. There is no one that lives upon the earth but what is, more or less, enlightened by the Spirit of the Lord Jesus. It is said of him, that he is the light of the world. He lighteth every man that comes into the world and every person, at times, has the light of the spirit of truth upon him [see John 1:9; 8:12; Moroni 7:16; D&C 84:46] (*DBY*, 32).

I do not believe for one moment that there has been a man or woman upon the face of the earth, from the days of Adam to this day, who has not been enlightened, instructed, and taught by the revelations of Jesus Christ. "What! the ignorant heathen?" Yes, every human being who has possessed a sane mind. I am far from believing that the children of men have been deprived of the privilege of receiving the Spirit of the Lord to teach them right from wrong (*DBY*, 32).

I . . . believe positively that there is nothing known except by the revelation of the Lord Jesus Christ, whether in theology, science, or art (*DBY*, 38).

There are men of talent, of thought, of reflection, and knowledge in all cunning mechanism; they are expert in that, though they do not know from whence they receive their intelligence. The Spirit of the Lord has not yet entirely [finished] striving with the people, offering them knowledge and intelligence; consequently, it reveals unto them, instructs them, teaches them, and guides them (*DBY,* 33).

God is here: his influence fills immensity. He has his messengers throughout all the works of his hands. He watches every one of his creatures; their acts, their affections, and thoughts are all known to him; for his intelligence and power fill immensity [see D&C 88:6–13]. Not that his person does, but his Spirit does; and he is here teaching, guiding and directing the nations of the earth (*DBY,* 32).

God speaks to His children through revelation.

This people believe in revelation. This people did believe and do believe that the Lord has spoken from the heavens. They did believe and do believe that God has sent angels to proclaim the everlasting Gospel, according to the testimony of John [see Revelation 14:6–7] (*DBY,* 38).

We often hear it said that the living oracles must be in the Church, in order that the Kingdom of God may be established and prosper on the earth. I will give another version of this sentiment. I say that the living oracles of God, or the Spirit of revelation must be in each and every individual, to know the plan of salvation and keep in the path that leads them to the presence of God (*DBY,* 38).

The Lord is not everywhere in person; but he has his agents speaking and acting for him. His angels, his messengers, his apostles and servants are appointed and authorized to act in his name. And his servants are authorized to counsel and dictate in the greatest and what might be deemed the most trifling matters, to instruct, direct and guide his Saints (*DBY,* 41).

No man can gain influence in this Kingdom, and maintain himself in it, magnify his calling without the power of God being with him. Persons must so live that they can enjoy the light of the Holy Spirit, or they will have no confidence in themselves, in their religion, or in their God, and will sooner or later turn from the faith (*DBY,* 33).

It was asked me by a gentleman how I guided the people by revelation. I teach them to live so that the Spirit of revelation may make plain to them their duty day by day that they are able to guide themselves. To get this revelation it is necessary that the people live so that their spirits are as pure and clean as a piece of blank paper that lies on the desk before the [writer], ready to receive any mark the writer may make upon it (*DBY,* 41).

No earthly argument, no earthly reasoning can open the minds of intelligent beings and show them heavenly things; that can only be done by the Spirit of revelation [see 1 Corinthians 2:9–14] (*DBY,* 37).

The revelations of the Lord Jesus Christ, the spirit of truth will detect everything, and enable all who possess it to understand truth from error, light from darkness, the things of God from the things not of God. It is the only thing that will enable us to understand the Gospel of the Son of God, the will of God, and how we can be saved. Follow it, and it will lead to God, the Fountain of light, where the gate will be open, and the mind will be enlightened so that we shall see, know and understand things as they are (*DBY,* 34).

No man can know Jesus the Christ except it be revealed from heaven to him [see 1 Corinthians 12:3] (*DBY,* 37).

Without revelation direct from heaven, it is impossible for any person to understand fully the plan of salvation (*DBY,* 38).

Without the revelations of God we know not who we are, whence we came, nor who formed the earth on which we live, move and have our being (*DBY,* 37).

When the Spirit of revelation from God inspires a man, his mind is opened to behold the beauty, order, and glory of the creation of this earth and its inhabitants, the object of its creation, and the purpose of its Creator in peopling it with his children. He can then clearly understand that our existence here is for the sole purpose of exaltation and restoration to the presence of our Father and God (*DBY,* 37).

In every part and portion of the revelations of God as given to the children of men, or to any individual in heaven or on earth, to understand them properly, a man needs the Spirit by which they were given—the Spirit that reveals such matters to the understanding, and makes them familiar to the mind (*DBY,* 39).

But we should all live so that the Spirit of revelation could dictate and write on the heart and tell us what we should do instead of the traditions of our parents and teachers. But to do this we must become like little children; and Jesus says if we do not we cannot enter the kingdom of heaven. How simple it is! Live free from envy, malice, wrath, strife, bitter feelings, and evil speaking in our families and about our neighbors and friends and all the inhabitants of the earth, wherever we meet them. Live so that our consciences are free, clean and clear (*DBY,* 36).

Should you receive a vision or revelation from the Almighty, one that the Lord gave you concerning yourselves, or this people, but which you are not to reveal on account of your not being the proper person, or because it ought not to be known by the people at present, you should shut it up and seal it as close, and lock it as tight as heaven is to you, and make it as secret as the grave. The Lord has no confidence in those who reveal secrets, for he cannot safely reveal himself to such persons (*DBY,* 40–41).

How do we know that prophets wrote the word of the Lord? By revelation. How do we know that Joseph Smith was called of God to establish his Kingdom upon the earth? By revelation. How do we know that the leaders of this people teach the truth? By revelation (*DBY,* 38).

How can you know the Latter-day work to be true? You can know it only by the spirit of revelation direct from heaven. What proved this work true to you . . . ? Was it not the spirit of revelation that rested upon you? . . . You should add to it day by day; you should add as the Lord gives—a little here and a little there, and treasure up truth in your faith and understanding, until you become perfect before the Lord and are prepared to receive the further things of the Kingdom of God (*DBY,* 36).

When you have labored faithfully for years, you will learn this simple fact—that if your hearts are aright, and you still continue to be obedient, continue to serve God, continue to pray, the Spirit of revelation will be in you like a well of water springing up to everlasting life [see D&C 19:38; 63:23]. Let no person give up prayer because he has not the spirit of prayer, neither let any earthly circumstance hurry you while in the performance of this important duty. By bowing down before the Lord to ask him to bless you, you will simply find this result—God will multiply blessings on you temporally and spiritually (*DBY,* 46).

One of our most important duties is to seek God's will in daily prayer.

Were I to draw a distinction in all the duties that are required of the children of men, from first to last, I would place first and foremost the duty of seeking unto the Lord our God until we open the path of communication from heaven to earth—from God to our own souls. Keep every avenue of your hearts clean and pure before him (*DBY,* 41).

If we draw near to him, he will draw near to us; if we seek him early, we shall find him; if we apply our minds faithfully and diligently day by day, to know and understand the mind and will of God, it is as easy as, yes, I will say easier than it is to know the minds of each other (*DBY,* 42).

Let us be humble, fervent, submissive, yielding ourselves to the will of the Lord, and there is no danger but that we shall have his Spirit to guide us. If we will open our lips and call upon our Heavenly Father, in the name of Jesus, we will have the spirit of prayer (*DBY,* 44).

The Lord says, I will be sought unto by my people for the blessings that they need. And instead of our classing prayer among the duties devolving upon us as Latter-day Saints, we should live so as to deem it one of the greatest privileges accorded to us; for were it not for the efficacy of prayer what would have become of us both as a people and as individuals? (*DBY,* 43).

The duty of the Latter-day Saints is to pray without ceasing, and in everything to give thanks, to acknowledge the hand of the Lord in all things, and to be subject to his requirements (*DBY,* 42).

Let every man and every woman call upon the name of the Lord, and that, too, from a pure heart, while they are at work as well as in their closet; while they are in public as well as while they are in private, asking the Father in the name of Jesus, to bless them, and to preserve and guide in, and to teach them, the way of life and salvation and to enable them so to live that they will obtain this eternal salvation that we are after (*DBY,* 43).

It matters not whether you or I feel like praying, when the time comes to pray, pray. If we do not feel like it, we should pray till we do (*DBY,* 44).

Some of the brethren come to me and say, "Brother Brigham, is it my duty to pray when I have not one particle of the spirit of prayer in me?" True, at times, men are perplexed and full of care and trouble, their ploughs and other implements are out of order, their animals have strayed and a thousand things perplex them; yet our judgment teaches us that it is our duty to pray, whether we are particularly in the spirit of praying or not. My doctrine is, it is your duty to pray; and when the time for prayer comes, John should say, "This is the place and this is the time to pray; knees bend down upon the floor, and do so at once." But John said, "I do not want to pray; I do not feel like it." Knees get down, I say; and down bend the knees, and he begins to think and reflect. Can you say anything? Can you not say, God have mercy on me a sinner? Yes, he can do this, if he can rise up and curse his neighbor for some ill deeds. Now, John, open your mouth and say, Lord, have mercy upon me. "But I do not feel the spirit of prayer." That does not excuse you, for you know what your duty is (*DBY,* 45).

If the Devil says you cannot pray when you are angry, tell him it is none of his business, and pray until that species of insanity is dispelled and serenity is restored to the mind (*DBY,* 45).

When you get up in the morning, before you suffer yourselves to eat one mouthful of food, call your wife and children together, bow down before the Lord, ask him to forgive your sins, and protect you through the day, to preserve you from temptation and all evil, to guide your steps aright, that you may do something that day that shall be beneficial to the Kingdom of God on the earth. Have you time to do this? Elders, sisters, have you time to pray? (*DBY,* 44).

Say your prayers always before going to work. Never forget that. A father—the head of the family—should never miss calling his family together and dedicating himself and them to the Lord of Hosts, asking the guidance and direction of his Holy Spirit to lead them through the day—that very day. Lead us this day, guide us this day, preserve us this day, save us from sinning against thee or any being in heaven or on earth this day! If we do this every day, the last day we live we will be prepared to enjoy a higher glory (*DBY,* 44).

You know that it is one peculiarity of our faith and religion never to ask the Lord to do a thing without being willing to help him all that we are able; and then the Lord will do the rest (*DBY,* 43).

I shall not ask the Lord to do what I am not willing to do (*DBY,* 43).

If I ask him to give me wisdom concerning any requirement in life, or in regard to my own course, or that of my friends, my family, my children, or those that I preside over, and get no answer from him, and then do the very best that my judgment will teach me, he is bound to own and honor that transaction, and he will do so to all intents and purposes (*DBY,* 43).

Let every Saint, when he prays, ask God for the things he needs to enable him to promote righteousness on the earth. If you do not know what to ask for, let me tell you how to pray. When you pray in secret with your families, if you do not know anything to ask for, submit yourselves to your Father in Heaven and beseech him to guide you by the inspirations of the Holy Ghost, and to guide this people, and dictate the affairs of his Kingdom on the earth, and there leave it. Ask him to put you just where he wants you, and to tell you what he wants you to do, and feel that you are on hand to do it (*DBY,* 45–46).

Let all persons be fervent in prayer, until they know the things of God for themselves and become certain that they are walking in the path that leads to everlasting life; then will envy, the child of ignorance, vanish and there will be no disposition in any man to place himself above another; for such a feeling meets no countenance in the order of heaven. Jesus Christ never wanted to be different from his Father. They were and are one. If a people are led by the revelations of Jesus Christ, and they are cognizant of the fact through their faithfulness, there is no fear but they will be one in Jesus Christ, and see eye to eye (*DBY,* 42).

Suggestions for Study

The Spirit of Christ is given to all God's children to enlighten them and help them know good from evil.

- Think about the workings of the Light of Christ or Spirit of the Lord. (See also Bible Dictionary, "Light of Christ," 725; D&C 88:6–13; Moroni 7:12–19.) What does it mean to be "enlightened by the Spirit of the Lord Jesus"?

- How can we know eternal standards of "right from wrong"?

- According to President Young, in what ways is the Spirit of the Lord still "striving with the people"?

- By what power that "fills immensity" does the Lord influence His children? In what sense is God not far from every one of us? (See also Acts 17:27.) What evidence do you see that God influences events throughout the world?

God speaks to His children through revelation.

- Who is authorized by the Lord to receive revelation for the entire Church? (See also D&C 21:4–5; 28:2; 43:3–4; 90:3–5.) Who are the "living oracles"? What is our responsibility in relation to the living oracles?

- President Young said that the teachings of salvation can be known only by revelation. What revelations will the Lord grant to us as individuals? (See also 2 Nephi 32:5; Numbers 11:29.)

- According to President Young, how may we know that we are being led in accordance with the will of God? On what conditions may we receive guiding revelation "day by day" in our lives?

- What promise is made to those who labor "faithfully for years" in prayer, obedience, and service? What experiences have you had with prayer that have helped draw the Spirit into your life?

One of our most important duties is to seek God's will in daily prayer.

- According to President Young, what is our "first and foremost" duty as members of the Church?

- On what conditions are we likely to have the "Spirit to guide us"? (See also 3 Nephi 19:9, 24.)

- What specific counsel did President Young give concerning prayer?

- What is President Young's strong admonition to those who don't feel like praying?

"Jesus will never cease his work until all are brought up to the enjoyment of a kingdom in the mansions of his Father" (*DBY,* 56).

The Plan of Salvation

As a prophet and a teacher of the plan of salvation, President Brigham Young taught that the "design and intent [of] the Supreme Ruler" (DBY, 49) is to make it possible for His children to enjoy eternal happiness. According to this great "plan of happiness" (Alma 42:16), as God's children we each lived in His presence before coming into mortality, where we are privileged to obtain mortal tabernacles and to choose to obey God's commandments. According to our faithfulness, Jesus Christ will bring us to a kingdom of glory.

Teachings of Brigham Young

God wants us to grow forever in light, truth, and happiness.

This life that you and I possess is for eternity. Contemplate the idea of beings endowed with all the powers and faculties which we possess, becoming annihilated, passing out of existence, ceasing to be, and then try to reconcile it with our feelings and with our present lives. No intelligent person can do it. Yet it is only by the Spirit of revelation that we can understand these things [see 1 Corinthians 2:11]. By the revelations of the Lord Jesus we understand things as they were, that have been made known unto us; things that are in the life which we now enjoy, and things as they will be [see D&C 93:24], not to the fullest extent, but all that the Lord designs that we should understand, to make it profitable to us, in order to give us the experience necessary in this life to prepare us to enjoy eternal life hereafter (*DBY*, 47).

If we could so understand true philosophy as to understand our own creation, and what it is for—what design and intent the Supreme Ruler had in organizing matter and bringing it forth in the capacity that I behold you here today, we could comprehend that matter cannot be destroyed—that it is subject to organization and disorganization; and could understand that matter can be organized and brought forth into intelligence, and to possess more intelligence and to continue to increase in that intelligence; and could learn those principles that organized matter into animals, vegetables, and into intelligent beings; and could discern the Divinity acting, operating, and diffusing principles into matter to produce intelligent beings and to exalt them—to what? Happiness. Will nothing short of that fully satisfy the spirits implanted within us? No [see D&C 131:7] (*DBY,* 49).

We are the spirit children of God.

No human being has had power to organize his own existence. Then there is a greater than we. Are we our own in our bodies? Are we our own in our spirits? We are not our own. We belong to our progenitors—to our Father and our God [see Acts 17:29] (*DBY,* 50).

Things were first created spiritually; the Father actually begat the spirits [see D&C 76:24], and they were brought forth and lived with him. Then he commenced the work of creating earthly tabernacles, precisely as he had been created in this flesh himself, by partaking of the coarse material that was organized and composed this earth, . . . consequently the tabernacles of his children were organized from the coarse materials of this earth (*DBY,* 50).

I have heard that the celebrated Mr. [Henry Ward] Beecher, of Brooklyn, once said that the greatest misfortune that could ever happen to man was to be born; but I say that the greatest good fortune that ever happened or can happen to human beings is to be born on this earth, for then life and salvation are before them; then they have the privilege of overcoming death, and of treading sin and iniquity under their feet, of incorporating into their daily lives every principle of life and salvation and of dwelling eternally with the Gods (*DBY,* 51).

The spirits that live in these tabernacles were as pure as the heavens, when they entered them. They came to tabernacles that are contaminated, pertaining to the flesh, by the fall of man. The Psalmist says, "Behold, I was shapen in iniquity; and in sin did my mother conceive me" [Psalm 51:5]. This Scripture has established in the minds of some the doctrine of total depravity—that it is impossible for them to have one good thought, that they are altogether sinful, that there is no good, no soundness, and no spiritual health in them. This is not correct, yet we have a warfare within us. We have to contend against evil passions, or the seeds of iniquity that are sown in the flesh through the fall. The pure spirits that occupy these tabernacles are operated upon, and it is the right of him that sent them into these tabernacles to hold the pre-eminence, and to always give the Spirit of truth to influence the spirits of men, that it may triumph and reign predominantly in our tabernacles, the God and Lord of every motion (*DBY,* 51–52).

We are free to choose good over evil, exaltation over misery.

[The Father asked,] "Who will redeem the earth, who will go forth and make the sacrifice for the earth and all things it contains?" The Eldest Son said: "Here am I"; and then he added, "Send me." But the second one, which was "Lucifer, Son of the Morning," said, "Lord, here am I, send me, I will redeem every son and daughter of Adam and Eve that lives on the earth, or that ever goes on the earth." "But," says the Father, "that will not answer at all. I give each and every individual his agency; all must use that in order to gain exaltation in my kingdom; inasmuch as they have the power of choice they must exercise that power. They are my children; the attributes which you see in me are in my children and they must use their agency. If you undertake to save all, you must save them in unrighteousness and corruption" [see Abraham 3:23–28; Moses 4:1–4] (*DBY,* 53–54).

When there was rebellion in heaven, judgment was laid to the line and righteousness to the plummet, and the evil were cast out (*DBY,* 54).

The Lord Almighty suffered this schism in heaven to see what his subjects would do preparatory to their coming to this earth (*DBY,* 54).

But they [the rebellious spirits] must go from heaven, they could not dwell there, they must be cast down to the earth to try the sons of men, and to perform their labor in producing an opposite in all things, that the inhabitants of the earth might have the privilege of improving upon the intelligence given to them, the opportunity for overcoming evil, and for learning the principles which govern eternity, that they may be exalted therein (*DBY,* 54).

You cannot give any persons their exaltation unless they know what evil is, what sin, sorrow, and misery are, for no person could comprehend, appreciate and enjoy an exaltation upon any other principle (*DBY,* 55).

Do you think that the Lord has his eye upon a great many? . . . I do not think there is anybody now on the earth, that has lived before us, or that will come after us, but what he knew. He knew who would be his anointed; he had his eye upon them all the time, as he had upon Moses, Pharaoh, Abraham, Melchizedek, and Noah, who was a chosen vessel to build the ark and save a remnant from the flood (*DBY,* 55).

It is a mistaken idea that God has decreed all things whatsoever that come to pass, for the volition of the creature is as free as air. You may inquire whether we believe in foreordination; we do, as strongly as any people in the world. We believe that Jesus was foreordained before the foundations of the world were built, and his mission was appointed him in eternity to be the Savior of the world, yet when he came in the flesh he was left free to choose or refuse to obey his Father. Had he refused to obey

51

his Father, he would have become a son of perdition. We also are free to choose or refuse the principles of eternal life. God has decreed and foreordained many things that have come to pass, and he will continue to do so; but when he decrees great blessings upon a nation or upon an individual they are decreed upon certain conditions. When he decrees great plagues and overwhelming destructions upon nations or people, those decrees come to pass because those nations and people will not forsake their wickedness and turn unto the Lord. It was decreed that Nineveh should be destroyed in forty days, but the decree was stayed on the repentance of the inhabitants of Nineveh. God rules and reigns, and has made all his children as free as himself, to choose the right or the wrong, and we shall then be judged according to our works (*DBY,* 55).

According to our faithfulness, Jesus Christ will bring us to a kingdom of glory.

This is the plan of salvation. Jesus will never cease his work until all are brought up to the enjoyment of a kingdom in the mansions of his Father, where there are many kingdoms and many glories, to suit the works and faithfulness of all men that have lived on the earth. Some will obey the celestial law and receive of its glory, some will abide the terrestrial and some the telestial, and others will receive no glory (*DBY,* 56).

Millions of [people] have passed away, both in the Christian and in the heathen worlds, just as honest, virtuous and upright as any now living. The Christian world say they are lost; but the Lord will save them, or at least, all who will receive the Gospel. The plan of salvation which Jesus has revealed, and which we preach, reaches to the lowest and most degraded of Adam's lost race (*DBY,* 60–61).

Suggestions for Study

God wants us to grow forever in light, truth, and happiness.

- How can we know that the "life that you and I possess is for eternity"? What difference does it make to you to know that life is eternal?
- What was God's "design and intent" in organizing the world?
- President Young taught that a principal purpose of life is "to possess more intelligence and to continue to increase in that intelligence." What is the relationship between growing in intelligence, or light and truth (see also D&C 93:36; 130:19), and gaining eternal happiness? How has this been true in your own life?

We are the spirit children of God.

- How do you feel knowing that you are a literal spirit child of our Heavenly Father? What difference has that made in your life?

- Why is "to be born on this earth" the "greatest good fortune that . . . can happen to human beings"? Read and ponder Doctrine and Covenants 93:33. What blessings are associated with your spirit and body being inseparably connected?

- According to President Young, what is the consequence of the Fall of man? What mistaken conclusion do some people come to regarding the Fall? What is the role of the Spirit of Truth in the "warfare within us" between good and evil? How can we make the Spirit of Truth a more dominant force in our lives?

We are free to choose good over evil, exaltation over misery.

- According to President Young, what role does our agency play in gaining our exaltation? Why did God the Father reject Lucifer's proposal to act for each of us? (See also 2 Nephi 2:15–16.)

- Why did the Lord allow a "schism in heaven"? What is the "labor" of those who were cast out of Father's presence? Why must there be "an opposite in all things"? Why must we understand "what evil is" and "what sin, sorrow, and misery are" in order to obtain exaltation? (See also 2 Nephi 2:11.)

- What can you do to fulfill the Lord's wishes and grow to the height of your capacity?

- How can God decree or foreordain certain events and still leave us our freedom of choice?

According to our faithfulness, Jesus Christ will bring us to a kingdom of glory.

- When will Jesus Christ's saving work be finished?

- Through Christ's Atonement, all but the sons of perdition "are brought up to the enjoyment of a kingdom in the mansions of his Father." President Young also stated there are "many kingdoms and many glories." Why are there so many kingdoms? Who determines what kingdom a person will go to?

- How does the Savior's Atonement "reach to the lowest and most degraded" as well as to the "honest, virtuous and upright"?

The early Saints demonstrated great faith in the Lord as they left homes and native lands to gather to Zion under the direction of President Brigham Young.

Faith in the Lord Jesus Christ

Faith in Jesus Christ was a powerful motivating force in the life of President Brigham Young. His faith in the Savior and in the restored gospel of Jesus Christ enabled him to endure severe hardships and trials. By this faith, he embarked on numerous missions; he endured the hardships of Zion's Camp; and he remained steadfast and true to the gospel and to the Prophet Joseph Smith during the difficult times in Kirtland when many Saints left the Church. By this faith, he guided the Saints to the Salt Lake Valley and established the kingdom of God there. He said: "Every person who lives in this Church must be faithful. They cannot run by sight, but must actually exercise faith in the Lord Jesus Christ, in order to enjoy the light of the Holy Ghost. When they neglect this the spirit of the world takes possession of them, and they become cold and fruitless, and pine away into darkness, and spiritual death" (DNW, 25 Apr. 1855, 2).

Teachings of Brigham Young

Faith in the Lord Jesus Christ is the first principle of the gospel and can be understood only by the power of the Holy Ghost.

The Gospel that we preach is the power of God unto salvation; and the first principle of that Gospel is . . . faith in God, and faith in Jesus Christ his Son, our Savior. We must believe that he is the character he is represented to be in the Holy Scriptures. . . . We must believe that this same Jesus was crucified for the sins of the world (*DBY,* 153).

You can say that the Lord and his Gospel are not worthy of notice, or you can bow to them (*DBY,* 153).

To understand the first principles of the Gospel—to rightly understand them, a man must have the wisdom that comes from above; he must be enlightened by the Holy Ghost; . . . he must enjoy the blessings of salvation himself, in order to impart them to others (*DBY,* 152).

Every particle of truth that every person has received is a gift of God. We receive these truths, and go on from glory to glory, . . . gaining a knowledge of all things, and becoming Gods, even Sons of God. These are the celestial ones. These are they whom the Lord has chosen through their

Photograph of wagons in Salt Lake City in the early 1860s.

obedience. They have not spurned the truth, when they have heard it. These are they that have not spurned the Gospel, but have acknowledged Jesus and God in their true character; that have acknowledged the angels in their true character. These are they that work for the salvation of the human family (*DBY,* 152).

Faith in Christ is a gift of God obtained through belief, obedience, and righteous works.

When you believe the principles of the Gospel and attain unto faith, which is a gift of God, he adds more faith, adding faith to faith. He bestows faith upon his creatures as a gift; but his creatures inherently possess the privilege of believing the Gospel to be true or false (*DBY,* 154).

If we speak of faith in the abstract, it is the power of God by which the worlds are and were made, and is a gift of God to those who believe and obey his commandments. On the other hand, no living, intelligent being, whether serving God or not, acts without belief. He might as well undertake to live without breathing as to live without the principle of belief. But he must believe the truth, obey the truth, and practice the truth, to obtain the power of God called faith (*DBY,* 153).

We are under obligation to trust in our God; and this is the ground-work of all we can do ourselves (*DBY,* 154).

When you read the revelations, or when you hear the will of the Lord concerning you, for your own sakes never receive that with a doubtful heart (*DBY,* 155).

Our Heavenly Father does not always reveal to his children the secret workings of his providences, nor does he show them the end from the beginning; for they have to learn to trust in him who has promised to fight our battles, and crown us with victory, if we are faithful as was faithful Abraham (*DBY,* 156).

When men are in the habit of philosophising upon every point, only relying upon what we call human reason, they are constantly liable to error. But place a man in a situation where he is obliged or compelled, in order to sustain himself, to have faith in the name of Jesus Christ, and it brings him to a point where he will know for himself; and happy are those who pass through trials, if they maintain their integrity and their faith to their calling (*DBY,* 154).

Righteous works demonstrate and strengthen faith.

To explain how much confidence we should have in God, were I using a term to suit myself, I should say *implicit* confidence. I have faith in my God, and that faith corresponds with the works I produce. I have no confidence in faith without works (*DBY,* 155).

If the people will only be full of good works, I will insure that they will have faith in time of need (*DBY,* 154).

When faith springs up in the heart, good works will follow, and good works will increase that pure faith within them (*DBY,* 156).

My faith is, when we have done all we can, then the Lord is under obligation, and will not disappoint the faithful; he will perform the rest (*DBY,* 155).

When a person is placed in circumstances that he cannot possibly obtain one particle of anything to sustain life, it would then be his privilege to exercise faith in God to feed him, who might cause a raven to pick up a piece of dried meat from some quarter where there was plenty, and drop it over the famishing man. When I cannot feed myself through the means God has placed in my power, it is then time enough for him to exercise his providence in an unusual manner to administer to my wants. But while we can help ourselves, it is our duty to do so (*DBY,* 155).

A great many good people, who possess much of the Spirit of the Lord are naturally given to doubting, having so little self-reliance that they sometimes doubt whether they are Saints in truth or not. These often doubt when they should not. So long as they are walking humbly before God, keeping his commandments, and observing his ordinances, feeling willing to give all for Christ, and do everything that will promote his Kingdom, they need never doubt, for the Spirit will testify to them whether they are of God or not (*DBY*, 155).

If the Latter-day Saints will walk up to their privileges, and exercise faith in the name of Jesus Christ, and live in the enjoyment of the fulness of the Holy Ghost constantly day by day, there is nothing on the face of the earth that they could ask for, that would not be given to them. The Lord is waiting to be very gracious unto this people, and to pour out upon them riches, honor, glory and power, even that they may possess all things according to the promises he has made through his Apostles and Prophets (*DBY*, 156).

Suggestions for Study

Faith in the Lord Jesus Christ is the first principle of the gospel and can be understood only by the power of the Holy Ghost.

- Why does our faith in the Lord Jesus Christ give us hope?
- What specific things did President Young say we must believe to have faith in Jesus Christ?
- Why is faith in Jesus Christ the first principle of the gospel? (See also Moroni 7:33–34; Articles of Faith 1:4.) According to President Young, how can we come to understand faith in Christ as the first principle of the gospel?
- Who are "they that work for the salvation of the human family"?

Faith in Christ is a gift of God obtained through belief, obedience, and righteous works.

- How can we develop faith in Christ? What does it mean to add "faith to faith"? (See also Alma 32:26–28.)
- Why must we believe, obey, and practice truth to obtain faith? (See also Alma 32:21.)
- Why did President Young say that "we are under obligation to trust in our God"? (See also Ether 12:6–7.) How do we show our trust in God? (See also Ether 3:11–12.)

- How do doubt and human reason interfere with faith? How can we know for ourselves what our standing is with God? How does our faith in Jesus Christ influence our feelings about ourselves?

- President Young said, "Happy are those who pass through trials, if they maintain their integrity and their faith to their calling." How can we maintain our faith and integrity during difficult times? How have your faith and integrity enabled you to successfully face adversity? (See also Helaman 12:3; Alma 32:6.)

Righteous works demonstrate and strengthen faith.

- How did President Young explain the relationship of faith and works?

- What did President Young say we must do in order to have the help of the Lord? What does the Lord expect of those who feel "willing to give all for Christ, and do everything that will promote his Kingdom"?

- What did President Young promise those who "exercise faith in the name of Jesus Christ, and live in the enjoyment of the fulness of the Holy Ghost constantly"? If our prayers are accompanied by such faith and inspiration, what will be the result? (See also D&C 46:30; Helaman 10:5.)

John the Baptist baptizing Jesus Christ. Baptism is a requirement for entering the kingdom of God (see John 3:5).

Repentance and Baptism

On a cold, snowy day in April 1832, Brigham Young was baptized in the icy waters of his own millstream by Eleazer Miller, a four-month convert to the Church. Of this he said, "I felt a humble, childlike spirit, witnessing unto me that my sins were forgiven" (MHBY-1, 2–3). He taught that water itself does not have "any virtue to wash away sin" (DBY, 159) but that baptism is effective in cleansing us from sin when administered by those in authority to those who are accountable and when preceded by repentance and followed by sincere effort to honor baptismal covenants.

Teachings of Brigham Young

As our understanding increases, so do our accountability and responsibility.

Sin consists in doing wrong when we know and can do better, and it will be punished with a just retribution, in the due time of the Lord (*DBY,* 156).

Though we may do the best we know how at this time, can there be no improvement made in our lives? There can. If we do wrong ignorantly, when we learn it is wrong, then it is our duty to refrain from that wrong immediately and for ever (*DBY,* 156).

We can make the Atonement effective in our lives through sincere repentance.

If I have injured any person, I ought to confess to that person and make right what I did wrong (*DBY,* 158).

I believe in coming out and being plain and honest with that which should be made public, and in keeping to yourselves that which should be kept. . . . Tell to the public that which belongs to the public. If you have sinned against the people, confess to them. If you have sinned against a family or a neighborhood, go to them and confess. . . . If you have sinned against one individual, take that person by yourselves and make your confession to him (*DBY,* 158).

When men truly and heartily repent, and make manifest to the heavens that their repentance is genuine by obedience to the requirements made known to them through the laws of the Gospel, then are they entitled to the administration of salvation, and no power can withhold the good spirit from them (*DBY,* 156).

Some of our old traditions teach us that a man guilty of atrocious and murderous acts may savingly repent when on the scaffold; and upon his execution will hear the expression, "Bless God! he has gone to heaven, to be crowned in glory, through the all-redeeming merits of Christ the Lord." This is all nonsense. Such a character never will see heaven. Some will pray, "O that I had passed through the veil on the night of my conversion!" This proves the false ideas and vain notions entertained by the Christian world (*DBY,* 157).

Baptism is an essential ordinance for our salvation.

We, the Latter-day Saints, believe in being baptized by immersion for the remission of sins, according to the testimony of the disciples of Jesus and the revelations of the Lord given in these last days. Infants are pure, they have neither sorrow of heart, nor sins to repent of and forsake, and consequently are incapable of being baptized for the remission of sin. If we have sinned, we must know good from evil; an infant does not know this, it cannot know it; it has not grown into the idea of contemplation of good and evil; it has not the capacity to listen to the parent or teacher or to the priest when they tell what is right or wrong or what is injurious; and until these things are understood a person cannot be held accountable and consequently cannot be baptized for the remission of sin [see Moroni 8] (*DBY,* 158–59).

There is no ordinance that God has delivered by his own voice, through his Son Jesus Christ, or by the mouths of any of his Prophets, Apostles or Evangelists, that is useless. Every ordinance, every commandment and requirement is necessary for the salvation of the human family (*DBY,* 152).

If you have been righteous from your birth up, and have never committed known sins and transgressions, be baptized to fulfil all righteousness, as Jesus was. If you can say you have no sins to repent of, forsake your false theories, and love and serve God with an undivided heart (*DBY,* 159).

All Latter-day Saints enter the new and everlasting covenant when they enter this Church. They covenant to cease sustaining, upholding and cherishing the kingdom of the Devil and the kingdoms of this world. They enter the new and everlasting covenant to sustain the Kingdom of God and no other kingdom. They take a vow of the most solemn kind, before

Daniel D. MacArthur baptizing Qui-Tuss, chief of the Shivwits Indians, in 1875.
On that same day, 130 other members of the tribe were also baptized.

the heavens and earth, and that, too, upon the validity of their own salvation, that they will sustain truth and righteousness instead of wickedness and falsehood, and build up the Kingdom of God, instead of the kingdoms of this world (*DBY,* 160).

However much we may profess attachment to God and his cause we are not entitled to the blessings and privileges of his Kingdom until we become citizens therein. How can we do this? By repenting of our sins, and obeying the requirements of the Gospel of the Son of God which has been delivered to us. Hundreds and thousands of people have believed on the Lord Jesus Christ and repented of their sins, and have had the Holy Spirit to witness unto them that God is love, that they loved him and that he loved them, and yet they are not in his Kingdom. They have not complied with the necessary requirements, they have not entered in at the door (*DBY,* 152–53).

You have not the power to baptize yourselves, neither have you power to resurrect yourselves; and you could not legally baptize a second person for the remission of sins until some person first baptized you and ordained you to this authority (*DBY,* 160).

Has water, in itself, any virtue to wash away sin? Certainly not; but the Lord says, "If the sinner will repent of his sins, and go down into the waters of baptism, and there be buried in the likeness of being put into the earth and buried, and again be delivered from the water, in the likeness of being born—if in the sincerity of his heart he will do this, his sins shall be washed away." [See D&C 128:12–13.] Will the water of itself wash them away? No; but keeping the commandments of God will cleanse away the stain of sin (*DBY,* 159).

Suggestions for Study

As our understanding increases, so do our accountability and responsibility.

- How did President Young define sin? (See also James 4:17.)
- What did President Young teach about our responsibility as we increase in knowledge of right and wrong? (See also 2 Nephi 9:25–27.)
- What should be our attitude about improving our lives? (See also Alma 34:33.) What does this teach us about knowledge, accountability, and responsibility?

We can make the Atonement effective in our lives through sincere repentance.

- What is the consequence of true repentance? Why is obedience to the laws of the gospel a necessary part of repentance?
- What did President Young teach about deathbed repentance?

Baptism is an essential ordinance for our salvation.

- What part does baptism play in coming unto Christ? (See also Moroni 8:25–26.)
- What did President Young teach about who should and should not be baptized? Why is it inappropriate to baptize those who are not account-able? (See also Moroni 8:9–14.) What did President Young say to accountable people who say they have no sin?
- President Young taught that all the ordinances of the gospel, including baptism, are necessary for our salvation. How have the ordinances of the gospel blessed your life?

- President Young taught that "all Latter-day Saints enter the new and everlasting covenant when they enter this Church." When we are baptized, what do we covenant to do? What do we covenant to refrain from doing? (See also Mosiah 18:8–10.)

- Why is believing on the Lord Jesus Christ and loving Him not enough alone to enter in at the door of His kingdom?

- Why must one be "ordained . . . to this authority" to baptize?

- According to President Young, what is the significance and symbolism of baptism? (See also Romans 6:3–6, 11; Moses 6:58–60; 1 John 5:7–8.) President Young explained that "water, in itself, [has not] any virtue to wash away sin." What will cleanse us from sin?

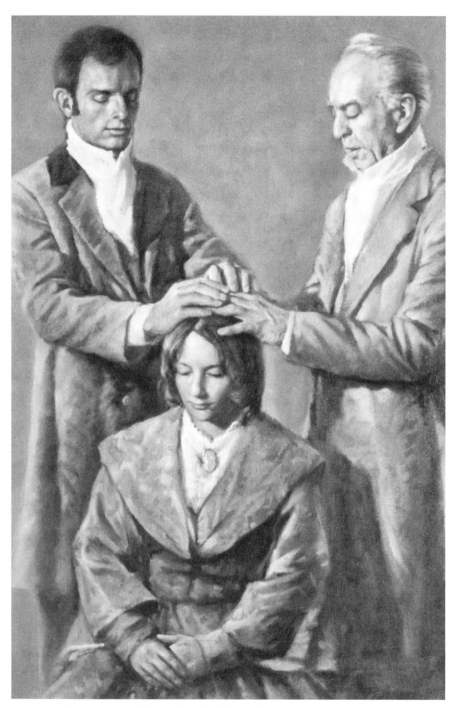

President Young taught that the gift of the Holy Ghost "brings all things to our remembrance . . . that are necessary for us to know" for our salvation (*DBY*, 160).

The Influence of the Holy Ghost

President Brigham Young said: "When I saw a man without eloquence, or talents for public speaking, who could only say, 'I know, by the power of the Holy Ghost, that the Book of Mormon is true, that Joseph Smith is a Prophet of the Lord,' the Holy Ghost proceeding from that individual illuminate[d] my understanding, and light, glory, and immortality [were] before me." He said that he was encircled and filled by them, and he knew for himself that the testimony of the man was true (DNW, 9 Feb. 1854, 4). President Young taught that the Holy Ghost is "the special gift of the Father" (DBY, 160), given according to our faithfulness, and can teach us all things and lead us to perfection.

Teachings of Brigham Young

The Holy Ghost is a gift from God that we enjoy according to God's wisdom and our faithfulness.

To understand the first principles of the Gospel—to rightly understand them, a man must have the wisdom that comes from above; he must be enlightened by the Holy Ghost; his mind must be in open vision; he must enjoy the blessings of salvation himself, in order to impart them to others (*DBY,* 152).

What is required of us as soon as we come to the years of accountability? It is required of us, for it is an institution of heaven, the origin of which you and I cannot tell, for the simple reason that it has no beginning, it is from eternity to eternity—it is required of us to go down into the waters of baptism. Here is a fountain or element, typical of the purity of the eternities. Go down into the waters, and there be baptized for the remission of sins, and then have hands laid upon us to confirm us members of the Church of Jesus Christ of Latter-day Saints. Then receive the Spirit of Truth, or the Holy Ghost (*DBY,* 159).

In the New Testament and Book of Mormon, we learn that when the Gospel is preached the people are taught to believe on the Lord Jesus Christ, to repent of their sins, be baptized for the remission of sin, and receive the Holy Ghost by the laying on of hands; the Holy Ghost is then the special gift of the Father and is his minister. He also gives intelligence by angels, as well as by the inspiration of the Holy Spirit, and by opening the minds of the Saints to behold in vision things as they are in eternity. When true doctrines are advanced, though they may be new to the hearers, yet the principles contained therein are perfectly natural and easy to be understood, so much so that the hearers often imagine that they had always known them. This arises from the influence of the Spirit of Truth upon the spirit of intelligence that is within each person [see D&C 6:15]. The influence that comes from heaven is all the time teaching the children of men (*DBY,* 160).

The gifts of the Gospel are given to strengthen the faith of the believer (*DBY,* 161).

We believe we are entitled to the gift of the Holy Ghost . . . according to the discretion and wisdom of God and our faithfulness; which gift brings all things to our remembrance, past, present, and to come, that are necessary for us to know, and as far as our minds are prepared to receive the knowledge of God revealed by that all-wise Agent. The Holy Ghost is God's minister, and is delegated to visit the sons and daughters of men. All intelligent beings pertaining to this earth are instructed from the same source (*DBY,* 160–61).

Listening to and acting on the promptings of the Holy Ghost can lead us to perfection.

My knowledge is, if you will follow the teachings of Jesus Christ and his Apostles, as recorded in the New Testament, every man and woman will be put in possession of the Holy Ghost. . . . They will know things that are, that will be, and that have been. They will understand things in heaven, things on the earth, and things under the earth, things of time, and things of eternity, according to their several callings and capacities (*DBY,* 161).

If you want the mind and will of God . . . , get it, it is just as much your privilege as of any other member of the Church and Kingdom of God. It is your privilege and duty to live so that you know when the word of the Lord is spoken to you and when the mind of the Lord is revealed to you. I say it is your duty to live so as to know and understand all these things (*DBY,* 163).

Then live according to every word that proceeds out of the mouth of God, through those men whom he has appointed here upon the earth, until we are perfect (*DBY,* 159).

Suggestions for Study

**The Holy Ghost is a gift from God that we enjoy according
to God's wisdom and our faithfulness.**

- What must a man possess to "rightly understand" the first principles of the gospel? Why? (See also Isaiah 55:8–9.)

- According to President Young, "when the Gospel is preached" what are the people taught? What have these blessings, which come from being taught the gospel, meant in your life?

- What is the role of the Holy Ghost in your life? Why does the influence of the Holy Ghost cause new doctrines to seem familiar? How can you tell whether feelings, ideas, and intuitions are from your own heart and mind or from the Holy Ghost?

- According to President Young, to what extent are we "entitled to the gift of the Holy Ghost"? What are the dangers of living without the influence of the Holy Ghost or under the influence of ungodly sources of knowledge?

- What things did President Young say that the Holy Ghost can help us know? What is our responsibility for obtaining such knowledge? What is our responsibility once we have obtained this knowledge?

**Listening to and acting on the promptings of the
Holy Ghost can lead us to perfection.**

- How can we know "the mind and will of God"? Why is knowing this important? What blessings come from seeking and following the promptings of the Holy Ghost and God's appointed servants?

- What experiences have you or others had that help you believe that the Holy Ghost can help you understand and obey the mind and will of God in your daily life? (See also 1 Nephi 22:2 and 2 Nephi 32:2–3.)

The early pioneers obeyed the call to gather to Zion, often traveling by covered wagon.

Choosing to Walk in Obedience

President Brigham Young directed the immigration of thousands of Saints to Zion, often giving instruction in such small details as not yoking tired animals with fresh ones. However, he also encouraged the Saints to show energetic self-reliance and to make intelligent choices. He counseled: "It is absolutely necessary for every man, woman, and child who embraces this work and gathers to Zion to do all that he or she can to forward the work of God to build up Zion, and to aid in the redemption thereof. . . . Our zeal in this labor . . . has a tendency to develop energy and self-reliance in the Saints that they could not otherwise have, were they not to be thrown on their resources" (LL, 220–21). President Young taught that "all the sacrifice that the Lord asks of his people is strict obedience to our own covenants" (DBY, 225).

Teachings of Brigham Young

We have agency to choose good or evil, but we cannot choose the consequences of our choices.

All rational beings have an agency of their own; and according to their own choice they will be saved or damned (*DBY,* 62).

Can the people understand that it is actually necessary for opposite principles to be placed before them, or this state of being would be no probation, and we should have no opportunity for exercising the agency given us? Can they understand that we cannot obtain eternal life unless we actually know and comprehend by our experience the principle of good and the principle of evil, the light and the darkness, truth, virtue, and holiness,—also vice, wickedness, and corruption? (*DBY,* 66).

Man can produce and control his own acts, but he has no control over their results (*DBY,* 63).

There is not an individual upon the earth but what has within himself ability to save or to destroy himself; and such is the case with nations (*DBY,* 67).

There are limits to agency, and to all things and to all beings, and our agency must not infringe upon that law. A man must choose life or death [see Helaman 14:31], and if he chooses death he will find himself abridged, and that the agency which is given to him is so bound up that he cannot exercise it in opposition to the law, without laying himself liable to be corrected and punished by the Almighty. (*DBY,* 63).

A man can dispose of his agency or of his birthright, as did Esau of old, but when disposed of, he cannot again obtain it; consequently, it behooves us to be careful, and not forfeit that agency that is given to us. The difference between the righteous and the sinner, eternal life or death, happiness or misery, is this, to those who are exalted there are no bounds or limits to their privileges, their blessings have a continuation, and to their kingdoms, thrones, and dominions, principalities, and powers there is no end, but they increase through all eternity; whereas, those who reject the offer, who despise the proffered mercies of the Lord, and prepare themselves to be banished from his presence, and to become companions of the devils, have their agency abridged immediately, and bounds and limits are put to their operations (*DBY,* 63–64).

The Lord does not compel any person to embrace the Gospel, and I do not think he will compel them to live it after they have embraced it (*DBY,* 64).

He has given them the privilege of choosing for themselves, whether it be good or evil; but the result of our choice is still in his hand (*DBY,* 62).

The eternal laws by which he and all others exist in the eternities of the Gods decree that the consent of the creature must be obtained before the Creator can rule perfectly (*DBY,* 65).

I am not going to drive a man or a woman to heaven. A great many think that they will be able to flog people into heaven, but this can never be done, for the intelligence in us is as independent as the Gods. People are not to be driven and you can put into a gnat's eye all the souls of the children of men that are driven into heaven by preaching hell-fire (*DBY,* 64).

You may know whether you are led right or wrong, as well as you know the way home; for every principle God has revealed carries its own convictions of its truth to the human mind, and there is no calling of God to man on earth but what brings with it the evidence of its authenticity (*DBY,* 65).

Does it follow that a man is deprived of his rights, because he lists in his heart to do the will of God? Must a man swear to prove that he has an agency? I contend there is no necessity for that, nor for stealing nor for doing any wrong. I can manifest to the heavens and to the inhabitants of the earth that I am free-born, and have my liberty before God, angels and men, when I kneel down to pray, certainly as much as if I were to go out and swear. I have the right to call my family together at certain hours for

Photograph of early Saints demonstrating their obedience by answering a call
from the prophet to settle the Big Horn Basin of Wyoming in 1900.

prayer, and I believe that this course proves that I am a free agent, as much as if I were to steal, swear, lie, and get drunk (*DBY,* 65).

In rendering that strict obedience, are we made slaves? No, it is the only way on the face of the earth for you and me to become free. . . . Now to say that I do not enjoy the volition of my own will just as much when I pray as I would to swear, is a false principle. . . . The man who yields strict obedience to the requirements of Heaven, acts upon the volition of his own will and exercises his freedom just as much as when he was a slave to passion. . . . All that the Lord requires of us is strict obedience to the laws of life. All the sacrifice that the Lord asks of his people is strict obedience to our own covenants that we have made with our God, and that is to serve him with an undivided heart (*DBY,* 225).

**Obedience to truth will enable us to dwell in the
presence of the Almighty.**

Obedience is one of the plainest, most every-day and home principles that you ever thought or know anything about (*DBY,* 220).

Blessed are they who obey when the Lord gives a direct commandment, but more blessed are they who obey without a direct commandment (*DBY,* 220).

73

If we hearken to counsel, we shall be the best people in the world; we shall be as a bright light set upon a hill, that cannot be hid, or like a candle upon a candlestick (*DBY,* 219).

If you wish to receive and enjoy the favor of our Heavenly Father, do his will (*DBY,* 223).

If our hearts are filled with the Spirit of truth, with the Spirit of the Lord, no matter what the true words from heaven are, when God speaks, all his subjects should shout, "Hallelujah! praise God! We are ready to receive those words, for they are true" (*DBY,* 219).

How I long to see the brethren, when they hear the words of truth poured upon them, ready to receive those words because they are perfectly congenial to their feelings, and every soul exclaim, "Those words savor of the Spirit that is in me; they are my delight, my meat, and my drink; they are the streams of eternal life. How congenial they are, instead of their being contrary to my feelings" (*DBY,* 219).

If you would always pause and say, I have no counsel for you, I have no answer for you on this subject, because I have no manifestation of the Spirit, and be willing to let everybody in the world know that you are ignorant when you are, you would become wise a great deal quicker than to give counsel on your own judgment, without the Spirit of revelation (*DBY,* 219).

Every man in the Kingdom of God would give the same counsel upon each subject, if he would wait until he had the mind of Christ upon it. Then all would have one word and mind, and all men would see eye to eye (*DBY,* 219).

This people have got to become of one heart and one mind. They have to know the will of God and do it, for to know the will of God is one thing, and to bring our wills, our dispositions, into subjection to that which we do understand to be the will of God is another (*DBY,* 221).

The Latter-day Saints who hearken to the words of the Lord, given to them touching their political, social, and financial concerns, I say, and say it boldly, that they will have wisdom which is altogether superior to the wisdom of the children of darkness, or the children of this world. I know this by the revelations of the Lord Jesus Christ, and by the results of my own actions. They who have hearkened to the counsels given to them in temporal matters, have invariably bettered their condition temporally and spiritually (*DBY,* 219–20).

All who receive eternal life and salvation will receive it on no other conditions than believing in the Son of God and obeying the principles that he has laid down. Can we devise any other means and plan of salvation? We cannot (*DBY,* 223–24).

The most effectual way to establish the religion of Heaven is to live it, rather than to die for it: I think I am safe in saying that there are many of the Latter-day Saints who are more willing to die for their religion than to live it faithfully. There is no other proof can be adduced to God, angels, and men, that a people faithfully live their religion, than that they repent truly of their sins, obey the law of baptism for the remission of sins, and then continue to do the works of righteousness day by day (*DBY,* 221).

Do you think that people will obey the truth because it is true, unless they love it? No, they will not. Truth is obeyed when it is loved. Strict obedience to the truth will alone enable people to dwell in the presence of the Almighty (*DBY,* 220).

Is there any particular art in making this people obedient? There is just one. If you, Elders of Israel, can get the art of preaching the Holy Ghost into the hearts of the people, you will have an obedient people. This is the only art required. Teach the people truth, teach them correct principles; show them what is for their greatest good and don't you think they will follow in that path? They will (*DBY,* 226).

We learn to obey willingly and bear chastisements when we accept the Spirit of Truth.

The Saints who live their religion will be exalted, for they never will deny any revelation which the Lord has given or may give, though, when there is a doctrine coming to them which they cannot comprehend fully, they may be found saying, "The Lord sendeth this unto me, and I pray that he will save and preserve me from denying anything which proceedeth from him, and give me patience to wait until I can understand it for myself" (*DBY,* 224).

Such persons will never deny, but will allow those subjects which they do not understand, to remain until the visions of their minds become open. This is the course which I have invariably pursued, and if anything came that I could not understand, I would pray until I could comprehend it (*DBY,* 224).

Do not reject anything because it is new or strange, and do not sneer nor jeer at what comes from the Lord, for if we do, we endanger our salvation (*DBY,* 224).

I believe that it is a hell intolerable for a people, a family or a single person, to strive to grasp truth with one hand, and error with the other, to profess to walk in obedience to the commandments of God, and, at the same time, mingle heart and hand with the wicked (*DBY,* 223).

The Lord has sent forth his laws, commandments, and ordinances to the children of men, and requires them to be strictly obeyed, and we do not wish to transgress those laws, but to keep them. We do not wish to change his ordinances, but to observe them; we do not wish to break the everlasting covenant, but to keep that with our fathers, with Jesus, with our Father in Heaven, with holy angels, and to live according to them (*DBY*, 220).

How shall we know that we obey him? There is but one method by which we can know it, and that is by the inspiration of the Spirit of the Lord witnessing unto our spirit that we are his, that we love him, and that he loves us. It is by the spirit of revelation we know this. We have no witness to ourselves internally, without the spirit of revelation. We have no witness outwardly, only by obedience to the ordinances (*DBY*, 224).

Anything that is impure must, sooner or later, perish; no matter whether it is in the faith and practice of an individual, town, nation, or government. That kingdom, principality, power or person that is not controlled by principles that are pure and holy must eventually pass away and perish (*DBY*, 227).

When salvation is sent to me, I can reject or receive it. In receiving it, I yield implicit obedience and submission to its great Author throughout my life, and to those whom he shall appoint to instruct me; in rejecting it, I follow the dictates of my own will in preference to the will of my Creator (*DBY*, 390).

God has placed within us a will, and we should be satisfied to have it controlled by the will of the Almighty (*DBY*, 264).

We as a people, will be chastened until we can wholly submit ourselves to the Lord and be Saints indeed (*DBY*, 226).

I know it is hard to receive chastisement, for no chastisement is joyous, but grievous at the time it is given [see Hebrews 12:11]; but if a person will receive chastisement and pray for the Holy Spirit to rest upon him, that he may have the Spirit of truth in his heart, and cleave to that which is pleasing to the Lord, the Lord will give him grace to bear the chastisement, and he will submit to and receive it, knowing that it is for his good (*DBY*, 227).

Suggestions for Study

We have agency to choose good or evil, but we cannot choose the consequences of our choices.

- Why is it "actually necessary for opposite principles to be placed before" God's children and for them to have "an agency of their own"?

- President Young taught that "man can produce and control his own acts, but he has no control over their results." (See also D&C 101:78.) In what ways do some people claim freedom of choice while trying to avoid the consequences of their choices?

- How does President Young define the "difference between the righteous and the sinner"? How might we limit or abridge our agency? President Young taught that the "exalted" have "no bounds or limits to their privileges." How does strict obedience actually increase our freedom?

- Why will God not "compel any person to embrace the Gospel . . . [or] to live it after they have embraced it"? (See also D&C 88:22–25, 32.)

- Why does President Young emphasize that obedience is just as much an exercise in agency as is disobedience? Why is "strict obedience . . . the only way on the face of the earth for you and me to become free"? (See also Mosiah 2:22–24.)

Obedience to truth will enable us to dwell in the presence of the Almighty.

- Why is obedience "one of the plainest, most every-day and home principles"? Why does obedience enable us to "receive and enjoy the favor of our Heavenly Father"?

- What does it mean to become "of one heart and one mind"? How does obedience help us do this?

We learn to obey willingly and bear chastisements when we accept the Spirit of Truth.

- According to President Young, what is our obligation when we don't understand a doctrine or revelation? (See also Ecclesiastes 12:13; John 7:17; Ether 12:6; D&C 11:20.)

- How can we know when we are obedient to God's will and how can we teach obedience?

- How does a willingness to submit our will to the will of the Almighty help us become more like the Savior? What does it mean to "wholly submit ourselves to the Lord"?

- To chasten is to correct and to purify. Why is chastisement often difficult to receive? (See also Hebrews 12:11.) What did President Young teach about how we can bear chastisement? Where can chastisement lead?

Judas betraying the Savior in the Garden of Gethsemane. President Young warned that "when a man begins to find fault" with Church leaders and teachings, "you may know that that person has more or less of the spirit of apostasy" (*DBY*, 83).

Preventing Personal Apostasy

While in Kirtland, President Brigham Young encountered a group of apostates who were plotting against the Prophet Joseph Smith within the very walls of the temple. He declared, "I rose up, and in a plain and forcible manner told them that Joseph was a Prophet, and I knew it, and they might rail and slander him as much as they pleased, they could not destroy the appointment of the Prophet of God, they could only destroy their own authority, cut the thread that bound them to the Prophet and to God and sink themselves to hell" ("History of Brigham Young," DNW, 10 Feb. 1858, 386). In Kirtland, Missouri, Nauvoo, and Utah, President Young witnessed the devastation that visits the personal lives of those who succumb to apostasy. Many of the apostates had been among his closest associates. He recognized that often "trifling affairs" were the commencement of their separation from the truth, and he emphatically warned each member to guard carefully against any degree of wrongdoing.

Teachings of Brigham Young

Apostasy is turning away from the Church and ultimately denying the faith.

What is that which turns people away from this Church? Very trifling affairs are generally the commencement of their divergence from the right path. If we follow a compass, the needle of which does not point correctly, a very slight deviation in the beginning will lead us, when we have traveled some distance, far to one side of the true point for which we are aiming (*DBY,* 83).

If the Saints neglect to pray, and violate the day that is set apart for the worship of God, they will lose his Spirit. If a man shall suffer himself to be overcome with anger, and curse and swear, taking the name of the Deity in vain, he cannot retain the Holy Spirit. In short, if a man shall do anything which he knows to be wrong, and repenteth not, he cannot enjoy the Holy Spirit, but will walk in darkness and ultimately deny the faith (*DBY,* 85).

It is most astonishing to every principle of intelligence that any man or woman will close their eyes upon eternal things after they have been made acquainted with them, and let the . . . things of this world, the lusts of the eye, and the lusts of the flesh, entangle their minds and draw them one hair's breadth from the principles of life (*DBY,* 82).

It was said here this morning that no person ever apostatized, without actual transgression. Omission of duty leads to commission (*DBY,* 82).

You hear many say, "I am a Latter-day Saint, and I never will apostatize;" "I am a Latter-day Saint, and shall be to the day of my death." I never make such declarations, and never shall. I think I have learned that of myself I have no power, but my system is organized to increase in wisdom, knowledge, and power, getting a little here and a little there. But when I am left to myself, I have no power, and my wisdom is foolishness; then I cling close to the Lord, and I have power in his name. I think I have learned the Gospel so as to know, that in and of myself I am nothing [see Alma 26:12] (*DBY,* 84).

Let a man or woman who has received much of the power of God, visions and revelations, turn away from the holy commandments of the Lord, and it seems that their senses are taken from them, their understanding and judgment in righteousness are taken away, they go into darkness, and become like a blind person who gropes by the wall [see Isaiah 59:9–10; Deuteronomy 28:29] (*DBY,* 82–83).

Many receive the Gospel because they know it is true; they are convinced in their judgment that it is true; strong argument overpowers them, and they are rationally compelled to admit the Gospel to be true upon fair reasoning. They yield to it, and obey its first principles, but never seek to be enlightened by the power of the Holy Ghost; such ones frequently step out of the way (*DBY,* 86).

When we find fault with Church leaders, we begin to separate ourselves from the Church.

Whenever there is a disposition manifested in any of the members of this Church to question the right of the President of the whole Church to direct in all things, you see manifested evidences of apostasy—of a spirit which, if encouraged, will lead to a separation from the Church and to final destruction; wherever there is a disposition to operate against any legally appointed officer of this Kingdom, no matter in what capacity he is called to act, if persisted in, it will be followed by the same results; they will "walk after the flesh in the lust of uncleanness, and despise government. Presumptuous are they, self-willed; they are not afraid to speak evil of dignities" [see 2 Peter 2:10] (*DBY,* 83).

When a man begins to find fault, inquiring in regard to this, that, and the other, saying, "Does this or that look as though the Lord dictated it?" you may know that that person has more or less of the spirit of apostasy. Every man in this Kingdom, or upon the face of the earth, who is seeking with all his heart to save himself, has as much to do as he can conveniently attend to, without calling in question that which does not belong to him. If he succeeds in saving himself, it has well occupied his time and attention. See to it that you are right yourselves; see that sins and folly do not manifest themselves with the rising sun (*DBY,* 83).

Many imbibe [conceive] the idea that they are capable of leading out in teaching principles that never have been taught. They are not aware that the moment they give way to this hallucination the Devil has power over them to lead them onto unholy ground; though this is a lesson which they ought to have learned long ago, yet it is one that was learned by but few in the days of Joseph (*DBY,* 77–78).

[Such a person] will make false prophecies, yet he will do it by the spirit of prophecy; he will feel that he is a prophet and can prophesy, but he does it by another spirit and power than that which was given him of the Lord. He uses the gift as much as you and I use ours (*DBY,* 82).

One of the first steps to apostasy is to find fault with your Bishop; and when that is done, unless repented of a second step is soon taken, and by and by the person is cut off from the Church, and that is the end of it. Will you allow yourselves to find fault with your Bishop? (*DBY,* 86).

No man gets power from God to raise disturbance in any Branch of the Church. Such power is obtained from an evil source (*DBY,* 72).

People do, however, leave this Church, but they leave it because they get into darkness, and the very day they conclude that there should be a democratic vote, or in other words, that we should have two candidates for the presiding Priesthood in the midst of the Latter-day Saints, they conclude to be apostates. There is no such thing as confusion, division, strife, animosity, hatred, malice, or two sides to the question in the house of God; there is but one side to the question there (*DBY,* 85).

Those who lose the Spirit are filled with darkness and confusion.

When men lose the spirit of the work in which we are engaged, they become infidel in their feelings. They say that they do not know whether the Bible is true, whether the Book of Mormon is true, nor about new revelations, nor whether there is a God or not. When they lose the spirit of this work, they lose the knowledge of the things of God in time and in eternity; all is lost to them (*DBY,* 83–84).

Men begin to apostatize by taking to themselves strength, by hearkening to the whisperings of the enemy who leads them astray little by little, until they gather to themselves that which they call the wisdom of man; then they begin to depart from God, and their minds become confused (*DBY,* 84).

What have the Latter-day Saints got to apostatize from? Everything that there is good, pure, holy, God-like, exalting, ennobling, extending the ideas, the capacities of the intelligent beings that our Heavenly Father has brought forth upon this earth. What will they receive in exchange? I can comprehend it in a very few words. These would be the words that I should use: death, hell and the grave. That is what they will get in exchange. We may go into the particulars of that which they experience. They experience darkness, ignorance, doubt, pain, sorrow, grief, mourning, unhappiness; no person to condole [lament] with in the hour of trouble, no arm to lean upon in the day of calamity, no eye to pity when they are forlorn and cast down; and I comprehend it by saying death, hell and the grave. This is what they will get in exchange for their apostasy from the Gospel of the Son of God (*DBY,* 85).

You have known men who, while in the Church, were active, quick and full of intelligence; but after they have left the Church, they have become contracted in their understandings, they have become darkened in their minds and everything has become a mystery to them, and in regard to the things of God, they have become like the rest of the world, who think, hope and pray that such and such things may be so, but they do not know the least about it. This is precisely the position of those who leave this Church; they go into the dark, they are not able to judge, conceive or comprehend things as they are. They are like the drunken man—he thinks that everybody is the worse for liquor but himself, and he is the only sober man in the neighborhood. The apostates think that everybody is wrong but themselves (*DBY,* 84).

Those who leave the Church are like a feather blown to and fro in the air. They know not whither they are going; they do not understand anything about their own existence; their faith, judgment and the operation of their minds are as unstable as the movements of the feather floating in the air. We have not anything to cling to, only faith in the Gospel (*DBY,* 84).

We can stand firm by living our religion and seeking the Holy Spirit.

Will there still be apostasy? Yes, brethren and sisters, you may expect that people will come into the Church and then apostatize. You may expect that some people will run well for a season, and then fall out by the way (*DBY,* 85–86).

Why do people apostatize? You know we are on the "Old Ship Zion." We are in the midst of the ocean. A storm comes on, and, as sailors say, she

82

labors very hard. "I am not going to stay here," says one; "I don't believe this is the 'Ship Zion.'" "But we are in the midst of the ocean." "I don't care, I am not going to stay here." Off goes the coat, and he jumps overboard. Will he not be drowned? Yes. So with those who leave this Church. It is the "Old Ship Zion," let us stay in it (*DBY,* 85).

God is at the helm of this great ship, and that makes me feel good. . . . Let those apostatize who wish to, but God will save all who are determined to be saved (*DBY,* 86).

If the people would live their religion, there would be no apostasy and we would hear no complaining or fault-finding. If the people were hungry for the words of eternal life, and their whole souls even centered on the building up of the Kingdom of God, every heart and hand would be ready and willing and the work would move forward mightily and we would advance as we should do (*DBY,* 84).

We want to live so as to have the Spirit every day, every hour of the day, every minute of the day, and every Latter-day Saint is entitled to the Spirit of God, to the power of the Holy Ghost, to lead him in his individual duties (*DBY,* 82).

Suggestions for Study

Apostasy is turning away from the Church and ultimately denying the faith.

- President Young identified some of the departures from the truth which seem common or "trifling." He used the image of "a compass, the needle of which does not point correctly." How is the gospel like a true and accurate compass? What are some of the slight deviations in our lives that might over time lead us astray? What course corrections should we make?

- What cautions did President Young extend to the person who boasts, "I am a Latter-day Saint, and I never will apostatize"? (See also 2 Nephi 28:25; D&C 20:31–34.)

- What prophetic warning did President Young sound for those Saints who received the "power of God" and then turned "away from the holy commandments"?

- Why is intellectual reasoning not enough to keep us on the path to eternal life?

When we find fault with Church leaders, we begin to separate ourselves from the Church.

- In what ways will attending to our own callings rather than questioning the inspiration of current leaders strengthen us as individuals, families, wards, and Church members collectively?

- What was President Young's warning to those who criticize their ward or branch leadership? What can we do at church and at home to sustain the bishop of our ward, president of our branch, or other Church leaders? When honest differences arise, what course should we follow in order to become united? (See also Matthew 18:15; Luke 11:34.)

- According to President Young, there cannot be a "democratic vote" between "two candidates for the presiding Priesthood" in the Church. (See also D&C 28:2, 6–7.) How is sustaining by "common consent" different from a "democratic vote"? (See also D&C 20:65; 26:2.)

- We are invited to give our sustaining vote to Church leaders. How does our willingness to sustain those leaders strengthen the whole Church? How does our unwillingness to sustain them weaken the Church?

Those who lose the Spirit are filled with darkness and confusion.

- What did President Young mean when he said that apostates take to themselves strength? What is the danger in relying on our own strength? (See also Helaman 4:13.) Why do some choose the "wisdom of man" rather than the wisdom of God as revealed by the Spirit? (See also Isaiah 29:13–14; 1 Corinthians 2:12–14.)

- Read President Young's answers to these questions: "What have the Latter-day Saints got to apostatize from?" "What will they receive in exchange?"

- How can we exercise our faith to help those who are "like a feather blown to and fro in the air"?

We can stand firm by living our religion and seeking the Holy Spirit.

- Why will apostasy continue to exist in the Church? How can we keep the beginnings of apostasy from entering our lives? How have other Church members and the influence of the Spirit helped to keep you faithful when you might have been tempted to "run well [only] for a season"?

- If we stay with the "Old Ship Zion," what are we promised?

84

Preparing for Eternal Progression

President Brigham Young was a learner. He began as a furniture maker and later developed the skills necessary to become a missionary, colonizer, governor, and prophet. He saw this life as a time to live fully, grow, and prepare for eternity, not as a time to prepare to die. He encouraged the Saints to be engaged in worthwhile activities, to broaden and deepen their understanding, and to treasure up truth as they reached toward perfection. By so doing, they would eventually go forward to enter the spirit world and continue on the glorious path of eternal progression.

Teachings of Brigham Young

We prepare for eternal life by daily learning, improving, and building the kingdom of God.

What are we here for? To learn to enjoy more, and to increase in knowledge and in experience (*DBY,* 87).

The object of this existence is to learn, which we can only do a little at a time (*DBY,* 87). The whole mortal existence of man is neither more nor less than a preparatory state given to finite beings, a space wherein they may improve themselves for a higher state of being (*DBY,* 87).

The first great principle that ought to occupy the attention of mankind, that should be understood by the child and the adult, and which is the main spring of all action, whether people understand it or not, is the principle of improvement. The principle of increase, of exaltation, of adding to that we already possess, is the grand moving principle and cause of the actions of the children of men. No matter what their pursuits are, in what nation they were born, with what people they have been associated, what religion they profess, or what politics they hold, this is the main spring of the actions of the people, embracing all the powers necessary in performing the duties of life (*DBY,* 87).

We are placed on this earth to prove whether we are worthy to go into the celestial world, the terrestrial, or the telestial or to hell, or to any other kingdom, or place, and we have enough of life given to us to do this (*DBY,* 87).

This is a world in which we are to prove ourselves. The lifetime of man is a day of trial, wherein we may prove to God, in our darkness, in our weakness, and where the enemy reigns, that we are our Father's friends, and that we receive light from him and are worthy to be leaders of our children—to become lords of lords, and kings of kings—to have perfect dominion over that portion of our families that will be crowned in the celestial kingdom with glory, immortality, and eternal lives (*DBY,* 87).

Hear it, all ye Latter-day Saints! Will you spend the time of your probation for naught, and fool away your existence and being? You were organized, and brought into being, for the purpose of enduring forever, if you fulfil the measure of your creation, pursue the right path, observe the requirements of the celestial law, and obey the commandments of our God (*DBY,* 87).

Human beings are expected by their Creator to be actively employed in doing good every day of their lives, either in improving their own mental and physical condition or that of their neighbors (*DBY,* 88).

We are here to live, to spread intelligence and knowledge among the people. I am here to school my brethren, to teach my family the way of life, to propagate my species, and to live, if in my power, until sin, iniquity, corruption, hell, and the Devil, and all classes and grades of abominations are driven from the earth. That is my religion and the object of my existence. We are not here merely to prepare to die, and then die; but we are here to live and build up the Kingdom of God on the earth—to promote the Priesthood, overcome the powers of Satan, and teach the children of man what they are created for—that in them is concealed the germ of all intelligence. Here is the starting-point—the foundation that is laid in the organization of man for receiving a fulness of eternal knowledge and glory. Are we to go yonder to obtain it? No; we are to promote it on this earth (*DBY,* 88).

The Latter-day Saints throughout the valleys in these mountains and throughout the world ought to be learning what they are on this earth for. They are here to increase and multiply, to enlarge, to gather the House of Israel, redeem Zion, build up the Zion of our God, and to promote that eternal intelligence that dwells with the Gods, and begin to plant it in this earth, and make it take root downward and bring forth fruit upward to the glory of God, until every obnoxious principle in the hearts of men is destroyed, and the earth returns to its paradisiacal state, and the Lord comes and dwells with this people, and walks and talks with them as he did with Father Adam. That is our business, and not to suffer all our energies to be expended in merely preparing to die (*DBY,* 89).

The purpose of our life should be to build up the Zion of our God, to gather the House of Israel, bring in the fulness of the Gentiles, restore and bless the earth with our ability and make it as the Garden of Eden, store up treasures of knowledge and wisdom in our own understandings, purify our own hearts and prepare a people to meet the Lord when he comes (*DBY,* 88).

We are able to progress as we increase in knowledge and experience.

This work is a progressive work, this doctrine that is taught the Latter-day Saints in its nature is exalting, increasing, expanding and extending broader and broader until we can know as we are known, see as we are seen (*DBY,* 90).

We are in the school and keep learning, and we do not expect to cease learning while we live on earth; and when we pass through the veil, we expect still to continue to learn and increase our fund of information. That may appear a strange idea to some; but it is for the plain and simple reason that we are not capacitated to receive all knowledge at once. We must therefore receive a little here and a little there (*DBY,* 91).

He gives a little to his humble followers today, and if they improve upon it, tomorrow he will give them a little more, and the next day a little more. He does not add to that which they do not improve upon, but they are required to continually improve upon the knowledge they already possess, and thus obtain a store of wisdom (*DBY,* 90).

Simply to take the path pointed out in the Gospel by those who have given us the plan of salvation, is to take the path that leads to life, to eternal increase; it is to pursue that course wherein we shall never, never lose what we obtain, but continue to collect, to gather together, to increase, to spread abroad, and extend to an endless duration. Those persons who strive to gain eternal life, gain that which will produce the increase their hearts will be satisfied with. Nothing less than the privilege of increasing eternally, in every sense of the word, can satisfy the immortal spirit (*DBY,* 93).

We can still improve, we are made for that purpose, our capacities are organized to expand until we can receive into our comprehension celestial knowledge and wisdom, and to continue, worlds without end (*DBY,* 90).

Shall we ever be learning and never be able to come to a knowledge of the truth? [See 2 Timothy 3:7.] No, I say we shall not; but we shall come to the knowledge of the truth. This is my hope and anticipation, and this is my joy (*DBY,* 90–91). We have the principle within us, and so has every

Photograph of the Logan Temple. President Young taught that the ordinances
of salvation and personal faithfulness prepare us for "eternal progression"
to a "more glorious and exalted sphere" (*DBY,* 16).

being on this earth, to increase and to continue to increase, to enlarge and
receive and treasure up truth, until we become perfect (*DBY,* 91).

We are prepared for some things, and we receive just as fast as we
prepare ourselves (*DBY,* 95).

Instead of pleading with the Lord to bestow more upon you, plead with
yourselves to have confidence in yourselves, to have integrity in
yourselves, and know when to speak and what to speak, what to reveal,
and how to carry yourselves and walk before the Lord. And just as fast as
you prove to him that you will preserve everything secret that ought to

be—that you will deal out to your neighbors all which you ought, and no more, and learn how to dispense your knowledge to your families, friends, neighbors, and brethren, the Lord will bestow upon you, and give to you, and bestow upon you, until finally he will say to you, "You shall never fall; your salvation is sealed unto you; you are sealed up unto eternal life and salvation, through your integrity" (*DBY,* 93).

Eternal life is the ability to progress and increase forever.

This is the greatest gift that can be conferred on intelligent beings, to live forever and never be destroyed (*DBY,* 96).

It is written that the greatest gift God can bestow upon man is the gift of eternal life. The greatest attainment that we can reach is to preserve our identity to an eternal duration in the midst of the heavenly hosts. We have the words of eternal life given to us through the Gospel, which, if we obey, will secure unto us that precious gift (*DBY,* 96).

The intelligence that is in me to cease to exist is a horrid thought; it is past enduring. This intelligence must exist; it must dwell somewhere. If I take the right course and preserve it in its organization, I will preserve to myself eternal life (*DBY,* 96).

We are going to have the Kingdom of God in the fulness thereof, and all the heights and depths of glory, power, and knowledge; and we shall have fathers and mothers, and wives and children (*DBY,* 97).

Suppose it possible that you have the privilege of securing to yourselves eternal life—to live and enjoy these blessings forever; you will say this is the greatest blessing that can be bestowed upon you. . . . What blessing is equal to this? What blessing is equal to the continuation of life—to the continuation of our organization? (*DBY,* 96).

The Lord has blessed us with the ability to enjoy an eternal life with the Gods, and this is pronounced the greatest gift of God. The gift of eternal life, without a posterity, to become an angel, is one of the greatest gifts that can be bestowed; yet the Lord has bestowed on us the privilege of becoming fathers of lives. What is a father of lives as mentioned in the Scriptures? A man who has a posterity to an eternal continuance. That is the blessing Abraham received, and it perfectly satisfied his soul. He obtained the promise that he should be the father of lives (*DBY,* 97).

If men are faithful, . . . they and their Creator will always be one, they will always be of one heart and of one mind, working and operating together; for whatsoever the Father doeth so doeth the Son, and so they continue throughout all their operations to all eternity (*DBY,* 97).

The Lord would like to see us take the course that leads unto the strait gate, that we might be crowned sons and daughters of God, for such are the only ones in the heavens who multiply and increase. . . . The rest take an inferior kingdom, where this privilege is denied them. . . . It is for us to choose whether we will be sons and daughters, joint heirs with Jesus Christ, or whether we accept an inferior glory (*DNSW,* 8 Aug. 1876, 1).

Suggestions for Study

We prepare for eternal life by daily learning, improving, and building the kingdom of God.

- What truths do we learn from our trials in this life that will help us progress eternally? (See also D&C 122:7–8.) What does President Young say about the principle of "enduring forever"? (See also D&C 121:7–8; 3 Nephi 15:9.)

- How does being "actively employed in doing good every day" build a foundation "for receiving a fulness of eternal knowledge and glory"? (See also Alma 5:41; 26:22; D&C 58:26–29.)

- According to President Young, one of our major purposes in life is to learn. What can keep us from learning? How can we learn more from our gospel study? How can we learn from our experiences? What specific truth have you learned through experience and the influence of the Spirit?

- President Young mentions several purposes for being on the earth. How can we better accomplish these purposes? (See also D&C 81:5.)

- What are several ways to help "prepare a people to meet the Lord"? How can you specifically help do this?

We are able to progress as we increase in knowledge and experience.

- President Young said that we receive knowledge "a little here and a little there." How does this process apply to our gospel understanding, our parenting, and our service in the Church? (See also 2 Nephi 28:30; D&C 130:18–19.)

- What does President Young teach about eternal increase? (See also D&C 93:12–14.)

- President Young stated that "we have the principle within us . . . to increase and to continue to increase, to enlarge and receive and treasure up truth, until we become perfect." How do our efforts to gain knowledge help prepare us for exaltation? (See also D&C 50:40; 93:24, 26–30; 130:18–19.)

Eternal life is the ability to progress and increase forever.

- President Young stated that "the greatest gift that can be conferred upon intelligent beings [is] to live forever and never be destroyed." What does he say is the "greatest attainment," and how do we preserve it? (See also D&C 14:7; 130:20–21.)
- What does it mean to be "joint heirs with Jesus Christ"? (See also Romans 8:17.) What blessings belong only to those "crowned sons and daughters of God"?

Artist's rendering of Peter, James, and John restoring the keys of past dispensations. The dispensation of the fulness of times, President Young said, "will excel in magnificence and glory every dispensation that has ever been committed to the children of men" (*DBY,* 442).

Dispensations of the Gospel

God established and taught his gospel in the beginning, revealed it anew in various dispensations amid periods of apostasy, and has now restored it in this last age. President Brigham Young rejoiced over this final "dispensation of all dispensations," which, he said, "will excel in magnificence and glory every dispensation that has ever been committed to the children of men upon the earth" (DBY, 442).

Teachings of Brigham Young

God first revealed the plan of salvation to Adam in mortality and since then has periodically restored His kingdom through His prophets.

The great plan called the plan of salvation—the system of doctrine, ideas, and practices that pertain to all the intelligence that exists in eternity (*DBY,* 56) . . . [was] devised in the heavens for the redemption of mankind from sin, and their restoration to the presence of God (*DBY,* 448).

When this Kingdom is organized in any age [on earth], the Spirit of it dwells in the hearts of the faithful, while its visible department exists among the people, with laws, ordinances, helps, governments, officers, administrators, and every other appendage necessary for its complete operation to the attainment of the end in view [see Moses 6:7; D&C 22:3] (*DBY,* 441).

Adam. God was once known on the earth among his children . . . as we know one another. Adam was as conversant with his Father who placed him upon this earth as we are conversant with our earthly parents. The Father frequently came to visit his son Adam, and talked and walked with him; and the children of Adam were more or less acquainted with him, and the things that pertain to God and to heaven were as familiar among mankind in the first ages of their existence on the earth, as . . . our gardens are to our wives and children, or as the road to the Western Ocean is to the experienced traveler [see Moses 3:15–21; 4:14–30; 5:4–5, 9, 12; 6:51] (*DBY,* 104).

We are safe in saying that from the day that Adam was created and placed in the Garden of Eden to this day, the plan of salvation and the revelations of the will of God to man are unchanged, although mankind have not for many ages been favored therewith, in consequence of apostasy and wickedness. There is no evidence to be found in the Bible that the Gospel should be one thing in the days of the Israelites, another in the days of Christ and his Apostles, and another in the 19th century, but, on the contrary, we are instructed that God is the same in every age, and that his plan of saving his children is the same. The plan of salvation is one, from the beginning of the world to the end thereof [see Moses 6:51–68] (*DBY,* 103–4).

The Gospel was among the children of men from the days of Adam until the coming of the Messiah; this Gospel of Christ is from the beginning to the end [see Moses 5:58–59; D&C 20:25–26] (*DBY,* 103–4).

Enoch. Enoch possessed intelligence and wisdom from God that few men ever enjoyed, walking and talking with God for many years; yet, according to the history written by Moses, he was a great length of time in establishing his kingdom among men. The few that followed him enjoyed the fulness of the Gospel, and the rest of the world rejected it (*DBY,* 105).

Enoch had to talk with and teach his people during a period of three hundred and sixty years, before he could get them prepared to enter into their rest, and then he obtained power to translate himself and his people, with the region they inhabited, their houses, gardens, fields, cattle and all their possessions [see Moses 7:68–69] (*DBY,* 105).

Enoch and his party were taken from the earth, and the world continued to ripen in iniquity until they were overthrown by the great flood in the days of Noah; and, "as it was in the days of Noah, so shall it be in the days of the coming of the Son of Man" [see Genesis 6:5; Moses 6:26–7:69] (*DBY,* 105).

Noah. In the beginning, after this earth was prepared for man, the Lord commenced his work upon what is now called the American continent, where the Garden of Eden was made (*DBY,* 102).

The Lord sent forth his Gospel to the people; he said, I will give it to my son Adam, from whom Methuselah received it; and Noah received from Methuselah (*DBY,* 105).

In the days of Noah, in the days of the floating of the ark, he took the people to another part of the earth; the earth was divided, and there he set up his kingdom [see Genesis 6:1–8:21] (*DBY,* 102).

Abraham. Abraham was faithful to the true God; he overthrew the idols of his father and obtained the Priesthood after the order of Melchizedek [see D&C 84:14], which is after the order of the Son of God [see D&C 107:2–3], and a promise that of the increase of his seed there should be no end; when you obtain the holy Priesthood, which is after the order of Melchizedek, sealed upon you, and the promise that your seed shall be numerous as the stars in the firmament, or as the sands upon the seashore, and of your increase there shall be no end, you have then got the promise of Abraham, Isaac, and Jacob, and all the blessings that were conferred upon them [see Genesis 12:2–3; 13:16; 14:18–19; 15:5; Abraham 1:2–4, 18–19; 2:9–11; D&C 84:14] (*DBY,* 106).

Moses. The Gospel was among the children of men from the days of Adam until the coming of the Messiah; this Gospel of Christ is from the beginning to the end. Then why was the law of Moses given? In consequence of the disobedience of the Children of Israel, the elect of God; the very seed that he had selected to be his people, and upon whom he said he would place his name. This seed of Abraham so rebelled against him and his commands that the Lord said to Moses, "I will give you a law which shall be a schoolmaster to bring them to Christ" [see Galatians 3:24]. But this law is grievous; it is a law of carnal commandments [see D&C 84:23–27] (*DBY,* 104).

If they had been sanctified and holy, the Children of Israel would not have traveled one year with Moses before they would have received their endowments and the Melchizedek Priesthood [see D&C 84:23] (*DBY,* 106).

Jesus Christ. Jesus undertook to establish the Kingdom of God upon the earth. He introduced the laws and ordinances of the Kingdom [see Matthew 16:18–19; Ephesians 1:22–23; 4:11–15] (*DBY,* 29).

The priesthood and the full gospel of the kingdom were lost from the earth in the period of the Great Apostasy.

In the early days of the Christian Church we understand that there was a good deal of speculation among its members with regard to their belief and practice, and the propagation of these speculative ideas created divisions and schisms. Even in the days of the Apostles there was evidently considerable division, for we read that some were for Paul, some for Apollos, and others for Cephas [see 1 Corinthians 1:10–13]. The people in those days had their favorites, who taught them peculiar doctrines not generally received and promulgated (*DBY,* 107).

Why have they wandered so far from the path of truth and rectitude? Because they left the Priesthood and have had no guide, no leader, no means of finding out what is true and what is not true. It is said the Priesthood was taken from the Church, but it is not so, the Church went from the Priesthood and continued to travel in the wilderness, turned from the commandments of the Lord, and instituted other ordinances [see Galatians 1:6–8; 2 Timothy 1:15; 3 John 1:9–10] (*DBY,* 107).

But that was the time they commenced little by little to transgress the laws, change the ordinances, and break the everlasting covenant, and the

Gospel of the kingdom that Jesus undertook to establish in his day and the Priesthood were taken from the earth [see Isaiah 24:5; 2 Thessalonians 2:1–12; Revelation 12:6; D&C 1:15] (*DBY*, 107).

The Lord has restored His gospel and priesthood authority in this final dispensation through the Prophet Joseph Smith.

Generations have come and gone without the privilege of hearing the sound of the Gospel, which has come to you through Joseph Smith—that was revealed to him from heaven by angels and visions. We have the Gospel and the keys of the holy Priesthood [see D&C 1:17–23, 30; 27:5–13; 110:11–16; 128:18–21] (*DBY*, 107–8).

We are a people whose rise and progress from the beginning, has been the work of God our Heavenly Father, which in his wisdom he has seen proper to commence for the re-establishment of his Kingdom upon the earth (*DBY*, 108).

But as it was in the days of our Savior, so was it in the advent of this new dispensation. It was not in accordance with the notions, traditions, and pre-conceived ideas of the American people. The messenger did not come to an eminent divine of any of the so-called orthodoxy, he did not adopt their interpretation of the Holy Scriptures. The Lord did not come with the armies of heaven in power and great glory, nor send his messengers [armored] with aught else than the truth of heaven, to communicate to the meek, the lowly, the youth of humble origin, the sincere enquirer after the knowledge of God. But he did send his angel to this same obscure person, Joseph Smith, Jr., who afterwards became a Prophet, Seer, and Revelator, and [the Lord] informed him that he should not join any of the religious sects of the day, for they were all wrong; that they were following the precepts of men instead of the Lord Jesus; that he had a work for him to perform, inasmuch as he should prove faithful before him [see Joseph Smith—History 1:11–26] (*DBY*, 108).

It was decreed in the counsels of eternity, long before the foundations of the earth were laid, that he, Joseph Smith, should be the man, in the last dispensation of this world, to bring forth the word of God to the people, and receive the fulness of the keys and power of the Priesthood of the Son of God. The Lord had his eyes upon him, and upon his father, and upon his father's father, and upon their progenitors clear back to Abraham, and from Abraham to the flood, from the flood to Enoch, and from Enoch to Adam. He has watched that family and that blood as it has circulated from its fountain to the birth of that man. He was fore-ordained in eternity to preside over this last dispensation [see 2 Nephi 3:6–15] (*DBY*, 108).

The interior of the restored log home of Peter Whitmer, in Fayette, New York. The Church was organized in the original home on 6 April 1830.

The Lord has been operating for centuries to prepare the way for the coming forth of the contents of that Book [the Book of Mormon] from the bowels of the earth, to be published to the world, to show to the inhabitants thereof that he still lives, and that he will, in the latter days, gather his elect from the four corners of the earth. . . . The Lord has dictated and directed the whole of this, for the bringing forth, and establishing of his Kingdom in the last days [see 1 Nephi 13; D&C 20:6–16] (*DBY,* 109).

Here is the Book of Mormon. We believe it contains the history of the aborigines of [the American] continent, just as the Old Testament contains the history of the Jewish nation. In that book we learn that Jesus visited this continent, delivered his Gospel and ordained Twelve Apostles. We believe all this, but we do not ask you to believe it. What we do ask is that you will believe what is recorded in the Holy Bible concerning God and his revelations to the children of men. Do this in all honesty and sincerity, then you will know that the Book of Mormon is true. Your minds will be opened and you will know by . . . the Spirit of God that we teach the truth (*DBY,* 109).

What did Oliver Cowdery (one of the Three Witnesses to the Book of Mormon) say, after he had been away from the Church years and years? He saw and conversed with the angels, who showed him the plates, and he handled them. He left the Church because he lost the love of truth; and after he had traveled alone for years, a gentleman walked into his law office and said to him, "Mr. Cowdery, what do you think of the Book of Mormon now? Do you believe that it is true?" He replied, "No, sir, I do not!" "Well," said the gentleman, "I thought as much; for I concluded that you had seen the folly of your ways and had resolved to renounce what you once declared to be true." "Sir, you mistake me; I do not believe that the Book of Mormon is true; I am past belief on that point, for I *know* that it is true, as well as I know that you now sit before me." "Do you still testify that you saw an angel?" "Yes, as much as I see you now; and I know the Book of Mormon to be true" (*DBY,* 110).

Joseph Smith has laid the foundation of the Kingdom of God in the last days (*DBY,* 458).

I feel like shouting Hallelujah, all the time, when I think that I ever knew Joseph Smith, the Prophet whom the Lord raised up and ordained, and to whom he gave keys and power to build up the Kingdom of God on earth and sustain it. These keys are committed to this people, and we have power to continue the work that Joseph commenced, until everything is prepared for the coming of the Son of Man. This is the business of the Latter-day Saints (*DBY,* 458).

This kingdom they [the wicked] cannot destroy, because it is the last dispensation—because it is the fulness of times. It is the dispensation of all dispensations, and will excel in magnificence and glory every dispensation that has ever been committed to the children of men upon the earth. The Lord will bring again Zion, redeem his Israel, plant his standard upon the earth, and establish the laws of his Kingdom, and those laws will prevail (*DBY,* 442).

Suggestions for Study

God first revealed the plan of salvation to Adam in mortality and since then has periodically restored His kingdom through His prophets.

- How did President Young describe the "great plan called the plan of salvation"? (See also Abraham 3:21–28.)
- When the Lord reveals the plan of salvation to men and organizes His kingdom on earth, what is essential for its "complete operation"?
- According to President Young, when did God introduce the plan of salvation and the priesthood to His children on the earth? (See also Moses 5:58–59; 6:7.)

- What was the special calling of each prophet who headed one of the major dispensations of the gospel?

The priesthood and the full gospel of the kingdom were lost from the earth in the period of the Great Apostasy.

- According to President Young, why was Christ's early Church withdrawn from the earth?
- What are some evidences that Christ's early Church and priesthood were lost from the earth? (See also Joseph Smith—History 1:17–20.) What did members of the early Church do to wander "so far from the path of truth"? How has the priesthood been a "means of finding out what is true and what is not true" in your life?

The Lord has restored His gospel and priesthood authority in this final dispensation through the Prophet Joseph Smith.

- God communicated His truth to a meek, lowly youth of humble origin, a "sincere enquirer after the knowledge of God." What does this mean for you and all others who sincerely seek the truth?
- What characteristics did Joseph have that helped him fulfill his calling to be "the man, in the last dispensation of this world, to bring forth the word of God to the people"?
- What role does the Book of Mormon have in the restoration of the gospel? (See also D&C 20:6–16.) What can you learn from Oliver Cowdery's testimony of the Book of Mormon?
- What was President Young's testimony concerning "the business of the Latter-day Saints"?

In 1848 a plague of crickets threatened to destroy the crops of the Saints. In answer to fervent prayer, the Lord sent seagulls to stop the crickets, as depicted in this painting.

The Settlement in the West

President Brigham Young declared: "God has shown me that this is the spot to locate this people, and here is where they will prosper. . . . As the Saints gather here and get strong enough to possess the land, God will temper the climate and we shall build a city and a temple to the Most High God in this place. We will extend our settlements to the east and west, to the north and to the south, and we will build towns and cities by the hundreds, and thousands of Saints will gather in from the nations of the earth. This will become the great highway of nations" (JSB).

Teachings of Brigham Young

Conflict in Illinois and the flight of the Saints to the West.

I do not wish men to understand I had anything to do with our being moved here [to the Salt Lake Valley], that was the providence of the Almighty; it was the power of God that wrought out salvation for this people, I never could have devised such a plan (*DBY,* 480).

I did not devise the great scheme of the Lord's opening the way to send this people to these mountains. Joseph contemplated the move for years before it took place, but he could not get here (*DBY,* 480).

In the days of Joseph we have sat many hours at a time conversing about this very country. Joseph has often said, "If I were only in the Rocky Mountains with a hundred faithful men, I would then be happy, and ask no odds of mobocrats" (*DBY,* 480).

We lived in Illinois from 1839 to 1844, by which time [enemies of the Church] again succeeded in kindling the spirit of persecution against Joseph and the Latter-day Saints. Treason! Treason! Treason! they cried, calling us murderers, thieves, liars, adulterers, and the worst people on the earth. . . . They took Joseph and Hyrum, and as a guarantee for their safety, Governor Thomas Ford pledged the faith of the State of Illinois. They were imprisoned [in Carthage, Illinois], on the pretense of safekeeping, because the mob was so enraged and violent. The Governor left them in the hands of the mob, who entered the prison and shot them dead. John Taylor, who is present with us today, was in the prison, too, and was also shot, and was

As depicted by this artist, in 1847 President Young led the Saints west to "the best place we could find. It was impossible for any person to live here unless he labored hard . . . , but it was a first-rate place to raise Latter-day Saints" (*DBY,* 474).

confined to his bed for several months afterwards. After the mob had committed these murders, they came upon us and burned our houses and grain. When the brethren would go out to put out the fire, the mob would lie concealed under fences, and in the darkness of the night, they would shoot them (*DBY,* 473).

In the year 1845 I addressed letters to all the Governors of states and territories in the Union, asking them for an asylum, within their borders, for the Latter-day Saints. We were refused such privilege, either by silent contempt or a flat denial in every instance. They all agreed that we could not come within the limits of their territory or state (*DBY,* 474).

Three congressmen came [to Nauvoo] in the fall of 1845, and had a conference with the Twelve and others; they were desirous that we should leave the United States. We told them we would do so, we had stayed long enough with them; we agreed to leave the State of Illinois in consequence of that religious prejudice against us that we could not stay in peace any longer. These men said the people were prejudiced against us. Stephen A. Douglas, one of the three, had been acquainted with us. He said, "I know you, I know Joseph Smith; he was a good man," and this people are a good people; but the prejudices of the . . . ungodly are such that, said he, "Gentlemen, you cannot stay here and live in peace." We agreed to leave. We left Nauvoo in February, 1846 (*DBY,* 473).

I crossed the Mississippi River, with my brethren, for this place, not knowing, at that time, whither we were going, but firmly believing that the Lord had in reserve for us a good place in the mountains, and that he would lead us directly to it (*DBY,* 482).

We were menaced on every side by the cruel persecutions of our inveterate enemies; hundreds of families, who had been forced from their homes, and compelled to leave behind them their all, were wandering as exiles in a state of abject destitution (*DBY,* 482).

We were migrating, we knew not whither, except that it was our intention to go beyond the reach of our enemies. We had no home, save our wagons and tents, and no stores of provisions and clothing; but had to earn our daily bread by leaving our families in isolated locations for safety, and going among our enemies to labor (*DBY,* 478).

We travelled west, stopping in places, building settlements, where we [temporarily] left the poor who could not travel any farther with the company (*DBY,* 474).

Recruitment and march of the Mormon Battalion.

When we were right in the midst of Indians, who were said to be hostile, five hundred men were called to go to Mexico to fight [in the Mexican War, 1846–48] (*DBY,* 476).

I went myself, in company with a few of my brethren, between one and two hundred miles along the several routes of travel, stopping at every little camp, using our influence to obtain volunteers, and on the day appointed for the rendezvous [16 July 1846 at Council Bluffs, Iowa] the required complement was made up; and this was all accomplished in about twenty days from the time that the requisition was made known (*DBY,* 479).

That battalion took up their line of march from Fort Leavenworth by way of Santa Fe, and over the desert and dreary route, and planted themselves in the lower part of California, to the joy of all the officers and men that were loyal. At the time of their arrival, General [Stephen W.] Kearny was in a [difficult] position, and Colonel P. St. George Cooke [the battalion's new leader] promptly marched the battalion to his relief, and said to him, "We have the boys here now that can put all things right." The boys in that battalion performed their duty faithfully. I never think of that little company of men without the next thoughts being, "God bless them for ever and for ever." All this we did to prove to the Government that we were loyal (*DBY,* 477).

Our battalion went to the scene of action, not in easy berths on steamboats, nor with a few months' absence, but on foot over two thousand miles across trackless deserts and barren plains, experiencing every degree of privation, hardship, and suffering during some two years' absence before they could rejoin their families. Thus was our deliverance again affected by the interposition of that All-wise Being who can discern the end from the beginning (*DBY,* 479).

Under . . . trying circumstances we were required to turn out of our traveling camps five hundred of our most efficient men, leaving the old, the young, the women upon the hands of the residue, to take care of and support (*DBY,* 478).

Those of us who remained behind labored and raised all that we needed to feed ourselves in the wilderness. We had to pay our own schoolteachers, raise our own bread and earn our own clothing, or go without, there was no other choice (*DBY,* 476).

The "camp of the poor" was preserved by the mercies of the Lord.

There remained behind a few of the very poor, the sick and the aged, who suffered again from the violence of the mob; they were whipped and beaten, and had their houses burned (*DBY,* 473–74).

[These] brethren who tarried by the way [along the riverbank above Montrose, Iowa] were toiling through poverty and distress. At one time, I was told, they would have perished from starvation, had not the Lord sent quails among them. These birds flew against their wagons, and they either killed or stunned themselves, and the brethren and sisters gathered them up, which furnished them with food for days, until they made their way in the wilderness. [Brigham Young sent rescue companies to bring these Saints on to join relatives and friends in camps further along the trail.] (*DBY,* 474).

Brigham Young's pioneer company of 1847 piloted the way to the Salt Lake Valley.

Some of the time we followed Indian trails, some of the time we ran by the compass; when we left the Missouri river we followed the Platte [River]. And we killed rattlesnakes by the cord in some places; and made roads and built bridges till our backs ached. Where we could not build bridges across rivers, we ferried our people across (*DBY,* 480).

When we met Mr. Bridger [proprietor of Fort Bridger, Wyoming] on the Big Sandy River [28 June 1847], said he, "Mr. Young, I would give a thousand dollars if I knew an ear of corn could be ripened in [these mountains]." Said I, "Wait eighteen months and I will show you many of them." Did I say this from knowledge? No, it was my faith; but we had not the least encouragement—from natural reasoning and all that we could learn of this country—of its sterility, its cold and frost, to believe that we could ever raise anything. . . . We had faith that we could raise grain; was there any harm in this? Not at all. If we had not had faith, what would have become of us? We would have gone down in unbelief, have closed up every resource for our sustenance and should never have raised anything (*DBY,* 481).

[On 30 June 1847,] when the Pioneer company reached Green River [about 80 miles east of the Great Salt Lake Valley], we met Samuel Brannan and a few others from [San Francisco,] California, and they wanted us to go there. I remarked, "Let us go to California, and we cannot stay there over five years; but let us stay in the mountains, and we can raise our own potatoes, and eat them; and I calculate to stay here." We are still on the backbone of the animal, where the bone and the sinew are, and we intend to stay here, and all hell cannot help themselves (*DBY,* 475).

Myself, with others, came out of what we named Emigration Canyon; we crossed the Big and Little mountains, and came down the valley about three quarters of a mile south of this. [Orson Pratt and Erastus Snow entered the Salt Lake Valley on 21 July 1847; the advance and main companies arrived on 22 July. The rear company with President Brigham Young, who was suffering from the effects of mountain fever, entered the valley on 24 July.] We located, and we looked about, and finally we came and camped between the two forks of City Creek, one of which ran southwest and the other west. Here we planted our standard on this temple block and the one above it; here we pitched our camps and determined that here we would settle and stop (*DBY,* 474).

Through faith in God the Saints surmounted their difficulties in the West.

We arrived here, where we found a few . . . Indians, a few wolves and rabbits, and any amount of crickets; but as for a green tree or a fruit tree, or any green field, we found nothing of the kind, with the exception of a few cottonwoods and willows on the edge of City Creek. For some 1200 or 1300 miles we carried every particle of provision we had when we arrived here. When we left our homes we picked up what the mob did not steal of our horses, oxen and calves and some women drove their own teams here. Instead of 365 pounds of breadstuff when they started from the Missouri river, there was not half of them had half of it. We had to bring our seed grain, our farming utensils, bureaus, secretaries [desks], sideboards, sofas, pianos, large looking glasses, fine chairs, carpets, nice shovels and tongs and other fine furniture, with all the parlor, cook stoves, etc., and we had to bring these things piled together with some women and children, helter skelter, topsy-turvy, with broken-down horses, . . . oxen with three legs, and cows with one teat. This was our only means of transportation, and if we had not brought our goods in this manner we would not have had them, for there was nothing here (*DBY*, 480).

The Saints were poor when they came into this valley (*DBY*, 475).

They picked up a few buckskins, antelope skins, sheep skins, buffalo skins, and made leggings and moccasins of them, and wrapped the buffalo robes around them. Some had blankets and some had not; some had shirts, and I guess some had not. One man told me that he had not a shirt for himself or family (*DBY*, 475–76).

I will venture to say that not one of four out of my family had shoes to their feet when we came to this valley (*DBY*, 476).

We have faith, we live by faith; we came to these mountains by faith. We came here, I often say, though to the ears of some the expression may sound rather rude, naked and barefoot, and comparatively this is true (*DBY*, 481).

We prayed over the land, and dedicated it and the water, air and everything pertaining to them unto the Lord, and the smiles of heaven rested on the land and it became productive, and today yields us the best of grain, fruit and vegetables (*DBY*, 483).

Until the Latter-day Saints came here, not a person among all the mountaineers and those who had traveled here, so far as we could learn, believed that an ear of corn would ripen in these valleys. We know that corn and wheat produce abundantly here, and we know that we have an excellent region wherein to raise cattle, horses, and every other kind of domestic animal that we need (*DBY*, 485).

There never has been a land, from the days of Adam until now, that has been blessed more than this land has been blessed by our Father in Heaven; and it will still be blessed more and more, if we are faithful and humble, and thankful to God for the wheat and the corn, the oats, the fruit, the vegetables, the cattle and everything he bestows upon us, and try to use them for the building up of his Kingdom on the earth (*DBY*, 483).

We are the pioneers of this country (*DBY*, 474).

We printed the first papers, except about two, set out the first orchards, raised the first wheat, kept almost the first schools, and made the first improvements in our pioneering, in a great measure, from the Mississippi river to the Pacific Ocean; and here we got at last, so as to be out of the way of everybody, if possible. We thought we would get as far as we could from the face of man; we wanted to get to a strange land, like Abraham, that we might be where we should not be continually wrong with somebody or other (*DBY*, 476).

We wish strangers to understand that we did not come here out of choice, but because we were obliged to go somewhere, and this was the best place we could find. It was impossible for any person to live here unless he labored hard and battled and fought against the elements, but it was a first-rate place to raise Latter-day Saints, and we shall be blessed in living here, and shall yet make it like the Garden of Eden; and the Lord Almighty will hedge about his Saints and will defend and preserve them if they will do his will. The only fear I have is that we will not do right; if we do [right] we will be like a city set on a hill, our light will not be hid (*DBY,* 474).

It is but seven years since we left Nauvoo, and we are now ready to build another temple. I look back upon our labors with pleasure. Here are hundreds and thousands of people that have not had the privileges that some of us have had. Do you ask, what privileges? Why, of running the gauntlet, of passing through the narrows. They have not had the privilege of being robbed and plundered of their property, of being in the midst of mobs and death, as many of us have (*DBY,* 482).

You inquire if we shall stay in these mountains. I answer yes, as long as we please to do the will of God our Father in Heaven. If we are pleased to turn away from the holy commandments of the Lord Jesus Christ, as ancient Israel did, every man turning to his own way, we shall be scattered and peeled, driven before our enemies and persecuted, until we learn to remember the Lord our God and are willing to walk in his ways (*DBY,* 483).

Many may inquire, "How long shall we stay here?" We shall stay here just as long as we ought to. "Shall we be driven, when we go?" If we will so live as to be satisfied with ourselves, and will not drive ourselves from our homes we shall never be driven from them. Seek for the best wisdom you can obtain, learn how to apply your labor, build good houses, make fine farms, set out apple, pear, and other fruit trees that will flourish here, also the mountain currant and raspberry bushes, plant strawberry beds, and build up and adorn a beautiful city (*DBY,* 483–84).

Mark our settlements for six hundred miles in these mountains and then mark the path that we made coming here, building the bridges and making the roads across the prairies, mountains and canyons! We came here penniless in old wagons, our friends . . . telling us to "take all the provisions you can; for you can get no more! Take all the seed grain you can, for you can get none there!" We did this, and in addition to all this we have gathered all the poor we could, and the Lord has planted us in these valleys, promising that he would hide us up for a little season until his wrath and indignation passed over the nations. Will we trust in the Lord? Yes (*DBY,* 475).

By the favor of heaven, we have been enabled to surmount all these difficulties, and can assemble here today in the chamber of these mountains, where there are none to make us afraid, far from our persecutors, far from the turmoil and confusion of the old world (*DBY,* 482).

Suggestions for Study

Conflict in Illinois and the flight of the Saints to the West.

- To whom did President Young give credit for the plan to move the Saints to the Rocky Mountains and the Salt Lake Valley?
- What circumstances prompted the exile of the Saints from Illinois? How did President Young know where to lead the Saints?

Recruitment and march of the Mormon Battalion.

- Why did Church leaders encourage 500 volunteers to join the Mormon Battalion and leave their families at such a critical time in their westward movement?
- The Mormon Battalion never had to fight in the war because the battle was over by the time they reached their destination. What did the Saints suffer because of the government's call for a battalion? Why do you think it was important for them to make that sacrifice? What benefits resulted from this experience?

The "camp of the poor" was preserved by the mercies of the Lord.

- How did the Lord relieve the Saints' hunger for a time? How has the Lord helped you in times of need?

Brigham Young's pioneer company of 1847 piloted the way to the Salt Lake Valley.

- Doctrine and Covenants 136 contains "the Word and Will of the Lord concerning the Camp of Israel in their journeyings to the West" (verse 1). This revelation was given to President Young at Winter Quarters on 14 January 1847. In addition to the organization described in this section, what other counsel was given to the Saints traveling west?

- What concern did Jim Bridger express to President Young? What was the basis of President Young's strong response to Mr. Bridger? How have you experienced success that resulted primarily from an exercise of faith?
- Why did President Young choose to stay in the Rocky Mountains rather than continue into California?

Through faith in God the Saints surmounted their difficulties in the West.

- In what ways did the Saints seek to find solutions to their poverty?
- President Young said, "There never has been a land, from the days of Adam until now, that has been blessed more than this land has been blessed by our Father in Heaven." What is required of the Saints wherever they dwell to ensure a continuation of those blessings? What does it mean to live by faith? What can we do to more completely live by faith in Jesus Christ?
- What did the Saints accomplish as pioneers of the Rocky Mountains? What can you do to build the Church where you live?
- President Young made the unusual statement, "Here are hundreds and thousands of people that have not had the privileges that some of us have had. . . . They have not had the privilege of being robbed and plundered of their property, of being in the midst of mobs and death, as many of us have." What do you think he meant? Why was the Salt Lake Valley "a first-rate place to raise Latter-day Saints"? How have difficulties blessed your life? What can we do to turn even the most challenging trial into a chance to grow?

President Brigham Young was known as a great colonizer. He dedicated the site for the Manti Temple (shown here under construction) in 1877.

Building Zion

President Brigham Young's whole soul was dedicated to establishing Zion. He oversaw the gathering of nearly one hundred thousand Latter-day Saints to the valleys of the Rocky Mountains and colonized some four hundred cities and towns. He built temples and tabernacles, organized stakes and wards throughout the western United States, and sent missionaries to nearly every corner of the earth. No one understood better the sacrifice and effort required, but, as he said, "we are not going to wait for angels, . . . we are going to build [Zion ourselves]" (DBY, 443).

Teachings of Brigham Young

Zion is the pure in heart.

Let me say a few words with regard to Zion. We profess to be Zion. If we are the pure in heart we are so, for "Zion is the pure in heart" [see D&C 97:21] (*DBY,* 118). Where is Zion? Where the organization of the Church of God is. And may it dwell spiritually in every heart; and may we so live as to enjoy the spirit of Zion always! (*DBY,* 118).

This is the Gospel; this is the plan of salvation; this is the Kingdom of God; this is the Zion that has been spoken and written of by all the Prophets since the world began. This is the work of Zion which the Lord has promised to bring forth (*DBY,* 118).

Zion will extend, eventually, all over this earth. There will be no nook or corner upon the earth but what will be in Zion. It will all be Zion (*DBY,* 120).

Our purpose in life should be to sanctify ourselves and build the Zion of our God.

The purpose of our life should be to build up the Zion of our God, to gather the House of Israel, bring in the fulness of the Gentiles, restore and bless the earth with our ability and make it as the Garden of Eden, store up treasures of knowledge and wisdom in our own understandings, purify our own hearts and prepare a people to meet the Lord when he comes (*DBY,* 88).

We have no business here other than to build up and establish the Zion of God. It must be done according to the will and law of God [see D&C 105:5], after that pattern and order by which Enoch built up and perfected the former-day Zion, which was taken away to heaven, hence the saying went abroad that Zion had fled [see Moses 7:69]. By and by it will come back again, and as Enoch prepared his people to be worthy of translation, so we, through our faithfulness, must prepare ourselves to meet Zion from above when it shall return to earth, and to abide the brightness and glory of its coming (*DBY,* 443).

We look forward to the day when the Lord will prepare for the building of the New Jerusalem, preparatory to the City of Enoch's going to be joined with it when it is built upon this earth [see Moses 7:62–64]. We are anticipating to enjoy that day, whether we sleep in death previous to that, or not. We look forward, with all the anticipation and confidence that children can possess in a parent, that we shall be there when Jesus comes; and if we are not there, we will come with him: in either case we shall be there when he comes (*DBY,* 120).

The purpose of building Zion is to sanctify the children of God through the ordinances of salvation.

We have been gathered . . . for the express purpose of purifying ourselves, that we may become polished stones in the temple of God. We are here for the purpose of establishing the Kingdom of God on the earth. To be prepared for this work it has been necessary to gather us out from the nations and countries of the world [to receive] the ordinances of the holy Priesthood of the Son of God, which are necessary for the perfection of the Saints preparatory to his coming (*DBY,* 121).

The ordinance of sealing must be performed here [son] to [father], and woman to man, and children to parents, etc., until the chain of generation is made perfect in the sealing ordinances back to Father Adam; hence, we have been commanded to gather ourselves together, to come out of Babylon [see D&C 133:5, 7, 14], and sanctify ourselves, and build up the Zion of our God, by building cities and temples, redeeming countries from the solitude of nature, until the earth is sanctified and prepared for the residence of God and angels (*DBY,* 407).

The Lord has provided the means for the Saints to build Zion.

Do we realize that if we enjoy a Zion in time or in eternity we must make it for ourselves? That all, who have a Zion in the eternities of the Gods,

Photograph of the Salt Lake Temple under construction. President Young dedicated
his life to establishing Zion and taught that "the purpose of our life
should be to build up the Zion of our God" (*DBY,* 88).

organized, framed, consolidated, and perfected it themselves, and consequently are entitled to enjoy it? (*DBY,* 118).

When we conclude to make a Zion we will make it, and this work
commences in the heart of each person. When the father of a family
wishes to make a Zion in his own house, he must take the lead in this good
work, which it is impossible for him to do unless he himself possesses the
spirit of Zion. Before he can produce the work of sanctification in his
family, he must sanctify himself, and by this means God can help him to
sanctify his family (*DBY,* 118).

The Lord has done his share of the work; he has surrounded us with
elements containing wheat, meat, flax, wool, silk, fruit, and everything
with which to build up, beautify and glorify the Zion of the last days, and
it is our business to mould these elements to our wants and necessities,
according to the knowledge we now have and the wisdom we can obtain
from the heavens through our faithfulness. In this way will the Lord bring
again Zion upon the earth, and in no other (*DBY,* 294).

There is not one thing wanting in all the works of God's hands to make
a Zion upon the earth when the people conclude to make it. We can make
a Zion of God on earth at our pleasure, upon the same principle that we
can raise a field of wheat, or build and inhabit. There has been no time
when the material has not been here from which to produce corn, wheat,
etc., and by the judicious management and arrangement of this ever-existing
material a Zion of God can always be built on the earth (*DBY,* 118).

Building Zion requires sacrifice and great effort.

We want all the Latter-day Saints to understand how to build up Zion. The City of Zion, in beauty and magnificence, will outstrip anything that is now known upon the earth. The curse will be taken from the earth and sin and corruption will be swept from its face. Who will do this great work? Is the Lord going to convince the people that he will redeem the center Stake of Zion, beautify it and then place them there without an exertion on their part? No. He will not come here to build a Temple, a Tabernacle, a Bowery, or to set out fruit trees, make aprons of fig leaves or coats of skins, or work in brass and iron, for we already know how to do these things. . . . We have to build up Zion, if we do our duty (*DBY,* 120).

I see men and women in this congregation—only a few of them—who were driven from the central Stake of Zion [in Jackson County, Missouri; see D&C 57:2–3]. Ask them if they had any sorrow or trouble; then let them look at the beautiful land that the Lord would have given them if all had been faithful in keeping his commandments, and had walked before him as they should; and then ask them with regard to the blessings they would have received. If they tell you the sentiments of their minds, they will tell you that the yoke of Jesus would have been easy and his burden would have been light, and that it would have been a delightful task to have walked in obedience to his commandments and to have been of one heart and one mind; but through the selfishness of some, which is idolatry, through their covetousness, which is the same, and the lustful desire of their minds, they were cast out and driven from their homes (*DBY,* 113–14).

Let us train our minds until we delight in that which is good, lovely and holy, seeking continually after that intelligence which will enable us effectually to build up Zion, which consists in building houses, tabernacles, temples, streets, and every convenience and necessity to embellish and beautify, seeking to do the will of the Lord all the days of our lives, improving our minds in all scientific and mechanical knowledge, seeking diligently to understand the great design and plan of all created things, that we may know what to do with our lives and how to improve upon the facilities placed within our reach (*DBY,* 247).

We have come here to build up Zion. How shall we do it? . . . We have got to be united in our efforts. We should go to work with a united faith like the heart of one man; and whatever we do should be performed in the name of the Lord, and we will then be blessed and prospered in all we do. We have a work on hand whose magnitude can hardly be told (*DBY,* 284).

Many Latter-day Saints think when they have obeyed the Gospel, made a sacrifice in forsaking their homes, perhaps their parents, husbands, wives, children, farms, native lands, or other things held dear, that the work is done; but it is only just commenced. The work of purifying ourselves and preparing to build up the Zion of God . . . has only just begun with us when we have got as far as that (*DBY,* 444).

Everything connected with building up Zion requires actual, severe labor. It is nonsense to talk about building up any kingdom except by labor; it requires the labor of every part of our organization, whether it be mental, physical, or spiritual, and that is the only way to build up the Kingdom of God (*DBY,* 291).

If we are to build up the Kingdom of God, or establish Zion upon the earth, we have to labor with our hands, plan with our minds, and devise ways and means to accomplish that object (*DBY,* 291).

I have Zion in my view constantly. We are not going to wait for angels, or for Enoch and his company to come and build up Zion, but we are going to build it. We will raise our wheat, build our houses, fence our farms, plant our vineyards and orchards, and produce everything that will make our bodies comfortable and happy, and in this manner we intend to build up Zion on the earth and purify it and cleanse it from all pollutions. Let there be an hallowed influence go from us over all things over which we have any power; over the soil we cultivate, over the houses we build, and over everything we possess; and if we cease to hold fellowship with that which is corrupt and establish the Zion of God in our hearts, in our own houses, in our cities, and throughout our country, we shall ultimately overcome the earth, for we are the lords of the earth; and, instead of thorns and thistles, every useful plant that is good for the food of man and to beautify and adorn will spring from its bosom (*DBY,* 443–44).

The Lord has blessed me; he has always blessed me; from the time I commenced to build up Zion, I have been extremely blessed. I could relate circumstances of so extraordinary a character in regard to the providences of God to me, that my brethren and sisters would say in their hearts, "I can hardly give credence to this" (*DBY,* 452).

My spiritual enjoyment must be obtained by my own life, but it would add much to the comfort of the community, and to my happiness, as one with them, if every man and woman would live their religion, and enjoy the light and glory of the Gospel for themselves, be passive, humble and faithful; rejoice continually before the Lord, attend to the business they are called to do, and be sure never to do anything wrong (*DBY,* 119).

All would then be peace, joy, and tranquility, in our streets and in our houses. Litigation would cease, there would be no difficulties before the High Council and Bishops' Courts, and courts, turmoil, and strife would not be known (*DBY,* 119).

Then we would have Zion, for all would be pure in heart (*DBY,* 119).

My heart has been set in me to do the will of God, to build up his Kingdom on the earth, to establish Zion and its laws, and to save the people; and I can say, truly and honestly, that the thought never came into my mind, in all my labors, what my reward will be, or whether my crown would be large or small, or any crown at all, a small possession, a large possession, or no possession. I have never had any thoughts or reflections upon this, or cared the first thing about it. All that I have had in my mind has been that it was my duty to do the will of God, and to labor to establish his Kingdom on the earth . . . because the principles which God has revealed for the salvation of the inhabitants of the earth are pure, holy and exalting in their nature. In them there is honor and eternal increase, they lead on from light to light, strength to strength, glory to glory, knowledge to knowledge, and power to power (*DBY,* 452).

Suggestions for Study

Zion is the pure in heart.

- How did President Young define Zion? (See also D&C 97:21.)
- Who are the rightful inhabitants of Zion, and where can Zion be found? (See also Psalm 102:16; 4 Nephi 1:15–17; D&C 109:39.)

Our purpose in life should be to sanctify ourselves and build the Zion of our God.

- President Young taught, "The purpose of our life should be to build up the Zion of our God." As a Church, what must we do to build up Zion? How can you as an individual help in this work?
- What is the "pattern and order" that Enoch used to build and perfect the former-day Zion? (See also Moses 7:10–11, 17–21.) How can we follow that same pattern in our families and wards or branches today?
- How can families create Zion in their own homes?

The purpose of building Zion is to sanctify the children of God through the ordinances of salvation.

- How can we sanctify ourselves and our families?
- Why have we been "commanded to gather ourselves together, to come out of Babylon" to Zion? (See also D&C 44:4–6; 133:14.) What is spiritual Babylon and how do we come out of it?

• What is the relationship between building Zion and the ordinances of the holy priesthood?

The Lord has provided the means for the Saints to build Zion.

• What has the Lord provided for us so we can contribute to the establishment of Zion?

• Zion begins in "the heart of each person." What gifts or talents do you have that can help you build Zion?

Building Zion requires sacrifice and great effort.

• In the early days of the Church, the location of the center stake of Zion was revealed (see also D&C 57:2–3). According to President Young, what prevented the Saints from entering into their inheritance and establishing Zion at that time?

• How will the Lord bring about the establishment of Zion? (See also D&C 105:5–6.)

• Why is it important that we "train our minds" as we strive to build Zion?

• President Young taught that to build Zion we must be united in our efforts. How can we achieve this unity in our families, quorums, and wards or branches?

• Why does the Lord require "actual, severe labor" from us in establishing Zion?

• President Young stated, "The Lord has blessed me; . . . from the time I commenced to build up Zion, I have been extremely blessed." What blessings are in store for those who keep their covenant to establish Zion? (See also Isaiah 51:11.)

By reading and praying about the Book of Mormon, Brigham Young gained a testimony of its truthfulness. He taught that if others would follow his example "in all honesty and sincerity, then [they] will know that the Book of Mormon is true" (*DBY,* 109).

The Scriptures

Every evening, President Brigham Young sounded the prayer bell and gathered his family around him to sing and hear counsel, study the word of God, and conduct family prayers. He believed in studying the scriptures and compared them to "a finger-post which points out the road we should travel. Where do they point? To the Fountain of light" (DBY, 127). He exhorted the Saints: "Do you read the Scriptures, my brethren and sisters, as though you were writing them a thousand, two thousand, or five thousand years ago? Do you read them as though you stood in the place of the men who wrote them? If you do not feel thus, it is your privilege to do so, that you may be as familiar with the spirit and meaning of the written word of God as you are with your daily walk and conversation, or as you are with your workmen or with your households" (DBY, 128).

Teachings of Brigham Young

Learning and living by the teachings of the scriptures bring inspiration and direction to our lives.

It is your privilege and duty to live so as to be able to understand the things of God. There are the Old and New Testaments, the Book of Mormon, and the book of Doctrine and Covenants, which Joseph has given us, and they are of great worth to a person wandering in darkness. They are like a lighthouse in the ocean, or a finger-post which points out the road we should travel. Where do they point? To the Fountain of light *(DBY,* 127).

I believe the words of the Bible. . . . I believe the doctrines concerning salvation contained in that book are true, and that their observance will elevate any people, nation or family that dwells on the face of the earth. The doctrines contained in the Bible will lift to a superior condition all who observe them; they will impart to them knowledge, wisdom, charity, fill them with compassion and cause them to feel after the wants of those who are in distress, or in painful or degraded circumstances. They who observe the precepts contained in the Scriptures will be just and true and virtuous and peaceable at home and abroad. Follow out the doctrines of the Bible, and men will make splendid husbands, women excellent wives, and children will be obedient; they will make families happy and the nations wealthy and happy and lifted up above the things of this life (*DBY,* 125).

I say we take this book [the Bible] for our guide, for our rule of action; we take it as the foundation of our faith. It points the way to salvation like a fingerboard pointing to a city, or a map which designates the locality of mountains, rivers, or the latitude and longitude of any place on the surface of the earth that we desire to find, and we have no better sense than to believe it; hence, I say that the Latter-day Saints have the most natural faith and belief of any people on the face of the earth (*DBY,* 125).

We consider the Bible . . . as a guide . . . pointing to a certain destination. This is a true doctrine, which we boldly advance. If you will follow the doctrines, and be guided by the precepts of that book, it will direct you where you may see as you are seen, where you may converse with Jesus Christ, have the visitation of angels, have dreams, visions, and revelations, and understand and know God for yourselves. Is it not a stay and a staff to you? Yes; it will prove to you that you are following in the footsteps of the ancients. You can see what they saw, understand what they enjoyed (*DBY,* 126).

There is no clash in the principles revealed in the Bible, the Book of Mormon, and the Doctrine and Covenants [the Pearl of Great Price was not yet canonized at the time of this statement]; and there would be no clash between any of the doctrines taught by Joseph the Prophet and by the brethren now, if all would live in a way to be governed by the Spirit of the Lord. All do not live so as to have the Spirit of the Lord with them all the time, and the result is that some get out of the way (*DBY,* 126).

We believe in the Book of Mormon, and the Doctrine and Covenants given by the Lord to Joseph Smith and by him to the Church. We also believe if we were destitute of the Spirit of the Lord, and our eyes were closed so that we could not see and understand things as they are by the spirit of revelation, we might say farewell to all these books, no matter how numerous. If we had all the revelation given since the days of Adam and were without the spirit of revelation to be and abide in the midst of the people, it would be impossible for us to be saved in the celestial kingdom of God (*DBY,* 128).

The book of Doctrine and Covenants is given for the Latter-day Saints expressly for their everyday walk and actions (*DBY,* 128).

The Bible contains the doctrines of salvation.

This Book, which is the Old and New Testament, preaches but one sermon from Genesis to Revelation (*DBY,* 126).

The doctrine that we preach is the doctrine of the Bible, it is the doctrine the Lord has revealed for the salvation of the children of God, and when men, who have once obeyed it, deny it, they deny it with their eyes wide open, and knowing that they deny the truth and set at naught the counsels of the Almighty (*DBY,* 126).

The Bible is true. It may not all have been translated aright, and many precious things may have been rejected in the compilation and translation of the Bible [see 1 Nephi 13:24–27]; but we understand, from the writings of one of the Apostles, that if all the sayings and doings of the Savior had been written, the world could not contain them [see John 21:25]. I will say that the world could not understand them. They do not understand what we have on record, nor the character of the Savior, as delineated in the Scriptures; and yet it is one of the simplest things in the world, and the Bible, when it is understood, is one of the simplest books in the world, for, as far as it is translated correctly [see Articles of Faith 1:8], it is nothing but truth, and in truth there is no mystery save to the ignorant. The revelations of the Lord to his creatures are adapted to the lowest capacity, and they bring life and salvation to all who are willing to receive them (*DBY,* 124).

We believe the New Testament, and consequently, to be consistent, we must believe in new revelation, visions, angels, in all the gifts of the Holy Ghost, and all the promises contained in these books, and believe it about as it reads (*DBY,* 124).

We have a holy reverence for and a belief in the Bible (*DBY,* 124).

By reading the Bible we find that the Gospel is contained not only in the New Testament, but also in the Old. Moses and the Prophets saw and predicted the apostasy of the Church. They saw that the Lord would strive with the children of men from time to time, that he would deliver to them the truth and the Priesthood; they also saw that through the wickedness of the people they would change his ordinances, break the covenants, and transgress his laws [see Isaiah 24:5], until the Priesthood would be taken from the earth, and its inhabitants be left in apostasy and darkness (*DBY,* 124–25).

We as Latter-day Saints have confessed before Heaven, before the heavenly hosts, and before the inhabitants of the earth, that we really believe the Scriptures as they are given to us, according to the best understanding and knowledge that we have of the translation, and the spirit and meaning of the Old and New Testaments (*DBY,* 125–26).

The Book of Mormon . . . declares that the Bible is true, and it proves it; and the two prove each other true. The Old and New Testaments are the stick of Judah [see Ezekiel 37:15–19]. You recollect that the tribe of Judah tarried in Jerusalem and the Lord blessed Judah, and the result was the writings of the Old and New Testaments. But where is the stick of Joseph?

Photograph of part of the original manuscript of the Book of Mormon.

Can you tell where it is? Yes. It was the children of Joseph who came across the waters to this continent [the Americas], and this land was filled with people, and the Book of Mormon or the stick of Joseph contains their writings, and they are in the hands of Ephraim. Where are the Ephraimites? They are mixed through all the nations of the earth. God is calling upon them to gather out, and he is uniting them, and they are giving the Gospel to all the world (*DBY*, 127).

The messages of the scriptures are plain and easy to understand for those who seek the Spirit of the Lord.

We are not in the same attitude that the people were a few thousand years ago—they were depending on the Prophet or Prophets, or on having immediate revelation for themselves to know the will of the Lord, without the record of their predecessors, while we have the records of those who have lived before us, also the testimony of the Holy Spirit; and, to the satisfaction of all who desire a testimony, we can turn to this book and read that which we believe, learn the object of our pursuit, the end that we expect to accomplish—the end of the race as far as mortality is concerned—and the fulness of the glory that is beyond this vale of tears; consequently we have the advantage of those who lived before us (*DBY*, 128).

The people on every hand are inquiring, "What does this scripture mean, and how shall we understand this or that passage?" Now I wish, my brethren and sisters, for us to understand things precisely as they are, and not as the flitting, changing imagination of the human mind may frame them (*DBY*, 128).

I ask you, brother B, how I must believe the Bible, and how shall you and every other follower of the Lord Jesus Christ believe it? . . . I believe it just as it is. I do not believe in putting any man's interpretation upon it whatever, unless it should be directed by the Lord himself in some way. I do not believe we need interpreters and expounders of the Scriptures, to wrest them from their literal, plain, simple meaning (*DBY*, 126).

The Bible is just as plain and easy of comprehension as the revelation which I have just read to you [see D&C 58], if you understand the Spirit of God—the Spirit of Revelation, and know how the Gospel of salvation is adapted to the capacity of weak man (*DBY*, 128).

With regard to the Bible, the phraseology is that which was customary centuries ago; but no matter what the language is, that is merely custom. But I will say that the doctrines taught in the Old and New Testaments concerning the will of God towards his children here on the earth; the history of what he has done for their salvation; the ordinances which he has instituted for their redemption; the gift of his Son and his atonement—all these are true, and we, the Latter-day Saints, believe in them (*DBY*, 129).

When we reflect and rightly understand, we learn how easy of comprehension the Gospel is, how plain it is in its plan, in every part and principle fitted perfectly to the capacity of mankind, insomuch that when it is introduced among the lovers of truth it appears very easy and very plain, and how very ready the honest are to receive it (*DBY*, 129).

We should all live so that the Spirit of revelation could dictate and write on the heart and tell us what we should do. . . . But to do this we must become like little children; and Jesus says if we do not we cannot enter the kingdom of heaven. How simple it is! Live free from envy, malice, wrath, strife, bitter feelings, and evil speaking in our families and about our neighbors and friends and all the inhabitants of the earth, wherever we meet them. Live so that our consciences are free, clean and clear (*DBY*, 36).

Suggestions for Study

**Learning and living by the teachings of the scriptures bring
inspiration and direction to our lives.**

- According to President Young, why should we study the doctrines of the Lord as contained in the scriptures? What promises does President Young make to those who will observe the precepts of the Bible and the other scriptures?

- In what way can records that are hundreds and thousands of years old guide our lives today? How have the scriptures directed your life?

- Why, according to President Young, was the Doctrine and Covenants given? How has the Doctrine and Covenants helped you in your

123

"everyday walk and actions"? (See also D&C 4:3–4; 84:43–44; 86:11; 121:41–42, 45.)

The Bible contains the doctrines of salvation.

- President Young taught that the Bible "preaches but one sermon from Genesis to Revelation." What is that sermon?
- How have the scriptures helped you understand "the character of the Savior"?
- What are the sticks of Judah and Joseph? What relation do the Bible and the Book of Mormon have to each other? According to President Young, for what purpose has the stick of Joseph been placed into the "hands of Ephraim"?

The messages of the scriptures are plain and easy to understand for those who seek the Spirit of the Lord.

- What was President Young's counsel to those who constantly seek man's interpretations of the scriptures?
- What advantages come to us because we have the records of the prophets in the scriptures?
- President Young invited us to look beyond the sometimes difficult language of the scriptures for valuable principles and doctrines to guide our lives. Which doctrines does he specifically mention? Why are these doctrines particularly important to us today?
- According to President Young, for whom are the scriptures plain and easy to understand?
- President Young taught that we should "live so that the Spirit of revelation could dictate and write on the heart and tell us what we should do." How can we cultivate the spirit of revelation in our lives so we can understand more clearly the messages of the scriptures?

The Priesthood

President Brigham Young was ordained as one of the original Twelve Apostles in this dispensation. As part of the blessing given him in his ordination, he was told that "the Holy Priesthood [was] conferred on him, that he may do wonders in the name of Jesus; that he may cast out devils, heal the sick, raise the dead, open the eyes of the blind, go forth from land to land and from sea to sea" (HC, 2:188–89). He declared that the priesthood that was conferred upon him is a "perfect system of government, of laws and ordinances," which, "when properly understood," empowers the righteous that they "may actually unlock the treasury of the Lord" (DBY, 130, 131).

Teachings of Brigham Young

The Lord directs His work in heaven and on earth through the priesthood.

If anybody wants to know what the Priesthood of the Son of God is, it is the law by which the worlds are, were, and will continue for ever and ever. It is that system which brings worlds into existence and peoples them, gives them their revolutions—their days, weeks, months, years, their seasons and times and by which they are rolled up as a scroll, as it were, and go into a higher state of existence (*DBY*, 130).

The Priesthood of the Son of God, which we have in our midst, is a perfect order and system of government, and this alone can deliver the human family from all the evils which now afflict its members, and insure them happiness and felicity hereafter (*DBY*, 130).

This Priesthood has been on the earth at various times. Adam had it, Seth had it, Enoch had it, Noah had it, Abraham and Lot had it, and it was handed down to the days of the Prophets, long after the days of the ancients. This High Priesthood rules, directs, governs, and controls all the Priesthoods, because it is the highest of all (*DBY*, 131).

When we talk of the celestial law which is revealed from heaven, that is, the Priesthood, we are talking about the principle of salvation, a perfect system of government, of laws and ordinances, by which we can be prepared to pass from one gate to another, and from one sentinel to another, until we go into the presence of our Father and God (*DBY*, 130).

It is not in my being called a Quaker, a Methodist or a "Mormon" that is the true cause of contention between these two great powers—Christ and Belial [the wicked]; but it is in the fact that God has established his Kingdom upon the earth and restored the holy Priesthood which gives men authority and power to administer in his name (*DBY*, 76).

The Gospel has brought to us the Holy Priesthood, which is again restored to the children of men. The keys of that Priesthood are here; we have them in our possession; we can unlock, and we can shut up. We can obtain salvation, and we can administer it (*DBY*, 130–31).

If you are satisfied, in your sensitive powers and faculties, that God has revealed the holy Priesthood, established his Kingdom upon the earth, restored the fulness of the Gospel, and set his hand to gather the House of Israel, this will answer your purpose just as well as though you went into heaven to see for yourselves (*DBY*, 429).

This law has not always been upon the earth; and in its absence, other laws have been given to the children of men for their improvement, for their education, for their government, and to prove what they would do when left to control themselves; and what we now call tradition has grown out of these circumstances (*DBY*, 130).

There is no act of a Latter-day Saint—no duty required—no time given, exclusive and independent of the Priesthood. Everything is subject to it, whether preaching, business, or any other act pertaining to the proper conduct of this life (*DBY*, 133).

The Lord Almighty will not suffer his Priesthood to be again driven from the earth (*DBY*, 131).

When the faithful Elders, holding this Priesthood, go into the spirit world they carry with them the same power and Priesthood that they had while in the mortal tabernacle (*DBY*, 132).

Much has been said about the power of the Latter-day Saints. Is it the people called Latter-day Saints that have this power, or is it the Priesthood? It is the Priesthood; and if they live according to that Priesthood, they can commence their work here and gain many victories, and be prepared to receive glory, immortality, and eternal life, that when they go into the spirit-world, their work will far surpass that of any other man or being that has not been blessed with the keys of the Priesthood here (*DBY*, 131–32).

The priesthood keys "unlock the treasury of the Lord."

The Priesthood is given to the people and the keys thereof, and, when properly understood, they may actually unlock the treasury of the Lord,

The First Presidency and the Quorum of the
Twelve Apostles in 1853.

and receive to their fullest satisfaction. But through our own weaknesses, through the frailty of human nature, we are not capable of doing so (*DBY,* 131).

Did they destroy it when they took the life of Joseph? No. "Mormonism" is here, the Priesthood is here, the keys of the Kingdom are here on the earth; and when Joseph went, they did not go. And if the wicked should succeed in taking my life, the keys of the Kingdom will remain with the Church (*DBY,* 134).

The ordinances of the house of God are for the salvation of the human family. We are the only ones on the earth at the present time, that we have any knowledge of, who hold the keys of salvation committed to the children of men from the heavens by the Lord Almighty; and inasmuch as there are those who hold these keys, it is important that they should be acted upon for the salvation of the human family. The building of temples, places in which the ordinances of salvation are administered, is necessary to carry out the plan of redemption, and it is a glorious subject upon which to address the Saints (*DBY,* 396–97).

We speak the truth and lie not, whosoever believes that Joseph Smith, Junior, was a Prophet sent of God, and was ordained by him to receive and hold the keys of the holy Priesthood, which is after the order of the Son of God, and power to build up the Kingdom of God upon the earth, to gather the House of Israel, to guide all who believe and obey to redemption, to restore that which has been lost through transgression—whosoever believes this, believing in the Lord, and obeying his commandments to the end of their lives, their names shall not be blotted out of the Lamb's book of life, and they shall receive crowns of glory, immortality, and eternal life (*DBY,* 5).

Receiving and exercising priesthood power requires personal righteousness.

An individual who holds a share in the Priesthood, and continues faithful to his calling, who delights himself continually in doing the things God requires at his hands, and continues through life in the performance of every duty will secure to himself not only the privilege of receiving, but the knowledge how to receive the things of God, that he may know the mind of God continually; and he will be enabled to discern between right and wrong, between the things of God and the things that are not of God. And the Priesthood—the Spirit that is within him, will continue to increase until it becomes like a fountain of living water; until it is like the tree of life; until it is one continued source of intelligence and instruction to that individual (*DBY,* 132).

Men who are vessels of the holy Priesthood, who are charged with words of eternal life to the world, should strive continually in their words and actions and daily deportment to do honor to the great dignity of their calling and office as ministers and representatives of the Most High (*DBY,* 130).

When the holy Priesthood is upon the earth, and the fulness of the Kingdom of God has come to the people, it requires a strict obedience to every point of law and doctrine and to every ordinance which the Lord reveals (*DBY,* 132).

Were your faith concentrated upon the proper object, your confidence unshaken, your lives pure and holy, every one fulfilling the duties of his or her calling according to the Priesthood and capacity bestowed upon you, you would be filled with the Holy Ghost, and it would be as impossible for any man to deceive and lead you to destruction as for a feather to remain unconsumed in the midst of intense heat (*DBY,* 132).

Until a selfish, individual interest is banished from our minds, and we become interested in the general welfare, we shall never be able to magnify our holy Priesthood as we should (*DBY,* 133).

The holy priesthood brings sacred blessings to individuals and families.

This Priesthood has been restored again, and by its authority we shall be connected with our fathers, by the ordinance of sealing, until we shall form a perfect chain from Father Adam down to the closing up scene [see D&C 128:18] (*DBY,* 400). I plead with the Elders of Israel day by day, when I have an opportunity, to live their religion—to live so that the Holy Ghost will be their constant companion; and then they will be qualified to be judges in Israel, to preside as Bishops, presiding Elders, and High Councilors, and as men of God, to take their families and friends by the hand and lead them in the path of truth and virtue, and eventually into the Kingdom of God (*DBY,* 136–37).

Suggestions for Study

The Lord directs His work in heaven and on earth through the priesthood.

- According to President Young, what is the priesthood? (See also D&C 84:17–22.)

- How should everything we do "pertaining to the proper conduct of this life" be subject to the priesthood? How would this affect your actions at home, at church, at school, and at work?

- What will the priesthood permit faithful elders to do in the spirit world?

- How do we, as members of the Church, live according to the principles and order of the priesthood? (See also D&C 20:38–60.) What influence has the priesthood had on your life? How can you make the priesthood's influence and power more effective in your life and in your family's life?

The priesthood keys "unlock the treasury of the Lord."

- Why didn't the keys of the priesthood leave the Church with the death of the Prophet Joseph Smith?

- How do the keys of the priesthood "unlock the treasury of the Lord" and bring salvation to the human family?

- What did President Young teach about priesthood keys? (See also D&C 107:18–20, 35; 132:7.) What do those keys authorize the Lord's servants to do?

Receiving and exercising priesthood power requires personal righteousness.

- How will a priesthood bearer's personal life influence his ability to act in behalf of the Lord? Why is personal righteousness so important? (See also D&C 107:99–100; 121:41–46.)

- How can "men who are vessels of the holy Priesthood" honor their office and calling? What blessings come to members who fulfill the duties of their callings?

- How are selfishness and priesthood power incompatible? Why must we banish selfishness if we are to magnify the priesthood? (See also D&C 121:37.) In what ways is selfishness a problem among us today? How can we overcome selfishness?

The holy priesthood brings sacred blessings to individuals and families.

- How has the priesthood blessed and strengthened your family? Why is priesthood power so important in forming eternal families? (See also D&C 128:18; 131:1–4; 132:19.)

- What might priesthood bearers do to "take their families and friends by the hand and lead them in the path of truth and virtue"?

The Relief Society and Individual Responsibility

The Female Relief Society of Nauvoo, organized by the Prophet Joseph Smith, was an important means of helping the poor and strengthening the sisters in Nauvoo from 1842 to 1844. Following Joseph's martyrdom, the Relief Society was discontinued for several years. In 1854, prompted by the sisters' work in behalf of the poor, President Brigham Young established Relief Societies in some wards in Utah. When the United States sent Johnston's army to Utah in 1857, however, ward organizations, including the Relief Society, were again discontinued. In late 1867 President Young decided that the needs of the poor could not be effectively addressed without the sisters being organized. He called on bishops to reestablish Relief Societies: "Now, Bishops, you have smart women for wives . . . ; let them organize Female Relief Societies in the various wards. We have many talented women among us, and we wish their help in this matter. Some may think this is a trifling thing, but it is not; and you will find that the sisters will be the mainspring of the movement. Give them the benefit of your wisdom and experience, give them your influence, guide and direct them wisely and well, and they will find rooms for the poor, and obtain the means for supporting them ten times quicker than even the Bishop could" (DEN, 14 Dec. 1867, 2). Today the sisters of the Relief Society work together to improve their families and communities and to build the kingdom of God.

Teachings of Brigham Young

Relief Society sisters help care for the poor, sick, and afflicted.

I have a short sermon for my sisters. I wish you, under the direction of your Bishops and wise men, to establish your Relief Societies, and organize yourselves under the direction of your brethren (*DBY,* 218).

Get women of good understanding to be your leaders, and then get counsel from men of understanding; and let your fashions proceed from yourselves, and become acquainted with those noble traits of character which belong to your sex (*DNSW,* 28 Apr. 1868, 2).

Let a sister appeal for the relief of suffering and poverty, and she is almost sure to be successful, especially if she appeals to those of her own sex. If you take this course you will relieve the wants of the poor a great deal better than they are now dealt by (*DEN,* 14 Dec. 1867, 2).

I will here say to the Latter-day Saints, if you will feed the poor with a willing heart and ready hand neither you nor your children will ever be found begging bread. In these things the people are right; they are right in establishing Female Relief Societies, that the hearts of the widow and the orphan may be made glad by the blessings which are so abundantly and so freely poured upon them (*DBY,* 217).

Sisters, do you see any children around your neighborhood poorly clad and without shoes? If you do, I say to you Female Relief Societies pick up these children and relieve their necessities, and send them to school. And if you see any young, middle-aged or old ladies in need find them something to do that will enable them to sustain themselves; but don't relieve the idle, for relieving those who are able but unwilling to work is ruinous to any community (*DBY,* 217).

Relieve the wants of every individual in need in your neighborhoods. This is in the capacity and in the power of the Female Relief Societies when it is not in the power of the Bishops (*DBY,* 218).

Look to yourselves in your capacity as Relief Societies in this city and throughout the mountains. Look at your condition! Consider it for yourselves, and decide whether you will go to and learn the influence which you possess, and then wield that influence for doing good and to relieve the poor among the people (*DNW,* 14 Aug. 1869, 2).

A record of the doings of all these Female Relief Societies will be kept, and it will be known who were fervent and faithful in carrying out the counsels given them in order to enable them to magnify their high callings here on the earth (*MS,* 31:269).

**Sisters who manage their resources wisely
can further God's work.**

I wish to call the attention of our sisters to our Relief Societies. We are happy to say that many of them have done a great deal. We wish them to continue and progress. In our Relief Societies we wish to introduce many improvements. We wish our sisters of experience to teach the young girls not to be so anxious for the gratification of their imaginary wants, but to confine themselves more to their real necessities. Fancy has no bounds. . . . We are too apt to give way to the imagination of our hearts, but if we will be guided by wisdom, our judgment will be corrected, and we will find that we can improve very much (*DBY,* 218).

Etching of Eliza R. Snow (1804–87). Often called "Zion's poetess," she was the first secretary of the Nauvoo Relief Society. She served as the second general president of the Relief Society for 20 years.

Ladies, if you are the means of plunging this whole people into debt so as to distress them, will there be anything required of you? I think there will, for you will be judged according to your works. Are not the men as extravagant as the women? Yes, they certainly are, and just as foolish (*DBY,* 213).

A good housekeeper will be saving and economical and teach her children to be good housekeepers, and how to take care of everything that is put in their charge (*DBY,* 213).

Let it be your delight that your children do not waste bread and other food. If you have bread to spare, give it to the poor, and see that your

133

children do not destroy it. Do not let them destroy valuable clothing, but put strong, durable cloth upon them, and save where you can, and give it to the gathering of the poor (*DNW*, 29 May 1861, 2).

We should learn how to take into our possession every blessing and every privilege that God has put within our reach, and know how to use our time, our talents and all our acts for the advancement of his Kingdom upon the earth (*DBY*, 53).

The time we spend here is our life, our substance, our capital, our fortune, and that time should be used profitably (*DBY*, 217).

Now, sisters, if you will consider these things you will readily see that time is all the capital stock there is on the earth; and you should consider your time golden, it is actually wealth, and, if properly used, it brings that which will add to your comfort, convenience, and satisfaction. Let us consider this, and no longer sit with hands folded, wasting time, for it is the duty of every man and of every woman to do all that is possible to promote the Kingdom of God on the earth (*DBY*, 214).

Sisters should "magnify, promote and honor the life they now possess."

Here are young, middle-aged and aged women, who all have experience according to that which they have passed through. . . . I shall commence by saying to these, my sisters, it is their imperative duty before God, their families and their brethren, to exercise themselves in the capacity in which they are placed, according to their ability, in order that they may magnify, promote and honor the life they now possess (*MS*, 31:267).

Let the sisters take care of themselves, and make themselves beautiful, and if any of you are so superstitious and ignorant as to say that this is pride, I can say that you are not informed as to the pride which is sinful before the Lord, you are also ignorant as to the excellency of the heavens, and of the beauty which dwells in the society of the Gods. Were you to see an angel, you would see a beautiful and lovely creature. Make yourselves like angels in goodness and beauty (*DBY*, 215).

Eve was a name or title conferred upon our first mother, because she was actually to be the mother of all the human beings who should live upon this earth. I am looking upon a congregation designed to be just such beings (*MS*, 31:267).

Permit me, sisters, to say, that we are endowed with a capacity to enjoy and to suffer and to be delighted. Are we delighted with that which is obnoxious? No; but with that which is beautiful and good (*MS*, 31:267).

Study order and cleanliness in your various occupations. Adorn your city and neighborhood. Make your homes lovely, and adorn your hearts with the grace of God (*DBY,* 200).

I can say to the sisters, if you have superior talents, arise and let your light shine. Prove to your neighbors and the community that you are capable of teaching those sisters whom you deem to be ignorant or neglectful (*DNW,* 15 June 1859, 2).

As I have often told my sisters in the Female Relief Societies, we have sisters here who, if they had the privilege of studying, would make just as good mathematicians or accountants as any man; and we think they ought to have the privilege to study these branches of knowledge that they may develop the powers with which they are endowed. We believe that women are useful not only to sweep houses, wash dishes, make beds, and raise babies, but that they should stand behind the counter, study law or physic [medicine], or become good book-keepers and be able to do the business in any counting house, and this to enlarge their sphere of usefulness for the benefit of society at large (*DBY,* 216–17).

The sisters in our Female Relief Societies have done great good. Can you tell the amount of good that the mothers and daughters in Israel are capable of doing? No, it is impossible. And the good they do will follow them to all eternity (*DBY,* 216).

Suggestions for Study

Relief Society sisters help care for the poor, sick, and afflicted.

- What blessing did President Young promise to those who "feed the poor with a willing heart and ready hand"? What other blessings can come to individuals, families, or the community when we share our resources? Why is it important to do this with a willing heart?

- Why is it "ruinous to any community" to give aid to those who are able but not willing to work? Why is work such an important principle?

- President Young counseled the sisters to "relieve the wants of every individual in need in your neighborhoods." What types of needs do people have? What specific needs have you and others observed around you? How can you serve those in need in your family, your ward or branch, or your community?

- How can Relief Society sisters "wield [their] influence for doing good"? When have you seen Relief Society sisters accomplish more together than individual women could alone?

- How can you support the work of the Relief Society? What blessings have you received through the Relief Society?

Sisters who manage their resources wisely can further God's work.

- President Young counseled Relief Society sisters to teach young girls to satisfy their needs but not necessarily their wants. How can you tell the difference between "imaginary wants" and "real necessities"? How can we learn to be more satisfied with what we have instead of longing for what we do not have?

- Why is it important to use our resources wisely and economically? How does frugal living by the Saints contribute to building up the kingdom of God? How can you use your resources more wisely?

- President Young referred to time as "capital," "our fortune," and "wealth." Why is time so valuable? How can we make sure we are using our time wisely?

Sisters should "magnify, promote and honor the life they now possess."

- How can we "magnify, promote and honor the life [we] now possess"?

- How can you contribute "order and cleanliness in your various occupations"? Why are order and cleanliness important? What does it mean to "adorn your hearts with the grace of God"? How can Latter-day Saint women "make [themselves] like angels in goodness and beauty"?

- Why is it important for women to develop their talents? What talents can you contribute to the building of the kingdom of God? How can you help advance the kingdom of God through your daily activities?

Church Organization and Government

In his 77th year, President Brigham Young organized the priesthood to give more clear direction to its labors, to unite the Saints, and to gather and care for the sheep of Israel. The effect of President Young's last major project was praised by his assistant counselor, Elder George Q. Cannon. He said that President Young "set the priesthood in order as it has never been since the organization of the Church upon the earth. He defined the duties of the Apostles, . . . Seventy, . . . High Priests, . . . Elders, . . . lesser priesthood, with plainness and distinction and power—the power of God— in a way that is left on record in such unmistakable language that no one need err who has the Spirit of God resting down upon him" (CHC, 5:507).

Teachings of Brigham Young

God reveals His will to the Church through the President of the Church.

In the setting forth of items of doctrine which pertain to the progress and further building up of the Kingdom of God upon the earth, and the revealing of his mind and will, he has but one mouth through which to make known his will to his people. When the Lord wishes to give a revelation to his people, when he wishes to reveal new items of doctrine to them, or administer chastisement, he will do it through the man whom he has appointed to that office and calling. The rest of the offices and callings of the Church are helps and governments for the edifying of the body of Christ and the perfection of the Saints, etc., every president, bishop, elder, priest, teacher, deacon and member standing in his order and officiating in his standing and degree of Priesthood as ministers of the words of life as shepherds to watch over departments and sections of the flock of God in all the world, and as helps to strengthen the hands of the Presidency of the whole Church (*DBY,* 137).

To possess and retain the spirit of the Gospel, gather Israel, redeem Zion, and save the world must be attended to first and foremost, and should be the prevailing desire in the hearts of the First Presidency, of the Elders of Israel, and of every officer in the Church and Kingdom of God (*DBY,* 137).

In trying all matters of doctrine, to make a decision valid, it is necessary to obtain a unanimous voice, faith and decision. In the capacity of a Quorum, the three First Presidents must be one in their voice; the Twelve Apostles must be unanimous in their voice, to obtain a righteous decision upon any matter that may come before them, as you may read in the Doctrine and Covenants. Whenever you see these Quorums unanimous in their declaration, you may set it down as true [see D&C 107:27]. Let the Elders get together, being faithful and true; and when they agree upon any point, you may know that it is true (*DBY,* 133).

The Lord Almighty leads this Church, and he will never suffer you to be led astray if you are found doing your duty. You may go home and sleep as sweetly as a babe in its mother's arms, as to any danger of your leaders leading you astray, for if they should try to do so the Lord would quickly sweep them from the earth. Your leaders are trying to live their religion as far as they are capable of doing so (*DBY,* 137).

The Twelve Apostles hold the priesthood keys for building the kingdom of God in the world.

The keys of the eternal priesthood, which is after the order of the Son of God, is comprehended by being an apostle. All the priesthood, all the keys, all the gifts, all the endowments and everything preparatory to entering back into the presence of the Father and of the Son, is composed of, circumscribed by, or I might say incorporated within the circumference of the apostleship (*MS,* 15:489).

After we returned from Missouri, my brother Joseph Young and myself had been singing after preaching in a meeting; and when the meeting was dismissed, Brother Joseph Smith said, "Come, go down to my house with me." We went and sung to him a long time, and talked with him. He then opened the subject of the Twelve and Seventies for the first time I ever thought of it. He said, "Brethren, I am going to call out Twelve Apostles. I think we will get together, by-and-by, and select Twelve Apostles, and select a Quorum of Seventies from those who have been up to Zion. . . ." In 1835 the last of January or in February, . . . we held our meetings from day to day, and Brother Joseph called out Twelve Apostles [on 14 February] (*DBY,* 141–42).

The calling of an Apostle is to build up the Kingdom of God in all the world; it is the Apostle that holds the keys of this power, and nobody else. If an Apostle magnifies his calling, he is the word of the Lord to his people all the time (*DBY,* 139).

I have tried to show you, brethren, as briefly as possible, the order of the Priesthood. When a man is ordained to be an Apostle, his Priesthood is without beginning of days, or end of life, like the Priesthood of Melchizedek; for it was his Priesthood that was spoken of in this language and not the man (*DBY,* 141).

It is the duty and privilege of the Twelve Apostles to have the Holy Ghost for their constant companion, and live always in the Spirit of Revelation, to know their duty and understand their calling; this is also the duty and privilege of the First Presidency of the Church (*DBY,* 139–40).

An Apostle of the Lord Jesus Christ has the keys of the holy Priesthood, and the power thereof is sealed upon his head, and by this he is authorized to proclaim the truth to the people, and if they receive it, well; if not, the sin be upon their own heads (*DBY,* 136).

The Lesser Priesthood, then, you perceive, comes within the purview [range of authority] of the Apostleship, because a man that holds it has a right to act or officiate as a High Priest, as one of the High Council, as a Patriarch, as a Bishop, Elder, Priest, Teacher, and Deacon, and in every other office and calling that is in the Church, from first to last, when duty demands it (*DBY,* 140).

You read in the revelation alluded to that when the Twelve were called and ordained, they possessed the same power and authority as the three First Presidents; and in reading further you find that there must needs be appendages and helps growing out of this Priesthood [see D&C 107:22–26]. The Seventies possess the same power and authority; [they receive delegated authority by assignment for the] establishing, building up, regulating, ordaining and setting in order the Kingdom of God in all its perfections upon the earth. We have a Quorum of High Priests, and there are a great many of them. They are a local body—they tarry at home; but the Seventies travel and preach; so also do the High Priests, when they are called upon. They possess precisely the same Priesthood that the Seventies and the Twelve and the First Presidency possess; but are they ordained in all the authority, power, and keys of this Priesthood? No, they are not. Still they are High Priests of God; and if they magnify their Priesthood [callings], they will receive at some time all the authority and power that it is possible for men to receive (*DBY,* 140).

The office of bishop belongs to the Aaronic Priesthood and holds the authority to minister in temporal and spiritual things.

The office of [Presiding] Bishop belongs to the lesser [Aaronic] Priesthood. He is the highest officer in the Aaronic Priesthood, and has . . . the administration of angels, if he has faith, and lives so that he can receive and enjoy the blessings Aaron enjoyed (*DBY,* 143).

A Bishop in his calling and duty is with the Church all the time; he is not called to travel abroad to preach, but is at home; he is not abroad in the world, but is with the Saints (*DBY,* 144).

The Bishops should be a perfect example to their Wards in all things (*DBY,* 144).

If a Bishop will act to the extent of his calling and office, and magnify it, there will not be an individual in his Ward that is not employed to the best advantage. He would see that all lived as they should, walking humbly with their God. There would not be a person in his Ward that he does not know, and he would be acquainted with their circumstances, conduct, and feeling [see 1 Timothy 3:1–4] (*DBY,* 145).

The Bishops should set those whom they have confidence in, those whom they know to be honest, to be watchmen on the tower, and let them find out who are suffering (*DBY,* 145).

Let each Bishop attend faithfully to his Ward, and see that every man and woman is well and faithfully and profitably employed; that the sick and aged are properly cared for that none suffer. Let each Bishop be a tender and indulgent father to his Ward, administering a word of comfort and encouragement here, a word of advice and counsel there, and a word of chastisement in another place, where needed, without partiality, wisely judging between man and man, caring for and seeking earnestly the welfare of all, watching over the flock of God with the eye of a true shepherd, that wolves and dogs may not enter among the flock to rend them (*DBY,* 144–45).

I say to the Bishop, . . . this is your business and calling. Do not let there be one place, in the habitations of the Saints in your Wards, about which you are uninformed (*DBY,* 146).

The Bishops should, through their teachers, see that every family in their Wards, who is able, should donate what they would naturally consume on the fast day to the poor (*DBY,* 145).

Church discipline can help people return to righteousness.

We shall never have the keys of authority committed to us to be rulers until we will rule just as God would rule if he were here himself (*DBY,* 146).

But the Kingdom of heaven, when organized upon the earth, will have every officer, law and ordinance necessary for the managing of those who are unruly, or who transgress its laws, and to govern those who desire to do right, but cannot quite walk to the line; and all these powers and authorities are in existence in the midst of this people (*DBY,* 146).

Bishops, do you have any trials? Are the feelings of the brethren in your Wards alienated? "Yes." What should they do in such cases? They should follow the rules laid down, and be reconciled to their brethren forthwith. I think that it can be shown that the great majority of difficulties between brethren arises from misunderstandings rather than from malice and a wicked heart, and instead of talking the matter over with each other in a saint-like spirit, they will contend with each other until a real fault is created, and they have brought a sin upon themselves. When we have done good ninety-nine times and then do an evil, how common it is, my brethren and sisters, to look at that one evil all the day long and never think of the good. Before we judge each other we should look at the design of the heart, and if it is evil, then chasten that individual, and take a course to bring him back again to righteousness (*DBY,* 149–50).

I would like to see the High Council and Bishops and all Judges filled with the power of the Holy Ghost, that when a person comes before them they can read and understand that person, and be able to decide a case quickly and justly. . . . I would like the Bishops and other officers to have sufficient power and wisdom from God to make them fully aware of the true nature of every case that may come before them (*DBY,* 133).

You may, figuratively speaking, pound one Elder over the head with a club, and he does not know but what you have handed him a straw dipped in molasses to suck. There are others, if you speak a word to them, or take a straw and chasten them, whose hearts are broken; they are as tender in their feelings as an infant, and will melt like wax before the flame. You must not chasten them severely; you must chasten according to the spirit that is in the person. Some you may talk to all day long, and they do not know what you are talking about. There is a great variety. Treat people as they are (*DBY,* 150).

When you are rebuked by each other—when brethren meet you and say, "This is wrong in you," you should receive it kindly, and express your thanks for the reproof, and acknowledge the wrong frankly, and admit that you may frequently do wrong when you do not know it, and say, "I wish you to enlighten my mind, to take me by the hand, and let me go along hand-in-hand and strengthen and sustain each other." What, in your weaknesses? Yes. Do you expect to see a perfect man? Not while you stay here (*DBY,* 150).

Let me say to the brethren and sisters, when you are chastened by any of your leaders, never consider that the enemy does it, but receive it always as a kindness from the hand of a friend and not as from an enemy. If your presidents were your enemies they would let you alone in your faults. If you are beloved of the Lord you will be chastened [see Hebrews 12:6]; receive it with joy (*DBY,* 133).

Suggestions for Study

God reveals His will to the Church through the President of the Church.

- How does the Lord use the President of the Church and the Council of the First Presidency and the Quorum of the Twelve Apostles to direct the Church? How do leaders holding other offices in the Church help them? (See also D&C 107:21–38; 132:7.)
- Why can we put full faith and confidence in the presiding quorums of the Church? (See also D&C 107:27.)
- Why will the Lord not allow the prophet to lead the Church astray? What promise did President Young make to those who do their duty? (See also D&C OD 1.)

The Twelve Apostles hold the priesthood keys for building the kingdom of God in the world.

- What are the priesthood keys of the apostleship?
- What are the duties of Apostles? (See also D&C 107:23–24, 33, 58.)
- Discuss the relationship between the calling of an Apostle and other offices in the Melchizedek and Aaronic Priesthood. (See also D&C 107:58.)
- What are the duties of the Seventy today as they function under the direction of the First Presidency and Quorum of the Twelve? (See also D&C 107:34.)

The office of bishop belongs to the Aaronic Priesthood and holds the authority to minister in temporal and spiritual things.

- What keys, powers, and authorities are held by a bishop? (See also D&C 84:26–27; 107:13–17.) What are the responsibilities of the bishop as the president of the Aaronic Priesthood? as the presiding high priest of a ward?

- According to Brigham Young, what does a bishop do who "attend[s] faithfully to his Ward"? (See also 1 Timothy 3:1–7.)

- How can we as home teachers or visiting teachers become more helpful in watching over the Church?

Church discipline can help people return to righteousness.

- How did President Young describe those who transgress?

- President Young said that the "majority of difficulties between [people] arises from misunderstandings rather than from malice and a wicked heart." What was his counsel for handling misunderstandings?

- What would President Young like to see in disciplinary councils? (See also D&C 107:71–84; 134:10.) How can the "power and wisdom from God" help those rendering judgment in a disciplinary council? (See also D&C 121:41–42.)

- In what way are those who conduct Church disciplinary councils to "read and understand" those being disciplined?

- What did President Young say about "chasten[ing] according to the spirit that is in the person"? (See also 3 Nephi 18:28–32.)

- How did President Young say we should respond when we are chastened by our leaders? (See also D&C 95:1.)

The sacrament is a necessary ordinance "to witness unto the Father . . . that [we] are believers in and desire to follow him . . . with an undivided heart" (*DBY*, 171).

144

Honoring the Sabbath and the Sacrament

On the day after arriving in the Salt Lake Valley, President Brigham Young spoke briefly to the pioneer camp concerning observance of the Sabbath. With a wilderness to tame, crops to be planted, and other pressing work of the time, he "informed the brethren . . . they must not work on Sunday, that [if they did] they would lose five times as much as they would gain by it, and they must not hunt or fish on that day." He remarked that "there would be a meeting every Sabbath in this place or wherever we stop" (WWJ, 25 July 1847). President Young continually admonished the Saints to keep the Sabbath "in remembrance of our God and our holy religion" (DBY, 165).

Teachings of Brigham Young

Keeping the Sabbath day holy brings temporal and spiritual blessings.

Take this book (the book of Doctrine and Covenants) and you will read here that the Saints are to meet together on the Sabbath day [see D&C 59:9–16]. . . . This people called Latter-day Saints, are required by the revelations that the Lord has given, to assemble themselves together on this day. In this commandment we are required to come together and repent of our sins and confess our sins and partake of the [sacrament] in commemoration of the death and sufferings of our Lord and Savior (*DBY,* 164).

When people assemble to worship they should leave their worldly cares where they belong, then their minds are in a proper condition to worship the Lord, to call upon him in the name of Jesus, and to get his Holy Spirit, that they may hear and understand things as they are in eternity, and know how to comprehend the providences of our God. This is the time for their minds to be open, to behold the invisible things of God, that he reveals by his Spirit (*DBY,* 167).

Every person should be silent when we meet here to worship God. Remember and try to keep perfectly quiet, and do not whisper, talk, nor scrape your feet (*DBY,* 167–68).

By forsaking our fields for a season, to gather together to worship our God, I can assure you that our crops will be better than they would be if we were to spend all our time in our fields. We may water and plant and toil, but we should never forget that it is God who gives the increase; and by meeting together, our health and spirits will be better, we will look better, and the things of this world will increase around us more, and we will know better how to enjoy them (*DBY,* 167).

We should observe [the Sabbath] for our own temporal good and spiritual welfare. When we see a farmer in such a hurry, that he has to attend to his harvest, and to haying, fence-making, or to gathering his cattle on the Sabbath day, as far as I am concerned, I count him weak in the faith. He has lost the spirit of his religion, more or less. Six days are enough for us to work [see Exodus 20:9–11], and if we wish to play, play within the six days; if we wish to go on excursions, take one of those six days, but on the seventh day, come to the place of worship (*DBY,* 165).

Instead of suffering our labors to occupy the Sabbath, . . . we should do as little as possible; if it is necessary to cook food, do so; but even if that could be dispensed with, it would be better. As to keeping the Sabbath according to the Mosaic law, indeed, I do not; for it would be almost beyond my power. Still, under the new covenant, we should remember to preserve holy one day in the week as a day of rest—as a memorial of the rest of the Lord and the rest of the Saints; also for our temporal advantage, for it is instituted for the express purpose of benefiting man. It is written in this book (the Bible), that the Sabbath was made for man. It is a blessing to him. As little labor as possible should be done upon that day; it should be set apart as a day of rest, to assemble together in the place appointed, according to the revelation [see D&C 59:10–12], confessing our sins, bringing our tithes and offerings, and presenting ourselves before the Lord (*DBY,* 164).

Now, remember, my brethren, those who go skating, buggy riding or on excursions on the Sabbath day—and there is a great deal of this practiced—are weak in the faith. Gradually, little by little, little by little, the spirit of their religion leaks out of their hearts and their affections, and by and by they begin to see faults in their brethren, faults in the doctrines of the Church, faults in the organization, and at last they leave the Kingdom of God and go to destruction. I really wish you would remember this, and tell it to your neighbors (*DBY,* 165).

Whether we are poor or rich, if we neglect our prayers and our sacrament meetings, we neglect the Spirit of the Lord, and a spirit of darkness comes over us (*DBY,* 170).

We are under the necessity of assembling here from Sabbath to Sabbath, and in Ward meetings, . . . to teach, talk, pray, sing, and exhort. What for? To keep us in remembrance of our God and our holy religion. Is this custom necessary? Yes; because we are so liable to forget—so prone to wander, that we need to have the Gospel sounded in our ears as much as once, twice, or thrice a week, or, behold, we will turn again to our idols (*DBY*, 165).

The Lord has planted within us a divinity; and that divine immortal spirit requires to be fed. Will earthly food answer for that purpose? No; it will only keep this body alive as long as the spirit stays with it, which gives us an opportunity of doing good. That divinity within us needs food from the Fountain from which it emanated. It is not of the earth, earthy, but is from heaven. Principles of eternal life, of God and godliness, will alone feed the immortal capacity of man and give true satisfaction (*DBY*, 165).

Coming to this Tabernacle to worship and do the will of God for one day in the week, and following our own inclinations and doing our own will at all other times, is a folly; it is useless, and a perfect burlesque on the service of God. We should do the will of God, and spend all our time for the accomplishment of his purposes, whether we are in this Tabernacle or elsewhere (*DBY*, 166).

Monday, Tuesday, Wednesday, Thursday, Friday, and Saturday must be spent to the glory of God, as much as Sunday, or we shall come short of the object of our pursuit [see D&C 59:11] (*DBY*, 166).

We meet together to strengthen and be strengthened.

Today [on the Sabbath] we are able to meet together to speak to each other, to strengthen and do each other good (*DBY*, 167).

While we have the privilege of speaking to each other, let us speak words of comfort and consolation. When you are influenced by the Spirit of holiness and purity, let your light shine; but if you are tried and tempted and buffeted by Satan, keep your thoughts to yourselves—keep your mouths closed; for speaking produces fruit, either of a good or evil character (*DBY*, 166).

When [an individual] opens or closes a meeting with prayer, every man, woman, and child in the congregation who professes to be a Saint should have no desire or words in their hearts and mouths but what are being offered by the [person] who is mouth for all the congregation (*DBY*, 170).

If any of you feel that there is no life in your meetings, as I occasionally hear some of the brethren say, then it becomes your duty to go and instill life into that meeting, and do your part to produce an increase of the Spirit and power of God in the meetings in your locality (*DBY*, 170).

I will take the liberty of suggesting to my brethren who address the congregation that our sermons should be short, and if they are not filled with life and spirit let them be shorter, for we have not time at this

Rachel Ridgeway Grant (front center), president of the Salt Lake City 13th Ward Relief Society, and her counselors and secretaries in 1875. The Relief Society has blessed sisters throughout the world by teaching them to observe all the commandments of God.

Conference to let all the Elders who speak preach a long sermon, but we have time to say a few words in bearing testimony, to give a few words of counsel to encourage the Saints, to strengthen the weak, to endeavor to confirm those who are wavering, and so forward the Kingdom of God (*DBY,* 167).

Brethren and sisters, I will make one request of you. When you speak, speak so that we can hear and understand you. . . . If you have nothing to say, take my counsel, and keep your seat. If you have anything to say, say it; and when you get through, stop. Let your feelings be governed and controlled by the principles of eternal life, as should the children of God, delighting in truth and righteousness (*DBY,* 167).

My greatest desire to my Father and God is that I may so speak that my remarks will be acceptable to him and beneficial to those who hear me (*DBY,* 168).

When I have endeavored to address a congregation, I . . . ask God my Heavenly Father, in the name of Jesus Christ, to give me his Spirit, and put into my heart the things he wishes me to speak (*DBY,* 168).

I need the attention of the congregation and the faith of those who have faith; I need the wisdom of God and his Spirit to be in my heart to enable me to speak to the edification of the people. Although I have been a public speaker for thirty-seven years, it is seldom that I rise before a congregation without feeling a child-like timidity; if I live to the age of Methuselah I do not know that I shall outgrow it. There are reasons for this which I understand. When I look upon the faces of intelligent beings I look upon the image of the God I serve. There are none but what have a certain portion of divinity within them; and though we are clothed with bodies which are in the image of our God, yet this mortality shrinks before that portion of divinity which we inherit from our Father. This is the cause of my timidity (*DBY,* 168).

In addressing a congregation, though the speaker be unable to say more than half a dozen sentences, and those awkwardly constructed, if his heart is pure before God, those few broken sentences are of more value than the greatest eloquence without the Spirit of the Lord and of more real worth in the sight of God, angels, and all good men. In praying, though a person's words be few and awkwardly expressed, if the heart is pure before God, that prayer will avail more than the eloquence of a Cicero [a first century B.C. Roman orator]. What does the Lord, the Father of us all, care about our mode of expression? The simple, honest heart is of more avail with the Lord than all the pomp, pride, splendor, and eloquence produced by men. When he looks upon a heart full of sincerity, integrity, and child-like simplicity, he sees a principle that will endure forever— "That is the spirit of my own kingdom—the spirit I have given to my children" (*DBY,* 169).

I believe it is our duty to imitate everything that is good, lovely, dignified and praiseworthy. We ought to imitate the best speakers, and study to convey our ideas to each other in the best and choicest language, especially when we are dispensing the great truths of the Gospel of peace to the people. I generally use the best language I can command (*DBY,* 169).

[However,] I believe . . . that if I had all the mastery of language that has ever been obtained by the learned, my spirit would delight more in childlike conversation, and that too, in a simple language, than in the most learned literary style that is used. A plain, clear method of expressing ideas is the most pleasing to me (*DBY,* 169).

Fast day is given to help the needy and strengthen testimonies.

You know that the first Thursday in each month [now the first Sunday] we hold as a fast day. How many here know the origin of this day? Before tithing was paid, the poor were supported by donations. They came to Joseph and wanted help, in Kirtland, and he said there should be a fast day, which was decided upon. It was to be held once a month, as it is now, and all that would have been eaten that day, of flour, or meat, or butter, or fruit, or anything else, was to be carried to the fast meeting and put into the hands of a person selected for the purpose of taking care of it and distributing it among the poor (*DBY,* 169).

In our fast-day meetings, the Saints meet to express their feelings and to strengthen each other in their faith in the holy Gospel (*DBY,* 169).

Do you not receive as much of the spirit of intelligence, of the spirit of knowledge, and the consoling influences of the Holy Ghost, to have people rise and testify of the things of God which they do know, of those things which they have experienced themselves? Does not that vividly bring to your minds the goodness of the Lord in revealing to you the truths of the Gospel? Does not that strengthen your faith, give you an increase of confidence and witness to you that you are a child of God? Most assuredly it does. Therefore, when any testify of the things of God, it strengthens their brethren, precisely as it did in days of old when they observed the counsel to, "Speak often one to another," "strengthen the brethren," and so on (*DBY,* 170).

By partaking of the sacrament, we remember the Savior and renew our covenants with our Heavenly Father.

I say to the brethren and sisters, in the name of the Lord, it is our duty and it is required of us, by our Father in Heaven, by the spirit of our religion, by our covenants with God and each other, that we observe the ordinances of the house of God, and especially on the Sabbath day, to attend to the Sacrament of the Lord's Supper. Then attend the Ward meetings and the Quorum meetings (*DBY,* 171).

In the ordinance [sacrament] we here attend to . . . , we show to the Father that we remember Jesus Christ, our Elder Brother; we testify to him that we are willing to take upon us his name. When we are doing this, I want the minds here as well as the bodies. I want the whole man here when you come to meeting (*DBY,* 171).

I would exhort my brethren and sisters to receive this ordinance every Sabbath, when [you] meet together. . . . I do pray you, my brethren and sisters, to contemplate this ordinance thoroughly, and seek unto the Lord with all your hearts that you may obtain the promised blessings by obedience to it. Teach its observance to your children; impress upon them its necessity. Its observance is as necessary to our salvation as any other of the ordinances and commandments that have been instituted in order that the people may be sanctified, that Jesus may bless them and give unto them his spirit, and guide and direct them that they may secure unto themselves life eternal. Impress the sacredness of this important ordinance upon the minds of your children (*DBY,* 171–72).

We [partake of the sacrament] in remembrance of the death of our Savior; it is required of his disciples until he comes again, no matter how long that may be. No matter how many generations come and go, believers in him are required to eat bread and drink wine [or water, today] in remembrance of his death and sufferings until he comes again. Why are they required to do this? To witness unto the Father, to Jesus and to the angels that they are believers in and desire to follow him in the regeneration, keep his commandments, build up his Kingdom, revere his name and serve him with an undivided heart, that they may be worthy to eat and drink with him in his Father's Kingdom. This is why the Latter-day Saints partake of the ordinance of the Lord's Supper (*DBY,* 172).

In what consists the benefit we derive from this ordinance? It is in obeying the commands of the Lord. When we obey the commandments of our Heavenly Father, if we have a correct understanding of the ordinances of the house of God, we receive all the promises attached to the obedience rendered to his commandments (*DBY,* 172).

It is one of the greatest blessings we could enjoy, to come before the Lord, and before the angels, and before each other, to witness that we remember that the Lord Jesus Christ has died for us. This proves to the Father that we remember our covenants, that we love his Gospel, that we love to keep his commandments, and to honor the name of the Lord Jesus upon the earth (*DBY,* 172).

Suggestions for Study

Keeping the Sabbath day holy brings temporal and spiritual blessings.

• What are the Lord's requirements for keeping the Sabbath day holy? What are the benefits of keeping the Sabbath holy? (See also D&C 59:9–16.)

- President Young stated, "We are under the necessity of assembling . . . in meetings." What did he tell us to do when we "assemble to worship"? What can distract us from assembling to worship God on the Sabbath?

- According to President Young, what happens "little by little" when we do not obey the commandment to keep the Sabbath holy? Drawing on President Young's statements, what are some questions we could ask ourselves to determine the appropriateness of certain Sabbath day activities? (For example: Is the activity for our spiritual welfare? Does it nurture our faith? Does it help us bless others?)

- Why should we worship the Lord every day and not just on the Sabbath? (See also D&C 59:11.) How might worship on weekdays be the same or different from worship on the Sabbath? How can we spend every day "to the glory of God"?

We meet together to strengthen and be strengthened.

- Why is it important that we meet together to worship on the Sabbath? What should be our intent as we greet one another, speak, or teach in our Sabbath meetings? (See also D&C 43:8–9.) How does your association with other Latter-day Saints help you?

- What counsel did President Young give to those who are invited to speak in Church meetings? Why is the influence of the Holy Ghost more important than the use of eloquent words? What did President Young expect of the members in the congregation? How might we appropriately "instill life" in our meetings? (See also D&C 50:21–24.)

Fast day is given to help the needy and strengthen testimonies.

- According to President Young, why was fast day instituted?

- What influence does the giving of a generous fast offering have on the giver?

- On fast Sundays we have opportunity to bear testimony to one another. What does it mean to bear testimony? Why is it vital for us to bear testimony and to hear others do the same? How do we influence others when we testify of the things of God? How are we influenced in the process? How have the testimonies of others strengthened your faith?

By partaking of the sacrament, we remember the Savior and renew our covenants with our Heavenly Father.

- The most significant thing we do in our Sunday meetings is partake of the sacrament. Why does the Lord require thoughtful participation in the sacrament? (See also D&C 27:2.)

- What do we covenant when we partake of the sacrament? (See the sacramental prayers in D&C 20:75–79 or Moroni 4; 5.) What does it mean to take upon us the name of Christ? What does the Lord promise to those who partake of the sacrament with full intent? How can we receive these promised blessings?

- How can partaking of the sacrament strengthen our commitment to the Savior on all days of the week? (See also D&C 59:9–12.)

The Tithing Store in Salt Lake City about 1860. President Young taught that the law of tithing "is an eternal law that God has instituted for the benefit of the human family, for their salvation and exaltation" (*DBY,* 177).

Tithing and Consecration

Despite all the challenges that President Brigham Young faced, for him, "there [was] no such thing" as sacrifice (DNW, 24 Aug. 1854, 1) because everything belongs to God already and what we give up only blesses us and prepares us for exaltation. He viewed what we would call sacrifices as opportunities to exchange "a worse condition for a better one" (DNW, 24 Aug. 1854, 1). President Young taught that we can participate in the Lord's work by obeying the laws of tithing and consecration—acknowledging that all we possess belongs to our Father in Heaven and returning a portion of our possessions to Him.

Teachings of Brigham Young

Paying tithing allows us to participate in the Lord's work by returning a portion of that which belongs to Him.

I do not suppose for a moment, that there is a person in this Church, who is unacquainted with the duty of paying tithing, neither is it necessary to have revelation every year upon the subject. There is the Law—pay one-tenth (*DBY*, 174).

There has been so much inquiry it becomes irksome: the law is for a man to pay one-tenth . . . for the erecting of the House of God, the spread of the gospel, and the support of the priesthood. When a man comes into the church he wants to know if he must reckon his clothing, bad debts, lands, etc. It is the law to give . . . one-tenth of his increase [see D&C 119:4] (*HC*, 7:301). The law of tithing is an eternal law. The Lord Almighty never had his Kingdom on the earth without the law of tithing being in the midst of his people, and he never will. It is an eternal law that God has instituted for the benefit of the human family, for their salvation and exaltation. This law is in the Priesthood, but we do not want any to observe it unless they are willing to do so (*DBY*, 177).

The people are not compelled to pay their tithing, they do as they please about it, it is urged upon them only as a matter of duty between them and their God (*DBY*, 177).

We do not ask anybody to pay tithing, unless they are disposed to do so; but if you pretend to pay tithing, pay it like honest men (*DBY*, 177).

Everybody should pay their tenth. A poor woman ought to pay her tenth chicken, if she has to draw out ten times its value for her support (*DBY*, 178).

It is very true that the poor pay their tithing better than the rich do. If the rich would pay their tithing we should have plenty. The poor are faithful and prompt in paying their tithing, but the rich can hardly afford to pay theirs—they have too much. If he has only ten dollars he can pay one; if he has only one dollar he can pay ten cents; it does not hurt him at all. If he has a hundred dollars he can possibly pay ten. If he has a thousand dollars he looks over it a little and says, "I guess I will pay it; it ought to be paid anyhow;" and he manages to pay his ten dollars or his hundred dollars. But suppose a man is wealthy enough to pay ten thousand, he looks that over a good many times and says, "I guess I will wait until I get a little more, and then I will pay a good deal." And they wait and wait, like an old gentleman in the East; he waited and waited and waited to pay his tithing until he went out of the world, and this is the way with a great many. They wait and continue waiting, until, finally, the character comes along who is called Death, and he slips up to them and takes away their breath, then they are gone and cannot pay their tithing, they are too late, and so it goes (*DBY*, 175).

It is not for me to rise up and say that I can give to the Lord, for in reality I have nothing to give. I seem to have something. Why? Because the Lord has seen fit to bring me forth, and has blessed my efforts in gathering things which are desirable, and which are termed property (*DBY*, 176).

When my Bishop came to value my property, he wanted to know what he should take my tithing in. I told him to take anything I had, for I did not set my heart upon any one thing; my horses, cows, hogs, or any other thing he might take; my heart is set upon the work of my God, upon the public good of his great Kingdom (*DBY*, 176).

If we live our religion we will be willing to pay tithing (*DBY*, 176).

We are not our own, we are bought with a price, we are the Lord's; our time, our talents, our gold and silver, our wheat and fine flour, our wine and our oil, our cattle, and all there is on this earth that we have in our possession is the Lord's, and he requires one-tenth of this for the building up of his Kingdom. Whether we have much or little, one-tenth should be paid in for tithing (*DBY*, 176).

When a man wishes to give anything, let him give the best he has got. The Lord has given to me all I possess; I have nothing in reality, not a single dime of it is mine. You may ask, "Do you feel as you say?" Yes, I actually do. The coat I have on my back is not mine, and never was; the Lord put it in my possession honorably, and I wear it; but if he wishes for it, and all there is under it, he is welcome to the whole. I do not own a house, or a single farm of land, a horse, mule, carriage, or wagon . . . but what the Lord gave me, and if he wants them, he can take them at his pleasure, whether he speaks for them, or takes them without speaking (*DBY,* 175).

It is all the Lord's and we are only his stewards (*DBY,* 178).

I do not expect to see the day when I am perfectly independent, until I am crowned in the celestial kingdom of my Father, and made as independent as my Father in Heaven. I have not yet received my inheritance as my own, and I expect to be dependent until I do, for all that I have is lent to me (*DBY,* 177).

Our responsibility is to pay tithing and to sustain those who are responsible for the tithing funds.

Here is a character—a man—that God has created, organized, fashioned and made,—every part and particle of my system from the top of my head to the soles of my feet, has been produced by my Father in Heaven; and he requires one-tenth part of my brain, heart, nerve, muscle, sinew, flesh, bone, and of my whole system, for the building of temples, for the ministry, for sustaining missionaries and missionaries' families, for feeding the poor, the aged, the halt and blind, and for gathering them home from the nations and taking care of them after they are gathered. He has said, "My son, devote one-tenth of yourself to the good and wholesome work of taking care of your fellow-beings, preaching the Gospel, bringing people into the Kingdom; lay your plans to take care of those who cannot take care of themselves; direct the labors of those who are able to labor; and one-tenth part is all-sufficient if it is devoted properly, carefully and judiciously for the advancement of my Kingdom on the earth" (*DBY,* 176).

If the Lord requires one-tenth of my ability to be devoted to building temples, meetinghouses, schoolhouses, to schooling our children, gathering the poor from the nations of the earth, bringing home the aged, lame, halt and blind, and building houses for them to live in, that they may be comfortable when they reach Zion, and to sustaining the Priesthood, it is not my prerogative to question the authority of the Almighty in this, nor of his servants who have charge of it. If I am required to pay my tithing it is my duty to pay it (*DBY,* 174).

I like the term [tithing], because it is scriptural, and I would rather use it than any other. The Lord instituted tithing; it was practiced in the days of Abraham, and Enoch and Adam and his children did not forget their tithes and offerings. You can read for yourselves with regard to what the Lord requires. I want to say this much to those who profess to be Latter-day

Saints—if we neglect our tithes and offerings we will receive the chastening hand of the Lord. We may just as well count on this first as last. If we neglect to pay our tithes and offerings we will neglect other things and this will grow upon us until the spirit of the Gospel is entirely gone from us, and we are in the dark, and know not whither we are going (*DBY*, 174).

The Lord requires one-tenth of that which he has given me; it is for me to pay the one-tenth of the increase of my flocks and of all that I have, and all the people should do the same. The question may arise, "What is to be done with the tithing?" It is for the building of temples to God; for the enlarging of the borders of Zion; sending Elders on missions to preach the Gospel and taking care of their families. By and by we shall have some temples to go into, and we will receive our blessings, the blessings of heaven, by obedience to the doctrine of tithing. We shall have temples built throughout these mountains, in the valleys of this Territory and the valleys of the next Territory, and finally, all through these mountain valleys. We expect to build temples in a great many valleys. We go to the Endowment House, and before going, we get a recommendation from our Bishop that we have paid our tithing (*DBY*, 178).

It is my business to control the disbursements of the tithing paid by the Saints, and not the business of every Elder in the Kingdom who thinks the tithing belongs to him (*DBY*, 178).

You allow the devil to suggest to you that I am not leading you right, and allow that thought to abide in your hearts, and I will promise you that it will lead you to apostasy. You allow yourselves to doubt anything that God has revealed, and it will not be a great while before you begin to neglect your prayers, refuse to pay your Tithing, and find fault with the authorities of the Church. You will be repeating what apostates all say, "The Tithing is not used aright" (*DNSW*, 29 Aug. 1876, 1).

Consecration is a willingness to give all and an acknowledgment that all we have belongs to our Father in Heaven.

I have looked upon the community of Latter-day Saints in vision and beheld them organized as one great family of heaven, each person performing his several duties in his line of industry, working for the good of the whole more than for individual aggrandizement; and in this I have beheld the most beautiful order that the mind of man can contemplate, and the grandest results for the upbuilding of the Kingdom of God and the spread of righteousness upon the earth. Will this people ever come to this order of things? Are they now prepared to live according to that patriarchal order that will be organized among the true and faithful before God receives his own? We all concede the point that when this mortality falls off, and with it its cares, anxieties, love of self, love of wealth, and love of power, and all the conflicting interests which pertain to this flesh, that then, when our spirits have returned to God who gave them, we will be subject to every requirement that he may make of us, that we shall then live together as one great family; our interest will be a general, a common interest. Why can we not so live in this world? (*DBY,* 181).

Will the time ever come that we can commence and organize this people as a family? It will. Do we know how? Yes. . . . Do you think we will ever be one? When we get home to our Father and God, will we not wish to be in the family? Will it not be our highest ambition and desire to be reckoned as the sons of the living God, as the daughters of the Almighty, with a right to the household, and the faith that belongs to the household, heirs of the Father, his goods, his wealth, his power, his excellency, his knowledge and wisdom? (*DBY,* 179).

And when this people become one, it will be one in the Lord. They will not look alike. We will not all have grey, blue, or black eyes. Our features will differ one from another, and in our acts, dispositions, and efforts to accumulate, distribute, and dispose of our time, talents, wealth and whatever the Lord gives to us, in our journey through life, we will differ just as much as in our features. The point that the Lord wishes to bring us to is to obey his counsel and observe his word. Then every one will be dictated so that we can act as a family (*DBY,* 180).

We want to see a community organized in which every person will be industrious, faithful and prudent (*DBY,* 180).

Never want a thing you cannot get, live within your means (*DBY,* 180).

When the Lord gave the revelation instructing us in our duty as to consecrating what we have, if the people then could have understood things precisely as they are, and had obeyed that revelation, it would have been neither more nor less than yielding up that which is not their own, to him to whom it belongs. And so it is now (*DBY,* 178).

The Lord has declared it to be his will that his people enter into covenant, even as Enoch and his people did, which of necessity must be before we shall have the privilege of building the Center Stake of Zion, for the power and glory of God will be there, and none but the pure in heart will be able to live and enjoy it (*DBY,* 178).

There is another revelation [probably Doctrine and Covenants 42] . . . stating that it is the duty of all people who go to Zion to consecrate all their property to the Church of Jesus Christ of Latter-day Saints. This revelation . . . was one of the first commandments or revelations given to this people after they had the privilege of organizing themselves as a Church, as a body, as the Kingdom of God on the earth. I observed then, and I now think, that it will be one of the last revelations which the people will

159

receive into their hearts and understand, of their own free will and choice, and esteem it as a pleasure, a privilege, and a blessing unto them to observe and keep most holy (*DBY*, 179).

There is any amount of property, and gold and silver in the earth and on the earth, and the Lord gives to this one and that one—the wicked as well as the righteous—to see what they will do with it, but it all belongs to him. He has handed over a goodly portion to this people. . . . But it is not ours, and all we have to do is to try and find out what the Lord wants us to do with what we have in our possession, and then go and do it. If we step beyond this, or to the right or to the left, we step into an illegitimate train of business. Our legitimate business is to do what the Lord wants us to do with that which he bestows upon us and dispose of it just as he dictates, whether it is to give all, one-tenth, or the surplus (*DNW*, 23 Apr. 1873, 4).

How long have we got to live before we find out that we have nothing to consecrate to the Lord—that all belongs to the Father in heaven; that these mountains are His; the valleys, the timber, the water, the soil; in fine, the earth and its fulness? [see D&C 104:14–18, 55] (*DNW*, 20 June 1855, 5).

Where then is the sacrifice this people have ever made? There is no such thing. They have only exchanged a worse condition for a better one, every time they have been moved; they have exchanged ignorance for knowledge, and inexperience for its opposite (*DNW*, 24 Aug. 1854, 1).

Suppose we were called to leave what we have now, shall we call it a sacrifice? Shame on the man who would so call it; for it is the very means of adding to him knowledge, understanding, power, and glory, and prepares him to receive crowns, kingdoms, thrones, and principalities, and to be crowned in glory with the Gods of eternity. Short of this we can never receive that which we are looking for (*DNW*, 3 Aug. 1854, 2).

I will tell you what to do in order to gain your exaltation, which you cannot obtain except you take this course. If your affections are placed upon anything so as to hinder you in the least from dedicating them to the Lord, make a dedication of that thing in the first place, that the dedication of the whole may be complete (*DNW*, 5 Jan. 1854, 2).

What hinders this people from being as holy as the church of Enoch? I can tell you the reason in a few words. It is because you will not cultivate the disposition to be so: this comprehends the whole. If my heart is not fully given up to this work, I will give my time, my talents, my hands, and my possessions, until my heart consents to be subject; I will make my hands labour in the cause of God, until my heart bows in submission to it (*DNW*, 5 Jan. 1854, 2).

I have now told you what course to pursue to obtain an exaltation. The Lord must be first and foremost in our affections; the building up of his cause and kingdom demands our first consideration (*DNW*, 5 Jan. 1854, 2).

Suggestions for Study

Paying tithing allows us to participate in the Lord's work by returning a portion of that which belongs to Him.

- Identify each sentence in which President Young used the term "one-tenth," and then list all that he included in our tithing obligations. What constitutes tithing and who should pay it? (See also D&C 119:3–4.)
- Why did President Young say that he had nothing to give? (See also Mosiah 2:19–24; D&C 104:14–18, 55.) What is the source of all that we enjoy, including that which we pay in tithing? What then should be our attitude about the other nine-tenths of the Lord's possessions that He has entrusted to our care? (See also Jacob 2:17–19.) How does this attitude help us understand Malachi 3:8–12?
- Read carefully 2 Chronicles 31:5–6. When did these people pay their tithes? What should be our attitude about paying tithes?

Our responsibility is to pay tithing and to sustain those who are responsible for the tithing funds.

- What did President Young mean when he said that the Lord "requires one-tenth part of . . . my whole system"? In what ways can you "devote one-tenth of yourself" to building God's kingdom? How have you been blessed when you have donated your time and talents to building God's kingdom in addition to paying tithing?
- What consequences are mentioned by President Young for failing to pay one's tithing? How does failing to pay tithing affect both the Lord's Church and the individual member?
- What did President Young say that tithing is used for? Who is responsible for disbursing the tithing funds? (See also D&C 120.) What was President Young's attitude about questioning those who are responsible for the disbursement of tithing funds?

Consecration is a willingness to give all and an acknowledgment that all we have belongs to our Father in Heaven.

- What does it mean for the "community of Latter-day Saints" to become "one great family of heaven" and to be "heirs of the Father"?

- Why is the law of consecration "one of the last revelations which the people will receive into their hearts and understand, of their own free will and choice, and esteem it as a pleasure, a privilege, and a blessing unto them to observe and keep most holy"?

- Why does the Lord put property into our possession? What is our responsibility as stewards of God's possessions? According to President Young, what is "our legitimate business" regarding tithing and consecration? How can trying to do too much be as wrong as doing too little?

- What must we consecrate if we expect to receive all that God has? Why? (See also D&C 84:38.) In what specific ways can you consecrate all that you have and are to our Father in Heaven? How will this bless you, your family, fellow Church members, and others with whom you associate?

Understanding the New and Everlasting Covenant of Marriage

In the spring of 1847, President Brigham Young left his family at Winter Quarters and led the first company of Saints west. In a letter to his wife Mary Ann, describing the company's efforts to "prepare for moving," he said: "My dear companion partner in tribulation, . . . I thank you a thousand times for your kind letters to me more especially for your kind acts and still more for your kind heart. I pray for you and the children continually and for all of our family. I do think the Lord has blessed me with one of [the] best families that any man ever had on earth" (MAAY). For President Young, the gospel was to prepare the Saints for eternal life, a life which has marriage and family as the ultimate goal. The new and everlasting covenant of marriage lays the foundation "for worlds, for angels, and for the Gods" (DBY, 195).

Teachings of Brigham Young

The new and everlasting covenant of marriage lays the foundation for eternal life.

It [eternal marriage] is without beginning of days or end of years. . . . We can tell some things with regard to it; it lays the foundation for worlds, for angels, and for the Gods; for intelligent beings to be crowned with glory, immortality, and eternal lives. In fact, it is the thread which runs from the beginning to the end of the holy Gospel of Salvation—of the Gospel of the Son of God; it is from eternity to eternity (*DBY*, 195).

Let the father and mother, who are members of this Church and Kingdom, take a righteous course, and strive with all their might never to do a wrong, but to do good all their lives; if they have one child or one hundred children, if they conduct themselves towards them as they should, binding them to the Lord by their faith and prayers, I care not where those children go, they are bound up to their parents by an everlasting tie, and no power of earth or hell can separate them from their parents in eternity; they will return again to the fountain from whence they sprang (*DBY,* 208).

We find quite a large number of young people who have arrived at a marriageable age and still they remain single. . . . Our young men and women should consider their obligations to each other, to God, the earth, their parents, and to future generations for their salvation and exaltation among the Gods and for the glory of Him whom we serve (*DNSW,* 25 Oct. 1870, 2).

I will give each of the young men in Israel, who have arrived at an age to marry, a mission to go straightway and get married to a good sister, fence a city lot, lay out garden and orchard and make a home. This is the mission that I give to all young men in Israel (*DBY,* 196).

There is not a young man in our community who would not be willing to travel from here to England to be married right, if he understood things as they are; there is not a young woman in our community, who loves the Gospel and wishes its blessings, that would be married in any other way; they would live unmarried until they could be married as they should be, [even] if they lived until they were as old as Sarah before she had Isaac born to her [see Genesis 17:17]. Many of our brethren have married off their children without taking this into consideration, and thinking it a matter of little importance. I wish we all understood this in the light in which heaven understands it (*DBY,* 195–96).

One of the first transgressions of the family called Israel, was their going to other families or other nations to select partners. This was one of the great mistakes made by the children of Abraham, Isaac and Jacob, for they would go and marry with other families, although the Lord had forbidden them to do so, and had given them a very strict and stringent law on the subject [see Genesis 28:1–2]. He commanded them not to marry among the Gentiles, but they did and would do it [see Genesis 24:3] (*DBY,* 196).

Be careful, O ye mothers of Israel, and do not teach your daughters in future, as many of them have been taught, to marry out of Israel. Woe to you who do it; you will lose your crowns as sure as God lives (*DBY,* 196).

There are multitudes of pure and holy spirits waiting to take tabernacles, now what is our duty? . . . It is the duty of every righteous man and woman to prepare tabernacles for all the spirits they can (*DBY,* 197).

**Fathers should follow Christ as they love, instruct,
and provide for their families.**

Now let me say to the First Presidency, to the Apostles, to all the Bishops in Israel, and to every quorum, and especially to those who are presiding

Pioneer newlyweds Sarah Farr Smith and John Henry Smith in 1866. President Young taught that eternal marriage "is the thread which runs from the beginning to the end of the holy Gospel of Salvation . . . ; it is from eternity to eternity" (*DBY,* 195).

officers, Set that example before your [wife] and your children, before your neighbors and this people, that you can say: "Follow me, as I follow Christ." When we do this, all is right, and our consciences are clear (*DBY,* 198).

Let the husband and father learn to bend his will to the will of his God, and then instruct his [wife] and children in this lesson of self-government by his example as well as by precept, and his neighbors also, showing them how to be brave and steadfast, in subduing the rebellious and sinful disposition. Such a course as this will eventually subdue that unhallowed influence which works upon the human heart (*DBY,* 198).

Never cease a day of your life to have the Holy Ghost resting upon you; and never cease, fathers, to pray that your wives may enjoy this blessing, that their infants may be endowed with the Holy Ghost from their mother's womb. If you want to see a nation rise up full of the Holy Ghost and power, this is the way to bring it about (BYP, 8 Apr. 1852).

If we do not take the pains to train our children, to teach and instruct them concerning these revealed truths, the condemnation will be upon us, as parents, or at least in a measure (*DBY,* 207).

Let the father be the head of the family, the master of his own household; and let him treat them [his family] as an angel would treat them (*DBY,* 197–98).

It is for the husband to learn how to gather around his family the comforts of life, how to control his passions and temper, and how to command the respect, not only of his family but of all his brethren, sisters, and friends (*DBY,* 198).

Kind looks, kind actions, kind words, and a lovely, holy deportment towards [children] will bind our children to us with bands that cannot easily be broken; while abuse and unkindness will drive them from us, and break asunder every holy tie, that should bind them to us and to the everlasting covenant in which we are all embraced. If my family . . . will not be obedient to me on the basis of kindness, and a commendable life before all men, and before the heavens, then farewell to all influence (*DNW,* 7 Dec. 1864, 2).

The father should . . . endeavor to happify [please] and cheer the mother, that her heart may be comforted and her affections unimpaired in her earthly protector, that her love for God and righteousness may vibrate throughout her whole being, that she may bear and bring forth offspring impressed and endowed with all the qualities necessary to a being designed to reign king of kings and lord of lords (*DBY,* 199).

Let every man in the land . . . take a wife, and then go to work with your hands and cultivate the earth, or labor at some mechanical business, or some honest trade to provide an honest living for yourselves and those who depend upon you for their subsistence; observing temperance, and loving truth and virtue; then would the woman be cared for, be nourished, honored and blest, becoming honorable mothers of a race of men and women farther advanced in physical and mental perfection than their fathers. This would create a revolution in our country, and would produce results that would be of incalculable good (*DBY,* 194–95).

Let the husband make an improvement upon his kitchen and pantry and upon his bedrooms for the benefit of his family, and improve his gardens, walks, etc., beautifying your habitations and their surroundings, making pavements and planting shade trees (*DBY,* 198).

Mothers should love and instruct their families and have a good influence on the world around them.

When I reflect upon the duties and responsibilities devolving upon our mothers and sisters, and the influence they wield, I look upon them as the mainspring and soul of our being here. It is true that man is first. Father Adam was placed here as king of the earth, to bring it into subjection. But when Mother Eve came she had a splendid influence over him. A great many thought it was not very good; I think it was excellent (*DBY,* 199).

The duty of the mother is to watch over her children and give them their early education, for impressions received in infancy are lasting. You know, yourselves, by experience, that the impressions you have received in the dawn of your mortal existence, bear, to this day, with the greatest weight upon your mind. The child reposes implicit confidence in the mother, you behold in him a natural attachment, no matter what her appearance may be, that makes him think his mother is the best and handsomest mother in the world. I speak for myself. Children have all confidence in their mothers; and if mothers would take proper pains, they can instill into the hearts of their children what they please (*DBY,* 201).

You will, no doubt, recollect reading in the Book of Mormon, of two thousand young men, who were brought up to believe that, if they put their whole trust in God, and served him, no power would overcome them. You also recollect reading of them going out to fight, and so bold were they, and so mighty their faith, that it was impossible for their enemies to slay them. This power and faith they obtained through the teachings of their mothers (*DBY,* 201).

It is the calling of the wife and mother to know what to do with everything that is brought into the house, laboring to make her home desirable to her husband and children, making herself an Eve in the midst of a little paradise of her own creating, securing her husband's love and confidence, and tying her offspring to herself, with a love that is stronger than death, for an everlasting inheritance (*DBY,* 198).

Many of the sisters grieve because they are not blessed with offspring. You will see the time when you will have millions of children around you. If you are faithful to your covenants, you will be mothers of nations (*DBY,* 200).

It is not my general practice to counsel the sisters to disobey their husbands, but my counsel is—obey your husbands; and I am sanguine and most emphatic on that subject. But I never counselled a woman to follow her husband to the Devil (*DBY,* 200–201).

The mothers are the moving instruments in the hands of Providence to guide the destinies of nations. . . . Consequently, you see at once what I wish to impress upon your minds is, that the mothers are the machinery that gives zest to the whole man, and guide the destinies and lives of men upon the earth (*DBY,* 199–200).

Suggestions for Study

The new and everlasting covenant of marriage lays the foundation for eternal life.

- President Young stated that eternal marriage "lays the foundation for worlds . . . [and] for intelligent beings to be crowned with glory." How can we dedicate our marriages to that eternal purpose? What specific things can you do to maintain that perspective each day?

- What did President Young say is the mission of every young man? How does that apply to you?

- What did President Young refer to when he counseled young people to be "married right"? What blessings come to those who do all things necessary to "raise up a kingdom"? (See also Abraham 2:9–11.)

- "One of the great mistakes" made by some of the children of Abraham, Isaac, and Jacob was to marry outside of the new and everlasting covenant of marriage. (See also Genesis 28:1–2.) What blessings are denied those who marry outside of the new and everlasting covenant of marriage? What can you do to ensure that you remain worthy of this marriage covenant and can receive its blessings someday?

- What is the "duty of every righteous man and woman"? Why is creating physical bodies for God's spirit children such an important responsibility of a marriage in the new and everlasting covenant? How does a couple determine when they have fulfilled this responsibility according to God's will for them? (See also your bishop or branch president regarding the counsel given in the *General Handbook of Instructions.*)

Fathers should follow Christ as they love, instruct, and provide for their families.

- What example should every father set before his wife and children? What does it mean for a man to follow Christ? How does a man "learn to bend his will to the will of his God"? What have you learned from fathers who have submitted themselves to doing God's will?

- What truths are parents to teach to their children? (See also D&C 68:25.)

- According to President Young, how should a father preside in the family? (See also D&C 121:41–46.) How should a man treat his family?

What actions "break asunder every holy tie, that should ˙
and to the everlasting covenant"? How does a man filleᴅ
and the Spirit enable his wife and children to fulfill their ro.

- What did President Young say would result if a husband ᵪ
provides for his family? (See also D&C 83:1–2.) How could this "ᴄ
a revolution"?

**Mothers should love and instruct their families and have a
good influence on the world around them.**

- According to President Young, what are the duties and callings of a wife
and mother?

- What comfort does President Young give to those who do not or cannot
have children?

- How have Latter-day Saint women influenced you, your family, and your
community? How can they do so in the future?

- What did President Young mean when he said, "I never counselled a
woman to follow her husband to the Devil"? How can a wife know
whether her husband is following Christ? What blessings come to
husbands and wives who together submit to God's will?

- President Young stated that mothers will "guide the destinies of
nations." How can women fulfill this promise?

Edward Martin with his family in 1870. Edward was captain of the ill-fated Martin Handcart Company of 1856. He survived to become a photographer in Salt Lake City.

Teaching the Family

"Let us live so that the spirit of our religion will live within us, then we have peace, joy, happiness and contentment, which makes such pleasant fathers, pleasant mothers, pleasant children, pleasant households, neighbors, communities and cities. That is worth living for, and I do think that the Latter-day Saints ought to strive for this" (DBY, 204).

Teachings of Brigham Young

The family is a divine institution in time and in eternity.

If every person who professes to be a Latter-day Saint, was actually a Saint, our home would be a paradise, there would be nothing heard, nothing felt, nothing realized, but praise to the name of our God, doing our duty, and keeping his commandments (*DBY,* 203).

When a man and woman have received their endowments and sealings [in the temple for eternity], and then had children born to them afterwards, those children are legal heirs to the Kingdom and to all its blessings and promises, and they are the only ones that are [legal heirs] on this earth (*DBY,* 195).

The ordinance of sealing must be performed here . . . woman to man, and children to parents, etc., until the chain of generation is made perfect in the sealing ordinances back to Father Adam; hence, we have been commanded to gather ourselves together to come out of Babylon, and sanctify ourselves, and build up the Zion of our God, . . . until the earth is sanctified and prepared for the residence of God and angels (*DBY,* 407).

Parents should teach their children to keep God's commandments.

We see the infant in its mother's arms. What is this infant here for? What is the design in the creation of this little infant child? . . . You see this foundation, the starting point, the germ of intelligence embodied in this infant, calculated to grow and expand into manhood [or womanhood], then to the capacity of an angel, and so onward to eternal exaltation. But here is the foundation. . . . Here is the first place where we learn, this is the foot of the hill (*DBY,* 205–6).

I have often thought and said, "How necessary it is for mothers, who are the first teachers of their children and who make the first impressions on their young minds, to be strict." How careful they should be never to impress a false idea on the mind of a child! They should never teach them anything unless they know it is correct in every respect. They should never say a word, especially in the hearing of a child, that is improper (*DBY,* 206–7).

Let mothers commence to teach their children while in their laps, there do you teach them to love the Lord, and keep his commandments (*DBY,* 206).

If you mothers, will live your religion, then in the love and fear of God teach your children constantly and thoroughly in the way of life and salvation, training them up in the way they should go, when they are old they will not depart from it [see Proverbs 22:6]. I promise you this, it is as true as the shining sun, it is an eternal truth. In this duty we fail (*DBY,* 206).

Bring up your children in the love and fear of the Lord; study their dispositions and their temperaments, and deal with them accordingly, never allowing yourself to correct them in the heat of passion; teach them to love you rather than to fear you, and let it be your constant care that the children that God has so kindly given you are taught in their early youth the importance of the oracles of God, and the beauty of the principles of our holy religion, that when they grow to the years of man and womanhood they may always cherish a tender regard for them and never forsake the truth (*DBY,* 207).

Parents, teach your children by precept and example, the importance of addressing the Throne of grace; teach them how to live, how to draw from the elements the necessaries of life, and teach them the laws of life that they may know how to preserve themselves in health and be able to minister to others. And when instructing them in the principles of the Gospel, teach them that they are true, truth sent down from heaven for our salvation, and that the Gospel incorporates every truth whether in heaven, in earth, or in hell; and teach them, too, that we hold the keys of eternal life, and that they must obey and observe the ordinances and laws pertaining to this holy Priesthood, which God has revealed and restored for the exaltation of the children of men (*DBY,* 207).

If we do not take the pains to train our children, to teach and instruct them concerning these revealed truths, the condemnation will be upon us, as parents, or at least in a measure (*DBY,* 207).

As parents lead by proper example, they help set a righteous course for their family.

We should never allow ourselves to teach our children one thing and practice another (*DBY,* 206).

We should never permit ourselves to do anything that we are not willing to see our children do. We should set them an example that we wish them to imitate. Do we realize this? How often we see parents demand obedience, good behavior, kind words, pleasant looks, a sweet voice and a bright eye from a child or children when they themselves are full of bitterness and scolding! How inconsistent and unreasonable this is! (*DBY,* 208).

If parents will continually set before their children examples worthy of their imitation and the approval of our Father in Heaven, they will turn the current, and the tide of feelings of their children, and they, eventually, will desire righteousness more than evil (*DBY,* 208).

Let the father and mother, who are members of this Church and Kingdom, take a righteous course, and strive with all their might never to do a wrong, but to do good all their lives; if they have one child or one hundred children, if they conduct themselves towards them as they should, binding them to the Lord by their faith and prayers, I care not where those children go, they are bound up to their parents by an everlasting tie, and no power of earth or hell can separate them from their parents in eternity; they will return again to the fountain from whence they sprang (*DBY,* 208).

Our children will have the love of the truth, if we but live our religion. Parents should take that course that their children can say, "I never knew my father to deceive or take advantage of a neighbor; I never knew my father to take to himself that which did not belong to him, never, never! No, but he said, 'Son, or daughter, be honest, true, virtuous, kind, industrious, prudent and full of good works.'" Such teachings from parents to their children will abide with them forever, unless they sin against the Holy Ghost (*DBY,* 209).

We can guide, direct, and prune a tender sprout, and it inclines to our direction, if it is wisely and skillfully applied. So, if we surround a child with healthy and salutary influences, give him suitable instructions and store his mind with truthful traditions, may be that will direct his feet in the way of life (*DBY,* 209).

Self-restraint and kind discipline help build strong families.

To gain the spiritual ascendancy over ourselves, and the influences with which we are surrounded, through a rigid course of self-discipline, is our first consideration, it is our first labor, before we can pave the way for our children to grow up without sin unto salvation (*DBY,* 203).

What did you promise your little girl if she would do so and so? Did you promise her a present for well doing? "Yes." Have you recollected it? "No, it has gone from my mind," says the mother. If she does ill have you promised her a chastisement? "Yes." Did you keep your word? You have not, and the child forms the conclusion in its own mind directly that the mother tells that which is not true—she says she will do this or that, and she does not do it. It is an easy lesson for mothers to learn to pass their time with their children and never give them a false impression. Think before you speak. . . . If you wish to make them presents, do so; if you promise a chastisement, keep your word, but be cautious! (*DBY,* 210).

Parents should never drive their children, but lead them along, giving them knowledge as their minds are prepared to receive it. Chastening may be necessary betimes, but parents should govern their children by faith rather than by the rod, leading them kindly by good example into all truth and holiness (*DBY,* 208).

I can pick out scores of men in this congregation who have driven their children from them by using the wooden rod. Where there is severity there is no affection or filial feeling in the hearts of either party; the children would rather be away from father than be with him (*DBY,* 203).

In our daily pursuits in life, of whatever nature and kind, Latter-day Saints, and especially those who hold important positions in the Kingdom of God, should maintain a uniform and even temper, both when at home and when abroad. They should not suffer reverses and unpleasant circumstances to sour their natures and render them fretful and unsocial at home, speaking words full of bitterness and biting acrimony . . . , creating gloom and sorrow in their habitations, making themselves feared rather than loved by their families. Anger should never be permitted to rise in our bosoms, and words suggested by angry feelings should never be permitted to pass our lips. "A soft answer turneth away wrath, but grievous words stir up anger" [Proverbs 15:1]. "Wrath is cruel, and anger is outrageous" [Proverbs 27:4]; but "the discretion of a man deferreth his anger; and it is his glory to pass over a transgression" [Proverbs 19:11] (*DBY,* 203–4).

You see, hear and witness a good deal of contention among children—some of you do, if not all—and I will give you a few words with regard to your future lives, that you may have children that are not contentious, not quarrelsome. Always be good-natured yourselves, is the first step. Never allow yourselves to become out of temper and get fretful. . . . They have so much vitality in them that their bones fairly ache with strength. They have such an amount of vitality—life, strength and activity, that they must dispose of them; and the young ones will contend with each other. Do not be out of temper yourselves. Always sympathize with them and soothe them. Be mild and pleasant (*DBY,* 209–10).

In my experience I have learned that the greatest difficulty that exists in the little bickerings and strifes of man with man, woman with woman, children with children, parents with children, brothers with sisters, and sisters with brothers, arises from the want of rightly understanding each other (*DBY,* 203).

Suggestions for Study

The family is a divine institution in time and in eternity.

- Why is the sealing of families for eternity so important? (See also D&C 128:18.) How can understanding the eternal importance and divine nature of family relations help us in our interactions with family members?

- What can you do to strengthen the family ties between generations in your family? How can your actions affect your ancestors and your descendants?

Parents should teach their children to keep God's commandments.

- Who has the primary responsibility for teaching children? When should parents begin teaching their children to be righteous? What counsel did President Young give to parents regarding their roles as their children's first teachers?

- President Young said that parents should "bring up [their] children in the love and fear [respect] of the Lord." (See also D&C 68:25–28.) How can you teach children to love and respect Heavenly Father and Jesus Christ?

- What principles did President Young outline for parents to teach their children? What might happen if parents do not teach their children properly?

As parents lead by proper example, they help set a righteous course for their family.

- Why is example such a powerful way of teaching children? What kind of example are you setting for the children around you?

- President Young stated that children will "return again to the fountain from whence they sprang." Why might this promise be particularly comforting to parents whose children go astray? What can parents do to help wayward children want to return to their families?

- What positive values did you learn from your parents? What are some of the values you want your children to learn from you? How can you teach these values? What evidence do you have that your children are learning values from you?

- How can "truthful traditions" help your children become more committed to righteousness? What righteous traditions have strengthened your family? What righteous traditions would you like to establish in your family?

Self-restraint and kind discipline help build strong families.

- What is the difference between "driving" children and "leading" them? Why is leading children more effective in teaching children righteousness?

- Why is it essential to "maintain a uniform and even temper" when dealing with others, especially children?

- Quarreling and fighting are sometimes common parts of family life. Why are these things detrimental to the family? (See also Mosiah 4:14.) What did President Young say is the primary reason these things happen? How can you promote better communication and understanding within your family? What have you done that has helped your family to show their love for each other more frequently?

Cultivating Gratitude, Humility, and Honesty

President Brigham Young believed in and lived according to simple, true principles. From his experiences as a carpenter and contractor, he learned to value honest workers who built walls that would last, hung doors that would not need repair, and did not leave a job site with the owner's tools or nails in their pockets. He counseled people in every walk of life to "have their eyes opened to see and understand where honesty and uprightness are" (DNW, 2 Dec. 1857, 4). President Young also encouraged the early Saints who suffered from trials such as persecution, poverty, and starvation to accept their afflictions with gratitude and humility, for the Lord truly strengthened them in their suffering. His words and his life emphasized that our duty is to show integrity and gratitude by improving on whatever the Lord has blessed us with.

Teachings of Brigham Young

Acknowledging the Lord's hand in our lives cultivates gratitude.

I do not know of any, excepting the unpardonable sin, that is greater than the sin of ingratitude (*DBY*, 228).

I might say something with regard to the hard times. You know that I have told you that if any one was afraid of starving to death, let him leave, and go where there is plenty. I do not apprehend the least danger of starving, for until we eat up the last mule, from the tip of the ear to the end of the fly whipper, I am not afraid of starving to death. There are many people who cannot now get employment, but the spring is going to open upon us soon, and we are not going to suffer any more than what is for our good. I am thankful for the hand of the Lord which is visible; I am as thankful for this providence of his as for any that I ever received. I have told you, years ago, my feelings with regard to their sympathies, their faith, gratitude and thankfulness, and their acknowledgement of the hand of the Lord and of the dispensations of his providence. My soul has been grieved to bleeding, to see the waste, and the prodigal feeling of this people in the use of their bountiful blessings. Many have walked them underfoot, and have been ready to curse God who bestowed them. They wanted gold and silver, instead of wheat and corn, and fine flour, and the best vegetables that ever grew upon the earth. They walked them underfoot, and set at nought the choice blessings of the Lord their God (*DNW*, 6 Feb. 1856, 4).

We rejoice because the Lord is ours, because we are sown in weakness for the express purpose of attaining to greater power and perfection. In everything the Saints may rejoice—in persecution, because it is necessary to purge them, and prepare the wicked for their doom; in sickness and in pain, though they are hard to bear, because we are thereby made acquainted with pain, with sorrow, and with every affliction that mortals can endure, for by contact all things are demonstrated to our senses. We have reason to rejoice exceedingly that faith is in the world, that the Lord reigns, and does his pleasure among the inhabitants of the earth. Do you ask if I rejoice because the Devil has the advantage over the inhabitants of the earth, and has afflicted mankind? I most assuredly answer in the affirmative; I rejoice in this as much as in anything else. I rejoice because I am afflicted. I rejoice because I am poor. I rejoice because I am cast down. Why? Because I shall be lifted up again. I rejoice that I am poor because I shall be made rich; that I am afflicted, because I shall be comforted, and prepared to enjoy the felicity of perfect happiness, for it is impossible to properly appreciate happiness except by enduring the opposite (*DBY*, 228).

We talk about our trials and troubles here in this life; but suppose that you could see yourselves thousands and millions of years after you have proved faithful to your religion during the few short years in this time, and have obtained eternal salvation and a crown of glory in the presence of God? Then look back upon your lives here, and see the losses, crosses, and disappointments, the sorrows . . . ; you would be constrained to exclaim, "but what of all that? Those things were but for a moment, and we are now here. We have been faithful during a few moments in our mortality, and now we enjoy eternal life and glory, with power to progress in all the boundless knowledge and through the countless stages of progression, enjoying the smiles and approbation of our Father and God, and of Jesus Christ our elder brother" (*DNW*, 9 Nov. 1859, 1).

There is another item which I will now notice, and until we learn such things I will promise you that we shall never inherit the Celestial Kingdom. We are gathered together for the purpose of learning what to do with this present life and with the present blessings bestowed upon us. If we do not learn these lessons, how can we expect to be trusted with the riches of eternity; for he that is faithful over a few things shall be made ruler over many things [see Matthew 25:21]. . . . When we are blessed with an increase of cattle, and we disregard this blessing which the Lord bestows upon us, we thereby incur His displeasure, and lay ourselves liable to punishment. What earthly father would bestow blessings upon a son with satisfaction and pleasure while that son would continue to squander them and gamble them away for nothing? After a time that father would withhold his favors, and bestow them upon the more worthy child. The Lord is more merciful than we are; but there may be a termination to His gifts, if we do not receive them with gratitude and take good care of them when we have them in our possession. Let the people take care of their cattle and horses, and the man who does not do it will lay himself liable to censure in the eyes of justice (*DNSW,* 29 Oct. 1865, 2).

What is our duty? It is our duty to improve upon every blessing the Lord gives to us. If he gives us land, improve it; if he gives us the privilege of building houses, improve it; if he gives us wives and children, try and teach them the ways of the Lord, and exalt them above the dark, degraded, and sunken state of mankind. . . . In his providence he has called the Latter-day Saints from the world, has gathered them from other nations, and given them a place upon the earth. Is this a blessing? Yes one of the greatest the people can enjoy, to be free from the wickedness of the wicked, from the calamities and clamor of the world. By this blessing we can show to our Father in Heaven that we are faithful stewards; and more, it is a blessing to have the privilege of handing back to him that which he has put in our possession. . . . Then it is plain that what I seem to have I do not in reality own, and I will hand it back to the Lord when he calls for it; it belongs to him, and it is his all the time. I do not own it, I never did (*DN,* 20 June 1855, 4).

There is not a single condition of life [or] one hour's experience but what is beneficial to all those who make it their study, and aim to improve upon the experience they gain (*DNW,* 9 July 1862, 1).

Those who are humble recognize their dependence on the Lord.

We have to humble ourselves and become like little children in our feelings—to become humble and childlike in spirit, in order to receive the first illuminations of the spirit of the Gospel, then we have the privilege of growing, of increasing in knowledge, in wisdom, and in understanding (*DBY,* 228).

We are nothing only what the Lord makes us (*DNW,* 28 Oct. 1857, 5).

When a person sees things as they are, . . . if he finds that he is pleasing God and his brethren, he is exceedingly rejoiced, and feels an increase of humility and resignation. When a man is proud and arrogant, flattery fills him with vanity and injures him; but it is not so when he is increasing in the faith of God (*DBY,* 228).

179

Who has the greatest reason to be thankful to his God—the man that has no strong passion or evil appetite to overcome, or the one that tries day by day to overcome, and yet is overtaken in a fault? The power of his strength, faith, and judgment is overcome, and he is found in fault through his evil propensities, though he is striving, day after day, and night after night, to overcome. Who has reason to be the most thankful? The being that has comparatively no strong passion to overcome ought constantly to walk in the vale of humility, rather than boast of his righteousness over his brother. We are under obligation, through the filial feeling and ties of humanity, to more or less fellowship those who do evil. We must endure this until the Lord shall see fit to separate the wheat from the chaff—until the righteous are gathered out, and the wicked are bound in bundles prepared for the burning [see D&C 86]—until the sheep are separated from the goats [see Matthew 25:31–34]. Those who have not strong passions to contend with, day by day, and year by year, should walk in the vale of humiliation; and if brethren and sisters are overtaken in fault, your hearts should be filled with kindness—with brotherly, angelic feeling—to overlook their faults as far as possible (*DNW,* 22 Aug. 1860, 1).

The hearts of the meek and humble are full of joy and comfort continually (*DBY,* 228).

Those who are honest are true to themselves, to others, and to the Lord.

Men must be honest, they must live faithfully before their God, and honor their calling and being on the earth. You ask if that is possible? Yes; the doctrine which we have embraced takes away the stony hearts (*DBY,* 232).

We need to learn, practice, study, know and understand how angels live with each other. When this community comes to the point to be perfectly honest and upright, you will never find a poor person; none will lack, all will have sufficient. Every man, woman, and child will have all they need just as soon as they all become honest. When the majority of the community are dishonest, it maketh the honest portion poor, for the dishonest serve and enrich themselves at their expense (*DBY,* 232).

I have tried to suppress dishonesty in individuals, and have tried thereby to make them honest. If I hire a carpenter and pay him three dollars a day, and he is three days in making a six panel door that a good workman can make in one, or even a door and a half, I do not want to pay him three dollars a day for that labor. Yet some who are here have no more judgment, discretion, or idea of right or wrong, than to want to be paid for labor they do not perform; and that they consider to be honesty: but it is just as dishonest as anything in the world (*DNW,* 2 Dec. 1857, 4).

Let [all workers] try to improve. . . . There has a great improvement taken place in the midst of this people, and we will still continue to improve. Let us seek unto the Lord for wisdom . . . and so continue to improve, until we come up to the standard of truth in all our acts and words; so that when I employ a mason to lay me up a wall he will do it honestly, and so on with every other workman. Then if a man does not earn his wages, he will not ask them or take them. . . . Honesty never comes into the hearts of such persons; their rule is to keep what they have got and to get all they can, whether honestly or not, and pray for more (*DNW,* 2 Dec. 1857, 5).

Woe to those who profess to be Saints and are not honest. Only be honest with yourselves, and you will be honest to the brethren (*DBY,* 231–32).

Children should be taught honesty, and they should grow up with the feeling within them that they should never take a pin that is not their own; never displace anything, but always put everything in its place. If they find anything seek for the owner. If there is anything of their neighbor's going to waste, put it where it will not waste, and be perfectly honest one with another (*DNW,* 23 Oct. 1872, 5).

Honest hearts produce honest actions—holy desires produce corresponding outward works. Fulfil your contracts and sacredly keep your word. I have no fellowship for a man that will make a promise and not fulfil it. Simple truth, simplicity, honesty, uprightness, justice, mercy, love, kindness, do good to all and evil to none, how easy it is to live by such principles! A thousand times easier than to practice deception! (*DBY,* 232).

It is much better to be honest; to live here uprightly, and forsake and shun evil, than it is to be dishonest. It is the easiest path in the world to be honest,—to be upright before God; and when people learn this, they will practice it (*DBY,* 232).

Suggestions for Study

Acknowledging the Lord's hand in our lives cultivates gratitude.

- President Young suggested that the Saints should be grateful for wheat, corn, and vegetables rather than gold and silver. What should each of us be grateful for? (See also D&C 59:7, 21.) How have you expressed your gratitude to God, your family, and others?
- Why do you think President Young taught the Saints to rejoice in persecution, sickness, pain, and affliction? What blessings can result from

these conditions? How can suffering and trials be for our good? How can we learn to appreciate and value life's difficulties while we are experiencing hard times?

- President Young said, "We are [here] for the purpose of learning what to do with this present life and with the present blessings bestowed upon us." What will happen if we do not show gratitude by learning what to do with our present blessings? (See also Mosiah 2:20–21.) What can we do to show gratitude for our blessings? How can we "improve upon every blessing the Lord gives to us"?

Those who are humble recognize their dependence on the Lord.

- President Young spoke of the need to become childlike to "receive the first illuminations of the spirit of the Gospel" and said that a person can then grow in knowledge and wisdom. What evidence have you seen in yourself or others that this is true? What characteristics do children have that can guide adults in becoming humble?

- President Young taught, "We are nothing only what the Lord makes us." How can we know what the Lord wants to make of us? How will our being humble enable the Lord to guide us? (See also Mosiah 3:19.) How has the Lord guided your life and helped you become a better person?

- President Young said, "The being that has comparatively no strong passion to overcome ought constantly to walk in the vale of humility, rather than boast of his righteousness over his brother." How can comparing our strengths to another's weaknesses lead to pride? What blessings come to those who are humble? (See also Ether 12:27.)

Those who are honest are true to themselves, to others, and to the Lord.

- How can angels serve as a model for how families and communities should live with each other?

- President Young stated that in a community of honest people none would lack and all would have sufficient. Why would this be true? How does dishonesty affect our communities? How does honesty benefit our communities?

- How can we teach our children to be honest? Why is it important to be honest in all aspects of our lives?

- According to President Young, why is being honest "a thousand times easier than [practicing] deception" and "the easiest path in the world"?

Happiness and Social Enjoyment

President Brigham Young knew that true happiness comes only through righteous living, but he also knew that much enjoyment in life can come through wholesome recreation and entertainment. He was fond of the theater, dancing, and other social amusements and provided opportunities for the Saints to enjoy these pastimes, believing that they were important to the people's well-being. In Salt Lake City he supervised the building of the Social Hall, in which were held dances and theatrical performances. In referring to the Social Hall he stated: "That is our fun hall, and not a place in which to administer the sacrament. We dedicated it to the purpose for which it was built. . . . You know what spirit attends that room. There we have had governors, judges, doctors, lawyers, merchants, passers-by, etc., who did not belong to our church, and what has been the universal declaration of each and every one? 'I never felt so well before in all my life at any party as I do here;' and the Saints do not feel as well in any other place of amusement. . . . Every thing in its time, and every thing in its place" (DNW, 26 Mar. 1862, 1).

Teachings of Brigham Young

True happiness is found in righteousness and service.

What principal object have human beings in view? Happiness. Give me glory, give me power, give me wealth, give me a good name, give me influence with my fellow-men, give me all these, and it does not follow that I am thereby made happy; that depends altogether upon what principle those acquisitions were gained (*DBY*, 235).

We are all searching for happiness; we hope for it, we think we live for it, it is our aim in this life. But do we live so as to enjoy the happiness we so much desire? (*DBY*, 236).

Where is happiness, real happiness? Nowhere but in God. By possessing the spirit of our holy religion, we are happy in the morning, we are happy at noon, we are happy in the evening; for the spirit of love and union is

183

with us, and we rejoice in the spirit because, it is of God, and we rejoice in God, for he is the giver of every good thing. Every Latter-day Saint, who has experienced the love of God in his heart, after having received the remission of his sins, through baptism, and the laying on of hands, realizes that he is filled with joy, and happiness, and consolation. He may be in pain, in error, in poverty, or in prison, if necessity demands, still, he is joyful. This is our experience, and each and every Latter-day Saint can bear witness to it (*DBY*, 236).

How do you feel, Saints, when you are filled with the power and love of God? You are just as happy as your bodies can bear (*MSS*, 15:48).

The whole world are after happiness. It is not found in gold and silver, but it is in peace and love (*DBY*, 235).

What will give a man joy? That which will give him peace (*DBY*, 235).

If the heart is cheerful, all is light and glory within; there is no sorrow (*DBY*, 235).

When man is industrious and righteous, then is he happy (*DBY*, 235).

It is a mistaken idea in the inhabitants of the earth to conclude that it will not do for them to yield obedience to the commandments of heaven, lest it should abridge them in their comforts and in their enjoyments; for there is no real peace, there is no real happiness in anything in heaven or on the earth, except to those who serve the Lord. In his service there is joy, there is happiness, but they are not to be found anywhere else. In it there are peace and comfort, but when the soul is filled with joy, with peace and with glory, and is perfectly satisfied therewith, a person even then has but little idea of that which is in store for all the faithful (*DNW*, 15 July 1857, 4).

We are made to enjoy all that God enjoys, to inherit all he inherits, to possess all the power that he possesses, all the excellency with which he is endowed—all things are to be brought into subjection to him by his faithful children, that they may enjoy all things with him; these considerations bring peace to the heart that is opened to understanding (*DBY*, 237).

There is only one way for Latter-day Saints to be happy, which is simply to live their religion, or in other words believe the Gospel of Jesus Christ in every part, obeying the gospel of liberty with full purpose of heart, which sets us free indeed. If we will, as a community, obey the law of God, and comply with the ordinances of salvation, then we may expect to find the happiness we so much desire (*DBY*, 236).

As I have frequently thought, and said, when duty requires I am happy in going from home and I am happy in returning, for it is my greatest joy and comfort to do what the Lord requires of me and what I know to be my duty, no matter what it is if the Lord requires it of me. This course gives joy and peace (*DN*, 6 Feb. 1856, 4).

American Fork, Utah, brass band, 1866. The Saints loved music,
and almost every community had a band.

Truly happy is that man or woman, or that people, who enjoys the privileges of the Gospel of the Son of God, and who know how to appreciate his blessings (*DBY,* 236).

We want to see every countenance full of cheerfulness, and every eye bright with the hope of future happiness (*DBY,* 236).

I say, if you want to enjoy exquisitely, become a Latter-day Saint, and then live the doctrine of Jesus Christ (*DNSW,* 30 June 1874, 1).

The person who enjoys the experience of the knowledge of the Kingdom of God on the earth, and at the same time has the love of God within him, is the happiest of any individuals on the earth (*DBY,* 235).

Recreation in the proper spirit can increase our physical and spiritual well-being.

We are to learn how to enjoy the things of life—how to pass our mortal existence here. There is no enjoyment, no comfort, no pleasure, nothing that the human heart can imagine, with all the spirit of revelation we can get, that tends to beautify, happify [make happy], make comfortable and peaceful, and exalt the feelings of mortals, but what the Lord has in store for his people. He never objected to their taking comfort. He never revealed any doctrine, that I have any knowledge of, but what in its nature is calculated to fill with peace and glory, and lift every sentiment and impulse of the heart above every low, sad, deathly, false and grovelling feeling. The Lord wishes us to live that we may enjoy the fulness of the glory that pertains to the upper world, and bid farewell to all that gloomy, dark, deathly feeling that is spread over the inhabitants of the earth (*DBY,* 237).

Is there anything immoral in recreation? If I see my sons and daughters enjoying themselves, chatting, visiting, riding, going to a party or a dance, is there anything immoral in that? I watch very closely, and if I hear a word, see a look, or a sneer at divine things or anything derogatory to a good moral character, I feel it in a moment, and I say, "If you follow that it will not lead to good, it is evil; it will not lead to the fountain of life and intelligence; follow, only, the path that leads to life everlasting" (*DBY,* 237).

It is the privilege of the Saints to enjoy every good thing, for the earth and its fulness belong to the Lord [see D&C 104:14], and he has promised all to his faithful Saints; but it must be enjoyed without spirit of covetousness and selfishness—without the spirit of lust, and in the spirit of the Gospel; then the sun will shine sweetly upon us; each day will be filled with delight, and all things will be filled with beauty, giving joy, pleasure, and rest to the Saints (*DBY,* 237).

To make ourselves happy is incorporated in the great design of man's existence. I have learned not to fret myself about that which I cannot help. If I can do good, I will do it; and if I cannot reach a thing, I will content myself to be without it. This makes me happy all the day long (*DBY,* 236).

Then learn to be happy when you have the privilege (*DBY,* 235).

We are now enjoying our pastimes. We often meet together and worship the Lord by singing, praying, and preaching, fasting, and communing with each other in the Sacrament of the Lord's Supper. Now we are met in the capacity of a social community—for what? That our minds may rest, and our bodies receive that recreation which is proper and necessary to keep up an equilibrium, to promote healthy action to the whole system (*DBY,* 240).

I have frequently told the people at our places of recreation, if they cannot go there with the Spirit of the Lord, they had better stay at home (*DBY,* 240).

In all your social communications, or whatever your associations are, let all the dark, discontented, murmuring, unhappy, miserable feelings—all the evil fruit of the mind, fall from the tree in silence and unnoticed; and

President Brigham Young encouraged the Saints to participate in cultural and social activities. This 1858 photograph shows the Social Hall in Salt Lake City, where many Saints had the opportunity to develop and share their talents.

so let it perish, without taking it up to present to your neighbors. But when you have joy and happiness, light and intelligence, truth and virtue, offer that fruit abundantly to your neighbors, and it will do them good, and so strengthen the hands of your fellow-beings (*DBY,* 240).

We should seek wholesome entertainment that is consistent with gospel standards.

I built [the] theater to attract the young of our community and to provide amusement for the boys and girls, rather than have them running all over creation for recreation. Long before [it] was built I said to the Bishops, "Get up your parties and pleasure grounds to amuse the people" (*DBY,* 243).

Is there evil in the theater; in the ball room; in the place of worship; in the dwelling; in the world? Yes, when men are inclined to do evil in any of these places. There is evil in persons meeting simply for a chitchat, if they will allow themselves to commit evil while thus engaged (*DBY,* 243).

Upon the stage of a theater can be represented in character, evil and its consequences, good and its happy results and rewards; the weakness and the follies of man, the magnanimity of virtue and the greatness of truth. The stage can be made to aid the pulpit in impressing upon the minds of a community an enlightened sense of a virtuous life, also a proper horror of the enormity of sin and a just dread of its consequences. The path of sin with its thorns and pitfalls, its gins and snares can be revealed, and how to shun it (*DBY,* 243).

Tragedy is favored by the outside world; I am not in favor of it. I do not wish murder and all its horrors and the villainy leading to it portrayed before our women and children; I do not want the child to carry home with it the fear of . . . the sword, the pistol, or the dagger, and suffer in the night from frightful dreams. I want such plays performed as will make the spectators feel well; and I wish those who perform to select a class of plays that will improve the public mind, and exalt the literary taste of the community (*DBY,* 243–44).

If you wish to dance, dance; and you are just as much prepared for a prayer meeting after dancing as ever you were, if you are Saints. If you desire to ask God for anything, you are as well prepared to do so in the dance as in any other place, if you are Saints (*DBY,* 243).

[However,] those who cannot serve God with a pure heart in the dance should not dance (*DBY,* 243).

I want it distinctly understood, that fiddling and dancing are no part of our worship. The question may be asked, What are they for, then? I answer, that my body may keep pace with my mind. My mind labors like a man logging, all the time; and this is the reason why I am fond of these pastimes—they give me a privilege to throw everything off, and shake myself, that my body may exercise, and my mind rest. What for? To get strength, and be renewed and quickened, and enlivened, and animated, so that my mind may not wear out (*DBY*, 242).

There are many of our aged brethren and sisters, who, through the traditions of their fathers and the requirements of a false religion, were never inside a ball-room or a theater until they became Latter-day Saints, and now they seem more anxious for this kind of amusement than are our children. This arises from the fact they have been starved for many years for that amusement which is designed to buoy up their spirits and make their bodies vigorous and strong, and tens of thousands have sunk into untimely graves for want of such exercises to the body and the mind. They require mutual nourishment to make them sound and healthy. Every faculty and power of both body and mind is a gift from God. Never say that means used to create and continue healthy action of body and mind are from hell (*DBY*, 242).

If you want to dance, run a foot race, . . . or play at ball, do it, and exercise your bodies, and let your minds rest (*DBY*, 243).

Those that have kept the covenants and served their God, if they wish to exercise themselves in any way to rest their minds and tire their bodies, go and enjoy yourselves in the dance, and let God be in all your thoughts in this as in all other things, and he will bless you (*DBY*, 242).

Our work, our every-day labor, our whole lives are within the scope of our religion. This is what we believe and what we try to practice. Yet the Lord permits a great many things that he never commands. . . . The Lord never commanded me to dance, yet I have danced: you all know it, for my life is before the world. Yet while the Lord has never commanded me to do it, he has permitted it. I do not know that he ever commanded the boys to go and play at ball, yet he permits it. I am not aware that he ever commanded us to build a theater, but he has permitted it, and I can give the reason why. Recreation and diversion are as necessary to our well-being as the more serious pursuits of life (*DBY*, 238).

I am satisfied that those persons who stamp, clap hands, whistle, and make other noisy and boisterous demonstrations in the theaters, so untimed and uncalled for, have but little sense, and know not the difference between a happy smile of satisfaction to cheer the countenance of a friend, or a contemptuous sneer that brings the curses of man upon man (*DBY*, 241).

[But] let our minds sing for joy, and let life diffuse itself into every avenue of the body; for the object of our meeting is for its exercise, for its good (*DBY*, 240).

Suggestions for Study

True happiness is found in righteousness and service.

- Why do human beings seek happiness? Why do so many people seem unable to find it? Where can we find true happiness? How can the gospel provide happiness even to those "in pain, in error, in poverty, or in prison"?

- Many people believe that obeying God's commandments will restrict their freedom and make them less happy. What situations have you experienced or observed that demonstrate that the opposite is actually true—that obedience to the commandments makes us happy, while disobedience makes us unhappy?

- How do you feel knowing that you are "made to enjoy all that God enjoys" and that Heavenly Father and Jesus Christ want you to be happy?

- What did President Young say is the only way for Latter-day Saints to be happy? How does living the gospel make you happy?

Recreation in the proper spirit can increase our physical and spiritual well-being.

- Why do you think President Young encouraged recreation? (See also D&C 136:28.) How can our recreational activities "fill [us] with peace and glory, and lift every sentiment and impulse of the heart"?

- What obligations must we fulfill before participating in recreation, if our activities are to bless us spiritually as well as physically?

- President Young taught that recreation must be done in the proper spirit. How can we ensure that we have the Spirit of the Lord with us in our recreation?

We should seek wholesome entertainment that is consistent with gospel standards.

- Why is it important to participate in a variety of activities, including entertainment and recreational activities? What did President Young say are some specific benefits of music, dancing, and the theater? What does he say to those who believe that the theater and the ballroom are places of evil?

- What should be our criteria for selecting appropriate entertainment? How can you ensure that "God [is] in all your thoughts" even when you are participating in entertainment or recreational activities? How can parents set a good example for their children by the type of entertainment they choose?

- Why is recreation "as necessary to our well-being as the more serious pursuits of life"?

- How can you help provide safe and wholesome recreation and entertainment for yourself, your children, or others in your community?

Photograph of Karl G. Maeser, the first instructor at Brigham Young Academy, which later became Brigham Young University.

Learning by Study and by Faith

*Although President Brigham Young had only 11 days of formal schooling,
he understood the need for learning both the things of the world and the
wisdom of God. He never ceased learning from books, from the scriptures,
and from the revelations of the Lord, and he taught the Saints to establish
schools and to delight in learning. In 1850 he founded the University of
Deseret, which later became the University of Utah; in 1875 he founded an
academy in Provo, Utah, which later became Brigham Young University.
Brigham Young College at Logan, Utah, was established in 1877 to train
teachers for schools throughout the Latter-day Saint settlements.
Consistent with this commitment to education, he also maintained a family
schoolhouse near his home for the last 12 years of his life. A founder of
universities and a profound teacher, President Young taught that if we wish
to become like Heavenly Father, we must grow continually in knowledge
and wisdom.*

Teachings of Brigham Young

We are "duty bound to study," learn, and live by eternal principles.

While the inhabitants of the earth are bestowing all their ability, both
mental and physical, upon perishable objects, those who profess to be
Latter-day Saints, who have the privilege of receiving and understanding
the principles of the holy gospel, are in duty bound to study and find out,
and put in practice in their lives, those principles that are calculated to
endure, and that tend to a continual increase in this, and in the world to
come (*DNW,* 20 July 1854, 1).

Not only does the religion of Jesus Christ make the people acquainted
with the things of God, and develop within them moral excellence and
purity, but it holds out every encouragement and inducement possible, for
them to increase in knowledge and intelligence, in every branch of mechanism, or in the arts and sciences, for all wisdom, and all the arts and
sciences in the world are from God, and are designed for the good of his
people (*DBY,* 247).

Every art and science known and studied by the children of men is comprised within the Gospel. Where did the knowledge come from which has enabled man to accomplish such great achievements in science and mechanism within the last few years? We know that knowledge is from God, but why do they not acknowledge him? Because they are blind to their own interests, they do not see and understand things as they are. Who taught men to chain the lightning? Did man unaided of himself discover that? No, he received the knowledge from the Supreme Being. From him, too, has every art and science proceeded, although the credit is given to this individual, and that individual. But where did they get the knowledge from, have they it in and of themselves? No, they must acknowledge that, if they cannot make one spear of grass grow, nor one hair white or black [see Matthew 5:36] without artificial aid, they are dependent upon the Supreme Being just the same as the poor and the ignorant. Where have we received the knowledge to construct the labor-saving machinery for which the present age is remarkable? From Heaven. Where have we received our knowledge of astronomy, or the power to make glasses to penetrate the immensity of space? . . . From [God] has every astronomer, artist and mechanician that ever lived on the earth obtained his knowledge (*DBY,* 246).

The greatest difficulty we have to meet is what may be termed ignorance, or want of understanding in the people (*DBY,* 247).

The religion embraced by the Latter-day Saints, if only slightly understood, prompts them to search diligently after knowledge [see D&C 88:118]. There is no other people in existence more eager to see, hear, learn, and understand truth (*DBY,* 247).

Put forth your ability to learn as fast as you can, and gather all the strength of mind and principle of faith you possibly can, and then distribute your knowledge to the people (*DBY,* 247).

Let us train our minds until we delight in that which is good, lovely and holy, seeking continually after that intelligence which will enable us effectually to build up Zion, . . . seeking to do the will of the Lord all the days of our lives, improving our minds in all scientific and mechanical knowledge, seeking diligently to understand the great design and plan of all created things, that we may know what to do with our lives and how to improve upon the facilities placed within our reach (*DBY,* 247).

We are called to grow in grace and knowledge for eternity.

This is our labor, our business, and our calling—to grow in grace and in knowledge from day to day and from year to year (*DBY,* 248).

I shall not cease learning while I live, nor when I arrive in the spirit-world; but shall there learn with greater facility; and when I again receive my body, I shall learn a thousand times more in a thousand times less time; and then I do not mean to cease learning, but shall still continue my researches (*DBY,* 248).

We shall never see the time when we shall not need to be taught, nor when there will not be an object to be gained. I never expect to see the time that there will not be a superior power and a superior knowledge, and, consequently, incitements to further progress and further improvements (*DBY,* 248).

Could we live to the age of Methuselah . . . and spend our lives in searching after the principles of eternal life, we would find, when one eternity had passed to us, that we had been but children thus far, babies just commencing to learn the things which pertain to the eternities of the Gods (*DBY,* 249).

We might ask, when shall we cease to learn? I will give you my opinion about it: never, never (*DBY,* 249).

Experience has taught us that it requires time to acquire certain branches of mechanism, also principles and ideas that we wish to become masters of. The closer people apply their minds to any correct purpose the faster they can grow and increase in the knowledge of the truth. When they learn to master their feelings, they can soon learn to master their reflections and thoughts in the degree requisite for attaining the objects they are seeking. But while they yield to a feeling or spirit that distracts their minds from a subject they wish to study and learn, so long they will never gain the mastery of their minds (*DBY,* 250).

A firm, unchangeable course of righteousness through life is what secures to a person true intelligence (*DBY,* 245).

We should educate ourselves and our children in the learning of the world and the things of God.

Teach the children, give them the learning of the world and the things of God; elevate their minds, that they may not only understand the earth we walk upon, but the air we breathe, the water we drink, and all the elements pertaining to the earth (*DBY,* 251).

See that your children are properly educated in the rudiments of their mother tongue, and then let them proceed to higher branches of learning; let them become more informed in every department of true and useful learning than their fathers are. When they have become well acquainted with their language, let them study other languages, and make themselves fully acquainted with the manners, customs, laws, governments and litera-ture of other nations, peoples, and tongues. Let them also learn all the truth pertaining to the arts and sciences, and how to apply the same to their temporal wants. Let them study things that are upon the earth, that are in the earth, and that are in the heavens (*DBY,* 252).

Every accomplishment, every polished grace, every useful attainment in mathematics, music, and in all science and art belongs to the Saints, and they should avail themselves as expeditiously as possible of the wealth of knowledge the sciences offer to every diligent and persevering scholar (*DBY,* 252).

I am happy to see our children engaged in the study and practice of music. Let them be educated in every useful branch of learning, for we, as a people, have in the future to excel the nations of the earth in religion, science and philosophy (*DBY,* 256).

There are hundreds of young men here who can go to school, which is far better than to waste their time. Study languages, get knowledge and understanding; and while doing this, get wisdom from God, and forget it not, and learn how to apply it, that you may be good with it all the days of your lives (*DBY,* 252).

Go to school and study. . . . I want to have schools to entertain the minds of the people and draw them out to learn the arts and sciences. Send the old children to school, and the young ones also; there is nothing I would like better than to learn chemistry, botany, geology, and mineral-ogy, so that I could tell what I walk on, the properties of the air I breathe, what I drink, etc. (*DBY,* 253).

We should be a people of profound learning.

We should be a people of profound learning pertaining to the things of the world. We should be familiar with the various languages, for we wish to send missionaries to the different nations and to the islands of the sea. We wish missionaries who may go to France to be able to speak the French language fluently, and those who may go to Germany, Italy, Spain, and so on to all nations, to be familiar with the languages of those nations (*DBY,* 254).

We also wish them to understand the geography, habits, customs, and laws of nations and kingdoms. . . . This is recommended in the revelations given to us [see D&C 88:78–80; 93:53]. In them we are taught to study the best books, that we may become as well acquainted with the geography of the world as we are with our gardens, and as families with the people—so far at least as they are portrayed in print—as we are with our families and neighbors (*DBY,* 254–55).

We are in a great school, and we should be diligent to learn, and continue to store up the knowledge of heaven and of earth, and read good books, although I cannot say that I would recommend the reading of all books, for it is not all books which are good. Read good books, and extract from them wisdom and understanding as much as you possibly can, aided by the Spirit of God (*DBY,* 248).

I would advise you to read books that are worth reading; read reliable history, and search wisdom out of the best books you can procure (*DBY,* 256).

How gladly would we understand every principle pertaining to science and art, and become thoroughly acquainted with every intricate operation of nature, and with all the chemical changes that are constantly going on around us! How delightful this would be, and what a boundless field of truth and power is open for us to explore! We are only just approaching the shores of the vast ocean of information that pertains to this physical world, to say nothing of that which pertains to the heavens, to angels and celestial beings, to the place of their habitation, to the manner of their life, and their progress to still higher degrees of perfection (*DBY,* 255).

The revelations of the Lord Jesus Christ to the human family are all the learning we can ever possess. Much of this knowledge is obtained from books which have been written by men who have contemplated deeply on various subjects, and the revelations of Jesus have opened their minds, whether they knew it or acknowledged it or not (*DBY,* 257–58).

Our religion will not clash with or contradict the facts of science in any particular. You may take geology, for instance, and it is true science; not that I would say for a moment that all the conclusions and deductions of its professors are true, but its leading principles are; they are facts—they are eternal; and to assert that the Lord made this earth out of nothing is preposterous and impossible [see Abraham 3:24; D&C 131:7]. God never made something out of nothing; it is not in the economy or law by which the worlds were, are, or will exist. There is an eternity before us, and it is full of matter; and if we but understand enough of the Lord and his ways we would say that he took of this matter and organized this earth from it. How long it has been organized it is not for me to say, and I do not care anything about it. . . . If we understood the process of creation there would be no mystery about it, it would be all reasonable and plain, for there is no mystery except to the ignorant. This we know by what we have learned naturally since we have had a being on the earth (*DBY,* 258–59).

The faculty of the Brigham Young Academy about 1885.

We have the privilege of searching out the wisdom of God.

It is the privilege of man to search out the wisdom of God pertaining to the earth and the heavens. Real wisdom is a real pleasure; real wisdom, prudence, and understanding, is a real comfort (*DBY,* 262).

The person that applies his heart to wisdom, and seeks diligently for understanding, will grow to be mighty in Israel (*DBY,* 261).

Let wisdom be sown in your hearts, and let it bring forth a bountiful harvest. It is more profitable to you than all the gold and silver and other riches of earth. Let wisdom spring up in your hearts, and cultivate it (*DBY,* 261).

As we prepare materials to build a house or temple, so man can prepare himself for the reception of eternal wisdom. We go where the materials for a house are, and prepare them to answer our purpose; so we may go to where eternal wisdom dwells and there diligently seek to possess it, for its price is above rubies [see Job 28:18] (*DBY,* 261–62).

After all our endeavors to obtain wisdom from the best books, etc., there still remains an open fountain for all; "If any man lack wisdom let him ask of God" [see James 1:5] (*DBY,* 261).

If you live so as to possess the Holy Ghost, . . . you will at once see the difference between the wisdom of men and the wisdom of God, and you can weigh things in the balance and estimate them at their true worth (*DBY,* 323).

Let every Latter-day Saint constantly practice himself in the performance of every good word and work, to acknowledge God to be God, to be strict in keeping his laws, and learning to love mercy, eschew [avoid] evil and delight in constantly doing that which is pleasing to God (*DBY,* 261).

There is only one Source whence men obtain wisdom, and that is God, the Fountain of all wisdom; and though men may claim to make their discoveries by their own wisdom, by meditation and reflection, they are indebted to our Father in Heaven for all (*DBY,* 259–60).

Suggestions for Study

We are "duty bound to study," learn, and live by eternal principles.

• While others "are bestowing all their ability . . . upon perishable objects," how should the Latter-day Saints invest their time and energies? What are "perishable objects"? List some of "those principles that are calculated to endure, and . . . increase . . . in the world to come."

- Who is the source of all great achievements in knowledge? Whom do people usually credit for these achievements?

- In what ways does the gospel encourage Church members to "increase in knowledge and intelligence"? Why is there "no other . . . people more eager to see, hear, learn, and understand truth"? Why should we seek to never stop learning?

- How can we "train our minds until we delight in that which is good, lovely and holy"? What results from "improving our minds"?

We are called to grow in grace and knowledge for eternity.

- According to President Young, when does a person stop learning?

- What course must we follow to gain mastery of our minds and to secure true intelligence?

We should educate ourselves and our children in the learning of the world and the things of God.

- President Young commanded us to teach our children. What are we to teach them? What can we do to encourage our children to gain an education?

- How can we balance obtaining secular knowledge with getting wisdom from God? In what ways do these goals work together?

- In teaching children, what are the responsibilities of teachers? of parents? of other adults?

We should be a people of profound learning.

- Why should we seek "profound learning"? What should we study? Why should we read more than just the scriptures?

- President Young exhorted us to "study the best books." What kinds of books did he refer to? How can we tell good books from bad? What books have you benefited from studying that you might classify as being among "the best books"? Aside from studying good books, how else might you gain knowledge?

- What is the source of "all the learning we can ever possess"? How can we learn more effectively from that source?

- According to President Young, what is the relationship between true religion and "the facts of science"?

We have the privilege of searching out the wisdom of God.

- President Young said that the wisdom of God "is more profitable to you than all the gold and silver and other riches of earth." How can true wisdom become a "pleasure" and a "comfort"?

- To whom do we go to obtain "eternal wisdom"? How must we prepare to receive eternal wisdom? How can we "see the difference between the wisdom of men and the wisdom of God"?

President Young taught the Saints to exercise self-control
in all aspects of their lives.

Exercising Self-Control

President Brigham Young learned through experience that leading people of strong and often independent wills to Zion brought moments of triumph and moments of exasperation. In 1848, the wagon train of 2,000 Saints that he led encountered a herd of buffalo. Although President Young appointed camp hunters to kill just enough buffalo to provide meat for the travelers, other men left their teams to ride after the animals all day, shooting them in abundance and leaving dead buffalo on the prairie to waste. He reproved the people for the course they had taken [see JTB]. He later said, "Learn to govern yourselves" (DNW, 15 Aug. 1860, 1). "Bless yourselves and friends, by conquering and controlling yourselves, [for] unless you control [your] passions [and] make all your faculties subservient to the principles God has revealed, you will never arrive at that state of happiness, glory, joy, peace, and eternal felicity that you are anticipating" (DNW, 15 Aug. 1860, 1).

Teachings of Brigham Young

We can control ourselves and submit to God's will.

Have we a will? Yes, it is an endowment, a trait of the character of the Gods, with which all intelligence is endowed, in heaven and on earth,—the power to accept or reject (*DBY,* 264).

Take people in every capacity of life, and their wills are first and foremost. You can gain and lead the affections of the people, but you cannot scare them, nor whip them, nor burn them to do right against their wills. The human family will die to gratify their wills. Then learn to rightly direct those wills, and you can direct the influence and power of the people (*DBY,* 264).

God has placed within us a will, and we should be satisfied to have it controlled by the will of the Almighty. Let the human will be indomitable for right. It has been the custom of parents to break the will until it is weakened, and the noble, God-like powers of the child are reduced to a comparative state of imbecility and cowardice. Let that heaven-born

203

property of human agents be properly tempered and wisely directed, instead of pursuing the opposite course, and it will conquer in the cause of right. Break not the spirit of any person, but guide it to feel that it is its greatest delight and highest ambition to be controlled by the revelations of Jesus Christ, then the will of man becomes God-like in overcoming the evil that is sown in the flesh, until God shall reign within us to will and do of his good pleasure (*DBY,* 264).

Learn to control yourselves; learn to be in the hands of God as clay in the hands of the potter (*DBY,* 265).

Let each person be determined, in the name of the Lord Jesus Christ, to overcome every besetment—to be the master of himself, that the Spirit God has put in your tabernacles shall rule; then you can converse, live, labor, go here or there, do this or that, and converse and deal with your brethren as you ought (*DBY,* 265–66).

We can control ourselves until we bring everything "into subjection to the law of Christ."

The sooner an individual resists temptation to do, say, or think wrong, while he has light to correct his judgment, the quicker he will gain strength and power to overcome every temptation to evil (*DBY,* 266).

The thousands and tens of thousands of incidents that make up the sum of human lives, whether for good or evil, depend on a momentary watchfulness and care (*DBY,* 267).

You cannot inherit eternal life, unless your appetites are brought in subjection to the spirit that lives within you, that spirit which our Father in Heaven gave. I mean the Father of your spirits, of those spirits which he has put into these tabernacles. The tabernacles must be brought in subjection to the spirit perfectly, or your bodies cannot be raised to inherit eternal life. . . . Seek diligently, until you bring all into subjection to the law of Christ (*DBY,* 266).

I am trying to civilize myself. Are you trying to do the same? If we have succeeded in this, then we have control over our words and over our actions, and also, so far as our influence goes, over our associates. If we are civilized ourselves, we shall be partially prepared to receive the things that our Father and God has in store for all such as prepare themselves to become recipients of his choice gifts—for enlightenment, for intelligence, for glory, for power, and for every qualification he wishes to bestow upon his children here upon the earth, to prepare them to dwell in mansions of eternal light (*DBY,* 266–67).

I have frequently said that the greatest endowment God ever gave to man is good, sound, solid sense to know how to govern ourselves (*DBY,* 265).

No man ever did, or ever will rule judiciously on this earth, with honor to himself and glory to his God, unless he first learn to rule and control himself. A man must first learn to rule himself rightly before his knowledge can be fully brought to bear for the correct government of a family, a neighborhood, or nation, over which it is his lot to preside (*DBY,* 265).

Until we can subdue our own passions, and bring every human feeling and aspiration into subjection to the will of God, we are not really capable of guiding and dictating others to the full possession of victory in the Kingdom of God. To conquer and subdue, and school ourselves until we bring everything into subjection to the law of Christ, is our work (*DBY,* 267).

We are trying to govern ourselves, and if we continue trying and faint not, we shall assuredly conquer (*DBY,* 265).

We can control our passions and emotions.

You have been taught the standard of right. Now subdue your rebellious passions, dismiss everything that you know or consider to be wrong, and embrace that which is better (*DBY,* 265).

In this probation, we have evil to contend with, and we must overcome it in ourselves, or we never shall overcome it anywhere else (*DBY,* 265).

A righteous person will never be discouraged, but will constantly contend against his evil passions, and against evil in his family and neighborhood (*DBY,* 267).

Many men will say they have a violent temper, and try to excuse themselves for actions of which they are ashamed. I will say, there is not a man in this house who has a more indomitable and unyielding temper than myself. But there is not a man in the world who cannot overcome his passion, if he will struggle earnestly to do so. If you find passion coming on you, go off to some place where you cannot be heard; let none of your family see you or hear you, while it is upon you, but struggle till it leaves you; and pray for strength to overcome. As I have said many times to the Elders, pray in your families; and if, when the time for prayer comes, you have not the spirit of prayer upon you, and your knees are unwilling to bow, say to them, "Knees, get down there"; make them bend, and remain there until you obtain the Spirit of the Lord. If the spirit yields to the body, it becomes corrupt; but if the body yields to the spirit it becomes pure and holy (*DBY,* 267).

Do not get so angry that you cannot pray; do not allow yourselves to become so angry that you cannot feed an enemy—even your worst enemy, if an opportunity should present itself. There is a wicked anger, and there is a righteous anger. The Lord does not suffer wicked anger to be in his heart; but there is anger in his bosom, and he will hold a controversy with the nations, and will sift them, and no power can stay his hand (*DBY,* 269).

When my feelings are aroused to anger by the ill-doings of others, I hold them as I would hold a wild horse, and I gain the victory. Some think and say that it makes them feel better when they are mad, as they call it, to give vent to their madness in abusive and unbecoming language. This, however, is a mistake. Instead of its making you feel better, it is making bad worse. When you think and say it makes you better you give credit to a falsehood. When the wrath and bitterness of the human heart are moulded into words and hurled with violence at one another, without any check or hindrance, the fire has no sooner expended itself than it is again re-kindled through some trifling course, until the course of nature is set on fire (*DBY,* 266).

Now I charge you again, and I charge myself not to get angry. Never let anger arise in your hearts. No, Brigham, never let anger arise in your heart, never, never! Although you may be called upon to chastise and to speak to the people sharply, do not let anger arise in you, no, never! (*DBY,* 265).

Cease your anger, and sullenness of temper, and serve the Lord with cheerfulness, and singleness of heart. You need not expect salvation, except you can administer the same salvation to others, both in precept and example. If you expect compassion from me, administer the same to me. If you wish kind words and kind treatment from me, give me the same blessing you desire yourself; and that is the way you will be saved (*DBY,* 268–69).

If you give way to your angry feelings, it sets on fire the whole course of nature, . . . and you are then apt to set those on fire who are contending with you. When you feel as though you would burst, tell the old boiler to burst, and just laugh at the temptation to speak evil. If you will continue to do that, you will soon be so masters of yourselves as to be able, if not to tame, to control your tongues—able to speak when you ought, and to be silent when you ought (*DBY,* 269).

We want the spirit, knowledge, power and principle within us to govern and control our tempers; there is no danger of having too much [anger] if we will only control [it] by the Spirit of the Almighty. Every intelligent being on the earth is tempered for glory, beauty, excellency and knowledge here, and for immortality and eternal lives in the worlds to come. But every being who attains to this must be sanctified before God and be completely under the control of his Spirit. If I am thus controlled by the

Spirit of the Most High, I am a king. I am supreme so far as the control of self is concerned (*DBY,* 264–65).

We can control our speech.

If you first gain power to check your words, you will then begin to have power to check your judgment, and at length actually gain power to check your thoughts and reflections (*DBY,* 267–68).

You should succeed in bringing your tongues into subjection, so as never to let them speak evil, so that they will perfectly obey your judgment and the discretion God has given you, and are perfectly obedient to the will of the holy Gospel (*DBY,* 268).

We often hear people excuse themselves for their uncouth manners and offensive language, by remarking "I am no hypocrite," thus taking to themselves credit for that which is really no credit to them. When evil arises within me, let me throw a cloak over it, subdue it, instead of acting it out upon the false presumption that I am honest and no hypocrite. Let not thy tongue give utterance to the evil that is in thine heart, but command thy tongue to be silent until good shall prevail over the evil, until thy wrath has passed away and the good Spirit shall move thy tongue to blessings and words of kindness (*DBY,* 266).

If any are in the habit of taking the name of God in vain, cease doing so today, tomorrow and throughout the coming week, and so continue, and you will soon gain strength to overcome the habit entirely; you will gain power over your words (*DBY,* 268).

Some are in the habit of talking about their neighbors, of vending stories they know nothing about, only that Aunt Sally said that Cousin Fanny told Aunt Betsy that old Aunt Ruth said something or other, or somebody had had a dream; and by the time the story or dream reaches you, it has assumed the semblance of a fact, and you are very foolishly spending your time in talking about things that amount to nothing, or that you have no concern with. A report is started that such a one has done wrong, and, by the time it has gone its round, has become anointed with the salve of the backbiter and tale-bearer—become endowed with their spirit. One and another falls in with it and says, "That is true—your cause is just, you are exactly right, and the other is surely wrong," when they know nothing about the matter, thereby engendering entirely groundless ill feelings against each other. Before we condemn, we should wait until the heavens clearly indicate a fault in a father, brother, sister, wife, husband, or neighbor. And if heaven declares a fault, wait until the Holy Ghost manifests to you that such is a fault. Let the Father reveal to you that the person you are thinking or talking about is actually wrong. Traduce [expose to shame or blame by falsehood] no person. When you know what right is, and are capable of correcting a person that is wrong, then it is time enough for you to judge (DBY, 268).

There is no man or woman on the earth in the habit of stealing, but what can cease the practice . . . if they are disposed. And so with the liar, he can stop lying, and lie no more, and tell the truth. [He or she] only [needs] the will to do it, and [this will] enable the liar to be truthful, the thief to be honest, and the swearer to stop his evil speaking (DBY, 264).

While we have the privilege of speaking to each other, let us speak words of comfort and consolation. When you are influenced by the Spirit of holiness and purity, let your light shine; but if you are tried and tempted and buffeted by Satan, keep your thoughts to yourselves—keep your mouths closed; for speaking produces fruit, either of a good or evil character (DBY, 166).

There is an old maxim, and in many cases an excellent one. It is, "Think twice before you speak, and three times before you act." If we train ourselves to think what we are about to do, before we do it, and have understanding to know, and power to perform the good, we can thereby avoid . . . evil (DBY, 268).

It is also a precious gift, that some people seem to be possessed of, to have knowledge enough not to talk until they can say something to advantage and benefit to themselves, or others, or both (DBY, 268).

Suggestions for Study

We can control ourselves and submit to God's will.

- President Young taught that will is "a trait of the character of the Gods." He also said that our will is an endowment, or gift, from God. By what process does the will of man become Godlike? (See also Mosiah 3:19.) How can parents and leaders "rightly direct" the wills of children and others but "break not the spirit of any person"? How have your parents or leaders successfully guided your will in the right way?

- What does it mean to be "in the hands of God as clay in the hands of the potter"? How can we completely submit to the Lord's will and still maintain our individuality?

We can control ourselves until we bring everything "into subjection to the law of Christ."

- How does resisting one temptation increase our ability to resist all temptation? President Young taught that bringing our appetites "in subjection to the spirit" is necessary to "be raised to inherit eternal life." How does obeying our spiritual inclinations rather than our physical appetites prepare us for exaltation?

- What "choice gifts" does control of self prepare us to receive from God?

- Why must we have self-control before we can lead others?

- What do you think President Young meant when he taught that "the greatest endowment God ever gave to man is good, sound, solid sense to know how to govern ourselves"? How can we govern ourselves and at the same time submit to doing only the Father's will?

We can control our passions and emotions.

- What are some "rebellious passions" that we are to control? How can we successfully subdue such passions and actions?

- How do we distinguish between "righteous anger," such as shown by the Savior on occasions, and "wicked anger"? (See also 2 Nephi 1:26.)

- What are the results of giving way to our angry feelings? (See also James 3:5–6.) What was President Young's advice for controlling anger? How does submission to the Spirit help us control our anger?

We can control our speech.

- How can we "gain power to check [our] thoughts and reflections"?

- How did President Young counsel those who say they speak offensively to avoid being hypocritical?

- How might we control our tongues when we are tempted to (1) take the name of God in vain, (2) gossip about our neighbors, (3) find fault with or disgrace the reputation of someone else (see also D&C 136:23–24), or (4) embarrass or demean a family member or a friend? (See also D&C 52:16.)

- What should we do if we have unkind thoughts about others?

The Word of Wisdom teaches that grains are among the healthy foods
that are good for our bodies.

Living the Word of Wisdom

For President Brigham Young the gospel of Jesus Christ was a practical religion. In an 1867 letter to two of his sons serving missions, President Young praised the Saints in Salt Lake City for observing the Word of Wisdom: "The merchants on Whiskey St. can scarcely get enough day by day to pay their rents. The people manifest the strongest disposition we have ever witnessed to carry into effect the counsels which have been given respecting the Word of Wisdom and obedience in temporal as well as spiritual matters. There has been no coercion used, no covenants required. The principle has been set forth and the people seemed prepared to receive and carry it out willingly. Peace and good health prevail throughout the Territory" (LBY, 88). He taught that the Lord revealed the Word of Wisdom to improve the quality of our mortal lives, to make us more effective workers in God's earthly kingdom, and to help us to fill the full measure of our creation.

Teachings of Brigham Young

We believe the Word of Wisdom is a commandment from God.

When the school of the prophets was inaugurated, one of the first revelations given by the Lord to His servant Joseph was the Word of Wisdom. The members of that school were but a few at first, and the prophet commenced to teach them in doctrine to prepare them to go out into the world to preach the gospel unto all people. . . . The prophet began to instruct them how to live, that they might be the better prepared to perform the great work they were called to accomplish (*DNSW,* 25 Feb. 1868, 2).

Bishops, Elders of Israel, High Priests, Seventies, the Twelve Apostles, the First Presidency, and all the House of Israel, hearken ye, O my people! keep the word of the Lord, observe the Word of Wisdom, sustain one another, sustain the household of faith (*DBY,* 183).

I know that some say the revelations upon these points are not given by way of commandment. Very well, but we are commanded to observe every word that proceeds from the mouth of God (*DBY,* 182–83).

The Spirit whispers to me to call upon the Latter-day Saints to observe the Word of Wisdom, to let tea, coffee, and tobacco alone, and to abstain from drinking spirituous drinks. This is what the Spirit signifies through me. If the Spirit of God whispers this to his people through their leader, and they will not listen nor obey, what will be the consequences of their disobedience? Darkness and blindness of mind with regard to the things of God will be their lot; they will cease to have the spirit of prayer, and the spirit of the world will increase in them in proportion to their disobedience until they apostatize entirely from God and his ways (*DBY*, 183).

The constitution that a person has should be nourished and cherished; and whenever we take anything into the system to force and stimulate it beyond its natural capacity, it shortens life. I am physician enough to know that. . . . If you will follow this counsel, you will be full of life and health, and you will increase your intelligence, your joy, and comfort (*DBY*, 183).

This Word of Wisdom which has been supposed to have become stale, and not in force, is like all the counsels of God, in force as much today as it ever was. There is life, everlasting life in it—the life which now is and the life which is to come (*DBY*, 184).

The Word of Wisdom is an inspired health code.

This Word of Wisdom prohibits the use of hot drinks and tobacco. I have heard it argued that tea and coffee are not mentioned therein; that is very true; but what were the people in the habit of taking as hot drinks when that revelation was given? Tea and coffee. We were not in the habit of drinking water very hot, but tea and coffee—the beverages in common use (*DBY*, 182).

Instead of doing two days' work in one day, wisdom would dictate to [the Saints], that if they desire long life and good health, they must, after sufficient exertion, allow the body to rest before it is entirely exhausted. When exhausted, some argue that they need stimulants in the shape of tea, coffee, spirituous liquors, tobacco, or some of those narcotic substances which are often taken to goad on the lagging powers to greater exertions. But instead of these kind of stimulants they should recruit by rest. Work less, wear less, eat less, and we shall be a great deal wiser, healthier, and wealthier people than by taking the course we now do. It is difficult to find anything more healthy to drink than good cold water, such as flows down to us from springs and snows of our mountains. This is the beverage we should drink. It should be our drink at all times. . . . It may be remarked that some men who use spirituous liquors and tobacco are healthy, but I argue that they would be much more healthy if they did not use it, and then they are entitled to the blessings promised to those who observe the advice given in the "Word of Wisdom" (*DBY*, 187).

When we go on a trip to the settlements and stop at the brethren's houses, it is, "Brother Brigham, let us manifest our feelings towards you and your company." I tell them to do so, but give me a piece of Johnny-cake [cornbread]; I would rather have it than their pies and tarts and sweet meats. Let me have something that will sustain nature and leave my stomach and whole system clear to receive the Spirit of the Lord and be free from headache and pains of every kind (*DBY,* 189).

The Americans, as a nation, are killing themselves with their vices and high living. As much as a man ought to eat in half an hour they swallow in three minutes, gulping down their food like the [dog] under the table, which, when a chunk of meat is thrown down to it, swallows it before you can say "twice." If you want a reform, carry out the advice I have just given you. Dispense with your multitudinous dishes, and, depend upon it, you will do much towards preserving your families from sickness, disease and death (*DBY,* 189).

Do you know that it is your privilege so to live that your minds may all the time be perfectly within your control? Study to preserve your bodies in life and health, and you will be able to control your minds (*DBY,* 190).

The thinking part is the immortal or invisible portion, and it is that which performs the mental labor; then the tabernacle, which is formed and organized for that express purpose, brings about or effects the result of that mental labor. Let the body work with the mind, and let them both labor fairly together, and, with but few exceptions, you will have a strong-minded, athletic individual, powerful both physically and mentally (*DBY,* 191).

Be careful of your bodies; be prudent in laying out your energies, for when you are old you will need the strength and power you are now wasting. Preserve your lives. Until you know and practice this, you are not thoroughly good soldiers nor wise stewards (*DBY,* 193).

Then let us not trifle with our mission, by indulging in the use of injurious substances. These lay the foundation of disease and death in the systems of men, and the same are committed to their children, and another generation of feeble human beings is introduced into the world. Such children have insufficient bone, sinew, muscle, and constitution, and are of little use to themselves, or to their fellow creatures; they are not prepared for life (*DBY,* 185–86).

Observing the Word of Wisdom can help us better fill our life's purpose.

It is a piece of good counsel which the Lord desires his people to observe, that they may live on the earth until the measure of their creation is full. This is the object the Lord had in view in giving that Word of

Wisdom. To those who observe it he will give great wisdom and understanding, increasing their health, giving strength and endurance to the faculties of their bodies and minds until they shall be full of years upon the earth. This will be their blessing if they will observe his word with a good and willing heart and in faithfulness before the Lord (*DBY,* 184).

So we see that almost the very first teachings the first Elders of this Church received were as to what to eat, what to drink, and how to order their natural lives that they might be united temporally as well as spiritually. This is the great purpose which God has in view in sending to the world, by his servants, the Gospel of life and salvation (*DBY,* 186).

A man who indulges in any habit that is pernicious to the general good in its example and influence, is not only an enemy to himself but to the community so far as the influence of that habit goes. A man who would not sacrifice a pernicious habit for the good it would do the community is, to say the least of it, lukewarm in his desires and wishes for public and general improvement (*DBY,* 186).

Prepare to die is not the exhortation in this Church and Kingdom; but prepare to live is the word with us, and improve all we can in the life hereafter, wherein we may enjoy a more exalted condition of intelligence, wisdom, light, knowledge, power, glory, and exaltation. Then let us seek to extend the present life to the uttermost, by observing every law of health, and by properly balancing labor, study, rest, and recreation, and thus prepare for a better life. Let us teach these principles to our children, that, in the morning of their days, they may be taught to lay the foundation of health and strength and constitution and power of life in their bodies (*DBY,* 186).

Suggestions for Study

We believe the Word of Wisdom is a commandment from God.

- How does living the Word of Wisdom better prepare us to do the Lord's work?

- President Young said that "we are commanded to observe every word that proceeds from the mouth of God," including the Word of Wisdom. (See also D&C 89:2.) How has knowing that the Word of Wisdom is a commandment and not just good advice helped you to live according to its principles? What did President Young say would be the consequences of disobeying the Word of Wisdom?

- What do you think President Young meant when he said, "There is life, everlasting life in" the Word of Wisdom?

The Word of Wisdom is an inspired health code.

- According to President Young, what is the purpose of the Word of Wisdom? (See also 1 Corinthians 3:16–17; D&C 89; 93:35.)
- What was President Young's counsel for avoiding exhaustion? How can you apply the principles governing his counsel in your life?
- How does obedience to the Word of Wisdom "let the body work with the mind"? How can you benefit from doing this? How can the Word of Wisdom prepare us to receive the Spirit?
- President Young said, "Let us not trifle with our mission, by indulging in the use of injurious substances." How do such substances impede our mission?

Observing the Word of Wisdom can help us better fill our life's purpose.

- How does living according to the Word of Wisdom help to fulfill our creation, individually and as a Church?
- How does living the Word of Wisdom improve our spirituality? How does disobeying the Word of Wisdom damage the soul?
- Why are we able to serve more effectively when we observe the Word of Wisdom?
- How can you follow President Young's counsel to "extend the present life to the uttermost, by observing every law of health, and by properly balancing labor, study, rest, and recreation"? How does obeying the Word of Wisdom help us live more fully?

The Savior used the story of the good Samaritan to teach us how we
should love our neighbors.

Developing Christlike Attitudes toward Others

President Brigham Young saw the need for charity, "the pure love of Christ," to smooth the path of life. His actions toward Lucy Groves are an example of his kindness and service to others: On the westward trek, Lucy fell under the wheel of the family wagon, breaking her leg and several ribs. President Young set the broken leg and gave her a blessing. A few days later Lucy's daughter stumbled over the leg and broke it a second time. In agony at every step the oxen took, Lucy asked her husband to pull out of the wagon train and let the others go on without them. President Young declared he would not leave them at the side of the road in dangerous territory. He instructed several men to cut the legs off Lucy's poster bed and suspend the frame from the wagon bows so the mattress and springs would swing easily, like a hammock. President Young then renewed his blessing to Lucy and rode by her side for several days to make sure she had no further trouble. "With his gentle kind manner," wrote Lucy's grandson, "he won the love of Lucy and her posterity forever" (HRF, 157–58).

Teachings of Brigham Young

Clothe yourselves with the bond of charity.

We are not here isolated and alone, differently formed and composed of different material from the rest of the human race. We belong to and are part of this family, consequently we are under obligations one to another (*DBY*, 271).

The Latter-day Saints have got to learn that the interest of their brethren is their own interest, or they never can be saved in the celestial kingdom of God (*DBY*, 271).

The Lord will bless that people that is full of charity, kindness and good works (*DBY*, 280).

Charity. There is one virtue, attribute, or principle, which, if cherished and practiced by the Saints, would prove salvation to thousands upon thousands. I allude to charity, or love, from which proceed forgiveness, long suffering, kindness, and patience (*DNW,* 11 Jan. 1860, 1).

We should have charity; we should do all we can to reclaim the lost sons and daughters of Adam and Eve, and bring them back to be saved in the presence of our Father and God. If we do this, our charity will extend to the utmost extent that it is designed for the charity of God to extend in the midst of this people (*DBY,* 273).

Love your neighbor as yourself [see Matthew 22:39]; do unto others as you would that others should do unto you [see Matthew 6:12] (*DNW,* 20 Mar. 1852, 3).

It is folly in the extreme for persons to say that they love God; when they do not love their brethren [see 1 John 4:20] (*DBY,* 271).

We should commence our labors of love and kindness with the family to which we belong; and then extend them to others (*DBY,* 271).

Be steadfast, always abiding in the truth. Never encourage malice or hatred in your hearts; that does not belong to a Saint (*DBY,* 273).

Do I say, Love your enemies? Yes, upon certain principles. But you are not required to love their wickedness; you are only required to love them so far as concerns a desire and effort to turn them from their evil ways, that they may be saved through obedience to the Gospel (*DBY,* 272).

Do any of your neighbors do anything wrong? They do. People come here from different parts of the earth, to make this their adopted country, and the old residents expect them to at once conform to and adopt their manners, customs, and traditions, or they think the new comers are not worthy of their fellowship. In other words, "if every man, woman, and child does not act, think, and see as I do, they are sinners." It is very necessary that we have charity that will cover a multitude of what we may suppose to be sins (*DNW,* 11 Jan. 1860, 1).

It should be satisfactory evidence that you are in the path of life, if you love God and your brethren with all your hearts (*DBY,* 271).

Make sure the path for your own feet to walk to eternal life, and take as many with you as you can. Take them as they are, understand them as they are, and deal with them as they are; look at them as God looks at them (*DBY,* 274).

Kindness. Be kind to all as our Father in Heaven is kind. He sends his rain upon the just and the unjust; and gives the sun to shine upon the evil and the good [see Matthew 5:45]. So let our goodness extend to all the works of his hands, where we can; but do not yield to the spirit and influence of evil (*DBY,* 272).

Away with all little meannesses, and deal out kindness to all. Chasten, where chastening will answer best; but try persuasion before you try the rod (*DBY,* 277).

If you are ever called upon to chasten a person, never chasten beyond the balm you have within you to bind up [see D&C 121:43] (*DBY,* 278).

It has never altered my feelings towards individuals, as men or as women, whether they believe as I do or not. Can you live as neighbors with me? I can with you; and it is no particular concern of mine whether you believe with me or not (*DBY,* 278–79).

In our [dealings] with outsiders—do not call them Gentiles—let our example be such as is worthy of imitation; then every one among them who is honest will say, "I guess you are right, I think I will come and stay with you" (*DBY,* 279).

To be gentle and kind, modest and truthful, to be full of faith and integrity, doing no wrong is of God; goodness sheds a halo of loveliness around every person who possesses it, making their countenances beam with light, and their society desirable because of its excellency. They are loved of God, of holy angels, and of all the good on earth, while they are hated, envied, admired and feared by the wicked (*DBY,* 280).

Good Works. The genius of our religion is to have mercy upon all, do good to all, as far as they will let us do good to them (*DBY,* 272).

Let us have compassion upon each other, and let the strong tenderly nurse the weak into strength, and let those who can see guide the blind until they can see the way for themselves (*DBY,* 271).

Pray always for all who are within the reach of mercy (*DBY,* 279).

When you see a neighbor begin to slip, pray for him that he may have the Spirit of the Gospel as he once had. And if you feel this Spirit within yourselves, pray for an increase of that light you received when you first received the Gospel, and you will save yourself and house (*DBY,* 272).

Suppose that in this community there are ten beggars who beg from door to door for something to eat, and that nine of them are imposters who beg to escape work, and with an evil heart practice imposition upon the generous and sympathetic, and that only one of the ten who visit your doors is worthy of your bounty; which is best, to give food to the ten, to make sure of helping the truly needy one, or to repulse the ten because you do not know which is the worthy one? You will all say, administer charitable gifts to the ten, rather than turn away the only truly worthy and truly needy person among them. If you do this, it will make no difference in your blessings, whether you administer to worthy or unworthy persons, inasmuch as you give alms with a single eye to assist the truly needy (*DBY,* 274).

Condemn not; judge righteous judgment.

Judge not, that ye be not judged [see Matthew 7:1]. Let no man judge his fellow being, unless he knows he has the mind of Christ within him [see Moroni 7:16–18]. We ought to reflect seriously upon this point; how often it is said—"Such a person has done wrong, and he cannot be a Saint, or he would not do so." How do you know? . . . Do not judge such persons, for you do not know the design of the Lord concerning them; therefore, do not say they are not Saints. . . . A person who would say another is not a Latter-day Saint, for some trifling affair in human life proves that he does not possess the Spirit of God. Think of this, brethren and sisters; write it down, that you may refresh your memories with it; carry it with you and look at it often. If I judge my brethren and sisters, unless I judge them by the revelations of Jesus Christ, I have not the Spirit of Christ; if I had, I should judge no man (*DBY,* 277–78).

It floods my heart with sorrow to see so many Elders of Israel who wish everybody to come to their standard and be measured by their measure. Every man must be just so long, to fit their iron bedstead [see Isaiah 28:20], or be cut off to the right length; if too short, he must be stretched, to fill the requirement (*DBY,* 279).

If they see an erring brother or sister, whose course does not comport with their particular ideas of things, they conclude at once that he or she cannot be a Saint, and withdraw their fellowship, concluding that, if they are in the path of truth, others must have precisely their weight and dimensions (*DBY,* 279).

Let us be patient with one another. I do not altogether look at things as you do. My judgment is not in all things like yours, nor yours like mine. When you judge a man or woman, judge the intentions of the heart. It is not by words, particularly, nor by actions, that men will be judged in the great day of the Lord; but, in connection with words and actions, the sentiments and intentions of the heart will be taken, and by these will men be judged [see D&C 137:9] (*DBY,* 273–74).

Let all Latter-day Saints learn that the weaknesses of their brethren are not sins. When men or women undesignedly commit a wrong, do not attribute that to them as a sin. Let us learn to be compassionate one with another; let mercy and kindness soften every angry and fretful temper, that we may become long-suffering and beneficial in all our communications one with another (*DBY,* 273).

Serve the Lord, and try not to find fault with each other [see D&C 88:124]. Live so that you will not have any fault to find with yourselves, and never mind the faults of your brethren, for each person has enough of his own to attend to (*DBY,* 280).

Handcart companies were often supported by contributions from the Saints to the Perpetual Emigrating Fund, which President Young established to help the poorer Saints gather to Zion.

You may see, or think you see, a thousand faults in your brethren; yet they are organized as you are; they are flesh of your flesh, bone of your bone; they are of your Father who is in heaven; we are all His children, and should be satisfied with each other as far as possible (*DBY,* 271).

Respect one another; do not speak lightly of each other. Some, if they get a little pique against an individual, are disposed to cast him down to hell, as not worthy of a place upon earth. O fools! not to understand that those you condemn are the workmanship of God, as well as yourselves! God overlooks their weaknesses; and so far as they do good, they are as acceptable as we are. Thank God that you know better, and be full of mercy and kindness (*DBY,* 274).

God bless the humble and the righteous, and may He have compassion upon us because of the weakness that is in our nature. And considering the great weakness and ignorance of mortals, let us have mercy upon each other (*DBY,* 272).

The merciful man shall find mercy [see Matthew 5:7] (*DBY,* 273).

I am very thankful that it is not our province, in our present condition, to judge the world; if it were, we would ruin everything. We have not sufficient wisdom, our minds are not filled with the knowledge and power of God; the spirit needs to contend with the flesh a little more until it shall be successful in subduing its passions, until the whole soul is brought into perfect harmony with the mind and will of God. And we must also acquire the discretion that God exercises in being able to look into futurity, and to ascertain and know the results of our acts away in the future, even in eternity, before we will be capable of judging (*DBY,* 278).

Build faith in one another and avoid contention.

If we could obtain that faith and confidence in each other, and in our God, that when we ask a favor, we could do so with a full assurance and knowledge that we should receive, do you not perceive that it would lead us directly to do as we would be done by, in every transaction and circumstance of life? It would prompt us to do, not only as much as requested, but more. If your brother should request you to go with him a mile, you would go two; if he should sue you for your coat, you would give him your cloak also [see Matthew 5:40–41]. This principle prompts us to do all we can to promote the interest of each other, the cause of God on the earth, and whatever the Lord desires us to do; makes us ready and willing to perform it at once (*DBY,* 275).

But if we lack confidence in each other, and be jealous of each other, our peace will be destroyed. If we cultivate the principles of unshaken confidence in each other, our joy will be full (*DBY,* 275).

The work in which you and I have enlisted is to restore confidence in the minds of the people; and when I hear of circumstances transpiring in which brethren forfeit their word I regard it as a blot upon the character of this people. We should keep our word with each other. And if we have difficulty or misunderstanding with each other, talk it over, canvass the subject thoroughly, seriously and discreetly, and we shall find that all difficulties will be remedied in this way easier than any other; and we shall also find that nearly every difficulty that arises in the midst of the inhabitants of the earth, is through misunderstanding; and if a wrong in intent and design really exists, if the matter is canvassed over, the wrong-doer is generally willing to come to terms (*DBY,* 276).

When a difference of judgment exists between two parties, let them come together and lay their difficulties at each other's feet, laying themselves down in the cradle of humility, and say, "Brother (or sister) I want to do right; yea, I will even wrong myself, to make you right." Do you not think that a man or woman, acting in that manner towards his or her neighbor, would be justified by the law of righteousness? Their judgments come together, and they are agreed: there would, consequently, be no need of calling in a third person to settle the difference. After taking this course, if you cannot come together, then call in a third person and settle it (*DBY,* 276–77).

Contentions frequently arise to so alienating a degree that brethren have no faith in each other's honesty and integrity, when, perhaps, both parties have stumbled over a little, selfish, ignorant, personal misunderstanding, are carrying it to the extent of wishing to cut each other off from the Church. Very frequently such cases are presented before me. Unravel the difficulty, and it is found to have started in a trifling misunderstanding in relation to some small matter; all the trouble has arisen from a most frivolous cause. Avoid nursing misunderstandings into difficulties (*DBY*, 277).

If your neighbors talk about you, and you think that they do wrong in speaking evil of you, do not let them know that you ever heard a word, and conduct yourselves as if they always did right (*DBY*, 277).

Let us from this time forth live so as to create confidence in all men with whom we deal and come in contact; and treasure up each particle of confidence we obtain as one of the most precious possessions mortals can possibly possess. When by my good actions I have created confidence in my neighbor towards me, I pray that I may never do anything that will destroy it (*DBY*, 276).

Suggestions for Study

Clothe yourselves with the bond of charity.

- What "obligations one to another" do we have as members of the human family? How do our attitudes and actions toward others affect our own salvation? How can charity help us "reclaim the lost sons and daughters of Adam and Eve"?

- Why can't we truly love God if we do not love other people? Why is it vital to "look at [others] as God looks at them"? How can you increase your ability to do this?

- Charity, "the pure love of Christ," can be expressed in many ways (see, for example, Moroni 7:45–47). What are some expressions of charity that President Young emphasized? In what ways can you show more charity to those with whom you come in contact? How have others shown charity to you?

Condemn not; judge righteous judgment.

- What did President Young counsel about judging one another? How can you apply this counsel when interacting with those who may think or behave differently than you do?

- What can be the consequences if we judge our fellow human beings unrighteously? What can help us judge righteously if we are in a position where we must judge another person? (See also Moroni 7:14–18.) Why is it important for us to show mercy to each other?

- How can remembering that we are all children of God help us in our relationships with our family members, friends, and acquaintances?

Build faith in one another and avoid contention.

- How do we build faith and confidence in each other? What are the results if we do? What will happen if we do not have confidence in each other?

- What are some sources of contention? (See also 2 Nephi 26:32–33.) What is contention and how can we avoid it? What have you done in the past to successfully avoid contention? How did President Young counsel us to behave when disagreements or conflicts do arise?

- Why do you think President Young described the confidence of others as "one of the most precious possessions mortals can possibly possess"? What specific things can you do to increase other people's trust and confidence in you?

Thrift, Industry, and Self-Reliance

President Brigham Young knew the value of hard work in preparing the Saints to build the kingdom of God. He counseled the pioneers, "Instead of searching after what the Lord is going to do for us, let us inquire what we can do for ourselves" (DBY, 293). President Heber C. Kimball, President Young's friend and Counselor in the First Presidency, worked many days in the fields with him and later remembered that time as follows: "[Brother] Brigham and myself used to work hard, side by side, for fifty cents a day and board ourselves; we had seventy-five cents a day when we worked in the hayfield; we would work from sunrise to sunset, and until nine o'clock at night if there was sign of rain. We would rake and bind after a cradler for a bushel of wheat a day, and chop wood, with snow to our waist for eighteen cents a cord, and take our pay in corn at seventy-five cents a bushel" (DNW, 30 July 1862). President Young emphasized the importance of thrift, industry, and self-reliance, saying: "They who secure eternal life are doers of the word as well as hearers" (DBY, 290).

Teachings of Brigham Young

We should work hard and use our time wisely to serve our families and build up the kingdom of God.

What have we? Our time. Spend it as you will. Time is given to you; and when this is spent to the best possible advantage for promoting truth upon the earth, it is placed to our account, and blessed are you; but when we spend our time in idleness and folly it will be placed against us (*DBY,* 290).

We have to give an account of the days we spend in folly (*DBY,* 290).

Of the time that is allotted to man here on the earth there is none to lose or to run to waste. After suitable rest and relaxation there is not a day, hour or minute that we should spend in idleness, but every minute of every day of our lives we should strive to improve our minds and to increase the faith of the holy Gospel, in charity, patience, and good works, that we may grow in the knowledge of the truth as it is spoken and prophesied of and written about (*DBY,* 290).

Idleness and wastefulness are not according to the rules of heaven. Preserve all you can, that you may have abundance to bless your friends and your enemies (*DBY,* 290).

Everything connected with building up Zion requires actual, severe labor [see 2 Nephi 5:17]. It is nonsense to talk about building up any kingdom except by labor; it requires the labor of every part of our organization, whether it be mental, physical, or spiritual, and that is the only way to build up the Kingdom of God (*DBY,* 291).

Is not the upbuilding of the Kingdom of God on earth a temporal labor all the time? (*DBY,* 290–91).

This is the greatest wealth we possess—to know how to direct our labors rightly, spending every hour advantageously for the benefit of our wives and children and neighbors (*DBY,* 290).

We will have to go to work and get the gold out of the mountains to lay down, if we ever walk in streets paved with gold. The angels that now walk in their golden streets, and they have the tree of life within their paradise, had to obtain that gold and put it there. When we have streets paved with gold, we will have placed it there ourselves. When we enjoy a Zion in its beauty and glory, it will be when we have built it. If we enjoy the Zion that we now anticipate, it will be after we redeem and prepare it. If we live in the city of the New Jerusalem, it will be because we lay the foundation and build it. If we do not as individuals complete that work, we shall lay the foundation for our children and our children's children, as Adam has. If we are to be saved in an ark, as Noah and his family were, it will be because we build it. If the Gospel is preached to the nations, it is because the Elders of Israel . . . preach the Gospel to the uttermost parts of the earth (*DBY,* 291).

My faith does not lead me to think the Lord will provide us with roast pigs, bread already buttered, etc.; he will give us the ability to raise the grain, to obtain the fruits of the earth, to make habitations, to procure a few boards to make a box, and when harvest comes, giving us the grain, it is for us to preserve it—to save the wheat until we have one, two, five, or seven years' provisions on hand, until there is enough of the staff of life saved by the people to [provide] bread [for] themselves and those who will come here seeking for safety (*DBY,* 291–92).

The Lord has provided an abundance in the earth for our use.

I say to my brethren and sisters, come let us learn how to gather around us from the elements an abundance of every comfort of life, and convert

226

Cooperative stores in Salt Lake City around 1869. President Young encouraged home industry, thrift, and self-reliance among the Saints.

them to our wants and happiness [see D&C 59:18–20]. Let us not remain ignorant, with the ignorant, but let us show the ignorant how to be wise (*DBY,* 294).

The Lord has done his share of the work; he has surrounded us with elements containing wheat, meat, flax, wool, silk, fruit, and everything with which to build up, beautify and glorify the Zion of the last days, and it is our business to mould these elements to our wants and necessities, according to the knowledge we now have and the wisdom we can obtain from the heavens through our faithfulness. In this way will the Lord bring again Zion upon the earth, and in no other (*DBY,* 294).

It is our duty to be active and diligent in doing everything we can to sustain ourselves, to build up His Kingdom, to defend ourselves against our enemies, to lay our plans wisely, and to prosecute [perform] every method that can be devised to establish the Kingdom of God on the earth, and to sanctify and prepare ourselves to dwell in His presence (*DBY,* 294–95).

While we have a rich soil in this valley, and seed to put in the ground, we need not ask God to feed us, nor follow us round with a loaf of bread begging of us to eat it. He will not do it, neither would I, were I the Lord. We can feed ourselves here; and if we are ever placed in circumstances where we cannot, it will then be time enough for the Lord to work a miracle to sustain us (*DBY,* 294).

People are contending, quarreling, seeking how to get the advantage of each other, and how to get all the wealth there is in the world. . . . But suppose we go to work to gather up all that there is in the bosom and upon the surface of our mother earth and bring it into use, is there any lack? There is not, there is enough for all. Then do look at these things as they are, Latter-day Saints, and you who are not Latter-day Saints, look at things as they are. And I do hope and pray for your sakes, outsiders, and for the sakes of those who profess to be Latter-day Saints, that we shall have good peace for a time here, so that we can build our furnaces, open our mines, make our railroads, till the soil, follow our mercantile business uninterrupted; that we may attend to the business of beautifying the earth (*DBY,* 295).

We should be wise in using the resources the Lord has given us.

The riches of a kingdom or nation do not consist so much in the fulness of its treasury as in the fertility of its soil and the industry of its people (*DBY,* 297).

Time and the ability to labor are the capital stock of the whole world of mankind, and we are all indebted to God for the ability to use time to advantage and he will require of us a strict account of the disposition we make of this ability; and he will not only require an account of our acts, but our words and thoughts will also be brought into judgment (*DBY,* 301).

All the capital there is upon the earth is the bone and sinew of working-men and women. . . . Labor builds our meetinghouses, temples, court-houses, fine halls for music and fine schoolhouses; it is labor that teaches our children, and makes them acquainted with the various branches of education, that makes them proficient in their own language and in other languages, and in every branch of knowledge understood by the children of men (*DBY,* 300).

Never let anything go to waste. Be prudent, save everything, and what you get more than you can take care of yourselves, ask your neighbors to help you consume (*DBY,* 292).

Take things calm and easy, pick up everything, let nothing go to waste (*DBY,* 292).

Never consider that you have bread enough around you to suffer your children to waste a crust or a crumb of it. If a man is worth millions of bushels of wheat and corn, he is not wealthy enough to . . . sweep a single kernel of it into the fire; let it be eaten by something and pass again into the earth, and thus fulfil the purpose for which it grew. Remember it, do not waste anything, but take care of everything (*DBY,* 292).

It is to our advantage to take good care of the blessings God bestows upon us; if we pursue the opposite course, we cut off the power and glory God designs we should inherit. It is through our own carefulness, frugal-ity, and judgment which God has given us, that we are enabled to preserve our grain, our flocks and herds, . . . houses and lands, and increase them around us, continually gaining power and influence for ourselves as individuals and for the Kingdom of God as a whole (*DBY,* 292).

Use just enough of your earnings to make your bodies and your families happy and comfortable, and save the residue (*DBY,* 292).

If you wish to get rich, save what you get. A fool can earn money; but it takes a wise man to save and dispose of it to his own advantage (*DBY,* 292).

We should build good homes and create beautiful communities.

Let the people build good houses, plant good vineyards and orchards, make good roads, build beautiful cities in which may be found magnificent edifices for the convenience of the public, handsome streets skirted with shade trees, fountains of water, crystal streams, and every tree, shrub and flower that will flourish in this climate, to make our mountain home a paradise and our hearts wells of gratitude to the God of Joseph, enjoying it all with thankful hearts, saying constantly, "not mine but thy will be done, O Father" (*DBY,* 302).

Beautify your gardens, your houses, your farms; beautify the city. This will make us happy, and produce plenty. The earth is a good earth, the elements are good if we will use them for our own benefit, in truth and righteousness. Then let us be content, and go to with our mights to make ourselves healthy, wealthy, and beautiful, and preserve ourselves in the best possible manner, and live just as long as we can, and do all the good we can (*DBY,* 302).

Every improvement that we make not only adds to our comfort but to our wealth (*DBY,* 302).

It is your right, wives, to ask your husbands to set out beautiful shade and fruit trees, and to get you some vines and flowers with which to adorn the outside of your dwellings; and if your husbands have not time, get them yourselves and plant them out. Some, perhaps, will say, "Oh, I have nothing but a log house, and it is not worth that." Yes; it is worth it. Whitewash and plaster it up, and get vines to run over the door, so that everybody who passes will say, "What a lovely little cottage!" This is your privilege and I wish you to exercise yourselves in your own rights (*DBY,* 200).

Make good houses; learn how to build; become good mechanics and business men, that you may know how to build a house, a barn, or a store-house, how to make a farm, and how to raise stock, and take every care of it by providing proper shelter and every suitable convenience for keeping it through the winter; and prove yourselves worthy of the greater riches that will be committed to you than this valley and what it can produce (*DBY,* 302).

I have been into houses which have not had the least convenience for the women, not so much as a bench to set their water pails on, and they have to set them on the floor, and yet their husbands will sit there year after year, and never make so much improvement as a bench to set the pail on. Yet they have the ability, but they will not exercise it (*DBY,* 198–99).

Let the husband make an improvement upon his kitchen and pantry and upon his bedrooms for the benefit of his family, and improve his gardens, walks, etc., beautifying your habitations and their surroundings, making pavements and planting shade trees (*DBY,* 198).

We should be self-reliant as families and as a people.

We want you henceforth to be a self-sustaining [self-reliant] people [see D&C 78:14]. Hear it, O Israel! hear it, neighbors, friends and enemies, this is what the Lord requires of this people (*DBY,* 293).

William Carter plowing at his home, St. George, Utah, 1893.

Ye Latter-day Saints, learn to sustain yourselves. If you cannot obtain all you wish for today, learn to do without that which you cannot purchase and pay for; and bring your minds into subjection that you must and will live within your means (*DBY*, 293).

Who are deserving of praise? The persons who take care of themselves or the ones who always trust in the great mercies of the Lord to take care of them? It is just as consistent to expect that the Lord will supply us with fruit when we do not plant the trees; or that when we do not plow and sow and are saved the labor of harvesting, we should cry to the Lord to save us from want, as to ask him to save us from the consequences of our own folly, disobedience and waste (*DBY*, 293).

Implied faith and confidence in God is for you and me to do everything we can to sustain and preserve ourselves; and the community that works together, heart and hand, to accomplish this, their efforts will be like the efforts of one man (*DBY*, 293).

Brethren, learn. You have learned a good deal, it is true; but learn more; learn to sustain yourselves; lay up grain and flour, and save it against a day of scarcity. Sisters, do not ask your husbands to sell the last bushel of grain you have to buy something for you out of the stores, but aid your husbands in storing it up against a day of want, and always have a year's, or two, provision on hand (*DBY*, 293).

Instead of searching after what the Lord is going to do for us, let us inquire what we can do for ourselves (*DBY,* 293).

Whatever the Latter-day Saints have gained has been obtained by sheer wrestling and unconquerable resolution (*DBY,* 294).

Suggestions for Study

We should work hard and use our time wisely to serve our families and build up the kingdom of God.

- What was President Young's counsel about the use of "every minute of every day"? (See also Alma 34:33.) Why is time such a precious gift? What principles have helped you improve the way you spend your time?
- Why are idleness and wastefulness contrary to the "rules of heaven"? (See also Doctrine and Covenants 42:42.)
- Why will building Zion require all types of labor? In what ways must we labor mentally, physically, and spiritually to build Zion?

The Lord has provided an abundance in the earth for our use.

- How will the Lord "bring again Zion upon the earth"? In what specific ways can we help build Zion?
- President Young said that "in the bosom and upon the surface of our mother earth . . . there is enough for all." Why then do you think there is so much poverty in the world? What can we do in our families, Church organizations, and communities to share with each other what the Lord has given us? (See also Jacob 2:18–19; D&C 104:14–18.)

We should be wise in using the resources the Lord has given us.

- Why should we "not waste anything, but take care of everything"? How might we apply President Young's counsel on this subject to food storage and emergency preparedness?
- How do we "cut off the power and glory God designs we should inherit"?
- How can we apply President Young's counsel, "A fool can earn money; but it takes a wise man to save and dispose of it to his own advantage"?

We should build good homes and create beautiful communities.

- What did President Young say the Saints should do to make their "home a paradise and [their] hearts wells of gratitude"? What can we do to make our homes and communities more beautiful? (See also D&C 82:14.) How do beautiful surroundings help us physically, emotionally, and spiritually?

We should be self-reliant as families and as a people.

- What was President Young's advice about how to live within our means? Why are these simple guidelines sometimes difficult to follow? What are some specific ways we can ensure that we live within our means?

- Evaluate what President Young said about sustaining ourselves, and consider what you have done to ensure that your family will be self-reliant in a time of need. Make a plan for increasing your self-reliance in your family and community.

- How is diligent labor a demonstration of faith? What is the relationship between self-reliance and relying on the merits of Christ?

- President Young urged the Saints to take care of themselves, but he also counseled them to unite in their communities. How do our efforts to sustain ourselves and build our communities work together? How have the efforts of others helped you to be more self-sustaining?

President Brigham Young taught that temporal wealth should be
dedicated to building up the kingdom of God.

Temporal Wealth and the Kingdom of God

President Brigham Young was a practical man who was not wasteful and who worked hard to provide material comforts for his family and for others. He built homes, businesses, and farms. But he did not set his heart on worldly things, warning that "our affections are often too highly placed upon paltry, perishable objects" (DNW, 16 July 1856, 2). "I know that the things of this world, from beginning to end, . . . make little or no difference in the happiness of an individual" (DNW, 11 Jan. 1860, 1). President Young taught that temporal wealth should be dedicated to building up the kingdom of God.

Teachings of Brigham Young

We should set our hearts on the things of God rather than on worldly things.

When I cast my eyes upon the inhabitants of the earth and see the weakness, and I may say, the height of folly in the hearts of the kings, rulers, and the great, and those who should be wise and good and noble; when I see them grovelling in the dust; longing, craving, desiring, contending for the things of this life, I think, O foolish men, to set your hearts on the things of this life! . . . A man or a woman who places the wealth of this world and the things of time in the scales against the things of God and the wisdom of eternity, has no eyes to see, no ears to hear, no heart to understand (*DBY*, 306–7).

I look around among the world of mankind and see them grabbing, scrambling, contending, and every one seeking to aggrandize himself, and to accomplish his own individual purposes, passing the community by, walking upon the heads of his neighbors—all are seeking, planning, contriving in their wakeful hours, and when asleep dreaming, "How can I get the advantage of my neighbor? How can I spoil him, that I may ascend the ladder of fame?" This is entirely a mistaken idea. . . . The man who seeks honor and glory at the expense of his fellow-men is not worthy of the society of the intelligent (*DBY*, 307).

The possession of wealth alone does not produce happiness, although it will produce comfort, when it can be exchanged for the essentials and luxuries of life. When wealth is obtained by purloining, or in any other unfair and dishonorable way, fear of detection and punishment robs the possessor of all human happiness. When wealth is honorably obtained by man, still the possession of it is embittered by the thought that death will soon strip them of it and others will possess it. What hopes have they in the future, after they get through with this sorrowful world? They know nothing about the future; they see nothing but death and hell. Solid comfort and unalloyed joy are unknown to them (*DBY,* 314).

The possession of all the gold and silver in the world would not satisfy the cravings of the immortal soul of man. The gift of the Holy Spirit of the Lord alone can produce a good, wholesome, contented mind. Instead of looking for gold and silver, look to the heavens and try to learn wisdom until you can organize the native elements for your benefit; then, and not until then, will you begin to possess the true riches (*DBY,* 305).

There is any amount of property, and gold and silver in the earth and on the earth, and the Lord gives to this one and that one—the wicked as well as the righteous—to see what they will do with it, but it all belongs to him. He has handed over a goodly portion to this people, and, through our faith, patience and industry, we have made us good, comfortable homes here, and there are many who are tolerably well off. . . . But it is not ours, and all we have to do is to try and find out what the Lord wants us to do with what we have in our possession, and then go and do it. If we step beyond this, or to the right or to the left, we step into an illegitimate train of business. Our legitimate business is to do what the Lord wants us to do with that which he bestows upon us, and dispose of it just as he dictates, whether it is to give all, one-tenth, or the surplus (*DBY,* 305).

Men and women who are trying to make themselves happy in the possession of wealth or power will miss it, for nothing short of the Gospel of the Son of God can make the inhabitants of the earth happy, and prepare them to enjoy heaven here and hereafter (*DBY,* 315).

The love of money leads to disappointment and loss of the Spirit.

Do you not know that the possession of your property is like a shadow, or the dew of the morning before the noonday sun, that you cannot have any assurance of its control for a single moment! It is the unseen hand of Providence that controls it (*DBY,* 305–6).

We cannot trust to the certainty of mortal possessions; they are transitory, and a dependence upon them will plunge into hopeless disappointment all those who trust in them (*DBY,* 306).

How the Devil will play with a man who so worships gain! (*DBY*, 306).

I am more afraid of covetousness in our Elders than I am of the hordes of hell (*DBY*, 306).

Those who are covetous and greedy, anxious to grasp the whole world, are all the time uneasy, and are constantly laying their plans and contriving how to obtain this, that, and the other (*DBY*, 306).

Men are greedy for the vain things of this world. In their hearts they are covetous. It is true that the things of this world are designed to make us comfortable, and they make some people as happy as they can be here; but riches can never make the Latter-day Saints happy. Riches of themselves cannot produce permanent happiness; only the Spirit that comes from above can do that (*DBY*, 306).

The Latter-day Saints who turn their attention to money-making soon become cold in their feelings toward the ordinances of the house of God. They neglect their prayers, become unwilling to pay any donations; the law of tithing gets too great a task for them; and they finally forsake their God, and the providences of heaven seem to be shut from them—all in consequence of this lust after the things of this world, which will certainly perish in handling, and in their use they will fade away and go from us (*DBY*, 315).

Patient labor brings temporal possessions and eternal riches.

To possess this world's goods is not in reality wealth, it is not riches, it is nothing more nor less than that which is common to all men, to the just and the unjust, to the Saint and to the sinner. The sun rises upon the evil and the good; the Lord sends his rain upon the just and upon the unjust [see Matthew 5:45]; this is manifest before our eyes, and in our daily experience. Old King Solomon, the wise man, says, the race is not to the swift, nor the battle to the strong, neither riches to men of wisdom [see Ecclesiastes 9:11]. The truth of this saying comes within our daily observation. . . . The weak, trembling, and feeble are the ones frequently who gain the battle; and the ignorant, foolish, and unwise will blunder into wealth (*DBY*, 308).

True wealth consists in the skill to produce conveniences and comforts from the elements. All the power and dignity that wealth can bestow is a mere shadow, the substance is found in the bone and sinew of the toiling millions. Well directed labor is the true power that supplies our wants. It gives regal grandeur to potentates, education and supplies to religious and political ministers, and supplies the wants of the thousands of millions of earth's sons and daughters (*DBY*, 309).

One-third or one-fourth of the time that is spent to procure a living would be sufficient, if your labor were rightly directed. People think they are going to get rich by hard work—by working sixteen hours out of the twenty-four; but it is not so. A great many of our brethren can hardly spend time to go to meeting. Six days is more time than we need to labor (*DBY,* 311).

This is the counsel I have for the Latter-day Saints today. Stop, do not be in a hurry. I do not know that I could find a man in our community but what wishes wealth, would like to have everything in his possession that would conduce to his comfort and convenience. Do you know how to get it? "Well," replies one, "if I do not, I wish I did; but I do not seem to be exactly fortunate—fortune is somewhat against me." I will tell you the reason of this—you are in too much of a hurry; you do not go to meeting enough, you do not pray enough, you do not read the Scriptures enough, you do not meditate enough, you are all the time on the wing, and in such a hurry that you do not know what to do first. This is not the way to get rich. I merely use the term "rich" to lead the mind along, until we obtain eternal riches in the celestial kingdom of God. Here we wish for riches in a comparative sense, we wish for the comforts of life. If we desire them let us take a course to get them. Let me reduce this to a simple saying—one of the most simple and homely that can be used—"Keep your dish right side up," so that when the shower of porridge does come, you can catch your dish full (*DBY,* 310).

When [individuals] act upon the principles which will secure to them eternal salvation, they are sure of obtaining all their hearts' desire, sooner or later; if it does not come today, it may come tomorrow; if it does not come in this time, it will in the next (*DBY,* 309).

We should be self-reliant and share our resources with the poor.

The poor are the people of God, and they shall inherit the earth (*DBY,* 316).

The man who is hungry and destitute has as good a right to my food as any other person, and I should feel as happy in associating with him, if he had a good heart, as with those who have an abundance, or with the princes of the earth. They all are esteemed by me, not according to the wealth and position they hold, but according to the character they have (*DBY,* 317).

The Lord's poor do not forget their covenants, while the Devil's poor pay no regard to their promises (*DBY,* 317).

Let the poor be honest, let the rich be liberal, and lay their plans to assist the poor, to build up the Kingdom of God, and at the same time enrich themselves, for that is the way to build up God's Kingdom (*DBY,* 317).

If the poor had all the surplus property of the rich many of them would waste it on the lusts of the flesh, and destroy themselves in using it. For this reason the Lord does not require the rich to give all their substance to the poor. It is true that when the young man came to Jesus to know what he must do to be saved, he told him, finally, "sell all that thou hast and distribute unto the poor, and thou shalt have treasure in heaven, and come, follow me;" and a great many think that he told the young man to give away all that he had, but Jesus did not require any such thing, neither did he say so, but simply, "distribute to the poor" [see Luke 18:18–23] (*DBY,* 317–18).

It is a disgrace to every man and woman that has sense enough to live, not to take care of their own relatives, their own poor, and plan for them to do something they are able to do (*DBY,* 318).

We should devote our temporal wealth to building up the kingdom of God.

What are riches for? For blessings, to do good. Then let us dispense that which the Lord gives us to the best possible use for the building up of his Kingdom, for the promotion of the truth on the earth, that we may see and enjoy the blessings of the Zion of God here upon this earth (*DBY,* 307).

If, by industrious habits and honorable dealings, you obtain thousands or millions, little or much, it is your duty to use all that is put in your possession, as judiciously as you have knowledge, to build up the Kingdom of God on the earth (*DBY,* 313–14).

If we possessed hundreds of millions of coin and devoted that means to building up the Kingdom of God and doing good to his creatures, with an eye single to his glory, we would be as much blessed and as much entitled to salvation as the poor beggar that begs from door to door; the faithful rich man is as much entitled to the revelations of Jesus Christ as is the faithful poor man (*DBY,* 314).

We must watch and pray, and look well to our walk and conversation, and live near to our God, that the love of this world may not choke the precious seed of truth, and feel ready, if necessary, to offer up all things, even life itself, for the Kingdom of Heaven's sake (*DBY,* 314).

Look out, ye men of Israel, and be careful that you love not the world or the things of the world in their present state, and in your loftiness and pride, forget the Lord your God. We ought to care no more for the silver and the gold, and the property that is so much sought for by the wicked world, than for the soil or the gravel upon which we tread (*DBY,* 314).

Though I possessed millions of money and property, that does not excuse me from performing the labor that it is my calling to perform, so far as I have strength and ability, any more than the poorest man in the community is excused. The more we are blessed with means, the more we are blessed with responsibility; the more we are blessed with wisdom and ability, the more we are placed under the necessity of using that wisdom and ability in the spread of righteousness, the subjugation of sin and misery, and the amelioration of the condition of mankind. The man that has only one talent and the man that has five talents have responsibility accordingly [see Matthew 25:14–30]. If we have a world of means, we have a world of responsibility (*DBY,* 315).

Suggestions for Study

We should set our hearts on the things of God rather than on worldly things.

- Why is it foolish to set our hearts on the things of this world? How can we set our hearts on the things of God?

- According to President Young, why are some blessed with riches? What dangers await those who fail to "do what the Lord wants [them] to do with that which he bestows upon [them]"? How can you know whether you are following an "illegitimate train of business"? What experiences have you had in sharing your temporal possessions as you have tried to live the gospel?

The love of money leads to disappointment and loss of the Spirit.

- Why does dependence on material wealth lead to disappointment? What evidence do you see that we should share President Young's concern about covetousness in the hearts of the people? How can we avoid such problems?

- What happens to those who "turn their attention to money-making"? How does a wrong devotion to money turn people away from the temple, prayer, and tithing?

Patient labor brings temporal possessions and eternal riches.

- What is "true wealth"? (See also D&C 6:7.)
- What was President Young's counsel to those who spend excessive amounts of time trying to obtain earthly possessions?
- What must we do to obtain "eternal riches in the celestial kingdom of God"?
- President Young said: "Do not be in a hurry. . . . This is not the way to get rich." What do you think he meant? How can you apply his counsel in your life?

We should be self-reliant and share our resources with the poor.

- What should be our attitude about helping the poor? What does the Lord require from the poor? from the rich? (See also Mosiah 4:16–28.)
- Why is character more important than temporal wealth?
- What is our responsibility to family members who are in need?

We should devote our temporal wealth to building up the kingdom of God.

- What are the responsibilities of those who receive temporal wealth?
- How can both the rich and the poor contribute generously to building the kingdom? What blessings are in store for those who do so?

Photograph of Elder Thomas C. Griggs, a missionary to the British Isles, in 1880.

Missionary Work

Few gave to the cause of missionary work as did President Brigham Young. The description of his arrival in Kirtland, Ohio—after serving a mission for about a year—is a tender account of the sacrifice he had made for this work: "When we arrived in Kirtland [in September 1833], if any man that ever did gather with the Saints was any poorer than I was—it was because he had nothing. . . . I had two children to take care of—that was all. I was a widower. 'Brother Brigham, had you any shoes?' No; not a shoe to my foot, except a pair of borrowed boots. I had no winter clothing, except a homemade coat that I had had three or four years. 'Any pantaloons?' No. 'What did you do? Did you go without?' No; I borrowed a pair to wear till I could get another pair. I had travelled and preached and given away every dollar of my property. I was worth a little property when I started to preach. . . . I had traveled and preached until I had nothing left to gather with; but Joseph said: 'come up'; and I went up the best I could" (DNSW, 9 Mar. 1867, 2).

Teachings of Brigham Young

The gospel will be preached to all people.

The Lord has called me to this work, and I feel as though I will do it. We will send the Gospel to the nations; and when one nation turns us away we will go to another and gather up the honest in heart, and the rest we care not for until we come on Mount Zion as saviors, to attend to the ordinances of the house of God for them [see Obadiah 1:21] (*DBY,* 319).

The Gospel must be preached to the world, that the wicked may be left without excuse (*DBY,* 319).

It is necessary that all have the privilege of receiving or rejecting eternal truth, that they may be prepared to be saved, or be prepared to be damned (*DBY,* 319).

Our Father in Heaven, Jesus, our Elder Brother and the Savior of the world, and the whole heavens, are calling upon this people to prepare to save the nations of the earth, also the millions who have slept without the Gospel (*DBY,* 319).

The Lord has restored the Priesthood in our day for the salvation of Israel. Does he design to save anybody else? Yes; he will save the House of Esau, and I hope to live until I see Mount Zion established, and saviors come up to save those poor, miserable beings who are continually persecuting us—all who have not sinned against the Holy Ghost. Our labor is to save ourselves, to save the House of Israel, to save the House of Esau, and all the Gentile nations—every one that can be saved (*DBY,* 319).

I shall be very happy when I can know that . . . the people on every island and continent, both the high and the low, the ignorant and intelligent, have received the words of eternal life, and have had bestowed upon them the power of the eternal Priesthood of the Son of God (*DBY,* 320).

The day will come when the Gospel will be presented to the kings and queens and great ones of the earth; but it will be presented with a different influence from that with which it has been presented to the poor, but it will be the same Gospel. We shall not present any other Gospel; it is the same from everlasting to everlasting (*DBY,* 320).

The Elders have also preached through the different nations of Europe so far as they were allowed to do so. In some countries the law would not permit them; but the Lord will yet revolutionize those nations until the door will be opened and the Gospel will be preached to all (*DBY,* 320).

We gather the poorest of the people, the unlearned, and a few of the learned; but generally, we gather those who are poor, who wish to be redeemed; who feel the oppression the high and the proud have made them endure; they have felt a wish to be delivered, and consequently their ears were open to receive the truth. Take those who are in the enjoyment of all the luxuries of this life, and their ears are stopped up; they cannot hear (*DBY,* 321).

And when you are called to preach the Gospel on foreign missions, take a course to save every person. There is no man or woman within the pale of saving grace but that is worth saving. There is no intelligent being, except those who have sinned against the Holy Ghost, but that is worth, I may say, all the life [efforts] of an Elder to save in the Kingdom of God (*DBY,* 321).

Missionaries should focus their minds and hearts on their missions and labor earnestly to bring souls to Christ.

There is neither man or woman in this Church who is not on a mission. That mission will last as long as they live, and it is to do good, to promote righteousness, to teach the principles of truth, and to prevail upon themselves and everybody around them to live those principles that they may obtain eternal life (*DBY,* 322).

When I came into this Church, I started right out as a missionary, and took a text, and began to travel on a circuit. Truth is my text, the Gospel of salvation my subject, and the world my circuit (*DBY,* 322).

We do not wish a man to enter on a mission, unless his soul is in it (*DBY,* 322).

The brethren who have been called upon foreign missions we expect to respond to the call cheerfully (*DBY,* 322).

Go forth and preach the Gospel, gain an experience, learn wisdom, and walk humbly before your God, that you may receive the Holy Ghost to guide and direct you, and teach you all things past, present, and to come (*DBY,* 322).

Go trusting in God, and continue to trust in him, and he will open your way and multiply blessings upon you, and your souls will be satisfied with his goodness. I cannot promise you any good in taking an unrighteous course; your lives must be examples of good works (*DBY,* 322).

I would like to impress upon the minds of the brethren, that he who goes forth in the name of the Lord, trusting in him with all his heart, will never want for wisdom to answer any question that is asked him, or to give any counsel that may be required to lead the people in the way of life and salvation, and he will never be confounded worlds without end. Go in the name of the Lord, trust in the name of the Lord, lean upon the Lord, and call upon the Lord fervently and without ceasing, and pay no attention to the world. You will see plenty of the world—it will be before you all the time—but if you live so as to possess the Holy Ghost you will be able to understand more in relation to it in one day than you could in a dozen days without it, and you will at once see the difference between the wisdom of men and the wisdom of God, and you can weigh things in the balance and estimate them at their true worth (*DBY,* 323).

If the Elders cannot go with clean hands and pure hearts, they had better stay here. Do not go thinking, when you arrive at the Missouri River, at the Mississippi, at the Ohio, or at the Atlantic, that then you will purify yourselves; but start from here with clean hands and pure hearts, and be pure from the crown of the head to the soles of your feet; then live so every hour [see Psalm 24:4]. Go in that manner, and in that manner labor, and return again as clean as a piece of pure white paper. This is the way to go; and if you do not do that, your hearts will ache (*DBY,* 323).

The travels and labors of the Elders about to go on missions will throw them into positions which will cause them to seek unto the Lord. They need to live their religion, to go forth with pure hearts and clean hands, and then preach the Gospel by the power of God sent down from heaven. They should touch not and taste not of sin, and when they return they should come pure and clean, ready to meet the Saints with open countenances (*DBY,* 325).

If you go on a mission to preach the Gospel with lightness and frivolity in your hearts, looking for this and that, and to learn what is in the world, and not having your minds riveted—yes, I may say riveted—on the cross of Christ, you will go and return in vain. Go forth weeping, bearing precious seed, full of the power of God, and full of faith to heal the sick even by the touch of your hand, rebuking and casting out foul spirits, and causing the poor among men to rejoice, and you will return bringing your sheaves with you [see Psalm 126:5–6]. Let your minds be centered on your missions and labor earnestly to bring souls to Christ (*DBY*, 325).

Dedicate them [your loved ones] to the Lord God of Israel, and leave them at home; and when you are in England, or among other nations, no matter where, when you pray for your families, pray for them . . . and do not bring them close to you, as though they were in your carpetbag. Pray for them where they are. You must feel—if they live, all right; if they die, all right; if I die, all right; if I live, all right; for we are the Lord's, and we shall soon meet again (*DBY*, 324).

When men enjoy the spirit of their missions and realize their calling and standing before the Lord and the people, it constitutes the happiest portions of their lives (*DBY*, 328).

The Spirit, not logic or debate, converts people to the gospel of Jesus Christ.

I had only traveled a short time to testify to the people, before I learned this one fact, that you might prove doctrine from the Bible till doomsday, and it would merely convince a people, but would not convert them. You might read the Bible from Genesis to Revelation, and prove every iota that you advance, and that alone would have no converting influence upon the people. Nothing short of a testimony by the power of the Holy Ghost would bring light and knowledge to them—bring them in their hearts to repentance. Nothing short of that would ever do. You have frequently heard me say that I would rather hear an Elder, either here or in the world, speak only five words accompanied by the power of God, and they would do more good than to hear long sermons without the Spirit. That is true, and we know it (*DBY*, 330).

Let one go forth who is careful to prove logically all he says by numerous quotations from the revelations, and let another travel with him who can say, by the power of the Holy Ghost, Thus saith the Lord, and tell what the people should believe—what they should do—how they should live, and teach them to yield to the principles of salvation,—though he may not be capable of producing a single logical argument, though he may tremble under a sense of his weakness, cleaving to the Lord for strength, as such

Missionaries of the Church in Echo Canyon, Utah, 1867. Early missionaries taught the gospel in England, Europe, and the islands of the Pacific Ocean.

men generally do, you will invariably find that the man who testifies by the power of the Holy Ghost will convince and gather many more of the honest and upright than will the merely logical reasoner (*DBY,* 330).

Debate and argument have not that saving effect that has testifying to the truth as the Lord reveals it to the Elder by the Spirit. I think you will all agree with me in this; at least, such is my experience. I do not wish to be understood as throwing a straw in the way of the Elders storing their minds with all the arguments they can gather to urge in defense of their religion, nor do I wish to hinder them in the least from learning all they can with regard to religions and governments. The more knowledge the Elders have the better (*DBY,* 330).

The spirit of truth will do more to bring persons to light and knowledge, than flowery words (*DBY,* 333).

The preacher needs the power of the Holy Ghost to deal out to each heart a word in due season, and the hearers need the Holy Ghost to bring forth the fruits of the preached word of God to his glory [see D&C 50:17–22] (*DBY,* 333).

No man ever preached a Gospel sermon, except by the gift and power of the Holy Ghost sent down from heaven. Without this power, there is no light in the preaching (*DBY,* 333).

If an Elder in preaching the Gospel, does not feel that he has the power to preach life and salvation, and legally to administer the ordinances, and that, too, by the power of God, he will not fill his mission to his own credit, nor to the good of the people, and the advancement and honor of the Kingdom of God. From all I can read, from all I can gather, from the revelations from God to man, and from the revelations of the Spirit to me, no man can successfully preach the Gospel and be owned, blessed, and acknowledged by the heavens, unless he preaches by the power of God through direct revelation (*DBY,* 336).

Continue to labor faithfully and keep the spirit of preaching and the gospel.

I wish to make this request: that the Elders who return from missions consider themselves just as much on a mission here as in England or in any other part of the world (*DBY,* 328).

We frequently call the brethren to go on missions to preach the Gospel, and they will go and labor as faithfully as men can do, fervent in spirit, in prayer, in laying on hands, in preaching to and teaching the people how to be saved. In a few years they come home, and throwing off their coats and hats, they will say, "Religion, stand aside, I am going to work now to get something for myself and my family." This is folly in the extreme. When a man returns from a mission where he has been preaching the Gospel he ought to be just as ready to come to this pulpit to preach as if he were in England, France, Germany, or on the islands of the sea. And when he has been at home a week, a month, a year, or ten years, the spirit of preaching and the spirit of the Gospel ought to be within him like a river flowing forth to the people in good words, teachings, precepts, and examples. If this is not the case he does not fill his mission (*DBY,* 328–29).

Come home with your heads up. Keep yourselves clean, from the crowns of your heads to the soles of your feet; be pure in heart,—otherwise you will return bowed down in spirit and with a fallen countenance, and will feel as though you never could rise again (*DBY,* 328).

Those faithful Elders who have testified of this work to thousands of people on the continents and islands of the seas will see the fruits of their labors, whether they have said five words or thousands. They may not see these fruits immediately, and perhaps, in many cases, not until the Millennium; but the savor of their testimony will pass down from father to son (*DBY,* 329).

Suggestions for Study

The gospel will be preached to all people.

- President Young said that when the gospel would be preached to kings and queens, it would be "presented with a different influence from that with which it has been presented to the poor." Why do different people respond to different teaching methods? How can we adapt our teaching methods to teach different people without compromising the truths of the gospel?

- President Young stated that the Lord would "revolutionize those nations" whose laws would not permit the gospel to be taught. How is this prophecy being fulfilled?

- According to President Young, who "is worth saving"? (See also D&C 18:10–16.)

Missionaries should focus their minds and hearts on their missions and labor earnestly to bring souls to Christ.

- According to President Young, every man and woman in this Church is on a mission. What are our responsibilities? What specific actions have brought you or others success in your missionary efforts? What have you learned from your missionary efforts that will help you become more effective in inviting people to come unto Christ? (See also Moroni 10:32.)

- President Young taught that missionaries should have their souls in the work. Based on what you have read in this chapter, what does that mean?

- What did President Young promise those who would preach the gospel and trust in God? Why should we seek the companionship of the Holy Ghost as we share the gospel?

- Why is it important that missionaries be clean before they begin their full-time service? What was President Young's counsel regarding missionaries being worthy while they serve and when they return?

- Why should missionaries have their minds "riveted" on our Savior, Jesus Christ? What was President Young's counsel to full-time missionaries who are dealing with homesickness?

The Spirit, not logic or debate, converts people to the gospel of Jesus Christ.

- Why are missionaries who testify of the gospel by the power of the Holy Ghost more effective than those who teach only with logic and reason? Why is debating an ineffective method of sharing the gospel?
- Why is there no light in the preaching of those who do not have the Holy Ghost with them?
- What did President Young promise those who preach "by the power of God through direct revelation" and trust in Him?

Continue to labor faithfully and keep the spirit of preaching and the gospel.

- Why is it "folly in the extreme" for missionaries to put aside their religion when they return home?
- When we are released from a calling, how can we keep "the spirit of preaching and the spirit of the Gospel . . . like a river flowing forth to the people in good words, teachings, precepts, and examples"?
- What did President Young promise faithful missionaries who testified of the Lord's work?

Strengthening the Saints through the Gifts of the Spirit

As a young man, Brigham Young earnestly sought a religion in which all the gifts of the gospel were manifest as recorded in the New Testament. Before his baptism he received a powerful testimony of the Church when the Holy Ghost illuminated his understanding (see DNW, 9 Feb. 1854, 4). During his first meeting with Joseph Smith in Kirtland, Brigham Young was blessed with the gift of tongues (see MHBY-1, 4–5). Although that was a rare occasion in his life, he always rejoiced in the diversity of spiritual gifts poured out on him and the Latter-day Saints. "If we have the religion of the Savior we are entitled to the blessings precisely as they were anciently. Not that all had visions, not that all had dreams, not that all had the gift of tongues or the interpretation of tongues, but every man received according to his capacity and the blessing of the Giver" (DNW, 27 Feb. 1856, 3).

Teachings of Brigham Young

The Lord gives gifts of the Spirit to strengthen and bless us, our families, and the Church.

The gifts of the Gospel are given to strengthen the faith of the believer (*DBY,* 161).

We are asked if signs follow the believer in our day as in days of old. We answer they do. The blind see, the lame leap, the deaf hear, the gift of prophecy is manifest, also the gift of healing, the gift of revelation, the gift of tongues and the interpretation of tongues. Jesus said that these signs should follow them that believe [see Mark 16:17]. His Church and Kingdom always have these signs which follow the believer in all ages when the true Church is in existence (*DNSW,* 19 May 1868, 1).

I have already said that Christ set in his Church Apostles and Prophets; he also set in his Church evangelists, pastors and teachers; also the gifts of the Spirit, such as diverse tongues, healing the sick, discernment of spirits, and various other gifts. Now, I would ask the whole world, who has

251

received revelation that the Lord has discontinued these offices and gifts in his Church? I have not. I have had revelation that they should be in the Church, and that there is no [true] Church without them (*DBY,* 136).

Suppose you obey the ordinances of the Gospel, and do not speak in tongues today, never mind that. Suppose you do not have the spirit of prophecy, no matter. Suppose you do not receive any particular gift attended by the rushing of a mighty wind, as on the day of Pentecost, there is not particular necessity that you should. On the day of Pentecost there was special need for it, it was a peculiarly trying time. Some special and powerful manifestation of the power of the Almighty was necessary to open the eyes of the people and let them know that Jesus has paid the debt, and they had actually crucified him who, by his death, had become the Savior of the world. It required this at that time to convince the people (*DBY,* 161–62).

Faith. When you believe the principles of the Gospel and attain unto faith, which is a gift of God, he adds more faith, adding faith to faith. He bestows faith upon his creatures as a gift; but his creatures inherently possess the privilege of believing the gospel to be true or false (*DBY,* 154).

The Gift of Healing. I am here to testify to hundreds of instances of men, women, and children being healed by the power of God, through the laying on of hands, and many I have seen raised from the gates of death, and brought back from the verge of eternity; and some whose spirits had actually left their bodies, returned again. I testify that I have seen the sick healed by the laying on of hands, according to the promise of the Savior (*DBY,* 162).

When I lay hands on the sick, I expect the healing power and influence of God to pass through me to the patient, and the disease to give way. I do not say that I heal everybody I lay hands on; but many have been healed under my administration (*DBY,* 162).

When we are prepared, when we are holy vessels before the Lord, a stream of power from the Almighty can pass through the tabernacle of the administrator to the system of the patient, and the sick are made whole; the headache, fever or other disease has to give way (*DBY,* 162).

I am sent for continually, though I only go occasionally, because it is a privilege of every father, who is an Elder in Israel, to have faith to heal his family, just as much so as it is my privilege to have faith to heal my family; and if he does not do it he is not living up to his privilege. It is just as reasonable for him to ask me to cut his wood and maintain his family, for if he had faith himself he would save me the trouble of leaving other duties to attend to his request (*DBY,* 163).

If we are sick, and ask the Lord to heal us, and to do all for us that is necessary to be done, according to my understanding of the Gospel of salvation, I might as well ask the Lord to cause my wheat and corn to grow, without my plowing the ground and casting in the seed. It appears consistent to me to apply every remedy that comes within the range of my knowledge, and to ask my Father in Heaven, in the name of Jesus Christ, to sanctify that application to the healing of my body (*DBY,* 163).

But suppose we were traveling in the mountains, . . . and one or two were taken sick, without anything in the world in the shape of healing medicine within our reach, what should we do? According to my faith, ask the Lord Almighty to . . . heal the sick. This is our privilege, when so situated that we cannot get anything to help ourselves. Then the Lord and his servants can do all. But it is my duty to do, when I have it in my power (*DBY,* 163).

We lay hands on the sick and wish them to be healed, and pray the Lord to heal them, but we cannot always say that he will (*DBY,* 162).

Prophecy, Revelation, and Knowledge. Every man and woman may be a revelator, and have the testimony of Jesus, which is the spirit of prophecy, and foresee the mind and will of God concerning them, eschew evil, and choose that which is good (*DBY,* 131).

My knowledge is, if you will follow the teachings of Jesus Christ and his Apostles, as recorded in the New Testament, every man and woman will be put in possession of the Holy Ghost. . . . They will know things that are, that will be, and that have been. They will understand things in heaven, things on the earth, and things under the earth, things of time, and things of eternity, according to their several callings and capacities [see D&C 88:78–79] (*DBY,* 161).

Seek diligently to know the will of God. How can you know it? In matters pertaining to yourselves as individuals, you can obtain it directly from the Lord; but in matters pertaining to public affairs [of the Church], his will is ascertained through the proper channel, and may be known by the general counsel that is given you from the proper source (*DBY,* 136).

If the Lord Almighty should reveal to a High Priest, or to any other than the head, things that are true, or that have been and will be, and show to him the destiny of this people twenty-five years from now, or a new doctrine that will in five, ten, or twenty years hence become the doctrine of this Church and Kingdom, but which has not yet been revealed to this people, and reveal it to him by the same Spirit, the same messenger, the same voice, the same power that gave revelations to Joseph when he was living, it would be a blessing to that High Priest, or individual; but he must rarely divulge it to a second person on the face of the earth, until God reveals it through the proper source to become the property of the people at large. Therefore when you hear Elders say that God does not reveal through the President of the Church that which they know, and tell wonderful things, you may generally set it down as a God's truth that the revelation they have had is from the Devil, and not from God. If they had received from the proper source, the same power that revealed to them would have shown them that they must keep the things revealed in their own bosoms, and they seldom would have a desire to disclose them to the second person (*DBY*, 338).

Other Gifts. The gift of seeing with the natural eyes is just as much a gift as the gift of tongues. The Lord gave that gift and we can do as we please with regard to seeing; we can use the sight of the eye to the glory of God, or to our own destruction.

The gift of communicating one with another is the gift of God, just as much so as the gift of prophecy, of discerning spirits, of tongues, of healing, or any other gift, though sight, taste, and speech, are so generally bestowed that they are not considered in the same miraculous light as are those gifts mentioned in the Gospel.

We can use these gifts, and every other gift God has given us, to the praise and glory of God, to serve Him, or we can use them to dishonor Him and His cause. . . .

These principles are correct in regard to the gifts which we receive for the express purpose of using them, in order that we may endure and be exalted, and that the organization we have received shall not come to an end, but endure to all eternity.

By a close application of the gifts bestowed upon us, we can secure to ourselves the resurrection of these bodies that we now possess, that our spirits inhabit, and when they are resurrected they will be made pure and holy; then they will endure to all eternity (*DNW*, 27 Aug. 1856, 2).

Miracles strengthen and confirm the faith of those who love and serve God.

Miracles, or these extraordinary manifestations of the power of God, are not for the unbeliever; they are to console the Saints, and to strengthen and confirm the faith of those who love, fear, and serve God, and not for outsiders (*DBY*, 341).

You have gathered the idea from me that it is not the miracles that are performed before a person's eyes that convince him that one is of God, or of the Devil; yet, if the Lord designs that a person should heal the sick, the individual can do so; but is that to convince the wicked that the operator is sent of God? No, it is a blessing on the Saints, and the wicked have nothing to do with it, they have no business to hear of it; that is for the Saints, it is especially for their benefit, and theirs alone (*DBY*, 340).

Camps of poor people were established across the Mississippi River from Nauvoo in 1847, as shown in this painting. The poor were saved when the Lord caused quail to fall from the sky to feed them.

The Gospel plan is so devised, that a miracle to make people believe would only be a condemnation to them. When you hear people tell what they have seen—that they have seen great and powerful miracles wrought, and they could not help believing, remember that "devils believe and tremble," because they cannot help it [see James 2:19]. When the voice of the Good Shepherd is heard, the honest in heart believe and receive it. It is good to taste with the inward taste, to see with the inward eyes, and to enjoy with the sensations of the ever-living spirit. No person, unless he is an adulterer [see Matthew 12:39], a fornicator, covetous, or an idolator, will ever require [demand] a miracle; in other words, no good, honest person ever will (*DBY,* 340).

Men who have professedly seen the most, known and understood the most, in this Church, and who have testified in the presence of large congregations, in the name of Israel's God, that they have seen Jesus, etc., have been the very men who have left this Kingdom, before others who had to live by faith [see Alma 32:21] (*DBY,* 342).

The providences of God are all a miracle to the human family until they understand them. There are no miracles, only to those who are ignorant.

255

A miracle is supposed to be a result without a cause, but there is no such thing. There is a cause for every result we see; and if we see a result without understanding the cause we call it a miracle (*DBY,* 339).

It is natural for me to believe that, if I plough the ground and sow wheat, in the proper season I shall reap a crop of wheat; this is the natural result. It was precisely so with the miracles that Jesus wrought upon the earth. At the wedding in Cana of Galilee [see John 2:1–11], when they had drunk all the wine, they went to the Savior and asked him what they should do. He ordered them to fill up their pots with water, and after having done so they drew forth of that water and found that it was wine. I believe that was real wine; I do not believe that it was done on the principle that such things are done in these days by wicked men, who, by means of what they term psychology, electro-biology, mesmerism, etc., influence men and make them believe that water is wine, and other things of a similar character. The Savior converted the water into wine. He knew how to call the necessary elements together in order to fill the water with the properties of wine. The elements are all around us; we eat, drink and breathe them, and Jesus, understanding the process of calling them together, performed no miracle except to those who were ignorant of that process. It was the same with the woman who was healed by touching the hem of his garment [see Matthew 9:20–22]; she was healed by faith, but it was no miracle to Jesus. He understood the process, and although he was pressed by the crowd, behind and before, and on each side, so that he could scarcely make his way through it, the moment she touched him he felt virtue leave him and enquired who touched him. This was no miracle to him. He had the issues of life and death in his power; he had power to lay down his life and power to take it up again [see John 10:17–18]. This is what he says, and we must believe this if we believe the history of the Savior and the sayings of the Apostles recorded in the New Testament. Jesus had this power in and of himself; the Father bequeathed it to him; it was his legacy, and he had the power to lay down his life and take it again. He had the streams and issues of life within him and when he said "Live" to individuals, they lived (*DBY,* 340–41).

If we have faith to feel that the issues of life and death are in our power, we can say to disease, "Be ye rebuked in the name of Jesus, and let life and health come into the system of this individual from God, to counteract this disease"; and our faith will bring this by the laying on of hands by administering the ordinance of the holy Gospel (*DBY,* 342).

The Holy Ghost unfolds the mysteries of the kingdom to those who seek the best gifts and keep the commandments.

What is a mystery? We do not know, it is beyond our comprehension. When we talk about mystery, we talk about eternal obscurity; for that which is known, ceases to be a mystery; and all that is known, we may know as we progress in the scale of our intelligence. That which is eternally beyond the comprehension of all our intelligence is mystery (*DBY,* 338–39).

If we were to examine the subject closely, we should learn that a very scanty portion of the things of the Kingdom were ever revealed, even to the disciples. If we were prepared to gaze upon the mysteries of the Kingdom, as they are with God, we should then know that only a very small portion of them has been handed out here and there. God, by his Spirit, has revealed many things to his people, but, in almost all cases, he has straightway shut up the vision of the mind. He will let his servants gaze upon eternal things for a moment, but straightway the vision is closed and they are left as they were, that they may learn to act by faith, or as the Apostle has it, not walking by sight, but by faith [see 2 Corinthians 5:7] (*DBY,* 339).

Just as fast as you will prove before your God that you are worthy to receive the mysteries, if you please to call them so, of the Kingdom of heaven—that you are full of confidence in God—that you will never betray a thing that God tells you—that you will never reveal to your neighbor that which ought not to be revealed, as quick as you prepare to be entrusted with the things of God, there is an eternity of them to bestow upon you [see Alma 26:22] (*DBY,* 93).

Now, brethren, preach the things that we verily believe, and when we come to points of doctrine that we do not know, even if we have good reason to believe them, [even] if our philosophy teaches us they are true, pass them by and teach only to the people that which we do know (*DBY,* 338).

If they will only live up to it, there has already been enough taught the brethren who have lived here for years to prepare them to enter into the strait gate and into New Jerusalem, and be prepared to enjoy the society of the holy angels (*DBY,* 339).

These are the mysteries of the Kingdom of God upon the earth, to know how to purify and sanctify our affections, the earth upon which we stand, the air we breathe, the water we drink, the houses in which we dwell and the cities which we build, that when strangers come into our country they may feel a hallowed influence and acknowledge a power to which they are strangers (*DBY,* 339).

If you say that you want mysteries, commandments, and revelations, I reply that scarcely a Sabbath passes over your heads, those of you who come here, without your having the revelations of Jesus Christ poured upon you like water on the ground (*DBY,* 343).

Suggestions for Study

The Lord gives gifts of the Spirit to strengthen and bless us, our families, and the Church.

- What are the gifts of the Spirit? Why is it important that they be available in the restored Church of Jesus Christ? (See also 1 Corinthians 12:4–11; D&C 46:10–26.)

- How can we know when the gifts of the Spirit are being manifest in our lives? How can we use them to bless others?

- Who is responsible for the discernment of spiritual gifts and their use in the Church? (See also D&C 46:27; 107:18.) How does the use of spiritual gifts in a Church calling differ from use of those gifts in a personal or family setting?

Miracles strengthen and confirm the faith of those who love and serve God.

- What are miracles? What is their purpose?

- What does it mean to hear "the voice of the Good Shepherd" and to "enjoy with the sensations of the ever-living spirit"? How can miracles confirm our faith and testimonies? Why are the whisperings of the Spirit more convincing than spectacular displays of power? How can we be more attentive to all the miracles in our lives? (See also 2 Nephi 27:23; Ether 12:12.)

The Holy Ghost unfolds the mysteries of the kingdom to those who seek the best gifts and keep the commandments.

- According to President Young, why does God reveal "a very scanty portion of the things of the Kingdom"? (See also D&C 78:17–18.)

- How can we prove ourselves "worthy to receive the mysteries"? (See also D&C 76:5–10.)

- According to President Young, what are the mysteries of the kingdom of God? (See also D&C 84:19–22.) How could a mystery to one person be a plain, simple truth to another? Why is it sometimes tempting to speculate about that which we do not know?

- President Young said, "Scarcely a Sabbath passes over your heads . . . without your having the revelations of Jesus Christ poured upon you like water on the ground." How can we prepare ourselves to receive those revelations as we receive the sacrament and keep the Sabbath day holy?

As depicted in this painting, the Saints were driven by mobs from their homes in Kirtland, Ohio; Jackson County, Missouri; and Nauvoo, Illinois.

CHAPTER 35

The Blessings of Trials, Chastening, and Persecution

President Brigham Young understood God's eternal purposes, and he applied this understanding to the tribulations he and other Saints endured. President Young said: "I have heard a great many tell about what they have suffered for Christ's sake. I am happy to say I never had occasion to. I have enjoyed a great deal, but so far as suffering goes I have compared it a great many times, in my feelings and before congregations, to a man wearing an old, worn-out, tattered and dirty coat, and somebody comes along and gives him one that is new, whole and beautiful. This is the comparison I draw when I think of what I have suffered for the Gospel's sake—I have thrown away an old coat and have put on a new one" (DBY, 348).

Teachings of Brigham Young

The Lord tests and tries us so we can prove ourselves worthy of celestial glory.

The people of the Most High God must be tried. It is written that they will be tried in all things, even as Abraham was tried [see D&C 101:1–4]. If we are called to go upon mount Moriah to sacrifice a few of our Isaacs, it is no matter; we may just as well do that as anything else. I think there is a prospect for the Saints to have all the trials they wish for or can desire. Now if you possess the light of the Holy Spirit, you can see clearly that trials in the flesh are actually necessary (*DBY*, 346).

We are now in a day of trial to prove ourselves worthy or unworthy of the life which is to come (*DBY*, 345).

All intelligent beings who are crowned with crowns of glory, immortality, and eternal lives must pass through every ordeal appointed for intelligent beings to pass through, to gain their glory and exaltation. Every calamity that can come upon mortal beings will be suffered to come upon the few, to prepare them to enjoy the presence of the Lord. If we obtain the glory that Abraham obtained, we must do so by the same means that he did. If we are ever prepared to enjoy the society of Enoch, Noah,

261

Melchizedek, Abraham, Isaac, and Jacob, or of their faithful children, and of the faithful Prophets and Apostles, we must pass through the same experience, and gain the knowledge, intelligence, and endowments that will prepare us to enter into the celestial kingdom of our Father and God. . . . Every trial and experience you have passed through is necessary for your salvation (*DBY*, 345).

Should our lives be extended to a thousand years, still we may live and learn. Every vicissitude we pass through is necessary for experience and example, and for preparation to enjoy that reward which is for the faithful (*DBY*, 345).

If Adam had not sinned, and if his posterity had continued upon the earth, they could not have known sin, or the bitter from the sweet, neither would they have known righteousness, for the plain and simple reason that every effect can only be fully manifested by its opposite. If the Saints could realize things as they are when they are called to pass through trials, and to suffer what they call sacrifices, they would acknowledge them to be the greatest blessings that could be bestowed upon them. But put them in possession of true principles and true enjoyments, without the opposite, and they could not know enjoyment, they could not realize happiness. They could not tell light from darkness, because they have no knowledge of darkness and consequently are destitute of a realizing sense of light. If they should not taste the bitter, how could they realize the sweet? They could not [see D&C 29:39] (*DBY*, 345–46).

We are the happiest people when we have what are called trials; for then the Spirit of God is more abundantly bestowed upon the faithful [see 1 Peter 3:14] (*DBY*, 347).

I say to the Latter-day Saints, all we have to do is to learn of God. Let the liars lie on, and let the swearers swear on, and they will go to perdition. All we have to do is to go onward and upward, and keep the commandments of our Father and God; and he will confound our enemies (*DBY*, 347).

We have passed through a great many scenes, we may say, of tribulation, though I would have all my brethren understand that I do not take this to myself, for all that I have passed through has been joy and joyful to me; but we have seemingly sacrificed a great deal, and passed through many scenes of trial and temptations, no doubt of this. We have had to suffer temptations, more or less, and we have taken the spoiling of our goods joyfully. I have, myself, five times before I came to this valley, left everything that the Lord had blessed me with pertaining to this world's goods, which, for the country where I lived, was not a very little (*DBY*, 347–48).

As to trials, why bless your hearts, the man or woman who enjoys the spirit of our religion has no trials; but the man or woman who tries to live according to the Gospel of the Son of God, and at the same time clings to the spirit of the world, has trials and sorrows acute and keen, and that, too, continually (*DBY,* 348).

Cast off the yoke of the enemy, and put on the yoke of Christ, and you will say that his yoke is easy and his burden is light. This I know by experience (*DBY,* 347–48).

The Lord helps the disobedient become humble by chastening them and allowing them to be persecuted.

When we look at the Latter-day Saints, we ask, is there any necessity of their being persecuted? Yes, if they are disobedient. Is there any necessity of chastening a son or a daughter? Yes, if they are disobedient [see D&C 105:6]. But suppose they are perfectly obedient to every requirement of their parents, is there any necessity of chastening them then? If there is, I do not understand the principle of it. I have not yet been able to see the necessity of chastening an obedient child, neither have I been able to see the necessity of chastisement from the Lord upon a people who are perfectly obedient. Have this people been chastened? Yes, they have (*DBY,* 350).

Those who turn away from the holy commandments will meet trials that are trials indeed. They will feel the wrath of the Almighty upon them. Those who are still and are good children will receive the rich blessings of their Father and God. Be still, and let your faith rest on the Lord Almighty [see D&C 101:16] (*DBY,* 351).

We are infinitely more blessed by the persecutions and injustice we have suffered, than we could have been if we had remained in our habitations from which we have been driven—than if we had been suffered to occupy our farms, gardens, stores, mills, machinery and everything we had in our former possessions (*DBY,* 346).

The righteous will be persecuted by the wicked, but God will lead His people, and His work will go forward.

Have no fears, for if the word of the Lord is true, you shall yet be tried in all things; or rejoice, and pray without ceasing, and in everything give thanks, even if it is in the spoiling of your goods, for it is the hand of God that leads us, and will continue so to do. Let every man and woman sanctify themselves before the Lord, and every providence of the Almighty shall be sanctified for good to them (*DBY,* 347).

[God] led this people in different parts of the United States, and the finger of scorn has been pointed at them. . . . The Lord has his design in

As rendered in this painting, local militias were sometimes
antagonistic and hostile towards the early Saints.

this. You may ask what his design is. You all know that the Saints must be
made pure, to enter into the celestial kingdom. It is recorded that Jesus
was made perfect through suffering [see Hebrews 5:8–9]. Why should we
imagine for one moment that we can be prepared to enter into the
kingdom of rest with him and the Father, without passing through similar
ordeals? (*DBY,* 346).

Joseph could not have been perfected, though he had lived a thousand
years, if he had received no persecution. If he had lived a thousand years,
and led this people, and preached the Gospel without persecution, he
would not have been perfected as well as he was at the age of [thirty-eight]
years. You may calculate, when this people are called to go through scenes
of affliction and suffering, are driven from their homes, and cast down, and
scattered, and smitten, and peeled, the Almighty is rolling on his work with
greater rapidity (*DBY,* 351).

Every time you kick "Mormonism" you kick it upstairs; you never kick it
downstairs. The Lord Almighty so orders it (*DBY,* 351).

If we did not have to bear the iron hand of persecution, the principles
we believe in, which attract the attention of the good and the evil upon

the earth and which occupy so many tongues and circumscribe their philosophy, would be embraced by thousands who are now indifferent to them (*DBY,* 351).

Every time they persecute and try to overcome this people, they elevate us, weaken their own hands, and strengthen the hands and arms of this people. And every time they undertake to lessen our number, they increase it. And when they try to destroy the faith and virtue of this people, the Lord strengthens the feeble knees, and confirms the wavering in faith and power in God, in light, and intelligence. Righteousness and power with God increase in this people in proportion as the Devil struggles to destroy it (*DBY,* 351).

Let us alone, and we will send Elders to the uttermost parts of the earth, and gather out Israel, wherever they are; and if you persecute us, we will do it the quicker, because we are naturally dull when let alone, and are disposed to take a little sleep, a little slumber, and a little rest. If you let us alone, we will do it a little more leisurely; but if you persecute us, we will sit up nights to preach the Gospel (*DBY,* 351).

Suggestions for Study

The Lord tests and tries us so we can prove ourselves worthy of celestial glory.

- Why do you think President Young called this life "a day of trial"? (See also Abraham 3:22–26.) How can trials prepare us to enter the celestial kingdom?

- Why is it necessary to experience the opposing forces of good and evil? (See also 2 Nephi 2:11–14.)

- Why do you think President Young was so grateful for the trials he and other early Saints received? How have trials helped you become a better Latter-day Saint?

- What does it mean to "put on the yoke of Christ"? (See also Matthew 11:28–30.) How does putting on the yoke of Christ help us be joyful when we face trials? (See also Mosiah 24:13–15.)

The Lord helps the disobedient become humble by chastening them and allowing them to be persecuted.

- Why does the Lord sometimes chasten us? (See also D&C 101:2–8.) What is the importance of our response to that chastening? How can learning this principle correctly help parents and children create better families?

• President Young said that the Saints were "infinitely more blessed by the persecutions and injustice [they had] suffered . . . than if [they] had been suffered to occupy . . . everything [in their] former possessions." Why is it a greater blessing to be punished for disobedience than to be allowed to remain comfortable in a sinful state?

The righteous will be persecuted by the wicked, but God will lead His people, and His work will go forward.

• President Young said that the disobedient would be persecuted, but he also spoke about obedient people—such as Jesus Christ, Joseph Smith, and missionaries—who have been persecuted. According to President Young, why does God allow the wicked to persecute the righteous?

• President Young said that persecution against the Church would only cause the Lord's work to go on "with greater rapidity." What does this tell us about how we should respond to attacks against the truth? What can we do to teach our children to overcome persecution?

Earthly Governments and the Kingdom of God

President Brigham Young—colonizer, statesman, and first governor of Utah—honored and served his government. In July 1846, while the Saints were preparing for the journey from Iowa to the Salt Lake Valley, they received a request from the United States government for assistance in the war with Mexico. Although the government had been unsupportive of the Saints during their trials in Missouri and Illinois, President Young directed the recruitment of the Mormon Battalion to aid in the war and promised the men that they would not have to fight if they conducted themselves properly. This promise was fulfilled. The enlisting of the Mormon Battalion also provided money to help the Saints move west. Five hundred men left the Camps of Israel for a grueling 2,000-mile march to California and the Pacific Ocean. Said President Young of the volunteers, "I never think of that little company of men without the next thoughts being, 'God bless them for ever and ever.' All this we did to prove to the Government that we were loyal" (DBY, 476). President Young consistently encouraged the Saints to be loyal to their government, to obey its laws, and to elect people of virtue and integrity to public office.

Teachings of Brigham Young

Earthly governments must be based on God's laws to endure.

If a nation transgresses wholesome laws and oppresses any of its citizens or another nation, until the cup of iniquity is full, through acts that are perfectly under its own control, God will hurl those who are in authority from their power, and they will be forgotten; and he will take another people, though poor and despised, a hiss and a by-word among the popular nations, and instill into them power and wisdom; and they will increase and prosper, until they in turn become a great nation on the earth (*DBY,* 357).

Great and mighty empires are raised to the summit of human greatness by him, to bring to pass his inscrutable purposes, and at his pleasure they are swept from existence and lost in the oblivion of antiquity. All these mighty changes are pointing to and preparing the way for the introduction of his Kingdom in the latter times, that will stand forever and grow in greatness and power until a holy, lasting, religious and political peace shall make the hearts of the poor among men exult with joy in the Holy One of Israel, and that his Kingdom is everywhere triumphant (*DBY,* 357).

A theocratic government [is] one in which all laws are enacted and executed in righteousness, and whose officers possess that power which proceedeth from the Almighty (*DBY,* 354).

If the Kingdom of God, or a theocratic government, was established on the earth, many practices now prevalent would be abolished (*DBY,* 354).

One community would not be permitted to array itself in opposition to another to coerce them to their standard; one denomination would not be suffered to persecute another because they differed in religious belief and mode of worship. Every one would be fully protected in the enjoyment of all religious and social rights, and no state, no government, no community, no person would have the privilege of infringing on the rights of another; one Christian community would not rise up and persecute another (*DBY,* 354).

Whoever lives to see the Kingdom of God fully established upon the earth will see a government that will protect every person in his rights. If that government was now reigning . . . you would see the Roman Catholic, the Greek Catholic, the Episcopalian, the Presbyterian, the Methodist, the Baptist, the Quaker, the Shaker, the [Hindi], the [Muslim], and every class of worshipers most strictly protected in all their municipal rights and in the privileges of worshiping who, what, and when they pleased, not infringing upon the rights of others. Does any candid person in his sound judgment desire any greater liberty? (*DBY,* 355).

How can a republican [freely elected] government stand? There is only one way for it to stand. It can endure; but how? It can endure, as the government of heaven endures, upon the eternal rock of truth and virtue; and that is the only basis upon which any government can endure (*DBY,* 355).

Those who govern should possess wisdom and integrity.

I like a good government, and then I like to have it wisely and justly administered. The government of heaven, if wickedly administered, would become one of the worst governments upon the face of the earth. No matter how good a government is, unless it is administered by righteous men, an evil government will be made of it (*DNW,* 3 June 1863, 2).

No being is fit to rule, govern, and dictate, until he has . . . yielded obedience to law, and proved himself worthy, by magnifying the law that was over him, to be master of that law (*DBY,* 357).

[A good government requires a leader who is] capable of communicating to the understanding of the people, according to their capacity, information upon all points pertaining to the just administration of the Government. He should understand what administrative policy would be most beneficial to the nation. He should also have the knowledge and disposition to wisely exercise the appointing power, so far as it is constitutionally within his control and select only good and capable men for the office. He should not only carry out the legal and just wishes of his constituents, but should be able to enlighten their understanding and correct their judgment. And all good officers in a truly republican administration will constantly labor for the security of the rights of all, irrespective of sect or party (*DBY,* 363).

The people should concentrate their feelings, their influence, and their faith to select the best man they can find to be their President, if he has nothing more to eat than potatoes and salt—a man who will not aspire to become greater than the people who appoint him, but be contented to live as they live, be clothed as they are clothed, and in every good thing be one with them (*DBY,* 363).

We want men to rule the nation who care more for and love better the nation's welfare than gold and silver, fame, or popularity (*DBY,* 364).

Members of the Church have a duty to be responsible citizens.

Individual self-government lies at the root of all true and effective government, whether in heaven or on earth. . . . Government in the hands of a wicked people must terminate in woe to that people, but in the hands of the righteous it is everlasting, while its power reaches to heaven (*DBY,* 355).

If we live our religion, honor our God and his Priesthood, then we shall honor every wholesome government and law there is upon the earth. . . . In the various nations, kingdoms and governments of the world are to be found laws, ordinances and statutes as good as can be made for mortal man (*DBY,* 358).

Are we a political people? Yes, very political indeed. But what party do you belong to or would you vote for? I will tell you whom we will vote for: we will vote for the man who will sustain the principles of civil and religious liberty, the man who knows the most and who has the best heart and brain for a statesman; and we do not care a farthing whether he is a whig, a democrat, . . . a republican, . . . or anything else. These are our politics (*DBY,* 358).

We, like all other good citizens, should seek to place those men in power, who will feel the obligations and responsibilities they are under to a mighty people; who would feel and realize the important trusts reposed in them by the voice of the people who call them to administer law (*DBY,* 362).

Whom do we want to fill our public offices? We want the best men that we can find for governor, president and statesmen, and for every other office of trust and responsibility; and when we have obtained them, we will pray for them and give them our faith [trust] and influence to do the will of God and to preserve themselves and the people in truth and righteousness (*DBY,* 358).

Suggestions for Study

Earthly governments must be based on God's laws to endure.

- Why must governments be based on God's laws to succeed? What will eventually happen to any government not based on righteous principles? (For examples of this result, consider the rise and fall of the Nephite and Lamanite kingdoms at various times throughout the Book of Mormon.)
- According to President Young, what is the purpose of earthly governments? (See also D&C 134:1.)
- How would society be different if a theocratic (God-directed) government were established on the earth? What did President Young consider to be the greatest liberty a theocratic government would provide? (See also D&C 134:4, 7, 9.)

Those who govern should possess wisdom and integrity.

- What qualities should a government leader possess? If government leaders are intelligent, knowledgeable, and hardworking, why is it important that they also have such qualities as honesty and virtue?
- Why must a potential leader have experience being governed before he or she is fit to govern? Why is it important for leaders to show that they have been obedient to the law?

Members of the Church have a duty to be responsible citizens.

- Why is "individual self-government" so important to the success of an earthly government? How does the righteousness of the people being governed affect the success of the government?
- Why is it important to vote when you are given the privilege? How should you decide whom to vote for?
- How can you fulfill your duty to be a responsible citizen? (See also D&C 134:5–6.)

Before ascending to His Father, the resurrected
Jesus Christ appeared to Mary.

Understanding Death and Resurrection

At the funeral services of Elder Thomas Williams on 13 July 1874, President Brigham Young spoke on the subject of death: "What a dark valley and a shadow it is that we call death! To pass from this state of existence as far as the mortal body is concerned, into a state of inanition [emptiness], how strange it is! How dark this valley is! How mysterious is this road, and we have got to travel it alone. I would like to say to you, my friends and brethren, if we could see things as they are, and as we shall see and understand them, this dark shadow and valley is so trifling that we shall turn round and look about upon it and think, when we have crossed it, why this is the greatest advantage of my whole existence, for I have passed from a state of sorrow, grief, mourning, woe, misery, pain, anguish and disappointment into a state of existence, where I can enjoy life to the fullest extent as far as that can be done without a body. My spirit is set free, I thirst no more, I want to sleep no more, I hunger no more, I tire no more, I run, I walk, I labor, I go, I come, I do this, I do that, whatever is required of me, nothing like pain or weariness, I am full of life, full of vigor, and I enjoy the presence of my heavenly Father, by the power of his Spirit. I want to say to my friends, if you will live your religion, live so as to be full of the faith of God, that the light of eternity will shine upon you, you can see and understand these things for yourselves" (DNSW, 28 July 1874, 1).

Teachings of Brigham Young

Earthly happiness cannot compare with "the glory, joy and peace and happiness of the soul" who departs mortality in righteous peace.

It is a great cause of joy and rejoicing and comfort to his friends to know that a person has passed away in peace from this life, and has secured to himself a glorious resurrection. The earth and the fulness of the earth and all that pertains to this earth in an earthly capacity is no comparison with the glory, joy and peace and happiness of the soul that departs in peace (*DBY*, 370).

Mourning for the righteous dead springs from the ignorance and weakness that are planted within the mortal tabernacle, the organization of this house for the spirit to dwell in. No matter what pain we suffer, no matter what we pass through, we cling to our mother earth, and dislike to have any of her children leave us. We love to keep together the social family relation that we bear one to another, and do not like to part with each other (*DBY,* 370).

It is true it is grievous to part with our friends. We are creatures of passion, of sympathy, of love, and it is painful for us to part with our friends. We would keep them in the mortal house, though they should suffer pain. Are we not selfish in this? Should we not rather rejoice at the departure of those whose lives have been devoted to doing good, to a good old age? (*DBY,* 371).

But could we have knowledge and see into eternity, if we were perfectly free from the weakness, blindness, and lethargy with which we are clothed in the flesh, we should have no disposition to weep or mourn (*DBY,* 370).

So live that when you wake in the spirit-world you can truthfully say, "I could not better my mortal life, were I to live it over again." I exhort you, for the sake of the House of Israel, for the sake of Zion which we are to build up, to so live, from this time, henceforth, and forever, that your characters may with pleasure be scrutinized by holy beings. Live godly lives, which you cannot do without living moral lives (*DBY,* 370).

At death the spirit separates from the body, the body returns to the earth, and the spirit enters the spirit world.

Every person possessing the principle of eternal life should look upon his body as of the earth earthy. Our bodies must return to their mother earth. True, to most people it is a wretched thought that our spirits must, for a longer or shorter period, be separated from our bodies, and thousands and millions have been subject to this affliction throughout their lives. If they understood the design of this probation and the true principles of eternal life, it is but a small matter for the body to suffer and die (*DBY,* 368).

The Lord has pleased to organize tabernacles here, and put spirits into them, and they then become intelligent beings. By and by, sooner or later, the body, this that is tangible to you, that you can feel, see, handle, etc., returns to its mother dust. Is the spirit dead? No. . . . The spirit still exists, when this body has crumbled into the earth again, and the spirit that God puts into the tabernacle goes into the world of spirits (*DBY,* 368).

Our bodies are composed of visible, tangible matter, as you all understand; you also know that they are born into this world. They then begin to partake of the elements adapted to their organization and growth, increase to manhood [or womanhood], become old, decay, and pass again into the dust. Now in the first place, though I have explained this many times, what we call death is the operation of life, inherent in the matter of which the body is composed, and which causes the decomposition after the spirit has left the body. Were that not the fact, the body, from which has fled the spirit, would remain to all eternity, just as it was when the spirit left it, and would not decay (*DBY*, 368).

Jesus Christ is the firstfruits of the resurrection.

Jesus is the first begotten from the dead, as you will understand. Neither Enoch, Elijah, Moses, nor any other man that ever lived on earth, no matter how strictly he lived, ever obtained a resurrection until after Jesus Christ's body was called from the tomb by the angel. He was the first begotten from the dead. He is the Master of the resurrection—the first flesh that lived here after receiving the glory of the resurrection (*DBY*, 374).

This was no miracle to him. He had the issues of life and death in his power; he had power to lay down his life and power to take it up again [see John 10:18]. This is what he says, and we must believe this if we believe the history of the Savior and the sayings of the Apostles recorded in the New Testament. Jesus had this power in and of himself; the Father bequeathed it to him; it was his legacy, and he had the power to lay down his life and take it again (*DBY*, 340–41).

The blood he spilled upon Mount Calvary he did not receive again into his veins. That was poured out, and when he was resurrected, another element took the place of the blood. It will be so with every person who receives a resurrection; the blood will not be resurrected with the body, being designed only to sustain the life of the present organization. When that is dissolved, and we again obtain our bodies by the power of the resurrection, that which we now call the life of the body, and which is formed from the food we eat and the water we drink will be supplanted by another element; for flesh and blood cannot inherit the Kingdom of God [see 1 Corinthians 15:50] (*DBY*, 374).

Our faithfulness can prepare us for a glorious resurrection, the reuniting of our body and spirit.

The Gospel of life and salvation reveals to each individual who receives it that this world is only a place of temporary duration, existence, trials, etc. Its present fashion and uses are but for a few days, while we were

Death was an ever-present reality for the Saints crossing
the plains, as depicted in this painting.

created to exist eternally. The wicked can see no further than this world is concerned. We understand that when we are unclothed in this present state, then we are prepared to be clothed upon with immortality—that when we put off these bodies we put on immortality [see Alma 11:43–44]. These bodies will return to dust, but our hope and faith are that we will receive these bodies again from the elements—that we will receive the very organization that we have here, and that, if we are faithful to the principles of [gospel] freedom, we shall then be prepared to endure eternally (*DBY*, 372).

After the spirit leaves the body, it remains without a tabernacle in the spirit world until the Lord, by his law that he has ordained, brings to pass the resurrection of the dead [see D&C 93:33–34]. When the angel who holds the keys of the resurrection shall sound his trumpet, then the peculiar fundamental particles that organized our bodies here, if we do honor to them, though they be deposited in the depths of the sea, and though one particle is in the north, another in the south, another in the east, and another in the west, will be brought together again in the twinkling of an eye, and our spirits will take possession of them. We shall then be prepared to dwell with the Father and the Son, and we never can be prepared to dwell with them until then. Spirits, when they leave their bodies, do not dwell with the Father and the Son, but live in the Spirit world, where there are places prepared for them. Those who do honor to their tabernacles, and love and believe in the Lord Jesus Christ, must put off this mortality, or they cannot put on immortality. This body must be changed, else it cannot be prepared to dwell in the glory of the Father (*DBY,* 372).

After the body and spirit are separated by death, what, pertaining to this earth, shall we receive first? The body; that is the first object of a divine affection beyond the grave. We first come in possession of the body. The spirit [of a righteous man or woman] has overcome the body, and the body is made subject in every respect to that divine principle God has planted in the person. The spirit within is pure and holy, and goes back pure and holy to God, dwells in the spirit world pure and holy, and, by and by, will have the privilege of coming and taking the body again. [Jesus Christ,] holding the keys of the resurrection, having previously passed through that ordeal, will be delegated to resurrect our bodies, and our spirits will be there and prepared to enter into [our] bodies. Then, when we are prepared to receive our bodies, they are the first earthly objects that bear divinity personified in the capacity of the man. Only the body dies; the spirit is looking forth (*DBY,* 373).

We are here in circumstances to bury our dead according to the order of the Priesthood. But some of our brethren die upon the ocean; they cannot be buried in a burying ground, but they are sewed up in canvas and cast into the sea, and perhaps in two minutes after they are in the bowels of the shark, yet those persons will come forth in the resurrection, and receive all the glory of which they are worthy, and be clothed upon with all the beauty of resurrected Saints, as much so as if they had been laid away in a gold or silver coffin, and in a place expressly for burying the dead (*DBY,* 373–74).

No man can enter the celestial kingdom and be crowned with a celestial glory, until he gets his resurrected body (*DBY,* 375).

The only true riches in existence are for you and me to secure for ourselves a holy resurrection (*DBY,* 372).

Suggestions for Study

Earthly happiness cannot compare with "the glory, joy and peace and happiness of the soul" who departs mortality in righteous peace.

• Though it is painful to part with our loved ones, in what sense might we rejoice and find comfort in their death?

- What did President Young counsel regarding our probationary time in mortality? He also taught that we should live so that our characters "may with pleasure be scrutinized by holy beings." How can we ensure that the Judgment Day will be a time of happiness for us?

At death the spirit separates from the body, the body returns to the earth, and the spirit enters the spirit world.

- Why is death part of the "operation of life"?
- What did President Young teach about the body once the spirit has departed?

Jesus Christ is the firstfruits of the resurrection.

- What enabled Jesus to be resurrected?
- What do we learn about resurrected beings from Christ's Resurrection? How will our bodies change when we are resurrected?

Our faithfulness can prepare us for a glorious resurrection, the reuniting of our body and spirit.

- According to President Young, how will the resurrection occur? (See also Alma 11:43; Philippians 3:21.)
- What does it mean to honor our tabernacles?
- Why is receiving "a holy resurrection" the "only true riches in existence"?

The Spirit World

While speaking at the funeral of Elder Thomas Williams, President Brigham Young spoke of the spirit world as follows: "How frequently the question arises in the minds of the people—'I wish I knew where I was going!' Can you find out? Well, you will go into the spirit world, where Brother Thomas now is. He has now entered upon a higher state of being, that is, his spirit has, than when in this body. 'Why cannot I see him? Why cannot I converse with his spirit? I wish I could see my husband or my father and converse with him!' It is not reasonable that you should, it is not right that you should; perhaps you would miss the very object of your pursuit if you had this privilege, and there would be the same trial of faith to exercise you, not so severe a path of affliction for you to walk in, not so great a battle to fight, nor so great a victory to win, and you would miss the very object you are in pursuit of. It is right just as it is, that this veil should be closed down; that we do not see God, that we do not see angels, that we do not converse with them except through strict obedience to his requirements, and faith in Jesus Christ (DNSW, 28 July 1874, 1).

Teachings of Brigham Young

The spirits of the dead go to the spirit world.

When you lay down this tabernacle, where are you going? Into the spiritual world (*DBY*, 376).

The wicked spirits that leave here and go into the spirit world, are they wicked there? Yes (*DNW*, 27 Aug. 1856, 3).

When the spirits leave their bodies, . . . they are prepared then to see, hear and understand spiritual things. . . .Can you see spirits in this room? No. Suppose the Lord should touch your eyes that you might see, could you then see the spirits? Yes, as plainly as you now see bodies, as did the servant of [Elisha] [see 2 Kings 6:16–17]. If the Lord would permit it, and it was his will that it should be done, you could see the spirits that have departed from this world, as plainly as you now see bodies with your natural eyes (*DBY*, 376–77).

Jesus opened the door of salvation to those in the spirit world.

Jesus was the first man that ever went to preach to the spirits in prison, holding the keys of the Gospel of salvation to them. Those keys were delivered to him in the day and hour that he went into the spirit world, and with them he opened the door of salvation to the spirits in prison (*DBY,* 378).

We want to sacrifice enough to do the will of God in preparing to bring up those who have not had the privilege of hearing the Gospel while in the flesh, for the simple reason that, in the spirit world, they cannot officiate in the ordinances of the house of God. They have passed the ordeals, and are beyond the possibility of personally officiating for the remission of their sins and for their exaltation, consequently they are under the necessity of trusting in their friends, their children and their children's children to officiate for them, that they may be brought up into the celestial kingdom of God (*DBY,* 406).

Compare those inhabitants on the earth who have heard the Gospel in our day, with the millions who have never heard it, or had the keys of salvation presented to them, and you will conclude at once as I do, that there is an almighty work to perform in the spirit world (*DBY,* 377).

Reflect upon the millions and millions and millions of people that have lived and died without hearing the Gospel on the earth, without the keys of the Kingdom. They were not prepared for celestial glory, and there was no power that could prepare them without the keys of this Priesthood (*DBY,* 378).

Father Smith [Joseph Smith Sr.] and Carlos [Smith] and Brother [Edward] Partridge, yes, and every other good Saint, are just as busy in the spirit world as you and I are here. They can see us, but we cannot see them unless our eyes were opened. What are they doing there? They are preaching, preaching all the time, and preparing the way for us to hasten our work in building temples here and elsewhere (*DBY,* 378).

Every faithful man's labor will continue as long as the labor of Jesus, until all things are redeemed that can be redeemed, and presented to the Father. There is a great work before us (*DBY,* 378).

The spirits that dwell in these tabernacles on this earth, when they leave them go directly into this world of spirits. What! A congregated mass of inhabitants there in spirit, mingling with each other, as they do here? Yes, brethren, they are there together, and if they associate together, and collect together, in clans and in societies as they do here, it is their privilege. No doubt they yet, more or less, see, hear, converse and have to do with each other, both good and bad. If the Elders of Israel in these latter times go and preach to the spirits in prison, they associate with them, precisely as our Elders associate with the wicked in the flesh, when they go to preach to them (*DBY,* 378).

The spirit world is an active place where growth and progression are possible.

When you are in the spirit world, everything there will appear as natural as things now do. Spirits will be familiar with spirits in the spirit world— will converse, behold, and exercise every variety of communication with one another as familiarly and naturally as while here in tabernacles. There, as here, all things will be natural, and you will understand them as you now understand natural things. You will there see that those spirits we are speaking of are active; they sleep not. And you will learn that they are striving with all their might—laboring and toiling diligently as any individual would to accomplish an act in this world (*DBY,* 380).

Spirits are just as familiar with spirits as bodies are with bodies, though spirits are composed of matter so refined as not to be tangible to this coarser organization. They walk, converse, and have their meetings; and the spirits of good men like Joseph and the Elders, who have left this Church on earth for a season to operate in another sphere, are rallying all their powers and going from place to place preaching the Gospel, and Joseph is directing them, saying, go ahead, my brethren, and if they hedge up your way, walk up and command them to disperse. You have the Priesthood and can disperse them, but if any of them wish to hear the Gospel, preach to them (*DBY,* 379).

I can say with regard to parting with our friends, and going ourselves, that I have been near enough to understand eternity so that I have had to exercise a great deal more faith to desire to live than I ever exercised in my whole life to live. The brightness and glory of the next apartment is inexpressible. It is not encumbered so that when we advance in years we have to be stubbing along and be careful lest we fall down. We see our youth, even, frequently stubbing their toes and falling down. But yonder, how different! They move with ease and like lightning. If we want to visit Jerusalem, or this, that, or the other place—and I presume we will be permitted if we desire—there we are, looking at its streets. If we want to behold Jerusalem as it was in the days of the Savior; or if we want to see the Garden of Eden as it was when created, there we are, and we see it as it existed spiritually, for it was created first spiritually and then temporally, and spiritually it still remains. And when there we may behold the earth as at the dawn of creation, or we may visit any city we please that exists upon its surface. If we wish to understand how they are living here on these western islands, or in China, we are there; in fact, we are like the light of the morning. . . . God has revealed some little things, with regard to his movements and power, and the operation and motion of the lightning furnish a fine illustration of the ability of the Almighty (*DBY*, 380).

When we pass into the spirit world we shall possess a measure of his power. Here, we are continually troubled with ills and ailments of various kinds. In the spirit world we are free from all this and enjoy life, glory, and intelligence; and we have the Father to speak to us, Jesus to speak to us, and angels to speak to us, and we shall enjoy the society of the just and the pure who are in the spirit world until the resurrection (*DBY*, 380–81).

Suppose, then, that a man is evil in his heart—wholly given up to wickedness, and in that condition dies, his spirit will enter into the spirit world intent upon evil. On the other hand, if we are striving with all the powers and faculties God has given us to improve upon our talents, to prepare ourselves to dwell in eternal life, and the grave receives our bodies while we are thus engaged, with what disposition will our spirits enter their next state? They will be still striving to do the things of God, only in a much greater degree—learning, increasing, growing in grace and in the knowledge of the truth (*DBY*, 379).

If we are faithful to our religion, when we go into the spirit world, the fallen spirits—Lucifer and the third part of the heavenly hosts that came with him, and the spirits of wicked men who have dwelt upon this earth, the whole of them combined will have no influence over our spirits. Is not that an advantage? Yes. All the rest of the children of men are more or less subject to them, and they are subject to them as they were while here in the flesh (*DBY*, 379).

Here [the faithful] shall be perplexed and hunted by him; but when we go into the spirit world there we are masters over the power of satan, and he cannot afflict us any more, and this is enough for me to know (*DNW*, 1 Oct. 1856, 3).

If a person is baptized for the remission of sins, and dies a short time thereafter, he is not prepared at once to enjoy a fulness of the glory promised to the faithful in the Gospel; for he must be schooled while in the spirit, in the other departments of the house of God, passing on from truth to truth, from intelligence to intelligence, until he is prepared to again receive his body and to enter into the presence of the Father and the Son. We cannot enter into celestial glory in our present state of ignorance and mental darkness (*DBY*, 378–79).

We have more friends behind the veil than on this side, and they will hail us more joyfully than you were ever welcomed by your parents and friends in this world; and you will rejoice more when you meet them than you ever rejoiced to see a friend in this life; and then we shall go on from

Between His death and resurrection, the Savior went to the spirit world
to begin the work of salvation among the dead.

step to step, from rejoicing to rejoicing, and from one intelligence and power to another, our happiness becoming more and more exquisite and sensible as we proceed in the words and powers of life (*DBY,* 379–80).

When we get through this state of being, to the next room, I may call it, we are not going to stop there. We shall still go on, doing all the good we can, administering and officiating for all whom we are permitted to administer and officiate for, and then go on to the next, and to the next, until the Lord shall crown all who have been faithful on this earth, and the work pertaining to the earth is finished, and the Savior, whom we have been helping, has completed his task, and the earth, with all things pertaining to it, is presented to the Father. Then these faithful ones will receive their blessings and crowns, and their inheritances will be set off to them and be given to them, and they will then go on, worlds upon worlds, increasing for ever and ever (*DBY,* 376).

Suggestions for Study

The spirits of the dead go to the spirit world.

- When the body dies, where does the spirit go? (See also Alma 40:11–14.) Why can't we see and converse with those in the spirit world?

Jesus opened the door of salvation to those in the spirit world.

- What does it mean that Jesus "opened the door of salvation to the spirits in prison"? (See also D&C 138; 1 Peter 3:18–19.)
- After Christ opened the doors of salvation in the spirit world, how has the gospel been preached there? (See also D&C 138:30.)
- If none of the ordinances that pertain to the flesh are administered in the spirit world, why is the gospel being preached to the spirits there? (See also D&C 138:58–59.) What can we do for those in the spirit world who have not received the ordinances of salvation? How can we actively participate in the redemption of the dead, even if a temple is not nearby?
- How does your life in mortality influence your life in the spirit world?

The spirit world is an active place where growth and progression are possible.

- What did President Young teach about life in the spirit world? How will life in the spirit world be like earth life? How will it be different? What aspects of life in the spirit world do you look forward to?
- What influence and power does Satan have in the spirit world?
- Why is a person who has just been baptized not immediately ready to receive a fulness of glory? What must that person do to prepare for this blessing? Where can this be done?

Eternal Judgment

"I have come to the conclusion," declared President Brigham Young, "that we shall be judged according to the deeds done in the body and according to the thoughts and intents of the heart" (DNW, *17 Aug. 1869, 2; see also D&C 137:9). He taught clearly that every man and woman will experience this judgment: "Each and every intelligent being will be judged . . . according to his works, faith, desires, and honesty or dishonesty before God; every trait of his character will receive its just merit or demerit, and he will be judged according to the law of heaven"* (DNW, *12 Sept. 1860, 2).*

Teachings of Brigham Young

**We will be judged according to our works, words,
thoughts, and response to the truth.**

This is a world in which we are to prove ourselves. The lifetime of man is a day of trial, wherein we may prove to God, in our darkness, in our weakness, and where the enemy reigns, that we are our Father's friends, and that we receive light from him and are worthy to be leaders of our children—to become lords of lords, and kings of kings—to have perfect dominion over that portion of our families that will be crowned in the celestial kingdom with glory, immortality, and eternal lives (*DBY,* 87).

I do know that the trying day will soon come to you and to me; and ere long we will have to lay down these tabernacles and go into the spirit world. And I do know that as we lie down, so judgment will find us, and that is scriptural; "as the tree falls so it shall lie" [see Ecclesiastes 11:3], or, in other words, as death leaves us so judgment will find us (*DBY,* 382).

Death levels the most powerful monarch with the poorest starving mendicant [beggar]; and both must stand before the judgment seat of Christ to answer for the deeds done in the body (*DBY,* 445).

Let every one believe as he pleases and follow out the convictions of his own mind, for all are free to choose or refuse; they are free to serve God or to deny him. We have the Scriptures of divine truth, and we are free to believe or deny them. But we shall be brought to judgment before God for all these things, and shall have to give an account to him who has the right to call us to an account for the deeds done in the body (*DBY,* 67).

Time and ability to labor are the capital stock of the whole world of mankind, and we are all indebted to God for the ability to use time to advantage, and he will require of us a strict account of the disposition we make of this ability (*DBY,* 301).

The children of men will be judged according to their works, whether they be good or bad. If a man's days be filled up with good works, he will be rewarded accordingly. On the other hand, if his days be filled up with evil actions, he will receive according to those acts. . . . When will the people realize that this is the period of time in which they should commence to lay the foundation of their exaltation for time and eternity, that this is the time to conceive, and bring forth from the heart fruit to the honor and glory of God, as Jesus did (*DNW,* 13 Apr. 1854, 1).

All who believe, have honest hearts, and bring forth fruits of righteousness, are the elect of God and heirs to all things. All who refuse to obey the holy commandments of the Lord and the ordinances of his house will be judged out of their own mouths, will condemn themselves as they do now, will be accounted unworthy and will have no part or lot with the righteous (*DBY,* 383–84).

"Well," says one, "if I am pretty sure to get a state of glory better than this, I guess I will not take the trouble to inherit anything more." Well, run the risk of it, every man on the earth has the privilege. The Gospel is preached, sin revives, some die and some contend against it [the gospel]—some receive it and some do not; but this is the sin of the people—truth is told them and they reject it. This is the sin of the world. "Light has come into the world, but men love darkness rather than light, because their deeds are evil" [see John 3:19]. So said Jesus in his day. We say, here is the Gospel of life and salvation, and everyone that will receive it, glory, honor, immortality and eternal life are theirs; if they reject it, they take their chance (*DBY,* 384).

When the light of the knowledge of God comes to a man, and he rejects it, that is his condemnation (*DBY,* 383).

The principles of eternal life that are set before us are calculated to exalt us to power and preserve us from decay. If we choose to take the opposite course and to imbibe and practice the principles that tend to death, the fault is with ourselves. If we fail to obtain the salvation we are seeking for, we shall acknowledge that we have secured to ourselves every reward that is due to us by our acts, and that we have acted in accordance with the independent agency given us, and we will be judged out of our own mouths, whether we are justified or condemned (*DNW,* 17 Aug. 1859, 1).

We will be judged for living "according to the best light [we] have."

It has appeared to me, from my childhood to this day, as a piece of complete nonsense, to talk about the inhabitants of the earth being thus irretrievably lost—to talk of my father and mother, and yours, or our ancestors, who have lived faithfully according to the best light they had; but because they had not the everlasting covenant and the holy Priesthood in their midst, that they should go to hell and roast there to all eternity. It is nonsense to me; it always was, and is yet (*DBY,* 384).

A man or woman must know the ways of God before they can become ungodly. Persons may be sinners, may be unrighteous, may be wicked, who have never heard the plan of salvation, who are even unacquainted with the history of the Son of Man, or who have heard of the name of the Savior, and, perhaps, the history of his life while on the earth, but have been taught unbelief through their tradition and education; but to be ungodly, in the strict sense of the word, they must measurably understand godliness (*DBY,* 384).

So far as mortality is concerned, millions of the inhabitants of the earth live according to the best light they have—according to the best knowledge they possess. I have told you frequently that they will receive according to their works; and all, who live according to the best principles in their possession, or that they can understand, will receive peace, glory, comfort, joy and a crown that will be far beyond what they are anticipating. They will not be lost (*DBY,* 384).

If [people] have a law, no matter who made it, and do the best they know how, they will have a glory which is beyond your imagination, by any description I might give; you cannot conceive of the least portion of the glory of God prepared for his beings, the workmanship of his hands (*DBY,* 385).

I say to every priest on the face of the earth, I do not care whether they be Christian, Pagan or [Muslim], you should live according to the best light you have; and if you do you will receive all the glory you ever anticipated (*DBY,* 384–85).

All except the sons of perdition will ultimately inherit a kingdom of glory.

The disciples of Jesus were to dwell with him. Where will the rest go? Into kingdoms prepared for them, where they will live and endure. Jesus will bring forth, by his own redemption, every son and daughter of Adam, except the sons of perdition, who will be cast into hell. Others will suffer the wrath of God—will suffer all the Lord can demand at their hands, or justice can require of them; and when they have suffered the wrath of God till the utmost farthing is paid, they will be brought out of prison. Is this dangerous doctrine to preach? Some consider it dangerous; but it is true that every person who does not sin away the day of grace, and become an angel to the Devil, will be brought forth to inherit a kingdom of glory (*DBY,* 382).

More will prove faithful than will apostatize. A certain class of this people will go into the celestial kingdom, while others cannot enter there, because they cannot abide a celestial law; but they will attain to as good a kingdom as they desire and live for (*DBY,* 383).

All these different glories are ordained to fit the capacities and conditions of men (*DNW,* 13 Aug. 1862, 2).

We read in the Bible that there is one glory of the sun, another glory of the moon, and another glory of the stars [see 1 Corinthians 15:40–42]. In the book of Doctrine and Covenants [see D&C 76], these glories are called telestial, terrestrial and celestial, which is the highest. These are worlds, different departments, or mansions, in our Father's house. Now those men, or those women, who know no more about the power of God, and the influences of the Holy Spirit, than to be led entirely by another person, suspending their own understanding, and pinning their faith upon another's sleeve, will never be capable of entering into the celestial glory, to be crowned as they anticipate; they will never be capable of becoming Gods. They cannot rule themselves, to say nothing of ruling others, but they must be dictated to in every trifle, like a child. They cannot control themselves in the least, but James, Peter, or somebody else must control them. They never can become Gods, nor be crowned as rulers with glory, immortality, and eternal lives. They never can hold sceptres of glory, majesty, and power in the celestial kingdom. Who will? Those who are valiant and inspired with the true independence of heaven, who will go forth boldly in the service of their God, leaving others to do as they please, determined to do right, though all mankind besides should take the opposite course (*DBY,* 382–83).

Were the wicked, in their sins, under the necessity of walking into the presence of the Father and Son, hand-in-hand with those who believe that all will be saved—that Jesus will leave none, their condition would be more excruciating and unendurable than to dwell in the lake that burns with fire and brimstone. The fatalist's doctrine consigns to hell the infant not a span long, while the adulterer, whoremonger, thief, liar, false swearer, murderer, and every other abominable character, if they but repent on the gallows or their death-beds, are, by the same doctrine, forced into the presence of the Father and the Son, which, could they enter there, would be a hell to them (*DBY,* 385).

The punishment of God is God-like. It endures forever, because there never will be a time when people ought not to be damned, and there must always be a hell to send them to. How long the damned remain in hell, I know not, nor what degree of suffering they endure. If we could by any means compute how much wickedness they are guilty of, it might be possible to ascertain the amount of suffering they will receive. They will receive according as their deeds have been while in the body. God's punishment is eternal, but that does not prove that a wicked person will remain eternally in a state of punishment (*DBY,* 383).

Suggestions for Study

We will be judged according to our works, words, thoughts, and response to the truth.

- President Young taught that "the lifetime of man is a day of trial." What are we to "prove to God" during our mortal existence?
- For what will we be held accountable in the day of judgment? (See also Alma 12:14; 41:3.)
- Who are the elect of God?
- President Young said that we will be "judged out of our own mouths." How do we determine "whether we [will be] justified or condemned"?
- President Young taught that we will be judged according to our use of time. Why is our use of time so important? How would you judge the way you spend your time now? What have you learned from other Church members, friends, and neighbors about how time can be used well?

We will be judged for living "according to the best light [we] have."

- What circumstances or conditions in people's lives will ease the Lord's judgments concerning them? How can we apply this principle to the way we esteem people whose beliefs are different from ours?
- According to President Young, on what condition will men receive in the hereafter "peace, glory, comfort . . . far beyond what they are anticipating"?

All except the sons of perdition will ultimately inherit a kingdom of glory.

- Why would the wicked who die in their sins not be able to endure dwelling with the Father and the Son? (See also Mormon 9:3–4; D&C 88:22.)

- President Young said that Heavenly Father's children "will attain to as good a kingdom as they desire and live for." How can we determine whether we are living worthy of attaining the kingdom that we desire?

- President Young taught that all people except the sons of perdition will ultimately inherit a kingdom of glory. What does this teach you about Heavenly Father's devotion to justice and mercy? What does it teach you about His love for His children?

Salvation through Jesus Christ

President Brigham Young asked, "Are there none going to be lost? Are there none going to suffer the wrath of the Almighty? I can say, in the first place, as I have said all my life, where I have been preaching, I never had the spirit to preach hell and damnation to the people. I have tried a great many times—I tried last Sabbath, and I have tried today to come to that point—the sufferings of the wicked. They will suffer, it seems; but I cannot get my heart upon anything else, only salvation for the people" (DBY, 388). President Young taught that "all will be resurrected" (DBY, 391). He spoke of a salvation that would "reach the whole human family" (DBY, 389). And he spoke of eternal life for those who strictly "obey the requirements of the law[s] of God, and continue in faithfulness" (DBY, 387).

Teachings of Brigham Young

The salvation that Jesus Christ offers reaches the whole human family.

Behold the goodness, the long-suffering, the kindness, and the strong parental feeling of our Father and God in preparing the way and providing the means to save the children of men—not alone the Latter-day Saints—not alone those who have the privilege of the first principles of the celestial law, but to save all. It is a universal salvation—a universal redemption (*DBY,* 388).

How many shall be preserved? All who do not deny and defy the power and character of the Son of God—all who do not sin against the Holy Ghost (*DBY,* 387).

All nations are going to share in these blessings; all are incorporated in the redemption of the Savior. He has tasted death for every man; they are all in his power, and he saves them all, as he says, except the sons of perdition; and the Father has put all the creations upon this earth in his power. The earth itself, and mankind upon it, the brute beasts, the fish of the sea, and the fowls of heaven, the insects, and every creeping thing, with all things pertaining to this earthly ball,—all are in the hands of the Savior, and he has redeemed them all (*DBY,* 388).

The names of every son and daughter of Adam are already written in the Lamb's Book of Life. Is there ever a time when they will be taken out of it? Yes, when they become sons of perdition, and not till then. Every person has the privilege of retaining it there for ever and ever. If they neglect that privilege, then their names will be erased, and not till then. All the names of the human family are written there, and the Lord will hold them there until they come to the knowledge of the truth, that they can rebel against him, and can sin against the Holy Ghost; then they will be thrust down to hell, and their names be blotted out from the Lamb's Book of Life (*DBY,* 387–88).

It will be a pleasure to know that we have saved all the Father gave into our power [stewardship]. Jesus said that he lost none except the sons of perdition. He will lose none of his brethren, except sons of perdition. Let us save all the Father puts in our power (*DBY,* 388).

Our religion is adapted to the capacity of the whole human family. It does not send a portion of the people to howl in torment for ever and ever, but it reaches after the last son and daughter of Adam and Eve, and will pluck them from the prison, unlock the doors, and burst the bonds and bring forth every soul who will receive salvation (*DBY,* 389).

All heaven is anxious that the people should be saved. The heavens weep over the people, because of their hard-heartedness, unbelief, and slowness to believe and act (*DBY,* 388–89).

When God revealed to Joseph Smith and Sidney Rigdon that there was a place prepared for all, according to the light they had received and their rejection of evil and practice of good, it was a great trial to many, and some apostatized because God was not going to send to everlasting punishment heathens and infants, but had a place of salvation, in due time, for all, and would bless the honest and virtuous and truthful, whether they ever belonged to any church or not. It was a new doctrine to this generation, and many stumbled at it (*DBY,* 390–91).

Is it not a glorious thought that there are kingdoms, mansions of glory and comfortable habitations prepared for all the sons and daughters of Adam, except the sons of perdition? All will not have part in the first resurrection, and perhaps many will not appear in the second; but all will be resurrected (*DBY,* 391).

Through Christ's Atonement, all who are faithful to the laws and ordinances of the gospel will be saved in the celestial kingdom.

There is a chance [for exaltation] for those who have lived and for those who now live. The Gospel has come. Truth and light and righteousness are sent forth into the world, and those who receive them will be saved in the celestial kingdom of God. And many of those who, through ignorance, through tradition, superstition, and the erroneous precepts of the fathers, do not receive them, will yet inherit a good and glorious kingdom, and will enjoy more and receive more than ever entered into the heart of man to conceive, unless he has had a revelation (*DBY,* 389).

These words [see D&C 88:21–24] set forth the fact to which Jesus referred when he said, "In my Father's house are many mansions" [John 14:2; D&C 98:18]. How many I am not prepared to say; but here are three distinctly spoken of: the celestial, the highest; the terrestrial, the next below it; and the telestial, the third. If we were to take the pains to read what the Lord has said to his people in the latter days we should find that he has made provision for all the inhabitants of the earth; every creature who desires, and who strives in the least, to overcome evil and subdue iniquity within himself or herself, and to live worthy of a glory, will possess one. We who have received the fulness of the Gospel of the Son of God, or the Kingdom of heaven that has come to earth, are in possession of those laws, ordinances, commandments and revelations that will prepare us, by strict obedience, to inherit the celestial kingdom, to go into the presence of the Father and the Son (*DBY,* 391).

No matter what the outward appearance is—if I can know of a truth that the hearts of the people are fully set to do the will of their Father in Heaven, though they may falter and do a great many things through the weaknesses of human nature, yet they will be saved (*DBY,* 389).

And if we accept salvation on the terms it is offered to us, we have got to be honest in every thought, in our reflections, in our meditations, in our private circles, in our deals, in our declarations, and in every act of our lives, fearless and regardless of every principle of error, of every principle of falsehood that may be presented (*DBY,* 389).

Though our interest is one as a people, yet remember, salvation is an individual work; it is every person for himself. I mean more by this than I have time to tell you in full, but I will give you a hint. There are those in this Church who calculate to be saved by the righteousness of others. They will miss their mark. They are those who will arrive just as the gate is shut, so in that case you may be shut out; then you will call upon some one, who, by their own faithfulness, through the mercy of Jesus Christ, have entered in through the celestial gate, to come and open it for you; but to do this is not their province. Such will be the fate of those persons who vainly hope to be saved upon the righteousness and through the influence of Brother [or Sister] Somebody. I forewarn you therefore to cultivate righteousness and faithfulness in yourselves, which is the only passport into celestial happiness (*DBY,* 390).

If Brother Brigham shall take a wrong track, and be shut out of the Kingdom of heaven, no person will be to blame but Brother Brigham. I am the only being in heaven, earth, or hell, that can be blamed (*DBY,* 390).

This will equally apply to every Latter-day Saint. Salvation is an individual operation. I am the only person that can possibly save myself. When salvation is sent to me, I can reject or receive it. In receiving it, I yield implicit obedience and submission to its great Author throughout my life, and to those whom he shall appoint to instruct me; in rejecting it, I follow the dictates of my own will in preference to the will of my Creator (*DBY,* 390).

There never was any person over-saved; all who have been saved, and that ever will be in the future, are only just saved, and then it is not without a struggle to overcome, that calls into exercise every energy of the soul (*DBY,* 387).

Where God and Christ dwell, that is a kingdom of itself—the celestial kingdom (*DBY,* 388).

The men and women, who desire to obtain seats in the celestial kingdom, will find that they must battle every day (*DBY,* 392).

As for a person being saved in the celestial kingdom of God without being prepared to dwell in a pure and holy place, it is all nonsense and ridiculous; and if there be any who think they can gain the presence of the Father and the Son by fighting for, instead of living, their religion, they will be mistaken, consequently the quicker we make up our minds to live our religion the better it will be for us (*DBY,* 392).

The economy of heaven is to gather in all, and save everybody who can be saved (*DBY,* 387).

People should understand that there is no man [or woman] born upon the face of the earth but what can be saved in the Kingdom of God, if he is disposed to be (*DBY,* 387).

All that have lived or will live on this earth will have the privilege of receiving the Gospel. They will have Apostles, Prophets, and ministers there, as we have here, to guide them in the ways of truth and righteousness, and lead them back to God. All will have a chance for salvation and eternal life (*DBY,* 387).

If our faith is one, and we are united to gain one grand object, and I, as an individual, can possibly get into the celestial kingdom, you and every other person, by the same rule, can also enter there (*DBY,* 387).

Heavenly Father will exalt His valiant children to live in His presence in power and glory forever.

Are all spirits endowed alike? No, not by any means. Will all be equal in the celestial kingdom? No. [See D&C 131:1–4.] Some spirits are more noble than others; some are capable of receiving more than others. There is the same variety in the spirit world that you behold here, yet they are of the same parentage, of one Father, one God (*DBY,* 391).

It is the design, the wish, the will, and mind of the Lord that the inhabitants of the earth should be exalted to thrones, kingdoms, principalities, and powers, according to their capacities. . . . They must all first be subjected to sin and to the calamities of mortal flesh, in order to prove themselves worthy; then the Gospel is ready to take hold of them and bring them up, unite them, enlighten their understandings, and make them one in the Lord Jesus, that their faith, prayers, hopes, affections, and all their desires may ever be concentrated in one (*DBY,* 391–92).

The difference between the righteous and the sinner, eternal life or death, happiness or misery, is this, to those who are exalted there are no bounds or limits to their privileges, their blessings have a continuation, and to their kingdoms, thrones, and dominions, principalities, and powers there is no end, but they increase through all eternity (*DBY,* 63).

Who can define the divinity of man? Only those who understand the true principles of eternity—the principles that pertain to life and salvation. Man, by being exalted, does not lose the power and ability naturally given to him; but, on the contrary, by taking the road that leads to life, he gains more power, more influence and ability during every step he progresses therein (*DBY,* 392).

The kingdom that this people are in pertains to the Celestial kingdom; it is a kingdom in which we can prepare to go into the presence of the Father and the Son. Then let us live to inherit that glory. God has promised you, Jesus has promised you, and the apostles and prophets of old and of our day have promised you that you shall be rewarded according to all you can desire in righteousness before the Lord, if you live for that reward (*DNW,* 31 Oct. 1860, 1).

Salvation is the full existence of man, of the angels, and the Gods; it is eternal life—the life which was, which is, and which is to come. And we, as human beings, are heirs to all this life, if we apply ourselves strictly to obey the requirements of the law of God, and continue in faithfulness (*DBY,* 387).

If you have gold and silver, let it not come between you and your duty. I will tell you what to do in order to gain your exaltation, the which you cannot obtain except you take this course. If your affections are placed upon anything so as to hinder you in the least from dedicating them to the Lord, make a dedication of that thing in the first place, that the dedication of the whole may be complete. . . . If my heart is not fully given up to this work, I will give my time, my talents, my hands, and my possessions to it, until my heart consents to be subject. I will make my hands labour in the cause of God, until my heart bows in submission to it. . . .

I have now told you what course to pursue to obtain an exaltation. The Lord must be first and foremost in our affections; the building up of his cause and kingdom demands our first consideration (*DNW,* 5 Jan. 1854, 2).

No man will be saved and come into the presence of the Father, only through the Gospel of Jesus Christ—the same for one as the other. The Lord has his cause, his ways, his work; he will finish it up. Jesus is laboring with his might to sanctify and redeem the earth and to bring back his brethren and sisters into the presence of the Father. We are laboring with him for the purification of the whole human family, that we and they may be prepared to dwell with God in his Kingdom (*DBY,* 389).

Suggestions for Study

The salvation that Jesus Christ offers reaches the whole human family.

- In what sense is the salvation that Jesus Christ offers "a universal salvation—a universal redemption"? How does this universal salvation show "the strong parental feeling" our Heavenly Father has for His children? How does this knowledge bring you joy?

- President Young said that many people apostatized when God revealed to Joseph Smith and Sidney Rigdon that all people could receive salvation. Why do you think that teaching was difficult for some members to accept? How can we avoid similar problems today with the teachings of modern prophets and apostles?

Through Christ's Atonement, all who are faithful to the laws and ordinances of the gospel will be saved in the celestial kingdom.

- What do you think President Young meant when he said that "salvation is an individual work"? Why does salvation require the "exercise [of] every energy of the soul"? (See also 2 Nephi 25:23.)

- Compare President Young's discussion of those "who calculate to be saved by the righteousness of others" with the Savior's parable of the wise and foolish virgins. (See also Matthew 25:1–13; D&C 33:17; 45:56–57.) President Young also said that "we are laboring with [Jesus] for the purification of the whole human family." Recognizing that "salvation is an individual work," how can we help others in their efforts to come to Jesus Christ and receive eternal life?

- Why do even the most faithful Saints need the mercy of Jesus Christ to enter the celestial kingdom?

- According to President Young, what does it mean to receive the salvation that is offered us? What does it mean to reject salvation? What experiences have helped you learn the importance of being submissive to God's will?

- Why is it "nonsense and ridiculous" to think that we could dwell in the presence of God without being prepared to do so? (See also Mormon 9:4.) How does faithful service in The Church of Jesus Christ of Latter-day Saints prepare us to enter the celestial kingdom? Why does this preparation require us to "battle every day"?

Heavenly Father will exalt His valiant children to live in His presence in power and glory forever.

- What did President Young mean when he said that the gospel can make us "one in the Lord Jesus"? (See also John 17; 4 Nephi 1:15–17; D&C 38:27.)

- President Young taught that "Jesus is laboring with his might . . . to bring back his brethren and sisters into the presence of the Father. We are laboring with him." In what ways can we labor with Him "for the purification of the whole human family"?

One of the few known photographs of the Nauvoo Temple. President Young and other members of the Twelve served day and night so that worthy Saints could receive their endowments in the Nauvoo Temple before leaving for the Salt Lake Valley.

Temple Ordinances

As persecution increased and the need to leave Nauvoo pressed upon the Saints, President Brigham Young labored in the temple to bless the Saints with sacred ordinances before their departure. He recorded that on one day, "one hundred and forty-three persons received their endowments in the Temple. . . . Such has been the anxiety manifested by the saints to receive the ordinances [of the Temple], and such the anxiety on our part to administer to them, that I have given myself up entirely to the work of the Lord in the Temple night and day, not taking more than four hours sleep, upon an average, per day, and going home but once a week" (HC, 7:567). When he arrived in the west, President Young immediately selected a site for a new temple. He directed the building of four temples in Utah—in Salt Lake City, St. George, Manti, and Logan; however, only the St. George Temple was completed in his lifetime. On 1 January 1877, with legs so weak that he had to be carried into the room in a chair, he addressed the congregation that had met to dedicate the lower story of the St. George Temple, declaring: "We enjoy privileges that are enjoyed by no one else on the face of the earth. . . . When I think upon this subject, I want the tongues of seven thunders to wake up the people" (DNSW, 16 Jan. 1877, 1).

Teachings of Brigham Young

Temples are houses of the Lord where sacred ordinances are administered to prepare the Saints for exaltation.

It may be asked why we build temples. We build temples because there is not a house on the face of the whole earth that has been reared to God's name which will in anywise compare with his character, and that he can consistently call his house. There are places on the earth where the Lord can come and dwell, if he pleases. They may be found on the tops of high mountains, or in some cavern or places where sinful man has never marked the soil with his polluted feet (*DBY*, 393–94).

He requires his servants to build him a house that he can come to and where he can make known his will (*DBY*, 394).

"Does the Lord require the building of a temple at our hands?" I can say that he requires it just as much as ever he required one to be built elsewhere. If you should ask, "Brother Brigham, have you any knowledge concerning this; have you ever had a revelation from heaven upon it?" I can answer truly, it is before me all the time (*DBY,* 411).

We are going to build temples. This law is given to the children of men (*DBY,* 393).

We cannot . . . administer the further ordinances of God, in the fullest sense of the word, legally unto the people . . . until we have a temple built for that purpose (*DBY,* 394–95).

Some say, "I do not like to do it, for we never began to build a temple without the bells of hell beginning to ring." I want to hear them ring again (*DBY,* 410).

We completed a temple in Kirtland and in Nauvoo; and did not the bells of hell toll all the time we were building them? They did, every week and every day (*DBY,* 410).

I have determined, by the help of the Lord and this people, to build him a house. You may ask, "Will he dwell in it?" He may do just as he pleases; it is not my prerogative to dictate to the Lord. But we will build him a house, that, if he pleases to pay us a visit, he may have a place to dwell in, or if he should send any of his servants, we may have suitable accommodations for them. I have built myself a house, and the most of you have done the same, and now, shall we not build the Lord a house? (*DBY,* 411).

Do we need a temple? We do, to prepare us to enter in through the gate into the city where the Saints are at rest. Ordinances necessary to this . . . cannot be [administered] in the absence of a suitable place. We wish a temple, not for the public congregation, but for the Priesthood, wherein to arrange and organize fully the Priesthood in its order and degrees [Aaronic and Melchizedek], to administer the ordinance of the Priesthood to the Saints for their exaltation (*DBY,* 394).

The temple will be for the endowments—for the organization and instruction of the Priesthood (*DBY,* 412).

We enjoy the privilege of entering into a temple, built to the name of God, and receiving the ordinances of his house, with all the keys and blessings preparatory to entering into the "lives" [see D&C 132:22]; we also enjoy the privilege of administering for our fathers and mothers, our grandfathers and grandmothers, for those who have slept without the Gospel (*DBY,* 394).

Those only who have shared with us in the temple ordinances know for themselves the satisfaction there is in realizing that we are indeed co-workers with our Lord and Savior; that we bear a humble part in the great

The St. George Temple was the first completed and dedicated temple in Utah.

work of salvation; that we have the privilege of receiving and obeying the truth, and of securing to ourselves that happiness which the Gospel alone affords; and not only of performing these ordinances for ourselves, but of doing the necessary work for our parents and forefathers who have slept without the Gospel, that they may partake also of the waters of life, and be judged according to men in the flesh [see 1 Peter 4:6]. This is a privilege, a blessing, which no one can sense unless he is in possession of it. We are happy to know by our faith and feelings through the spirit of revelation within us that our labors have been accepted of the Lord. We have enjoyed ourselves exceedingly in the society of each other; the aged, the middle-aged and the youth have rejoiced and been made glad in this glorious work (*DBY,* 419–20).

It is for us to do those things which the Lord requires at our hands, and leave the result with him. It is for us to labor with a cheerful good will; and if we build a temple that is worth a million of money, and it requires all our time and means, we should leave it with cheerful hearts, if the Lord in his providence tells us so to do. If the Lord permits our enemies to drive us from it, why, we should abandon it with as much cheerfulness of heart as we ever enjoy a blessing. It is no matter to us what the Lord does, or how he disposes of the labor of his servants. But when he commands, it is for his people to obey. We should be as cheerful in building this temple, if we knew beforehand that we should never enter into it when it was finished, as we would though we knew we were to live here a thousand years to enjoy it (*DBY,* 411).

You have got to do the work, or it will not be done. We do not want any whiners about this temple. If you cannot commence cheerfully, and go through the labor of the whole building cheerfully, start for California, and the quicker the better. Make you a golden calf, and worship it. If your care for the ordinances of salvation, for yourselves, your living, and dead, is not first and foremost in your hearts, in your actions, and in everything you possess, go! Pay your debts, if you have any, and go in peace, and prove to God and all his Saints that you are what you profess to be, by your acts (*DBY,* 417–18).

We . . . are enjoying a privilege that we have no knowledge of any other people enjoying since the days of Adam, that is, to have a temple completed, wherein all the ordinances of the house of God can be bestowed upon his people. Brethren and sisters, do you understand this? (*DBY,* 393).

The endowment enables us to return someday to the presence of the Lord.

The preparatory ordinances . . . administered [in the Kirtland Temple], though accompanied by the ministrations of angels, and the presence of the Lord Jesus, were but a faint similitude of the ordinances of the house of the Lord in their fulness; yet many, through the instigation of the Devil, thought they had received all, and knew as much as God; they have apostatized, and gone to hell. But be assured, brethren, there are but few, very few of the Elders of Israel, now on earth, who know the meaning of the word endowment. To know, they must experience; and to experience, a temple must be built (*DBY,* 415–16).

Let me give you a definition in brief. Your endowment is, to receive all those ordinances in the house of the Lord, which are necessary for you, after you have departed this life, to enable you to walk back to the presence of the Father, passing the angels who stand as sentinels (*DBY,* 416).

Who has received and understands such an endowment, in this assembly? . . . The keys to these endowments are among you, and thousands have received them, so that the Devil, with all his aids, need not suppose he can again destroy the holy Priesthood from the earth, by killing a few, for he cannot do it. God has set his hand, for the last time, to redeem his people, the honest in heart, and Lucifer cannot hinder him (*DBY,* 416).

It is absolutely necessary that the Saints should receive the further ordinances of the house of God before this short existence shall come to a close, that they may be prepared and fully able to pass all the sentinels leading into the celestial kingdom and into the presence of God (*DBY*, 395).

The ordinances of the house of God are for the salvation of the human family. We . . . hold the keys of salvation committed to the children of men from the heavens by the Lord Almighty; and inasmuch as there are those who hold these keys, it is important that they should be acted upon for the salvation of the human family. The building of temples, places in which the ordinances of salvation are administered, is necessary to carry out the plan of redemption, and it is a glorious subject upon which to address the Saints (*DBY*, 396–97).

I feel sometimes like lecturing men and women severely who enter into covenants without realizing the nature of the covenants they make, and who use little or no effort to fulfil them (*DBY*, 396).

Some Elders go to the nations and preach the Gospel of life and salvation, and return without thoroughly understanding the nature of the covenant. It is written in the Bible that every man should perform his own vows, even if to his own hurt [see Ecclesiastes 5:4–5]; in this way you will show to all creation and to God that you are full of integrity (*DBY*, 396).

The sealing ordinances can connect Adam's righteous posterity eternally through priesthood authority.

There are many of the ordinances of the house of God that must be performed in a temple that is erected expressly for the purpose. There are other ordinances that we can administer without a temple. You know that there are some which you have received—baptism, the laying on of hands for the gift of the Holy Ghost, . . . and many blessings bestowed upon the people, we have the privilege of receiving without a temple. There are other blessings, that will not be received, and ordinances that will not be performed according to the law that the Lord has revealed, without their being done in a temple prepared for that purpose. . . . When we come to . . . sealing ordinances [for the dead], ordinances pertaining to the holy Priesthood, to connect the chain of the Priesthood from Father Adam until now, by sealing children to their parents, being sealed for our forefathers, etc., they cannot be done without a temple. When the ordinances are carried out in the temples that will be erected, [children] will be sealed to their [parents], and those who have slept, clear up to Father Adam. This will have to be done, because of the chain of the Priesthood being broken upon the earth. The Priesthood has left the people, but in the first place the people left the Priesthood. They transgressed the laws, changed the ordinance, and broke the everlasting covenant [see Isaiah 24:5], and the Priesthood left them; but not until they had left the Priesthood. This Priesthood has been restored again, and by its authority we shall be connected with our fathers, by the ordinance of sealing, until we shall form a perfect chain from Father Adam down to the closing up scene [see D&C 128:18]. This ordinance will not be performed anywhere but in a temple; neither will children be sealed to their living parents in any other place than a temple. . . . Then parents, after receiving their endowments and being sealed for time and eternity, and they have other children; they are begotten and born under the covenant, and they are the rightful heirs to the kingdom, they possess the keys of the kingdom. Children born unto parents, before the latter enter into the fulness of the covenants, have to be sealed to them in a temple to become legal heirs of the Priesthood. It is true they can receive the ordinances, they can receive their endowments, and be blessed in common with their parents; but still the parents cannot claim them legally and lawfully in eternity unless they are sealed to them. Yet the chain would not be complete without this sealing ordinance being performed (*DBY*, 399–401).

Were it not for what is revealed concerning the sealing ordinances, children born out of the covenant could not be sealed to their parents (*DBY*, 397).

The ordinance of sealing must be performed here . . . until the chain of generation is made perfect in the sealing ordinances back to Father Adam; hence, we have been commanded to gather ourselves together to come out of Babylon [see D&C 133:14], and sanctify ourselves, and build up the Zion of our God, by building cities and temples, redeeming countries from the solitude of nature, until the earth is sanctified and prepared for the residence of God and angels (*DBY*, 407).

Suggestions for Study

Temples are houses of the Lord where sacred ordinances are administered to prepare the Saints for exaltation.

- Why do we build temples? Why does the building of temples cause "the bells of hell . . . to ring"? Why do you think President Young said, "I want to hear them ring again"?

- In what ways does temple service make us "co-workers with our Lord and Savior"? How can we know that our "labors have been accepted of the Lord"?

- President Young said, "We do not want any whiners about [the] temple." Why are "a cheerful good will" and willing obedience required for the building of temples and for temple worship? What have you done that has helped you not to complain about building temples and worshiping in temples? Why must the ordinances of salvation be "first and foremost" in our hearts and actions?

The endowment enables us to return someday to the presence of the Lord.

- What did President Young teach about the purpose of the temple endowment?

- What are the dangers of making covenants without recognizing their sacred nature? How can we understand the nature of our covenants and make an "effort to fulfil them"? How can we help our children understand the sacred nature of covenants made in the temple?

The sealing ordinances can connect Adam's righteous posterity eternally through priesthood authority.

- What does it mean to form "a perfect chain from Father Adam down to the closing up scene"? What is our responsibility in forming this chain? (See also D&C 128:18.) How can making such connections bless us and our families now and in the future?

- How does the sealing ordinance help us "come out of Babylon, and sanctify ourselves, and build up the Zion of our God"?

- What can you do to make the sealing ordinance of the temple fully effective in your life? How do you feel when you realize that you can make eternal family ties with your ancestors, your posterity, and your immediate family? How does this knowledge influence how you feel about living the gospel each day?

This is a recent photograph of the St. George Temple. The dedication
of this temple in April 1877 enabled the Saints to begin performing
endowments for the dead.

Temple Service

When the St. George Temple was dedicated in April 1877, President Brigham Young rejoiced that the Saints finally could begin to perform temple endowments for the dead. He reported that the Saints who began laboring there "had a blessed time, such a time as no other people on the earth have enjoyed for many centuries, that we have any knowledge of" (DBY, 419). "Since the completion of the temple at St. George," he wrote his son Lorenzo, "the spirit to look after the dead and to officiate for them, and also attend to the necessary ordinances for the living, has taken possession of the faithful members of the Church all through these valleys. The Saints probably have never felt such interest in these subjects since the organization of the Church as they do at the present. This will be attended with good results, and as the work of building temples progresses, this spirit will be felt with greater power through all the branches of the Church" (LBY, 288–89).

Teachings of Brigham Young

God gives those who have died the opportunity to enjoy temple blessings.

My father died before the endowments were given. None of his children have been sealed to him. If you recollect, you that were in Nauvoo, we were very much hurried in the little time we spent there after the temple was built. The mob was there ready to destroy us; they were ready to burn our houses, they had been doing it for a long time; but we finished the temple according to the commandment that was given to Joseph, and then took our departure. Our time, therefore, was short, and we had no time to attend to this. My father's children, consequently, have not been sealed to him. Perhaps all of his sons may go into eternity, into the spirit world, before this can be attended to; but this will make no difference; the heirs of the family will attend to this if it is not for a hundred years (*DBY,* 401).

Hundreds of millions of human beings have been born, lived out their short earthly span, and passed away, ignorant alike of themselves and of the plan of salvation provided for them. It gives great consolation, however, to know that this glorious plan devised by Heaven follows them into the next existence, offering for their acceptance eternal life and exaltation to thrones, dominions, principalities, and powers in the presence of their Father and God, through Jesus Christ, his Son (*DBY,* 404).

We are preaching to them the Gospel of Salvation—to the dead—through those who have lived in this dispensation [see D&C 138:57] (*DBY,* 397).

There is an opportunity for men who are in the spirit to receive the Gospel. Jesus, while his body lay in the grave two nights and one day, went to the world of spirits to show the brethren how they should build up the kingdom, and bring spirits to the knowledge of the truth in the spirit world; he went to set them the pattern there, as he had done on this earth. Hence you perceive that there, spirits have the privilege of embracing the truth.

You may ask if they are baptized there? No. Can they have hands laid upon them for the gift of the Holy Ghost? No. None of the outward ordinances that pertain to the flesh are administered there, but the light, glory, and power of the Holy Ghost are enjoyed just as freely as upon this earth; and there are laws which govern and control the spirit world, and to which they are subject (*DBY,* 397).

Can we do anything for them? Yes. What are we trying to build a temple for? And we shall not only build a temple here, if we are successful, and are blessed and preserved, but we shall probably commence two or three more, and so on as fast as the work requires, for the express purpose of redeeming our dead. When I get a revelation that some of my progenitors lived and died without the blessings of the Gospel, or even hearing it preached, but were as honest as I am, as upright as I am, or as any man or woman could be upon the earth; as righteous, so far as they knew how, as any Apostle or Prophet that ever lived, I will go and be baptized, confirmed, washed, and anointed, and go through all the ordinances and endowments for them, that their way may be opened to the celestial kingdom (*DBY,* 403).

This doctrine of baptism for the dead is a great doctrine, one of the most glorious doctrines that was revealed to the human family; and there are light, power, glory, honor and immortality in it (*DBY,* 399).

Many a man I know of, who has fallen asleep [died], we have been baptized for, since the Church was organized—good, honest, honorable men, charitable to all, living good, virtuous lives. We will not let them go down to hell; God will not. The plan of salvation is ample to bring them all up and place them where they may enjoy all they could anticipate (*DBY,* 403).

They have passed the ordeals [of mortality], and are beyond the possibility of personally officiating for the remission of their sins and for their exaltation, consequently they are under the necessity of trusting in their friends, their children and their children's children to officiate for them, that they may be brought up into the celestial kingdom of God (*DBY,* 406).

What do you suppose the fathers would say if they could speak from the dead? Would they not say, "We have lain here thousands of years, here in this prison house, waiting for this dispensation to come?" . . . What would they whisper in our ears? Why, if they had the power the very thunders of heaven would be in our ears, if we could realize the importance of the work we are engaged in. All the angels in heaven are looking at this little handful of people, and stimulating them to the salvation of the human family. So also are the devils in hell looking at this people, too, and trying to overthrow us, and the people are still shaking hands with the servants of the devil, instead of sanctifying themselves and calling upon the Lord and doing the work which he has commanded us and put into our hands to do (*DBY,* 403–4).

Heavenly Father will bless us for doing family history research for the salvation of our forefathers.

I think there is a work to be done [in the Millennium] which the whole world seems determined we shall not do. What is it? To build temples. We never yet commenced to lay the foundation of a temple but what all hell was in arms against us. . . . What are we going to do in these temples? Anything to be done there? Yes, and we will not wait for the Millennium and the fulness of the glory of God on the earth; we will commence as soon as we have a temple, and work for the salvation of our forefathers; we will get their genealogies as far as we can. By and by, we shall get them perfect. In these temples we will officiate in the ordinances of the Gospel of Jesus Christ for our friends (*DBY,* 402).

We are now baptizing for the dead . . . for our fathers, mothers, grandfathers, grandmothers, uncles, aunts, relatives, friends and old associates. . . . The Lord is stirring up the hearts of many . . . , and there is a perfect mania with some to trace their genealogies and to get up printed records of their ancestors. They do not know what they are doing it for, but the Lord is prompting them; and it will continue and run on from father to father, father to father, until they get the genealogy of their forefathers as far as they possibly can (*DBY,* 406).

When his Kingdom is established upon the earth, and Zion built up, the Lord will send his servants as saviors upon Mount Zion [see Obadiah 1:21]. The servants of God who have lived on the earth in ages past will reveal where different persons have lived who have died without the Gospel, give their names, and say, "Now go forth, ye servants of God, and exercise your rights and privileges; go and perform the ordinances of the house of God for those who have passed their probation without the Gospel, and for all who will receive any kind of salvation; bring them up to inherit the celestial, terrestrial, and telestial kingdoms," . . . for every person will receive according to his capacity and according to the deeds done in the body, whether good or bad, much or little (*DBY,* 407).

The Lord says, I have sent the keys of Elijah the Prophet—I have imparted that doctrine to turn the hearts of the fathers to the children, and the hearts of the children to the fathers [see D&C 2; 110:13–15]. Now, all you children, are you looking to the salvation of your fathers? Are you seeking diligently to redeem those that have died without the Gospel, inasmuch as they sought the Lord Almighty to obtain promises for you? For our fathers did obtain promises that their seed should not be forgotten. O ye children of the fathers, look at these things. You are to enter into the temples of the Lord and officiate for your forefathers (*DBY,* 408).

We become saviors on Mount Zion through performing temple ordinances for our kindred dead.

We are called, as it has been told you, to redeem the nations of the earth. The fathers cannot be made perfect without us; we cannot be made perfect without the fathers. There must be this chain in the holy Priesthood; it must be welded together from the latest generation that lives on the earth back to Father Adam, to bring back all that can be saved and placed where they can receive salvation and a glory in some kingdom. This Priesthood has to do it; this Priesthood is for this purpose (*DBY,* 407).

The doctrines of the Savior reveal and place the believers in possession of principles whereby saviors will come upon Mount Zion to save . . . all except those who have sinned against the Holy Ghost. Men and women will enter into the temples of God, and be, in comparison, pillars there [see Revelation 3:12], and officiate year after year for those who have slept thousands of years (*DBY,* 407).

To accomplish this work there will have to be not only one temple but thousands of them, and thousands and tens of thousands of men and women will go into those temples and officiate for people who have lived as far back as the Lord shall reveal (*DBY,* 394).

This is what we are going to do for the inhabitants of the earth. When I look at it, I do not want to rest a great deal, but be industrious all the day long; for when we come to think upon it, we have no time to lose, for it is a pretty laborious work (*DBY,* 410).

The priesthood the Lord has again bestowed upon those who will receive it, is for the express purpose of preparing them to become proficient in the principles pertaining to the law of the celestial kingdom. If we obey this law, preserve it inviolate, live according to it, we shall be prepared to enjoy the blessings of a celestial kingdom. Will any others? Yes, thousands and millions of the inhabitants of the earth who would have received and obeyed the law that we preach, if they had had the privilege. When the Lord shall bring again Zion, and the watchmen shall see eye to eye, and Zion shall be established, saviors will come upon Mount Zion and save all the sons and daughters of Adam that are capable of being saved, by administering for them (*DNW,* 16 May 1860, 1).

Our fathers cannot be made perfect without us; we cannot be made perfect without them. They have done their work and now sleep. We are now called upon to do ours; which is to be the greatest work man ever performed on the earth. Millions of our fellow creatures who have lived upon the earth and died without a knowledge of the Gospel must be officiated for in order that they may inherit eternal life (that is, all that would have received the Gospel). And we are called upon to enter into this work (*DBY,* 406).

Who will possess the earth and all its fulness? Will it not be those whom the Lord has reserved to this honor? And they will come upon Mount Zion as saviors to labor through the Millennium to save others (*DBY,* 407–8).

The work of the Millennium will include temple building and temple service.

We are trying to save the living and the dead. The living can have their choice, the dead have not. Millions of them died without the Gospel, without the Priesthood, and without the opportunities that we enjoy. We shall go forth in the name of Israel's God and attend to the ordinances for them. And through the Millennium, the thousand years that the people will love and serve God, we will build temples and officiate therein for those who have slept for hundreds and thousands of years—those who would have received the truth if they had had the opportunity; and we will bring them up, and form the chain entire, back to Adam (*DBY,* 404).

As I have frequently told you, that is the work of the Millennium. It is the work that has to be performed by the seed of Abraham, the chosen seed, the royal seed, the blessed of the Lord, those the Lord made covenants with. They will step forth, and save every son and daughter of Adam who will receive salvation here on the earth; and all the spirits in the spirit world will be preached to, conversed with, and the principles of salvation carried

311

to them, that they may have the privilege of receiving the Gospel; and they will have plenty of children here on the earth to officiate for them in those ordinances of the Gospel that pertain to the flesh (*DBY,* 403).

We trust in God. I reckon he will fight our battles and we will be baptized for and in behalf of the human family during a thousand years; and we will have hundreds of temples and thousands of men and women officiating therein for those who have fallen asleep, without having had the privilege of hearing and obeying the Gospel, that they may be brought forth and have a glorious resurrection, and enjoy the kingdom which God has prepared for them. The Devil will fight hard to hinder us, and we shall not take an inch of ground except by obedience to the power of, and faith in, the Gospel of the Son of God. The whole world is opposed to this doctrine. But is there any harm in it? If they could only see it as it is in the Lord, they would rejoice in it, and instead of fighting it, they would praise God for having revealed so glorious a doctrine (*DBY,* 401).

Suggestions for Study

God gives those who have died the opportunity to enjoy temple blessings.

- The "glorious plan" for redeeming those who died without having received the full blessings of the gospel was a "great consolation" to President Young. Why? What does that plan mean to you and your loved ones?

- How and when was the preaching of the gospel in the spirit world organized? Who continues in that labor now? (See also D&C 138:57.)

- What does it mean to redeem our dead and open to them the celestial kingdom? (See also D&C 138:58.)

- Why does Satan so actively oppose temple work? What evidence have you seen that Satan cannot prevent temples from being built nor stop the saving ordinance work from flourishing?

Heavenly Father will bless us for doing family history research for the salvation of our forefathers.

- President Young spoke of a time when we would perfect our genealogies or family histories. How will we do this? What can you personally do to contribute to your family history?

- According to President Young, who is "stirring up the hearts of many" to learn about their ancestors? What evidence have you seen that this is true today?

- What are "the keys of Elijah the Prophet"? (See also D&C 27:9; 110:13–15.)

We become saviors on Mount Zion through performing temple ordinances for our kindred dead.

- How can we become saviors on Mount Zion?
- Why is it impossible for our kindred dead to be made perfect without us? Why is it impossible for us to be made perfect without them?

The work of the Millennium will include temple building and temple service.

- What will be "the work of the Millennium"? Who will perform it?
- How can we overcome Satan's attempts to hinder the work? How do "obedience to the power of, and faith in, the Gospel of the Son of God" help us prepare for the Millennium?

Joseph Smith, a careful reader of the Bible, asked God for direction.

Our Search for Truth and Personal Testimony

President Brigham Young's search for the truth of God was finally resolved by the sincere and simple testimony of a "man without eloquence . . . who could only say, 'I know, by the power of the Holy Ghost, that the Book of Mormon is true, that Joseph Smith is a Prophet of the Lord.' " Said President Young, "The Holy Ghost proceeding from that individual illuminated my understanding, and light, glory, and immortality were before me" (DNW, 9 Feb. 1854, 4). Throughout his life, he sought to live gospel truths, declaring, "As I advance in years I hope to advance in the true knowledge of God and godliness. I hope to increase in the power of the Almighty and in influence to establish peace and righteousness upon the earth, and to bring . . . all who will hearken to the principles of righteousness, to a true sense of the knowledge of God and godliness, of themselves and the relation they sustain to heaven and heavenly beings. . . . I pray that this may be the case not only with myself but with all the Saints, that we may grow in grace and in the knowledge of the truth and be made perfect before Him" (DNW, 10 June 1857, 3).

Teachings of Brigham Young

Many desire to find the truth, but not all embrace it.

The greater portion of the inhabitants of the earth are inclined to do right. That is true. There is a monitor in every person that would reign there triumphantly, if permitted so to do, and lead to truth and virtue [see Moroni 7:15–17] (*DBY,* 423).

Honest hearts, the world over, desire to know the right way. They have sought for it, and still seek it. There have been people upon the earth all the time who sought diligently with all their hearts to know the ways of the Lord. Those individuals have produced good, inasmuch as they had the ability (*DBY,* 421).

Until they sin away the day of grace, there is something in all persons that would delight to rise up and reject the evil and embrace the truth.

315

There is not a person on the earth so vile but, when he looks into his own heart, honors the man of God and the woman of God—the virtuous and holy—and despises his comrades in iniquity who are like himself. There is not a man upon the earth, this side of saving grace, unless he has sinned so far that the Spirit of the Lord has ceased to strive with him and enlighten his mind, but delights in the good, in the truth, and in the virtuous (*DBY*, 421).

It is recorded that some have eyes to see, and see not; ears to hear, and hear not; hearts have they, but they understand not. You who are spiritually-minded, who have the visions of your minds opened, . . . can understand that the power that has given you physical sensation is the power of the same God that gives you understanding of the truth [see D&C 88:11–13]. The latter power is inward. . . . Thousands and thousands know, by their inward and invisible sensation, things that have been, things that are, and things that are in the future, as well as they know the color of a piece of cloth by means of their outward or physical vision. When this inner light is taken from them, they become darker than they were before, they cannot understand, and turn away from the things of God (*DBY*, 421–22).

The spirit which inhabits these tabernacles naturally loves truth, it naturally loves light and intelligence, it naturally loves virtue, God and godliness; but being so closely united with the flesh their sympathies are blended, and their union being necessary to the possession of a fulness of joy to both [see D&C 93:33–34], the spirit is indeed subject to be influenced by the sin that is in the mortal body, and to be overcome by it and by the power of the Devil, unless it is constantly enlightened by that spirit which enlighteneth every man that cometh into the world, and by the power of the Holy Ghost which is imparted through the Gospel (*DBY*, 422–23).

Wherever the Gospel of Jesus Christ has been preached, either in these or former days, it has met with a class of men to whom the truth looked lovely and God-like, and the spirit within would prompt them to embrace it; but they find themselves so advantageously connected in the world, and have so many interests at stake if they should embrace it, they conclude that it will not do, and here comes the warfare again. Some few will overcome the reasonings of the flesh, and follow the dictates of the spirit; while the great majority of this class of persons are won over by sordid considerations and cleave to their idols (*DBY*, 434).

Each of us is responsible to seek knowledge
and a witness of the truth.

What are we here for? To learn to enjoy more, and to increase in knowledge and experience (*DNW,* 27 Sept. 1871, 5).

We shall never cease to learn, unless we apostatize. . . . Can you understand that? (*DNW,* 27 Feb. 1856, 2).

If we can have the privilege we will enrich our minds with knowledge, filling these mortal tenements with the rich treasures of heavenly wisdom (*MS,* Oct. 1862, 630).

All our educational pursuits are in the service of God, for all these labors are to establish truth on the earth, and that we may increase in knowledge, wisdom, understanding in the power of faith and in the wisdom of God, that we may become fit subjects to dwell in a higher state of existence and intelligence than we now enjoy (*DNSW,* 25 Oct. 1870, 2).

It is possible for a man who loves the world to overcome that love, to get knowledge and understanding until he sees things as they really are, then he will not love the world but will see it as it is (*DNW,* 28 Nov. 1855, 2).

Let us seek the Lord with all our hearts, then shall we be weaned from the world; no man will love this, that, or the other thing, except to do good with it; to promote the eternal interests of mankind, and prepare them to be exalted in immortality. . . . It is for you and I to receive wisdom so as to be prepared for exaltation and eternal lives in kingdoms that now exist in eternity (*DNW,* 14 May 1853, 3).

A man or woman desirous of knowing the truth, upon hearing the Gospel of the Son of God proclaimed in truth and simplicity, should ask the Father, in the name of Jesus, if this is true. If they do not take this course, they try and argue themselves into the belief that they are as honest as any man or woman can be on the face of the earth; but they are not, they are careless as to their own best interests (*DBY,* 430).

Wait until you have searched and researched and have obtained wisdom to understand what we preach. . . . If it is the work of God, it will stand [see Acts 5:38–39] (*DBY,* 435).

It is both the duty and privilege of the Latter-day Saints to know that their religion is true (*DBY,* 429).

Let every one get a knowledge for himself that this work is true. We do not want you to say that it is true until you know that it is; and if you know it, that knowledge is as good to you as though the Lord came down and told you (*DBY,* 429).

It is a special privilege and blessing of the holy Gospel to every true believer, to know the truth for himself (*DBY,* 429).

I do not want men to come to me or my brethren for testimony as to the truth of this work; but let them take the Scriptures of divine truth, and there the path is pointed out to them as plainly as ever a guideboard indicated the right path to the weary traveler. There they are directed to go, not to . . . any Apostle or Elder in Israel, but to the Father in the name of Jesus, and ask for the information they need. Can they who take this course in honesty and sincerity receive information? Will the Lord turn away from the honest heart seeking the truth? No, he will not; he will prove it to them, by the revelations of his Spirit, the facts in the case. And when the mind is open to the revelations of the Lord it comprehends them quicker and keener than anything that is seen by the natural eye. It is not what we see with our eyes—they may be deceived—but what is revealed by the Lord from heaven that is sure and steadfast, and abides forever (*DBY,* 429–30).

We must have the testimony of the Lord Jesus to enable us to discern between truth and error, light and darkness, him who is of God, and him who is not of God, and to know how to place everything where it belongs. . . . There is no other method or process which will actually school a person so that he can become a Saint of God, and prepare him for a celestial glory; he must have within him the testimony of the spirit of the Gospel (*DBY,* 429).

You and I must have the testimony of Jesus within us, or it is of but little use for us to pretend to be servants of God. We must have that living witness within us (*DBY,* 430).

Truth commends itself to every honest person, it matters not how simply it is told, and when it is received it seems as though we had been acquainted with it all our lives. It is the testimony of the majority of the Latter-day Saints that when they first heard the Gospel preached, . . . although entirely new to them, it seemed as though they already understood it, and that they must have been "Mormons" from the beginning [see John 10:27] (*DBY,* 432).

The Holy Ghost grants us knowledge of the truth.

Men rise up here and say they do know that this is the work of God, that Joseph was a Prophet, that the Book of Mormon is true, that the revelations through Joseph Smith are true, and this is the last dispensation and the fulness of times, wherein God has set his hand to gather Israel for the last time, and redeem and build up Zion. . . . How do they know this? Persons know and will continue to know and understand many things by the manifestations of the Spirit, that through the organization of the tabernacle it is impossible otherwise to convey. Much of the most important information is alone derived through the power and testimony of the Holy Ghost. . . . This is the only way you can convey a knowledge of the invisible things of God [see 1 Corinthians 2:9–14; 12:3] (*DBY,* 430).

Nothing short of the Holy Spirit . . . can prove to you that this is the work of God. Men uninspired of God cannot by their worldly wisdom disprove it, or prevail against it; neither can they by wisdom alone prove it to be true, either to themselves or to others. Their not being able to prevail against it does not prove it to be the Kingdom of God, for there are many theories and systems on the earth, incontrovertible by the wisdom of the world, which are nevertheless false. Nothing less than the power of the Almighty, enlightening the understanding of men, can demonstrate this glorious truth to the human mind (*DBY,* 430–31).

How are we to know the voice of the Good Shepherd from the voice of a stranger? Can any person answer this question? I can. It is very easy. To every philosopher upon the earth, I say, your eye can be deceived, so can mine; your ear can be deceived, so can mine; the touch of your hand can be deceived, so can mine; but the Spirit of God filling the creature with revelation and the light of eternity, cannot be mistaken—the revelation which comes from God is never mistaken. When an individual, filled with the Spirit of God, declares the truth of heaven, the sheep hear that [see D&C 29:7], the Spirit of the Lord pierces their inmost souls and sinks deep into their hearts; by the testimony of the Holy Ghost light springs up within them, and they see and understand for themselves (*DBY,* 431).

There is but one witness—one testimony, pertaining to the evidence of the Gospel of the Son of God, and that is the Spirit that he diffused among his disciples. Do his will, and we shall know whether he speaks by the authority of the Father or of himself. Do as he commands us to do, and we shall know of the doctrine, whether it is of God or not [see John 7:16–17]. It is only by the revelations of the Spirit that we can know the things of God (*DBY,* 431–32).

Be diligent and prayerful. It is your privilege to know for yourself God lives and that He is doing a work in these last days and we are His honored ministers. Live for this knowledge and you will receive it. Remember your prayers and be fervent in spirit (*LBY,* 245).

My testimony is based upon experience, upon my own experience, in connection with that obtained by observing others. . . . The heavenly truth commends itself to every person's judgment and to their faith; and more especially to the sense of those who wish to be honest with themselves, with their God, and with their neighbor. . . . If persons can receive a little, it proves they may receive more. If they can receive the first and second principles with an upright feeling, they may receive still more (*DBY,* 433).

My testimony is positive. . . . I know that the sun shines, I know that I exist and have a being, and I testify that there is a God, and that Jesus Christ lives, and that he is the Savior of the world. Have you been to heaven and learned to the contrary? I know that Joseph Smith was a Prophet of God, and that he had many revelations. Who can disprove this testimony? Any one may dispute it, but there is no one in the world who can disprove it. I have had many revelations; I have seen and heard for myself, and know these things are true, and nobody on earth can disprove them. The eye, the ear, the hand, all the senses may be deceived, but the Spirit of God cannot be deceived; and when inspired with that Spirit, the whole man is filled with knowledge, he can see with a spiritual eye, and know that which is beyond the power of man to controvert. What I know concerning God, concerning the earth, concerning government, I have received from the heavens, not alone through my natural ability, and I give God the glory and the praise (*DBY*, 433).

Having received a witness of the truth, we should seek righteousness in the kingdom of God.

It is one of the first principles of the doctrine of salvation to become acquainted with our Father and our God. The Scriptures teach that this is eternal life, to "know Thee, the only true God, and Jesus Christ whom thou hast sent [see John 17:3];" this is as much as to say that no man can enjoy or be prepared for eternal life without that knowledge (*DNW*, 18 Feb. 1857, 4).

We have the promise, if we seek first the kingdom of God and its righteousness, that all necessary things will be added to us [see 3 Nephi 13:33]. We should not be distrustful, but seek first to know how to please our Father and God; seek to know how to save ourselves from the errors that are in the world, from darkness and unbelief, from the vain and delusive spirits that go abroad among the children of men to deceive, and learn how to save and preserve ourselves upon the earth to preach the gospel, build up the kingdom, and establish the Zion of our God (*DNW*, 11 Jan. 1860, 1).

I . . . love to reflect and talk on eternal principles. Our salvation consists in knowing them, and they are designed in their nature to cheer and comfort us. Is that eternal existence in me, that feeds upon eternal truth, organized to be destroyed? Is that organism ever to come to an end, so long as it lives upon eternal truth? No. . . . Seek unto the Lord for his Spirit, without any cessation in your efforts, until his Spirit dwells within you like eternal burnings. Let the candle of the Lord be lighted up within you, and all is right (*DNW*, 11 Jan. 1860, 2).

We have the words of eternal life, we have the privilege of obtaining glory, immortality, and eternal lives, now will you obtain these blessings?

Will you spend your lives to obtain a seat in the kingdom of God, or will you lie down and sleep, and go down to hell? (*DNW,* 1 Oct. 1856, 3)

Strive to be righteous, not for any speculation, but because righteousness is lovely, pure, holy, beautiful, and exalting; it is designed to make the soul happy and full of joy, to the extent of the whole capacity of man, filling him with light, glory, and intelligence (*DBY,* 428).

Suggestions for Study

Many desire to find the truth, but not all embrace it.

- According to President Young, what leads "the greater portion of the inhabitants of the earth" to do what is right and search for the truth?
- Why do many people fail to live righteously even after receiving a witness of the truth? What has helped you most to live according to the testimony that you have developed?

Each of us is responsible to seek knowledge and a witness of the truth.

- What should be the purposes of our educational pursuits? What can we do to overcome the love of worldly things?
- How can we know God's truths for ourselves? How does a testimony of Jesus Christ help us discern between truth and error?

The Holy Ghost grants us knowledge of the truth.

- What is the only way we can know that the gospel is true, that Jesus is the Christ, and that we are engaged in the work of the Lord? What experiences have taught you that the Holy Ghost can and will influence your life if you allow Him to do so?
- Why can worldly wisdom neither prove nor disprove the existence of God and the truth of the gospel? Though our physical senses may be deceived in the search for truth, what did President Young say "cannot be mistaken"?
- Why was President Young able to bear such powerful testimony? How can we strengthen our testimonies? What can you do to become a more powerful witness of the truth of God?

**Having received a witness of the truth, we should
seek righteousness in the kingdom of God.**

- What promise does the Lord make to those who "seek first the kingdom of God and its righteousness"?

- How does knowing the things of God help us gain salvation? How can we "obtain a seat in the kingdom of God"?

The Kingdom of God and the Gathering of Israel

On July 26, 1847, just a few days after the first pioneers entered the Salt Lake Valley, President Brigham Young and a small group of priesthood leaders climbed a hill north of the area that would later become Salt Lake City. They named the hill Ensign Peak in remembrance of the prophecy of Isaiah: "He will lift up an ensign to the nations from far . . . and, behold, they shall come with speed swiftly" (Isaiah 5:26). President Young later identified this hill as the place he had seen in a vision, a place where the Saints would flourish, where the kingdom of God could be built and the latter-day Israel gathered. In the years that followed, missionaries took the message of the gospel throughout the world, and thousands of newly converted Saints came to the Salt Lake Valley. Today the building of the kingdom and the gathering of Israel goes on in hundreds of nations. President Young said, "The gathering of Israel is so important a part of the great work in which we are engaged that it occupies much of our thoughts, and we are ever anxious to afford it all just facilities and influence" (BYL).

Teachings of Brigham Young

The people of God seek to build the kingdom of God.

The people that sit before me, in connection with the many thousands that are upon the earth, are the people of God. . . . Just as fast as we are capable of rightly dispensing the principles of power, of light, of knowledge, of intelligence, of wealth, of heaven, and of earth, just so fast will they be bestowed upon this people (*DBY,* 438).

Out of this Church will grow the Kingdom which Daniel saw. This is the very people that Daniel saw would continue to grow and spread and prosper [see Daniel 2:44]; and if we are not faithful, others will take our places, for this is the Church and people that will possess the Kingdom for ever and ever (*DBY,* 438).

Our work is to bring forth Zion, and produce the Kingdom of God in its perfection and beauty upon the earth (*DBY,* 443).

The Kingdom we are talking about, preaching about and trying to build up is the Kingdom of God on the earth, not in the starry heavens, nor in the sun. We are trying to establish the Kingdom of God on the earth to which really and properly everything that pertains to men—their feelings, their faith, their affections, their desires, and every act of their lives—belong, that they may be ruled by it spiritually and temporally (*DBY,* 339).

When the Kingdom of God is fully set up and established on the face of the earth, and takes the preeminence over all other nations and kingdoms, it will protect the people in the enjoyment of all their rights, no matter what they believe, what they profess, or what they worship (*DBY,* 440).

I have learned years ago that the Lord stands at the helm that guides Zion's ship. . . . Unless we work exactly to the line that is marked out by him, our works will be in vain. This has been my experience from the beginning. In every branch and avenue of our lives we must learn to work to the line of truth. It is for us to know what ought to be done, and then do it. Though there should be no earthly prospect of accomplishing it, we can certainly try; and if we try with all our might, that act will prove at least a resolute and determined mind, adorned with patience and perseverance. And if, with all our resolute endeavors we are still unable to accomplish our purpose, the Lord will be very likely to stretch forth his hand and give the victory (*DBY,* 441).

If this people live to the principles they have embraced, they will be capable of counselling the nations; for we build upon a just foundation, and our principles are truth, righteousness, and holiness. Let us stand by those principles until they crush out folly, . . . and we become teachers of wisdom to the nations (*DBY,* 441).

What will be the final result of the restoration of the Gospel, and the destiny of the Latter-day Saints? If they are faithful to the Priesthood which God has bestowed upon us, the Gospel will revolutionize the whole world of mankind; the earth will be sanctified, and God will glorify it, and the Saints will dwell upon it in the presence of the Father and the Son (*DBY,* 438).

The work of the kingdom of God includes gathering the house of Israel.

We have an object in view, and that is to gain influence among all the inhabitants of the earth for the purpose of establishing the Kingdom of God in its righteousness, power and glory, and to exalt the name of the Deity, and cause that name by which we live to be revered everywhere that he may be honored, that his works may be honored, that we may be honored ourselves, and deport ourselves worthy of the character of his children (*DBY,* 438–39).

We are to build up . . . Zion, gather the House of Israel, and redeem the nations of the earth [see D&C 115:4–6]. This people have this work to do, whether we live to see it or not. This is all in our hands (*DBY,* 437).

It is obligatory upon us to see that the House of Israel have the Gospel preached to them (*DBY,* 437).

We are now [1863] gathering the children of Abraham who have come through the loins of Joseph and his sons, more especially through Ephraim, whose children are mixed among all the nations of the earth (*DBY,* 437).

Who are Israel? They are those who are of the seed of Abraham, who received the promise through their forefathers [see Genesis 22:17–18]; and all the rest of the children of men, who receive the truth, are also Israel. My heart is always drawn out for them, whenever I go to the throne of grace (*DBY,* 437).

Israel is dispersed among all the nations of the earth; the blood of Ephraim is mixed with the blood of all the earth. Abraham's seed is mingled with the rebellious seed through the whole world of mankind (*DBY,* 437).

Those islanders [of the Pacific] and the natives of [America] are of the House of Israel—of the seed of Abraham, and to them pertain the promise; and every soul of them, sooner or later, will be saved in the Kingdom of God, or be destroyed root and branch (*DBY,* 437).

To possess and retain the spirit of the Gospel, gather Israel, redeem Zion, and save the world must be attended to first and foremost, and should be the prevailing desire in the hearts of the First Presidency, of the Elders of Israel, and of every officer in the Church and Kingdom of God (*DBY,* 137).

The kingdom of God cannot be destroyed.

God has commenced to set up his Kingdom on the earth, and all hell and its devils are moving against it. Hell is yawning and sending forth its devils and their imps. What for? To destroy the Kingdom of God from the earth. But they cannot do it (*DBY,* 442).

If there are any hearts or spirits in this city, or elsewhere, that are fearfully wondering whether or not we are going to be destroyed, or whether this Church will endure and become the mighty power in the earth, according to the predictions of the servants of God, I will say to all such trembling souls, you need entertain no such fears. You need have

Photograph of the Salt Lake Temple in 1892. This temple stands as a monument
to the faith and commitment of the early Saints.

only one fear, and that is with regard to yourselves, lest you should leave
the light that the Lord has imparted to you and wander into darkness,
returning to the beggarly elements of the world, lusting again after the
things of the world in their sinful state (*DBY*, 442).

When the wicked have power to blow out the sun, that it shines no
more; when they have power to bring to a conclusion the operations of
the elements, suspend the whole system of nature, and make a footstool
of the throne of the Almighty, they may then think to check "Mormonism"
in its course, and thwart the unalterable purposes of heaven [see D&C
121:33]. Men may persecute the people who believe its doctrines, report
and publish lies to bring tribulation upon their heads, earth and hell may
unite in one grand league against it, and exert their malicious powers to
the utmost, but it will stand as firm and immovable in the midst of it all as
the pillars of eternity. Men may persecute the Prophet, and those who
believe and uphold him, they may drive the Saints and kill them, but this
does not affect the truths of "Mormonism" one iota, for they will stand
when the elements melt with fervent heat, and the heavens are wrapt up
like a scroll and the solid earth is dissolved [see Isaiah 34:4; D&C 88:95]
(*DBY*, 442–43).

In that helpless infant upon its mother's breast we see a man, an Apostle, a Saint—yea, generations of men with kingdoms, thrones, and dominions. Then the life of that little frail mortal is fraught with great and mighty results, and its value is inestimable. If this be true of an infant, what may we expect to grow out of this infant Kingdom? We may look forward to all that belongs to greatness and goodness, to might and power, to dominion and glory. Then how jealously we ought to guard the rights of this infant power? How zealous and constant we should be in maintaining its interests and supporting its laws and sacred institutions! (*DBY,* 439).

My heart is comforted. I behold the people of God, that they have been hunted, cast out, driven from the face of men. The powers of earth and hell have striven to destroy this Kingdom from the earth. The wicked have succeeded in doing so in former ages; but this Kingdom they cannot destroy (*DBY,* 442).

"It is the Kingdom of God or nothing."

The Kingdom of God is all that is real worth [see Matthew 6:33]. All else is not worth possessing, either here or hereafter. Without it, all else would be like a dry tree prepared for the burning—it is all consumed and the ashes are driven to the four winds (*DBY,* 444).

To me it is the Kingdom of God or nothing upon the earth. Without it I would not give a farthing for the wealth, glory, prestige and power of all the world combined; for like the dew upon the grass, it passeth away and is forgotten, and like the flower of the grass it withereth, and is not. Death levels the most powerful monarch with the poorest starving mendicant [beggar]; and both must stand before the judgment seat of Christ to answer for the deeds done in the body [see Revelation 20:12] (*DBY,* 444–45).

With us, it is the Kingdom of God, or nothing; and we will maintain it, or die in trying—though we shall not die in trying. It is comforting to many to be assured that we shall not die in trying; but we shall live in trying. We will maintain the Kingdom of God, living; and if we do not maintain it, we shall be found dying not only a temporal, but also an eternal death. Then take a course to live (*DBY,* 445).

If you give anything for the building up of the Kingdom of God, give the best you have. What is the best thing you have to devote to the Kingdom of God? It is the talents God has given you. How many? Every one of them. What beautiful talents! What a beautiful gift! . . . Let us devote every qualification we are in possession of to the building up of God's Kingdom, and you will accomplish the whole of it (*DBY,* 445).

Suggestions for Study

The people of God seek to build the kingdom of God.

- How do you feel, knowing that as a member of the Church you are a part of the effort to build up the kingdom of God on the earth? What responsibilities does this involve? What blessings will come when the kingdom of God is fully established on the earth?

- How can we ensure that our actions are "exactly to the line that is marked out" by the Lord? What will happen if we do this?

- How can members of the Church become "teachers of wisdom to the nations" individually or collectively?

- What is "the destiny of the Latter-day Saints" if we are faithful?

The work of the kingdom of God includes gathering the house of Israel.

- How can we "deport [behave] ourselves worthy" of our position as children of God? How can your actions bring honor and reverence to the Lord and His works?

- Who belongs to the house of Israel? How can you participate in the gathering of the house of Israel?

The kingdom of God cannot be destroyed.

- What evidence do you see that Satan and his followers are indeed trying to destroy the kingdom of God today? How can we strengthen our families to resist their efforts? How can the knowledge that the kingdom of God cannot be destroyed give us strength to resist temptations and endure trials?

- According to President Young, what is the one fear that we must concern ourselves with as members of the Church? What can we do to make sure this fear does not come to pass? How can your faith in God and your study of the gospel help you eliminate other fears you may have?

"It is the Kingdom of God or nothing."

- Why do you think President Young said that the kingdom of God is the only thing worth possessing? What does "it is the kingdom of God or nothing" mean for you?

- What talents or gifts are you willing to dedicate to the building up of the kingdom of God?

Jesus Christ will come in clouds of glory to usher in the millennial era.

The Last Days

When Brigham Young was ordained an Apostle, he was given the charge to "go forth and gather the elect, preparatory to the great day of the coming of the Lord" (HC, 2:188). He served a mission to England, where he and his fellow Apostles launched a full program of proselyting, publishing, and preparing converts for emigration to the headquarters of the young Church in America. In a report to the Prophet Joseph Smith detailing their efforts, Elder Young stated: "The Gospel is spreading, the devils are roaring; as nigh as I can learn, . . . the tares they are binding up, the wheat is gathering, nations are trembling, and kingdoms are tottering: 'men's hearts are failing them for fear, and for looking for those things that are coming on the earth' " (HC, 4:114). As a Church leader for almost another 40 years, President Young taught the Saints to continue in the Lord's redemptive work and to be unafraid of the turmoil prophesied for the last days.

Teachings of Brigham Young

The last days will be a period of great turmoil.

All we have yet heard and we have experienced is scarcely a preface to the sermon that is going to be preached. When the testimony of the Elders ceases to be given, and the Lord says to them, "Come home; I will now preach my own sermons to the nations of the earth," all you now know can scarcely be called a preface to the sermon that will be preached with fire and sword, tempests, earthquakes, hail, rain, thunders and lightnings, and fearful destruction. What matters the destruction of a few railway cars? You will hear of magnificent cities, now idolized by the people, sinking in the earth, entombing the inhabitants. The sea will heave itself beyond its bounds, engulfing mighty cities. Famine will spread over the nations and nation will rise up against nation, kingdom against kingdom and states against states, in our own country and in foreign lands; and they will destroy each other, caring not for the blood and lives of their neighbors, of their families, or for their own lives (*DBY,* 111–12).

There never has been a day for ages and ages, not since the true church was destroyed after the days of the Apostles, that required the faith and the energy of godly men and godly women, and the skill, wisdom and power of the Almighty to be with them, so much as this people require it at the present time. There never was that necessity; there never has been a time on the face of the earth, from the time that the church went to destruction, and the Priesthood was taken from the earth, that the powers of darkness and the powers of earth and hell were so embittered, and enraged, and incensed against God and Godliness on the earth, as they are at the present (*DBY*, 112).

The Devil is just as much opposed to Jesus now as he was when the revolt took place in heaven. And as the Devil increases his numbers by getting the people to be wicked, so Jesus Christ increases his numbers and strength by getting the people to be humble and righteous. The human family are going to the polls by and by, and they wish to know which party is going to carry the day (*DBY*, 112).

Righteousness will triumph at the end of the world.

The time will come when every knee will bow, and every tongue confess to and acknowledge him, and when they who have lived upon the earth and have spurned the idea of a Supreme Being and of revelations from him, will fall with shamefacedness and humble themselves before him, exclaiming, "There is a God! O God, we once rejected thee and disbelieved thy word and set at naught thy counsels, but now we bow down in shame and we do acknowledge that there is a God, and that Jesus is the Christ." This time will come, most assuredly. We have the faith of the Gospel of the Lord Jesus (*DBY*, 112–13).

What will they do? They will hear of the wisdom of Zion and the kings and potentates of the nations will come up to Zion to inquire after the ways of the Lord, and to seek out the great knowledge, wisdom and understanding manifested through the Saints of the Most High (*DBY*, 113).

They will have to bow the knee and confess that he is God, and that Jesus Christ, who suffered for the sins of the world, is actually its Redeemer; that by the shedding of his blood he has redeemed men, women, children, beasts, birds, fish, the earth itself and everything that John saw and heard praising in heaven [see Revelation 5:13] (*DBY*, 113).

By and by the world will be overturned according to the words of the prophet, and we will see the reign of righteousness enter in, and sin and iniquity will have to walk off. But the power and principles of evil, if they can be called principles, will never yield one particle to the righteous march of the Savior, only as they are beaten back inch by inch, and we have got to take the ground by force. Yes, by the mental force of faith, and by good works, the march forth of the Gospel will increase, spread, grow and prosper, until the nations of the earth will feel that Jesus has the right to rule King of nations as he does King of Saints (*DBY,* 113).

Do you know that it is the eleventh hour of the reign of Satan on the earth? Jesus is coming to reign, and all you who fear and tremble because of your enemies, cease to fear them, and learn to fear to offend God, fear to transgress his laws, fear to do any evil to your brother, or to any being upon the earth, and do not fear Satan and his power, nor those who have only power to slay the body, for God will preserve his people (*DBY,* 114).

In the progress of the age in which we live, we discern the fulfilment of prophecy, and the preparation for the second coming of our Lord and Savior to dwell upon the earth. We expect that the refuge of lies will be swept away, and that city, nation, government, or kingdom which serves not God, and gives no heed to the principles of truth and religion, will be utterly wasted away and destroyed (*DBY,* 114).

**The Millennium will be a time of unity,
peace, and temple service.**

The Millennium consists in this—every heart in the Church and Kingdom of God being united in one; the Kingdom increasing to the overcoming of everything opposed to the economy of heaven, and Satan being bound, and having a seal set upon him. All things else will be as they are now, we shall eat, drink, and wear clothing (*DBY,* 115).

Let the people be holy, and the earth under their feet will be holy. Let the people be holy, and filled with the Spirit of God, and every animal and creeping thing will be filled with peace; the soil of the earth will bring forth in its strength, and the fruits thereof will be meat for man. The more purity that exists, the less is the strife; the more kind we are to our animals, the more will peace increase, and the savage nature of the brute creation vanish away. If the people will not serve the Devil another moment whilst they live, if this congregation is possessed of that spirit and resolution, here in this house is the Millennium. Let the inhabitants of this city be possessed of that spirit, let the people of the territory be possessed of that spirit, and here is the Millennium. Let the whole people . . . be possessed of that spirit and here is the Millennium, and so will it spread over all the world (*DBY,* 115–16).

In the Millennium, when the Kingdom of God is established on the earth in power, glory and perfection, and the reign of wickedness that has so long prevailed is subdued, the Saints of God will have the privilege of building their temples, and of entering into them, becoming, as it were, pillars in the temples of God [see Revelation 3:12], and they will officiate for their dead. Then we will see our friends come up, and perhaps some that we have been acquainted with here. . . . And we will have revelations to know our forefathers clear back to Father Adam and Mother Eve, and we will enter into the temples of God and officiate for them. Then [children] will be sealed to [parents] until the chain is made perfect back to Adam, so that there will be a perfect chain of Priesthood from Adam to the winding-up scene.

This will be the work of the Latter-day Saints in the Millennium (*DBY,* 116).

We should sanctify ourselves in preparation for the Second Coming of Jesus Christ.

Do not be too anxious for the Lord to hasten his work. Let our anxiety be centered upon one thing, the sanctification of our own hearts, the purifying of our own affections, the preparing of ourselves for the approach of the events that are hastening upon us. This should be our concern, this should be our study, this should be our daily prayer, and not to be in a hurry to see the overthrow of the wicked (*DBY,* 117).

Whether the world is going to be burned up within a year, or within a thousand years, does not matter a groat [a kernel of grain] to you and me. We have the words of eternal life, we have the privilege of obtaining glory, immortality, and eternal lives, now will you obtain these blessings? (*DBY,* 117).

We have the Kingdom of God to build up, Zion to redeem; we have to sanctify ourselves so that we may be prepared to be caught up with the Church of the Firstborn, and if we improve every day and hour, then if we die we shall be found justified. But if we continue to live, we must become Saints in very deed, or come short of the fulness of the glory of God that is to be revealed (*DBY,* 444).

The Lord's time is not for me to know; but he is kind, long-suffering, and patient, and his wrath endureth silently, and will until mercy is completely exhausted, and then judgment will take the reins. I do not know how, neither do I at present wish to know. It is enough for us to know how to serve our God and live our religion, and thus we will increase in the favor of God (*DBY,* 117–18).

Suggestions for Study

The last days will be a period of great turmoil.

- According to President Young, what trials will come in the last days? Why will these judgments fall on the earth?
- What did President Young say would be the only reason for persecution against the Church to stop?
- How is the war in heaven still being waged on the earth today? What is required of "godly men and godly women" in the last days?

Righteousness will triumph at the end of the world.

- How will the wicked people of the earth react when they "hear of the wisdom of Zion"?
- What should we learn to fear during this "eleventh hour of the reign of Satan on the earth"? How can we remain unafraid of the enemies of righteousness?
- President Young said that the wicked will be "beaten back" and the "march forth of the Gospel will increase" by the "mental force of faith, and by good works." How can faith be a "mental force"? How do good works overcome wickedness? How can we help the march of the gospel "increase, spread, grow and prosper"?

The Millennium will be a time of unity, peace, and temple service.

- According to President Young, what is the Millennium? (See also D&C 43:30–31; 88:110.)
- How will the earth and its inhabitants be made peaceful and holy?
- What will be the work of the Latter-day Saints during the Millennium?

We should sanctify ourselves in preparation for the Second Coming of Jesus Christ.

- President Young said that we should sanctify ourselves in preparation for Jesus Christ's Second Coming. How do we become sanctified? (See also Helaman 3:35; D&C 20:31.)
- Why should we not be concerned with the exact timing of the Second Coming?

The Beehive House, Brigham Young's home in Salt Lake City, Utah, where he held daily prayer and regular scripture study with members of his family.

Parental Responsibility

President Brigham Young loved children and believed in their purity before God. Many of his sermons contained advice to the Saints on how they should care for their children. For example, a small son of his had the habit of knocking his spoon and his bowl of bread and milk to the floor whenever it was placed in front of him. The child's mother was perplexed. Brigham counseled her: "The next time he knocks the dish from your hand lean him against the chair, do not say one word to him, [and] go to your work." The mother did this. The child at first stood by the chair and looked at his mother, then at what he had knocked onto the floor. Finally, he crawled to the spoon and the bowl and placed them back on the table. The child never knocked them from the table again. Of his wife's action President Young said, "She might have whipped him and injured him, as a great many others would have done; but if they know what to do, they can correct the child without violence" (LBY, xxv). That President Young lived the principles he taught is evidenced by his daughter Susa's description of him as "an ideal father. Kind to a fault, tender, thoughtful, just and firm. . . . None of us feared him; all of us adored him" (LSBY, 356).

Teachings of Brigham Young

Parents are guardians of God's children and are to train, educate, and care for them.

W̶e are the guardians of our children; their training and education are committed to our care, and if we do not ourselves pursue a course which will save them from the influence of evil, when we are weighed in the balance we shall be found wanting (*LBY*, xxiv).

Parents are responsible before the Lord for the way in which they educate and train their children, for "Lo, children are an heritage of the Lord; and the fruit of the womb is his reward. Happy is the man that hath his quiver full of them; they shall not be ashamed [Psalm 127:3–5]" (*DNW*, 7 Dec. 1864, 2).

Parents, seek to honor your children; bring them up in the nurture and admonition of the Lord. Teach them truth and not error, teach them to love and serve God [see Deuteronomy 6:5]; teach them to believe in Jesus Christ the Son of God and the Saviour of the world (*DNSW,* 8 Aug. 1877, 1).

The mothers are the moving instruments in the hands of Providence to guide the destinies of nations. Let the mothers of any nation teach their children not to make war, the children would grow up and never enter into it. Let the mothers teach their children, "War, war upon your enemies, yes, war to the hilt!" and they will be filled with this spirit. Consequently, you see at once what I wish to impress upon your minds is, that the mothers are the machinery that gives zest to the whole man, and guide the destinies and lives of men upon the earth (*DBY,* 199–200).

We can guide, direct, and prune a tender sprout, and it inclines to our direction, if it is wisely and skilfully applied. So, if we surround a child with healthy and salutary influences, give him suitable instructions and store his mind with truthful traditions, may be that will direct his feet in the way of life (*DBY,* 209).

Parents should rear their children in love and kindness.

Let parents treat their children as they themselves would wish to be treated, and set an example before them that is worthy of you as Saints of God (*DNW,* 7 Dec. 1864, 2).

Bring up your children in the love and fear of the Lord; study their dispositions and their temperaments, and deal with them accordingly, never allowing yourself to correct them in the heat of passion; teach them to love you rather than to fear you (*DBY,* 207).

In our daily pursuits in life, of whatever nature and kind, Latter-day Saints . . . should maintain a uniform and even temper, both when at home and when abroad. They should not suffer reverses and unpleasant circumstances to sour their natures and render them fretful and unsocial at home, speaking words full of bitterness and biting acrimony to their wives and children, creating gloom and sorrow in their habitations, making themselves feared rather than loved by their families. Anger should never be permitted to rise in our bosoms, and words suggested by angry feelings should never be permitted to pass our lips. "A soft answer turneth away wrath, but grievous words stir up anger [Proverbs 15:1]." "Wrath is cruel, and anger is outrageous;" but "the discretion of a man deferreth his anger; and it is his glory to pass over a transgression [Proverbs 19:11]" (*DBY,* 203–4).

In passing through the world I see that the most of parents are very anxious to govern and control their children. As far as my observations have gone I have seen more parents who were unable to control themselves than I ever saw who were unable to control their children. If a mother wishes to control her child, in the first place let her learn to control herself, then she may be successful in bringing the child into perfect subjection to her will. But if she does not control herself how can she expect a child,—an infant in understanding—to be more wise, prudent and better than one of grown age and matured? (*DNSW,* 12 July 1870, 2).

Parents should never drive their children, but lead them along, giving them knowledge as their minds are prepared to receive it. Chastening may be necessary, . . . but parents should govern their children by faith rather than by the rod, leading them kindly by good example into all truth and holiness [see D&C 121:43] (*DBY,* 208).

We cannot chastise a child for doing that which is contrary to our wills, if he knows no better; but when our children are taught better and know what is required of them, if they then rebel, of course, they expect to be chastised, and it is perfectly right that they should be (*DNSW,* 8 July 1873, 1).

I will here say to parents, that kind words and loving actions towards children, will subdue their uneducated nature a great deal better than the rod, or, in other words, than physical punishment. Although it is written that, "The rod and reproof give wisdom; but a child left to himself bringeth his mother to shame [Proverbs 29:15]," and, "He that spareth his rod hateth his son; but he that loveth him chasteneth him betimes [Proverbs 13:24];" these quotations refer to . . . wise and prudent corrections. Children who have lived in the sunbeams of parental kindness and affection, when made aware of a parent's displeasure, and receive a kind reproof from parental lips, are more thoroughly chastened than by any physical punishment that could be applied to their persons (*DNW,* 7 Dec. 1864, 2).

I can pick out scores of men in this congregation who have driven their children from them by using the wooden rod. Where there is severity there is no affection or filial feeling in the hearts of either party; the children would rather be away from father than be with him (*DBY,* 203).

It is not by the whip or the rod that we can make obedient children; but it is by faith and by prayer, and by setting a good example before them (*DNW,* 9 Aug. 1865, 3).

I do not believe in making my authority as a husband or a father known by brute force; but by a superior intelligence—by showing them that I am capable of teaching them. . . . If the Lord has placed me to be the head of a family, let me be so in all humility and patience, not as a tyrannical ruler, but as a faithful companion, an indulgent and affectionate father, a thoughtful and unassuming superior; let me be honored in my station through faithful diligence, and be fully capable, by the aid of God's Spirit, of filling my office in a way to effect the salvation of all who are committed to my charge (*DNW*, 23 July 1862, 2).

At times our children may not be in possession of a good spirit; but if the parent continues to possess the good Spirit, the children will have the bad spirit but a short time. . . . Rule in righteousness, and in the fear and love of God, and your children will follow you (*DNSW*, 7 Apr. 1868, 3).

Kind looks, kind actions, kind words, and a lovely, holy deportment towards them will bind our children to us with bands that cannot easily be broken; while abuse and unkindness will drive them from us, and break asunder every holy tie that should bind them to us and to the everlasting covenant in which we are all embraced. If my family, and my brethren and sisters will not be obedient to me on the basis of kindness, and a commendable life before all men, and before the heavens, then farewell to all influence (*DNW*, 7 Dec. 1864, 2).

Let us live so that the spirit of our religion will live within us, then we have peace, joy, happiness and contentment, which makes such pleasant fathers, pleasant mothers, pleasant children, pleasant households, neighbors, communities and cities. That is worth living for, and I do think that the Latter-day Saints ought to strive for this (*DBY*, 204).

Parents should kindly and firmly lead their children in righteous living.

You ought always to take the lead of your children in their minds and affections. Instead of being behind with the whip, always be in advance, then you can say, "Come along," and you will have no use for the rod. They will delight to follow you, and will like your words and ways, because you are always comforting them and giving them pleasure and enjoyment. If they get a little naughty, stop them when they have gone far enough. . . . When they transgress, and transcend certain bounds we want them to stop. If you are in the lead they will stop, they cannot run over you; but if you are behind they will run away from you (*DNSW*, 8 Dec. 1868, 2–3).

A child loves the smiles of its mother, but hates her frowns. I tell the mothers not to allow the children to indulge in evils, but at the same time to treat them with mildness. If a child is required to step in a certain direction, and it does not seem willing to do so, gently put it in the desired way, and say, There, my little dear, you must step when I speak to you. Children need directing and teaching what is right in a kind, affectionate manner (*DBY*, 209).

We should never permit ourselves to do anything that we are not willing to see our children do. We should set them an example that we wish them to imitate. Do we realize this? How often we see parents demand obedience, good behavior, kind words, pleasant looks, a sweet voice and a bright eye from a child or children when they themselves are full of bitterness and scolding! How inconsistent and unreasonable this is! (*DBY,* 208).

Children can be bound to their parents by an everlasting tie.

Let the father and mother, who are members of this Church and Kingdom, take a righteous course, and strive with all their might never to do a wrong, but to do good all their lives; if they have one child or one hundred children, if they conduct themselves towards them as they should, binding them to the Lord by their faith and prayers, I care not where those children go, they are bound up to their parents by an everlasting tie, and no power of earth or hell can separate them from their parents in eternity; they will return again to the fountain from whence they sprang (*DBY,* 208).

Suggestions for Study

Parents are guardians of God's children and are to train, educate, and care for them.

- According to President Young, how are parents only guardians of their children? How might this perspective influence how you think of rearing children?

- What does it mean to direct children in "the way of life"? What are some specific things that a parent can do to provide this direction?

- What does President Young say is the blessing of a faithful parent? How is this achieved?

Parents should rear their children in love and kindness.

- How can parents teach their children to love them rather than fear them? Why is this important?

- Why are some parents so "very anxious to govern and control their children"? What must parents do before they can govern their children righteously? How have you successfully gained control of yourself in angry moments?

- What is the difference between chastening an unruly child and physically or verbally abusing an unruly child? When and how is it appropriate to chasten a child?

- Why is kindness more effective than physical punishment in disciplining children?

- What do you think President Young meant when he said, "Children who live in the sunbeams of parental kindness and affection, when [they] . . . receive a kind reproof from parental lips, are more thoroughly chastened, than by any physical punishment that could be applied to their persons"?

- What actions will bind children to their parents? What actions will drive children away from their parents?

Parents should kindly and firmly lead their children in righteous living.

- When do children need direction? Why is it critical that "bounds" be given to children?

- According to President Young, what is the best way to give direction to children? What can parents do to lead their children rather than drive them?

Children can be bound to their parents by an everlasting tie.

- How can you bind your children to you with an everlasting tie?

President Brigham Young's Witness of the Prophet Joseph Smith

In one of many sermons to the Saints regarding Joseph's work and mission, President Brigham Young testified: "I feel like shouting Hallelujah, all the time, when I think that I ever knew Joseph Smith, the Prophet whom the Lord raised up and ordained, and to whom he gave keys and power to build up the Kingdom of God on earth and sustain it" (DBY, 458). Throughout his life as a Church leader, he expressed love and admiration for the Prophet Joseph Smith: "I can truly say, that I invariably found him to be all that any people could require a true prophet to be, and that a better man could not be, though he had his weaknesses; and what man has ever lived upon this earth who had none?" (Brigham Young to David P. Smith, 1 June 1853, BYP). President Young's lifelong conviction of the Seer and his work was confirmed at his deathbed in a final expression of recognition and anticipation: "Joseph, Joseph, Joseph" (LSBY, 362).

Teachings of Brigham Young

The Prophet Joseph Smith laid the foundation of the Church of Jesus Christ in this dispensation.

It was decreed in the counsels of eternity, long before the foundations of the earth were laid, that he, Joseph Smith, should be the man, in the last dispensation of this world, to bring forth the word of God to the people, and receive the fulness of the keys and power of the Priesthood of the Son of God. The Lord had his eyes upon him, and upon his father, and upon his father's father, and upon their progenitors clear back to Abraham, and from Abraham to the flood, from the flood to Enoch, and from Enoch to Adam. He has watched that family and that blood as it has circulated from its fountain to the birth of that man. He was fore-ordained in eternity to preside over this last dispensation (*DBY,* 108).

[The Lord] called upon his servant Joseph Smith, Jr., when he was but a boy, to lay the foundation of his Kingdom for the last time. Why did he call upon Joseph Smith to do it? Because he was disposed to do it. Was Joseph Smith the only person on earth who could have done this work? No doubt there were many others who, under the direction of the Lord, could have done that work; but the Lord selected the one that pleased him, and that is sufficient (*DBY,* 460).

How frequently it is cast at the Elders, when they are abroad preaching, that Joseph Smith, the founder of their Church and religion, was only a poor illiterate boy. That used to be advanced as one of the strongest arguments that could be produced against the doctrine of salvation, by the wise and learned of this world, though it is no argument at all. The Lord should have revealed himself to some of the learned priests or talented men of the age, say they, who could have done some good and borne off the Gospel by their influence and learning, and not to a poor, ignorant, unlettered youth. Not many wise, not many mighty, not many noble, speaking after the manner of men, are called; but God hath chosen the foolish things of the world to confound the wise, the weak things of the world to confound the things that are mighty; and base things of the world—things which are despised by the world, hath God in his wisdom chosen; yea, and things which are not, to bring to naught things that are, that no flesh should glory in his presence [see 1 Corinthians 1:26–29] (*DBY,* 321–22).

I felt in those days [before joining the Church], that if I could see the face of a prophet, such as had lived on the earth in former times, a man that had revelations, to whom the heavens were opened, who knew God and his character, I would freely circumscribe the earth on my hands and knees; I thought that there was no hardship but what I would undergo, if I could see one person that knew what God is and where he is, what was his character, and what eternity was (*DNW,* 8 Oct. 1856, 3).

What is the nature and beauty of Joseph's mission? . . . When I first heard him preach, he brought heaven and earth together (*DBY,* 458).

Joseph Smith has laid the foundation of the Kingdom of God in the last days; others will rear the superstructure (*DBY,* 458).

I never saw any one, until I met Joseph Smith, who could tell me anything about the character, personality and dwelling-place of God, or anything satisfactory about angels, or the relationship of man to his Maker. Yet I was as diligent as any man need to be to try and find out these things (*DBY,* 458).

He took heaven, figuratively speaking, and brought it down to earth; and he took the earth, brought it up, and opened up, in plainness and simplicity, the things of God; and that is the beauty of his mission. I had a testimony, long before that, that he was a Prophet of the Lord, and that was consoling. Did not Joseph do the same to your understandings? Would he

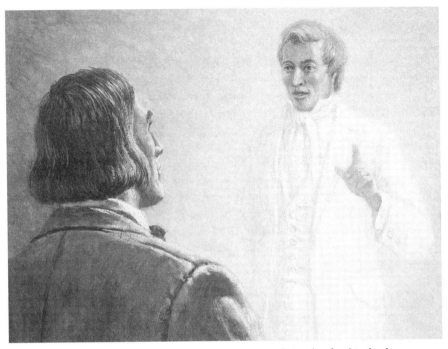

As portrayed in this painting, the Prophet Joseph Smith, after his death,
appeared in vision to President Brigham Young on 11 January 1847.

not take the Scriptures and make them so plain and simple that everybody
could understand? Every person says, "Yes, it is admirable; it unites the
heavens and the earth together," and as for time, it is nothing, only to
teach us how to live in eternity (*DBY,* 458–59).

I honor and revere the name of Joseph Smith. I delight to hear it; I love
it. I love his doctrine (*DBY,* 458).

What I have received from the Lord, I have received by Joseph Smith;
he was the instrument made use of. If I drop him, I must drop these principles; they have not been revealed, declared, or explained by any other
man since the days of the Apostles. If I lay down the Book of Mormon, I
shall have to deny that Joseph is a Prophet; and if I lay down the doctrine
and cease to preach the gathering of Israel and the building up of Zion, I
must lay down the Bible; and, consequently, I might as well go home as
undertake to preach without these three items (*DBY,* 458).

There is not that being that ever had the privilege of hearing the way of
life and salvation set before him as it is written in the New Testament, and
in the Book of Mormon, and in the book of Doctrine and Covenants, by a
Latter-day Saint, that can say that Jesus lives, that his Gospel is true, and at
the same time say that Joseph Smith was not a Prophet of God. That is
strong testimony, but it is true. No man can say that this book (laying his

hand on the Bible) is true, is the word of the Lord, is the way, is the guide-board in the path, and a charter by which we may learn the will of God; and at the same time say, that the Book of Mormon is untrue; if he has had the privilege of reading it, or of hearing it read, and learning its doctrines. There is not that person on the face of the earth who has had the privilege of learning the Gospel of Jesus Christ from these two books, that can say that one is true, and the other is false. No Latter-day Saint, no man or woman, can say the Book of Mormon is true, and at the same time say that the Bible is untrue. If one be true, both are; and if one be false, both are false. If Jesus lives, and is the Savior of the world, Joseph Smith is a Prophet of God, and lives in the bosom of his father Abraham. Though they have killed his body, yet he lives and beholds the face of his Father in Heaven; and his garments are pure as the angels that surround the throne of God; and no man on the earth can say that Jesus lives, and deny, at the same time, my assertion about the Prophet Joseph. This is my testimony, and it is strong (*DBY,* 459).

The Lord taught His servant Joseph Smith through revelation, "truth upon truth."

From the day that Joseph obtained the plates, and previous to that time, the Lord dictated him. He directed him day by day and hour by hour (*DBY,* 461).

Joseph continued to receive revelation upon revelation, ordinance upon ordinance, truth upon truth, until he obtained all that was necessary for the salvation of the human family (*DBY,* 461).

All the inhabitants of the earth are called of God; they are called to repent and be baptized for the remission of sins (*DBY,* 461).

We have passed from one thing to another, and I may say from one degree of knowledge to another. When Joseph first received the knowledge of the plates that were in the hill Cumorah, he did not then receive the keys of the Aaronic Priesthood, he merely received the knowledge that the plates were there, and that the Lord would bring them forth. . . . He received the knowledge that [early inhabitants of the Americas] were once in possession of the Gospel, and from that time he went on, step by step, until he obtained the plates, and the Urim and Thummim and had power to translate them. This did not make him an Apostle, it did not give to him the keys of the Kingdom, nor make him an Elder in Israel. He was a Prophet, and had the spirit of prophecy, and had received all this before the Lord ordained him. And when the Lord, by revelation, told him to go to Pennsylvania, he did so, and finished the translation of the Book of Mormon; and when the Lord, in another revelation, told him to come back, into New York State, and to go to old Father Whitmer's, who lived in a place opposite Waterloo, and there stop, he did so, and had meetings, and gathered up a few who believed in his testimony [see *HC,* 1:48–51]. He received the Aaronic Priesthood, and then he received the keys of the Melchizedek Priesthood, and organized the Church [see D&C 13; 20; 128:20]. He first received the power to baptize, and still did not know that he was to receive any more until the Lord told him there was more for him. Then he received the keys of the Melchizedek Priesthood, and had power to confirm after he had baptized, which he had not before. He would have stood precisely as John the Baptist stood, had not the Lord sent his other messengers, Peter, James and John, to ordain Joseph to the Melchizedek Priesthood. . . . And then [we] received other ordinances (*DBY,* 461–62).

At this time [1840] came a revelation that we could be baptized for our dead friends, but at first it was not revealed that a record should be kept of those who were baptized; but when he received an additional revelation to that effect, then a record was kept (*DBY,* 462).

The Prophet Joseph Smith plainly taught the truths of the gospel.

All that Joseph Smith did was to preach the truth—the Gospel as the Lord revealed it to him—and tell the people how to be saved, and the honest-in-heart ran together and gathered around him and loved him as they did their own lives. He could do no more than to preach true principles, and that will gather the Saints in the last days, even the honest-in-heart. All who believe and obey the Gospel of Jesus Christ are his witnesses to the truth of these statements (*DBY,* 463).

The excellency of the glory of the character of Brother Joseph Smith was that he could reduce heavenly things to the understanding of the finite. When he preached to the people—revealed the things of God, the will of God, the plan of salvation, the purposes of Jehovah, the relation in which we stand to him and all the heavenly beings, he reduced his teachings to the capacity of every man, woman, and child, making them as plain as a well-defined pathway. This should have convinced every person that ever heard of him of his divine authority and power, for no other man was able to teach as he could, and no person can reveal the things of God, but by the revelations of Jesus Christ (*DBY,* 463).

No man was to be found who could teach repentance and baptism for the remission of sins, with authority to administer in the ordinances, until God commissioned Joseph Smith, and sent him forth with his commandment to the people. Previous to that time, I searched everything pertaining to the churches; I searched high and low to find whether there was any such thing as pure religion upon the earth; I searched for a man that could tell me something of God, of heaven, of angels and of eternal life. I believed in God the Father, and in Jesus Christ, but I could not believe that the Church of Christ was upon the earth (*DBY,* 463).

I might have continued to study the Bible and all the books that have been written, and without revelation from God I would have been like the sounding brass or tinkling cymbal, having no knowledge of God, of true religion, of the redemption of the living or of the dead; I would have lived and died in ignorance; and this was the condition of all the inhabitants of the earth (*DBY,* 463).

The question was asked a great many times of Joseph Smith, by gentlemen who came to see him and his people, "How is it that you can control your people so easily? It appears that they do nothing but what you say; how is it that you can govern them so easily?" Said he, "I do not govern them at all. The Lord has revealed certain principles from the heavens by which we are to live in these latter days. The time is drawing near when the Lord is going to gather out his people from the wicked, and he is going to cut short his work in righteousness, and the principles which he has revealed I have taught to the people and they are trying to live according to them, and they control themselves."

Gentlemen, this is the great secret now in controlling this people. It is thought that I control them, but it is not so. It is as much as I can do to control myself and to keep myself straight and teach the people the principles by which they should live (*DBY,* 470).

I recollect many times when Brother Joseph, reflecting upon how many would come into the Kingdom of God and go out again, would say, "Brethren I have not apostatized yet, and don't feel like doing so." Many of you, no doubt, can call to mind his words. Joseph had to pray all the time, exercise faith, live his religion, and magnify his calling, to obtain the manifestations of the Lord, and to keep him steadfast in the faith (*DBY,* 469).

Now, as bad as myself and my brethren are, and as far as we are from the mark, and from the privileges we should enjoy, if Joseph Smith, Jr., the Prophet, could have seen the people in his day as willing to obey his voice, as they are today to obey the voice of their President, he would have been a happy man. He lived, labored, toiled, and worked; his courage was like the courage of an angel, and his will was like the will of the Almighty, and he labored till they killed him (*DBY,* 464).

The Prophet Joseph Smith sealed his testimony with his blood.

Many of the Prophets have sealed their testimony with their blood, that their testament might go forth with force. . . . As in ancient days, so in modern days. When Joseph Smith sealed his testimony with his blood, his testament from that moment was in force to all the world; and woe to those who fight against it (*DBY,* 467).

When [Joseph Smith] went to Carthage he said, "I go to death; I go like a lamb to the slaughter; I go to my fate" (*DBY,* 467).

Who delivered Joseph Smith from the hands of his enemies [until] the day of his death? It was God; though he was brought to the brink of death time and time again, and, to all human appearance, could not be delivered, and there was no probability of his being saved. When he was in jail in Missouri, and no person expected that he would ever escape from their hands, I had the faith of Abraham, and told the brethren, "As the Lord God liveth, he shall come out of their hands." Though he had prophesied that he would not live to be forty years of age, yet we all cherished hopes that that would be a false prophecy, and we should keep him forever with us; we thought our faith would outreach it, but we were mistaken—he at last fell a martyr to his religion. I said, "It is all right; now the testimony is in full force; he has sealed it with his blood" (*DBY,* 469–70).

His office is not taken from him, he has only gone to labor in another department of the operations of the Almighty. He is still an Apostle, still a Prophet, and is doing the work of an Apostle and Prophet; he has gone one step beyond us and gained a victory that you and I have not gained (*DBY,* 468).

I know that [Joseph Smith] was called of God, and this I know by the revelations of Jesus Christ to me, and by the testimony of the Holy Ghost. Had I not so learned this truth, I should never have been what is called a "Mormon," neither should I have been here to-day (*DNW,* 22 Oct. 1862, 2).

Suggestions for Study

The Prophet Joseph Smith laid the foundation of the Church of Jesus Christ in this dispensation.

• What role did Joseph Smith's ancestors play in preparing him to be the first prophet in this dispensation? In what ways has the faith of your ancestors influenced your life? What can you do to have a righteous influence on your posterity?

- What advantages came from the Lord's calling a mere boy to lay the foundation of his kingdom in these last days? How does this help you to see the hand of the Lord working in your life?

- President Young said that the Prophet Joseph Smith laid the foundation of Jesus Christ's latter-day Church and that others would rear the superstructure. What is that foundation? (See also D&C 5:9–10; 135:3.) What is the superstructure? What evidence have you seen that the superstructure of the Church is being built up? How can we all contribute to this work?

- What did President Young suggest was the "nature and beauty of Joseph's mission"? How can we follow the Prophet Joseph Smith's teaching approach in teaching our children and others?

- How did the Prophet Joseph Smith "teach us how to live in eternity"? How do these teachings apply to our lives in mortality?

The Lord taught His servant Joseph Smith through revelation, "truth upon truth."

- Why do you think the Lord reveals His truths "revelation upon revelation" rather than all at once? (See also D&C 93:11–14.) How was this true in the Prophet Joseph Smith's life? How has it been true in your life?

The Prophet Joseph Smith plainly taught the truths of the gospel.

- Why was the Prophet Joseph Smith such a beloved and influential teacher? What was his "great secret" for governing the Lord's people? How can we apply this principle to our responsibilities at home, at work, and in the Church?

- How was the Prophet Joseph able "to obtain the manifestations of the Lord, and to keep him[self] steadfast in the faith"? How can we know the will of the Lord concerning ourselves? Why must we continue to be faithful in order to maintain our testimonies of the gospel?

The Prophet Joseph Smith sealed his testimony with his blood.

- Why was it necessary for Joseph and Hyrum Smith to seal their testimonies with their blood? (See also D&C 135; 136:39.)

- President Young stated, "I know that [Joseph Smith] was called of God, and this I know by the revelations of Jesus Christ to me." How do you feel about the Prophet Joseph Smith? How can you appropriately share your feelings with your family, friends, and associates? Consider recording your feelings about the Prophet in some way for your posterity.

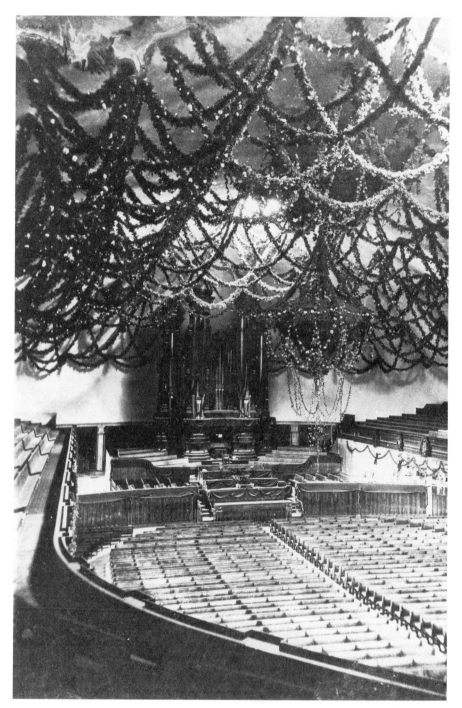

The Salt Lake Tabernacle draped for the funeral of President Brigham Young.

A Call for Unity, a Testimony, and a Blessing

In his youth Brigham Young searched for a religion that would satisfy his spiritual longings, but he was unable to find one. After being introduced to the Book of Mormon in 1830 and subsequently studying the restored gospel for almost two years, he knew that he had found the truth. He was baptized into the Church, and from that time forward he was unwavering in his testimony of the gospel, which, he said, "embraces all truth in heaven and on earth. . . . Wherever these principles are found among all the creations of God, the gospel of Jesus Christ, and His order and Priesthood, embrace them" (DNSW, 5 May 1866, 2). His strong testimony and complete devotion to the Church inspired the early Saints to meet the challenge of establishing homes in the wilderness and to unite in obeying the Lord's command to build His Church and preach His gospel throughout the world. He proclaimed: "God, angels and good men being my helpers, I will never cease to contend, inch by inch, until we gain the ground and possess the Kingdom. That is my feeling and faith, and we will accomplish it, I will prophesy, in the name of the Lord Jesus Christ, that we will possess the Kingdom of God upon the whole earth" (DBY, 453). President Brigham Young's testimony continues to inspire us today as we work together to build the kingdom of God.

Teachings of Brigham Young

**True disciples of Jesus Christ strive to be united—
of one heart and one mind.**

We have come here to build up Zion. How shall we do it? I have told you a great many times. There is one thing I will say in regard to it. We have got to be united in our efforts. We should go to work with a united faith like the heart of one man; and whatever we do should be performed in the name of the Lord, and we will then be blessed and prospered in all we do (*DBY,* 284).

The faith of the Gospel of Jesus Christ is calculated to unite the people in one, and to bring them back to the unity and faith of those who obeyed the Gospel anciently, and finally to bring them back to glory (*DBY,* 283).

I pray, my brethren, the Bishops, the Elders, the Seventies, the Apostles, yea, every man and woman and child who has named the name of Christ, to be of one heart and of one mind, for if we do not become of one heart and mind we shall surely perish by the way [see Moses 7:18] (*DBY,* 281).

A perfect oneness will save a people, because intelligent beings cannot become perfectly one, only by acting upon principles that pertain to eternal life. Wicked men may be partially united in evil; but, in the very nature of things, such a union is of short duration. The very principle upon which they are partially united will itself breed contention and disunion (*DBY,* 282).

The religion of heaven unites the hearts of the people and makes them one. You may gather a people together, and no matter how widely they differ in politics, the Gospel of Jesus Christ will make them one, even if among them were found members of all the political parties in the country (*DBY,* 285).

We have not in our society an aristocratic circle. Whether a brother wears a coon skin cap or a fine beaver hat is all the same to us. If a person is a faithful servant of God we do not object to his coming to meeting, though he has only a piece of buffalo skin to wear on his head. We partake of the Sacrament with him, hail him in the street as a brother and a friend, converse with him, meet him in social parties and greet him as an equal (*DBY,* 283–84).

The Savior sought continually to impress upon the minds of His disciples that a perfect oneness reigned among all celestial beings—that the Father and the Son and their Minister, the Holy Ghost, were one in their administration in heaven and among the people pertaining to this earth. . . . If the heavenly hosts were not one, they would be entirely unfit to dwell . . . with the Father and Ruler of the universe (*DBY,* 282).

Jesus . . . prayed the Father to make His disciples one, as He and His Father were one. He knew that if they did not become one, they could not be saved in the celestial Kingdom of God. If persons do not see as He did while in the flesh, hear as He heard, understand as He understood, and become precisely as He was, according to their several capacities and callings, they can never dwell with Him and His Father [see John 17:20–21; 3 Nephi 19:23] (*DBY,* 281).

How is it that the Latter-day Saints feel and understand alike, are of one heart and one mind, no matter where they may be when they receive the Gospel, whether in the north, or the south, the east or the west, even to the uttermost parts of the earth? They receive that which was promised by the Savior when He was about to leave the earth, namely, the Comforter, that holy function from on high which recognizes one God, one faith, one baptism [see Ephesians 4:5], whose mind is the will of God the Father, in whom there dwelleth unity of faith and action, and in whom there cannot be division or confusion; when they received this further light, it matters not whether they have seen each other or not, they have at once become brothers and sisters, having been adopted into the family of Christ through the bonds of the everlasting covenant, and all can then exclaim, in the beautiful language of Ruth, "Thy people shall be my people, and thy God my God"! [Ruth 1:16] (*DBY,* 282–83).

If we were one, we should then prove to heaven, to God our Father, to Jesus Christ our Elder Brother, to the angels, to the good upon the earth, and to all mankind that we are the disciples of the Lord Jesus Christ. If we are not one, we are not in the true sense of the word the disciples of the Lord Jesus [see D&C 38:27] (*DBY,* 281).

President Young continually bore testimony of the gospel of Jesus Christ.

The gospel of salvation is expressly designed to make Saints of sinners, to overcome evil with good, to make holy, good men of wicked, bad men, and to make better men of good. Wherein we are wicked, wherein we have evil passions, the Gospel will aid us in overcoming evil. It gives us the influence, the power, the knowledge, the wisdom, and the understanding to overcome our weaknesses and to purify ourselves before the Lord our God (*DBY,* 448–49).

Our religion teaches us truth, virtue, holiness, faith in God and in his Son Jesus Christ. It reveals mysteries, it brings to mind things past and present—unfolding clearly things to come. It is the foundation of mechanism; it is the Spirit that gives intelligence to every living being upon the earth. All true philosophy originates from that fountain from which we draw wisdom, knowledge, truth, and power. What does it teach us? To love God and our fellow creatures; to be compassionate, full of mercy, long suffering, and patient to the froward [disobedient] and to those who are ignorant. There is a glory in our religion that no other religion that has ever been established upon the earth, in the absence of the true priesthood, ever possessed—It is the fountain of all intelligence; it is to bring heaven to earth and exalt earth to heaven, to prepare all intelligence, that God has placed in the hearts of the children of men, to mingle with that intelligence which dwells in eternity, and to elevate the mind above the trifling and frivolous objects of time which tend downward to destruction. It frees the mind of man from darkness and ignorance, gives him that intelligence that flows from Heaven, and qualifies him to comprehend all things (*DNW*, 1 June 1859, 1).

Our belief will bring peace to all men and good will to all the inhabitants of the earth. It will induce all who sincerely follow its dictates to cultivate righteousness and peace; to live peaceably in their families; to praise the Lord morning and evening; to pray with their families, and will so fill them with the spirit of peace that they will never condemn or chasten any one unless it is well deserved. They will rise in the morning with their spirits as smooth and serene as the sun that is rising and giving life and heat to the world; just as calm and as smooth as the breeze on a summer evening. No anger, no wrath, no malice, contention or strife (*DBY*, 449–50).

When people receive this Gospel, what do they sacrifice! Why, death for life. This is what they give: darkness for light, error for truth, doubt and unbelief for knowledge and the certainty of the things of God (*DBY*, 450).

The Saints in all ages have been protected, sustained and upheld by an Almighty Power in their sufferings, and the power of the religion of Jesus Christ has ever sustained them (*DBY*, 450).

Our religion has been a continual feast to me. With me it is Glory! Hallelujah! Praise God! instead of sorrow and grief. Give me the knowledge, power, and blessings that I have the capacity of receiving, and I do not care how the Devil originated, nor anything about him; I want the wisdom, knowledge, and power of God. Give me the religion that lifts me higher in the scale of intelligence—that gives me the power to endure—that when I attain the state of peace and rest prepared for the righteous, I may enjoy to all eternity the society of the sanctified (*DBY*, 451).

I feel happy. "Mormonism" has made me all I am, and the grace, the power, and the wisdom of God will make me all that I ever will be, either in time or eternity (*DBY*, 451).

The Lord has blessed me; he has always blessed me; from the time I commenced to build up Zion, I have been extremely blessed. I could relate circumstances of so extraordinary a character in regard to the providences of God to me, that my brethren and sisters would say in their hearts, "I can hardly give credence to this." But my heart has been set in me to do the will of God, to build up his Kingdom on the earth, to establish Zion and its laws, and to save the people. . . . I do not love, serve or fear the Lord for the sake of getting rid of being damned, nor for the sake of getting some great gift or blessing in eternity, but purely because the principles which God has revealed for the salvation of the inhabitants of the earth are pure, holy and exalting in their nature. In them there is honor and eternal increase, they lead on from light to light, strength to strength, glory to glory, knowledge to knowledge, and power to power (*DBY*, 452).

I am so thankful . . . that I have the privilege of associating with the Saints, and of being a member in the Kingdom of God, and that I have friends in the Church of the Living God (*DBY,* 452).

"Mormonism" has done everything for me that ever has been done for me on the earth; it has made me happy; . . . it has filled me with good feelings, with joy and rejoicing. Whereas, before I possessed the spirit of the Gospel I was troubled with that which I hear others complain of, that is, with, at times, feeling cast down, gloomy, and despondent; with everything wearing to me, at times, a dreary aspect (*DBY,* 452).

But since I have embraced the Gospel not for one-half minute, to the best of my recollection, has anything worn to me a gloomy aspect (*DBY,* 453).

When surrounded by mobs, with death and destruction threatening on every hand, I am not aware but that I felt just as joyful, just as well in my spirits, as I do now. Prospects might appear dull and very dark, but I have never seen a time in this Gospel but what I knew that the result would be beneficial to the cause of truth and the lovers of righteousness, and I have always felt to joyfully acknowledge the hand of the Lord in all things (*DBY,* 453).

God, angels, and good men being my helpers, I will never cease to contend, inch by inch, until we gain the ground and possess the Kingdom. That is my feeling and faith, and we will accomplish it. I will prophesy, in the name of the Lord Jesus Christ, that we will possess the Kingdom of God upon the whole earth, and possess the earth (*DBY,* 453).

President Young promised blessings to the faithful Saints.

Brethren and sisters, inasmuch as I have the right and privilege, through the Priesthood, I bless you in the name of the Lord, and say, be you blessed. These are my feelings to the Latter-day Saints, and would be to all the human family, if they would receive my blessings (*DBY,* 456).

God bless every good man. God bless the works of nature, God bless his own work, overthrow the wicked and ungodly and them that would destroy their fellow beings, that war and contentions may cease on the earth. O Lord, remove these from office and place good men at the head of the nations, that they may learn war no more, but go to, like rational and civilized beings, sustain peace on the earth and do good to each other [see Isaiah 2:4] (*DBY,* 456).

I feel to bless you continually; my life is here, my interest, my glory, my pride, my comfort, my all are here, and all I expect to have, to all eternity is wrapped up in the midst of this Church (*DBY,* 456).

If I had power, I certainly would bless the people with everything their hearts could wish if they would not sin. . . . And if it were in my power I would bless all the inhabitants of the earth, with everything in which they could glorify God, and purify their own hearts (*DBY,* 457).

If the Lord had a people on the earth that he had perfect confidence in, there is not a blessing in the eternities of our God, that they could bear in the flesh, that he would not pour out upon them. Tongue cannot tell the blessings the Lord has for a people who have proved themselves before him [see 1 Corinthians 2:9–14] (*DBY,* 455).

Instead of the righteous being bound tighter and tighter, they will continue to have more and more liberty, as we are more and more faithful, and obtain more power with the heavens and more of the power of God upon us. Let us seek diligently unto the Lord, until we obtain the faith of Jesus in its fulness, for those who possess this are free indeed (*DBY,* 455).

I wish the people could realize that they walk, live, and abide in the presence of the Almighty. The faithful shall have eyes to see as they are seen, and you shall behold that you are in the midst of eternity and in the presence of holy beings, and be enabled ere long to enjoy their society and presence. You are greatly blessed (*DBY,* 454–55).

Do just as well as you know how in all things, never permitting yourself to commit an act unless the Spirit of God within you justifies you in doing it [see Moses 6:60]. And if you live every day of your lives according to the best light and understanding you possess, glorifying God, our Heavenly Father, just as far as your knowledge extends, I will promise you eternal life in the Kingdom of God (*DBY,* 455).

May God bless you! Peace be upon you! Be fervent in spirit, humble, teachable, and prayerful, taking care of yourselves, endeavoring to save yourselves, and all you have any influence over, which is my continual prayer for you, in the name of Jesus. Amen (*DBY,* 456).

Suggestions for Study

**True disciples of Jesus Christ strive to be united—
of one heart and one mind.**

- What does it mean for followers of Christ to "become perfectly one," or "be of one heart and of one mind"? (See also John 17:20–21.)

- Why is it essential that the Saints be united if we are to build up the kingdom of God? Why can't any of us be saved in the celestial kingdom if we do not become one with each other?

- How does the gospel enable Church members with social, economic, political, and cultural differences to be united in the work of the Lord?

- How can we become truly "of one heart and of one mind" with our fellow Saints and with our Savior, Jesus Christ?

President Young continually bore testimony of the gospel of Jesus Christ.

- What effects of the gospel did President Young describe? How have you seen these effects occur in your life or the lives of those around you?
- In what ways does the gospel help us "bring heaven to earth and exalt earth to heaven"?
- President Young referred to his religion as "a continual feast." How can we feast on the gospel? What teachings of President Young in this course of study have helped you better understand and appreciate the gospel?
- How has the gospel of Jesus Christ filled you with joy and rejoicing?

President Young promised blessings to the faithful Saints.

- How can members of the Church prove themselves before the Lord and show that they are worthy of the great blessings He has for them?
- How does being "more and more faithful" lead to "more and more liberty" and power? Why do obedience and faith make us free?
- How can you "live every day of your lives according to the best light and understanding you possess"?
- How have President Young's unwavering testimony and enthusiasm for the gospel influenced your life?

Works Cited and
Abbreviations Used

BYL   Brigham Young Letterbook, 6:33–36. Historical
             Department Archives. The Church of Jesus Christ of
             Latter-day Saints.

BYP   Brigham Young Papers: 1832–78. Historical
             Department Archives. The Church of Jesus Christ of
             Latter-day Saints.

CHC   Roberts, B. H. *A Comprehensive History of the Church.*

DBY   Young, Brigham. *Discourses of Brigham Young.*
             Selected by John A. Widtsoe. 1941.

DEN   *Deseret Evening News.*

DN   *Deseret News.*

DNSW   *Deseret News: Semi-Weekly.*

DNW   *Deseret News (Weekly).*

HC   *History of the Church.*

HRF   "A History of Ralph Frost, Great Grandson of Elisha
             and Lucy Groves." Special Collections. Brigham Young
             University.

JD   *Journal of Discourses.*

JH   Journal History of The Church of Jesus Christ of
             Latter-day Saints, 23 Feb. 1847. Historical Department
             Archives. The Church of Jesus Christ of Latter-day
             Saints.

JSB   Brown, James S. *Life of a Pioneer, Being the Autobiography of James S. Brown.* 1900. 121–22.

JTB   Journal of Thomas Bullock, 29–30 June, 2 July 1848. Historical Department Archives. The Church of Jesus Christ of Latter-day Saints.

LBY   Young, Brigham. *Letters of Brigham Young to His Sons.* Edited by Dean C. Jessee. 1974.

LL   Creel, George. "The Lion of the Lord." *Collier's,* 4 Sept. 1926. 11–12, 36.

LSBY   Gates, Susa Young, with Leah D. Widtsoe. *The Life Story of Brigham Young.* 1930.

MAAY   Letter from Brigham Young to Mary Ann Angell Young, 20 Apr. 1847. Historical Department Archives. The Church of Jesus Christ of Latter-day Saints. Spelling modernized.

MFP   Clark, James R., comp. *Messages of the First Presidency of The Church of Jesus Christ of Latter-day Saints.* 6 vols. 1965–75.

MHBY-1   Young, Brigham. *Manuscript History of Brigham Young, 1801–1844.* Compiled by Elden Jay Watson. 1968.

MHBY-2   Young, Brigham. *Manuscript History of Brigham Young, 1846–1847.* Compiled by Elden Jay Watson. 1971.

MS   *Millennial Star.*

MSS   *Millennial Star (Supplement).*

WWJ   *Wilford Woodruff's Journal.* Edited by Scott G. Kenney. 1983. Vol. 3, 25 July 1847. Spelling and punctuation modernized.

Index

in God sustained early Saints,
101–8

shown through good works, 57–58

Family

fathers lead in righteousness,
164–66

mothers love and instruct, 167–68

parents teach by example and
kindness, 171–75, 337–41

Family history, 307–12

Fast day, 150

Fathers. *See also* Parents

lead with kindness, 164–66

set an example of
righteousness, 164–66

Food storage, 231

Foreordination, leaves us free to
choose, 52

Free agency. *See* Agency

G

Gifts of the Spirit

gift of the Holy Ghost, 67–68

same today as in days of old,
251–54

strengthen the faith of the believer,
254–56

God the Father

attributes of, 29–31

created all spirits, 50–51

Gospel of Jesus Christ

contains all truth, 15–17, 347–49

encourages Saints to increase in
knowledge, 193–94

guide to everyday living, 23–25

living, makes us happy, 183–85

means of salvation, 18–19

same in every dispensation, 93–95

spiritual and temporal aspects are
the same, 22–23

system of law and order, 15–17

teaches self-reliance, 25–26

transforming power of, 21–22,
347–49

truths revealed line upon line,
21–22

will be preached to all people,
243–44

Gossip, avoid participating in, 207–8

Government

Church members' duty to, 269–70

leaders should be wise, 268–69

must be based on God's laws,
267–68

Gratitude, 177–79

H

Happiness

comes from living the gospel,
183–85

does not come only from wealth,
235–37

through proper recreation, 185–89

Healing the sick

should use all medical means
available, 252–53

worthy Melchizedek Priesthood
brethren have privilege of, 252–53

Holy Ghost

leads us to perfection, 67

loss of the, can lead to personal
apostasy, 81–83

mission of, 33, 67–68

missionaries should rely on, 246–48

reveals mysteries, 257–58

teaches all truth, 318–20

Holy Spirit. *See* Holy Ghost

Home storage, 231

Homes, should build good, 229–30

Honesty

all Saints should be, 180–81

in business dealings, 24

teach children, 181

House of Israel

definition of, 324–25

our duty to gather, 324–25

Humility, 179–80

Husbands. *See also* Marriage, eternal

build comfortable homes, 229–30

serve wife and family, 164–66

I

Idleness, contrary to the laws of heaven, 225–26

Initiative. *See* Self-reliance

Integrity, in business dealings, 24

Intelligence. *See also* Knowledge

attaining, through study and faith, 193–99

Israel. *See* House of Israel

J

Jesus Christ. *See also* Atonement of Jesus Christ

faith in, first principle, 55–58

miracles of, 255–56

mission of, 31–32

resurrected first of all God's children, 38–39, 275

role in plan of salvation, 49–52

salvation comes by no other name, 291–96

Second Coming of, 32–33

Spirit of, given to all people, 41–42

Judgment

based on our works in the flesh, 285–87

depends on the law given to us on earth, 287

determines the level of glory we receive, 288–89

withhold, unless you have the Spirit of Christ, 220–22

K

Kindness, show the same, as our Father in Heaven, 218–19

Kingdom of God

cannot be destroyed, 325–26

give everything for, 327–28

includes gathering the house of Israel, 324–25

seek righteousness in, 320–21

use wealth to build, 239–40

work hard to build, 225–26

Kingdoms of glory, 288–89, 291–96

Kirtland Temple, 4

Knowledge. *See also* Intelligence

all, comes from God, 193–94

God gives us more as we improve on our, 87

prepare for eternal life by gathering, 85–90, 193–99

we are responsible to seek, 317–18

L

Last days

great calamities will occur in the, 331–32

righteousness will triumph, 332–33

Learning, by study and faith, 193–99

Light of Christ, given to all people, 41–42

M

Marriage, eternal. *See also* Husbands; Wives

binds parents and children together, 163–64, 171

counsel to fathers, 164–66

counsel to mothers, 167–68

young men counseled to enter into, 164

Martyrdom, of Joseph and Hyrum
Smith, 6–7, 101–2, 349

Mercy, show, for one another,
217–19

Millennium

description of life during the,
333–34

will include temple service, 311–12

Miracles

of Jesus reflected the Father's will,
32, 255–56

strengthen faith of those who love
God, 254–56

Missionary service

counsel to missionaries, 244–46,
248

spirit, not debate, converts people,
246–48

we are all called to do, 243–44

Money. *See* Wealth

Mormon Battalion

organization and march of the,
103–4

showed the Saints' loyalty to the
government, 103–4

Mothers. *See also* Parents

instruct their children in
righteousness, 167–68, 171–72

Mourning, eased by knowledge of
eternity, 273–74

Music, uplifting power of, 188–89

Mysteries of the kingdom, 257–58

N

Nauvoo, exodus from, 101–2, 104–5

Nauvoo Temple, 6, 10–11

New and everlasting covenant.
See Marriage, eternal

O

Obedience

cannot choose consequences of
choices, 71–73

enables us to dwell in God's
presence, 73–75

learn to obey willingly, 75–76

Ordinances. *See* Temple ordinances

P

Parents. *See also* Fathers; Mothers

educate children, 196–97, 337–38

guide their children without anger,
171–75, 338–41

positive influence of Brigham
Young's, 1

teach righteousness by word and
example, 171–75, 337–41

Perdition, sons of. *See* Sons of
perdition

Persecution. *See also* Chastisement;
Trials

of early Saints, 101–2, 104–5

by the wicked strengthens the
Church, 263–65

Plan of salvation

through Jesus Christ, 291–96

provides eternal life to the
faithful, 49–52

revealed to prophets, 93–94

Poor

camp of, 104–5

importance of caring for the, 25–26,
217–19, 238–39

Prayer

can create the desire to pray, 45

gain a witness of the truth through,
317–18

family, 45–46

pray without ceasing, 44–46

Notes